GOOD HOUSEKEEPING

COMPLETE BOOK OF

DESSERTS

OVER 300 RECIPES, FROM SUMPTUOUS CHOCOLATE PUDDINGS
TO FRESH FRUIT SORBETS

Published in association with

GOOD HOUSEKEEPING

COMPLETE BOOK OF

DESSERTS

OVER 300 RECIPES, FROM SUMPTUOUS CHOCOLATE PUDDINGS TO FRESH FRUIT SORBETS

EBURY PRESS · LONDON

First published by Ebury Press
An imprint of Century Hutchinson Ltd
20 Vauxhall Bridge Road
London SW1V 2SA

British Library Cataloguing in Publication Data
Good housekeeping complete book of desserts.
1. Desserts, Recipes
I. Title
641.8'6

ISBN 0-85223-836-3

Editor: Barbara Croxford
Home Economists: Janet Smith, Emma-Lee Gow
Designer: Grahame Dudley Associates
Stylist: Sarah Wylie
Illustrations: Linda Smith
Photography: James Murphy
Additional photography: Grant Symon, Jan Baldwin, Laurie Evans, James Jackson,
Charlie Stebbings, Peter Myers, Paul Kemp, and Don Last

Filmset in Palatino by Advanced Filmsetters (Glasgow) Ltd
Printed and bound in Italy by New Interlitho S.p.a., Milan

Contents

COOKERY NOTES

1. Follow either metric or imperial measures for the recipes in this book as they are not interchangeable.

2. The metric equivalent for 4 oz is 100 g or 125 g, depending on the recipes.

3. All spoon measures are level unless otherwise stated.

4. Sets of measuring spoons are available in both metric and imperial size to give accurate measurement of small quantities.

5. When measuring milk the exact conversion of 568 ml (1 pint) has been used.

6. Size 2 eggs should be used except where otherwise stated.

7. Where margarine is stated use either block or soft tub margarine. Otherwise use as specified in the recipes.

8. Raw eggs are used in some recipes. We believe that at the time of going to press the proven risk for healthy people using fresh eggs is minimal. However, the elderly, pregnant women, the sick and very young should not eat raw eggs.

9. Where reference is made to microwave cooking, the wattage of the cooker used is 650. HIGH refers to 100% full power output, MEDIUM refers to 60% of full power, and LOW is 35% of full power.

OVEN TEMPERATURE SCALES

°Celsius Scale	Electric Scale °F	Gas Oven Marks
110°C	225°F	$\frac{1}{4}$
130	250	$\frac{1}{2}$
140	275	1
150	300	2
170	325	3
180	350	4
190	375	5
200	400	6
220	425	7
230	450	8
240	475	9

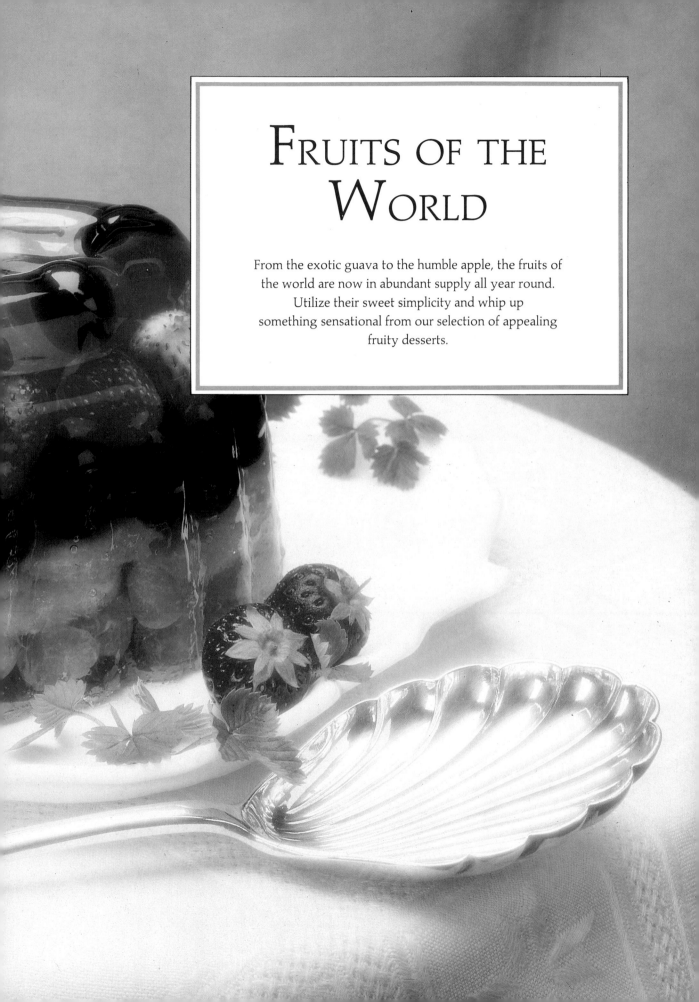

FRUITS OF THE WORLD

From the exotic guava to the humble apple, the fruits of the world are now in abundant supply all year round. Utilize their sweet simplicity and whip up something sensational from our selection of appealing fruity desserts.

Soft or crisp fleshed, juicy or firm, sweet or sharp, fruits make perfect crumbles and mousses. Simply washed, peeled and freed from any stems, stones or cores, they make a simple healthy dessert served au naturel with yogurt, cream or ice cream, or lightly poached in syrup, wine or fruit juice.

Ice Bowl

Serve a plate of perfectly prepared and prettily arranged fruit as a refreshing finale to a meal. For a more extravagant presentation, make an ice bowl: pour about 2.5 cm (1 inch) water into a large freezerproof bowl. Add flowers and leaves to decorate. Freeze until firm. Place a small freezerproof bowl inside the larger one. Add more flowers and leaves. Place a heavy weight inside the smaller bowl to keep it in place. Carefully fill the space between the two bowls with water. Freeze until firm. Remove the weight. Wipe the inner bowl with a damp hot cloth until it loosens. Repeat with the outside bowl. Return to the freezer until needed. Serve filled with fruit salad, decorated with more flowers and leaves.

Melon Basket

A melon basket is a good receptacle for fruit of all kinds and makes a pretty centrepiece. Choose a firm, ripe, melon. Lay it on its side and cut a small slice from the base so that it will sit securely without wobbling. Insert a sharp knife just above where the stalk was and cut lengthways, almost to the centre. Leave a space of 2.5 cm (1 inch) of the melon uncut, and continue cutting lengthways to the end of the melon. Repeat on the other side. Make the handle by cutting across the melon leaving 2.5 cm (1 inch) uncut across the centre. Remove the two end wedges of melon. Cut away the flesh about 1 cm (½ inch) from the rind, inside the handle. Scoop out the flesh and use to make a fruit salad. Store the melon basket in the refrigerator until required. Serve on a large platter, decorated with herbs, flowers and leaves and filled with fruit or fruit salad of your choice.

Frosted Fruits and Flowers

Frosted fruits and flowers make a pretty decoration for fruit desserts, gâteaux and mousses. Whisk the white of 1 egg and 10 ml (2 tsp) cold water together to give a frothy mixture. Using a small paintbrush, brush small firm fruits and flowers with a little of the mixture. Dip in caster sugar, shake off any excess, then spread out on greaseproof paper. Leave to dry for at least 24 hours.

SUMMER PUDDING
SERVES 8

You do not have to wait until summer to enjoy summer pudding; it can be made very successfully with frozen fruits. Traditionally, it is made with bread, but trifle sponge cakes can be used instead. Always make the day before serving.

175 g (6 oz) redcurrants, stalks removed
350 g (12 oz) blackcurrants, stalks removed
225–275 g (8–10 oz) granulated sugar
thinly pared rind of 1 large orange, in one continuous spiral if possible
225 g (8 oz) raspberries, hulled
225 g (8 oz) loganberries, hulled
12 thick slices of white bread, about 2 days old, crusts removed

1. Place the currants, sugar and orange rind in a large saucepan. Cover and cook gently until the juices flow and the sugar has dissolved. Add the raspberries and loganberries, and continue cooking for about 5 minutes until they are softened. (Alternatively, microwave in a covered bowl on HIGH for 5–7 minutes until softened, stirring occasionally.) Remove from the heat and leave to cool.
2. Cut a round from one of the slices of bread, large enough to fit in the base of a 1.7 litre (3 pint) pudding basin. Place the round in the basin, then line the sides of the basin with slightly overlapping slices of bread, reserve the rest for the centre and top.
3. Remove the orange rind from the fruit. Spoon half of the fruit and juice into the lined basin, then place a layer of bread on top. Add the remaining fruit and juice, then cover completely with the remaining bread.
4. Cover the top of the pudding with clingfilm, then place a small, flat plate on the top. Stand the basin on a plate to catch any juices that overflow. Place some heavy weights on top of the plate. Chill overnight.
5. To serve, gently loosen the pudding from the sides of the basin with a palette knife, then turn out on to a flat plate. Serve with Crème Chantilly (see page 248).

Not suitable for freezing.

VARIATION

Autumn Pudding Use 900 g (2 lb) mixed autumn fruit such as apples, blackberries, plums. Put the fruit, 90 ml (6 tbsp) water and 50 g (2 oz) sugar in a saucepan. Cover and cook as above. (Alternatively, microwave in a covered bowl on HIGH for 4–8 minutes, stirring occasionally.) Finish as above.

Previous Page: LAYERED FRUIT TERRINE (PAGE 16).
Opposite: SUMMER PUDDING.

BLACK FRUIT SALAD

SERVES 4–6

Serve this unusual fruit salad in a plain white or glass bowl for the most stunning effect. Other dark-skinned fruits may be added.

350 g (12 oz) blueberries or blackcurrants
350 g (12 oz) black cherries, stoned
350 g (12 oz) black grapes, seeded
finely grated rind and juice of 1 large orange
50–75 g (2–3 oz) light brown soft sugar

1. Mix the fruits together in a bowl with the orange rind and juice and the sugar.
2. Leave to stand for 3–4 hours or overnight, stirring occasionally. Serve the salad with Frozen yogurt (see page 226).

Not suitable for freezing.

RØDGRØD

SERVES 4–6

Rødgrød is a Danish dessert which essentially is a thick fruit soup. It is always made with fresh soft summer fruit, depending on what is available. An important point to remember is to mix at least two fruits together to provide good flavour and colour. In Russia, it is known as Kisel.

450 g (1 lb) redcurrants or blackcurrants, stalks removed
450 g (1 lb) raspberries or strawberries, hulled, or cherries, stoned
30 ml (2 tbsp) arrowroot
100–175 g (4–6 oz) caster sugar

FOR THE DECORATION
whipped cream
sprigs of mint

1. Place the currants and 60 ml (4 tbsp) water in a saucepan. Cover and simmer gently for about 20 minutes or until really soft. Leave to cool.
2. Meanwhile, purée half of the berries in a blender or food processor until smooth, then press through a nylon sieve.
3. Blend a little of the purée with the arrowroot. Put the rest into a pan and bring slowly to the boil. Stir into the blended mixture, then return it all to the pan. Bring to the boil again, cook for 4–5 minutes and sweeten to taste. Leave to cool for 10 minutes. Stir in the cooked currants and the remaining raspberries, strawberries or cherries.
4. Pour the Rødgrød into individual glasses and chill for 30 minutes. Top with whipped cream and mint sprigs just before serving.

To freeze: pack and freeze the cold Rødgrød. Thaw overnight in the refrigerator, then finish as above.

TROPICAL FRUIT SALAD WITH PASSION FRUIT CREAM

SERVES 6

The syrup of this delicious fruit salad is flavoured with the distinctive taste of fresh lime. It is a perfect background for the exotic mixture of fruit. The passion fruit cream and the fruit salad can both be prepared in the morning for dinner that night.

100 g (4 oz) granulated sugar
thinly pared rind and juice of 2 limes
1 ripe mango
1 ripe pawpaw (papaya)
1 cm (½ inch) thick slice of fresh pineapple
2 ripe kiwi fruit

FOR THE PASSION FRUIT CREAM
4 ripe passion fruit
150 ml (¼ pint) double cream
30 ml (2 tbsp) caster sugar

1. To make the tropical fruit salad, put the granulated sugar, 150 ml (¼ pint) water and lime rind and juice into a small saucepan. Heat gently until the sugar dissolves, then bring to the boil. Boil gently for 5 minutes. (Alternatively, put all of the ingredients into a bowl and microwave on HIGH for 3 minutes or until the sugar dissolves, stirring frequently. Continue to microwave on HIGH for 3 minutes.) Strain and leave to cool.
2. Peel the mango, then cut the flesh away from the stone. Cut the mango flesh into small cubes. Cut the pawpaw in half and scoop out the seeds. Peel the pawpaw, then cut each half into two lengthways and cut into slices crossways. Remove all the outer skin from the pineapple, and remove the hard centre core. Cut the pineapple into small pieces. Peel and slice the kiwi fruit.
3. Add all of the prepared fruits to the lime syrup. Cover and chill until serving.
4. To make the passion fruit cream, cut each passion fruit in half, then scoop out the seeds into a nylon sieve placed over a small bowl. Work the seeds in the sieve with the back of a spoon until all of the juice has been extracted into the bowl.
5. Whip the cream and caster sugar together in a bowl until it holds soft peaks. Gradually fold in the passion fruit juice. Spoon the cream into a serving bowl, cover and chill until ready to serve.
6. Transfer the tropical fruit salad to a serving bowl. Serve with the passion fruit cream.

Not suitable for freezing.

Above: RØDGRØD. Below: CRANBERRY AND ORANGE UPSIDE DOWN CAKE (PAGE 37).

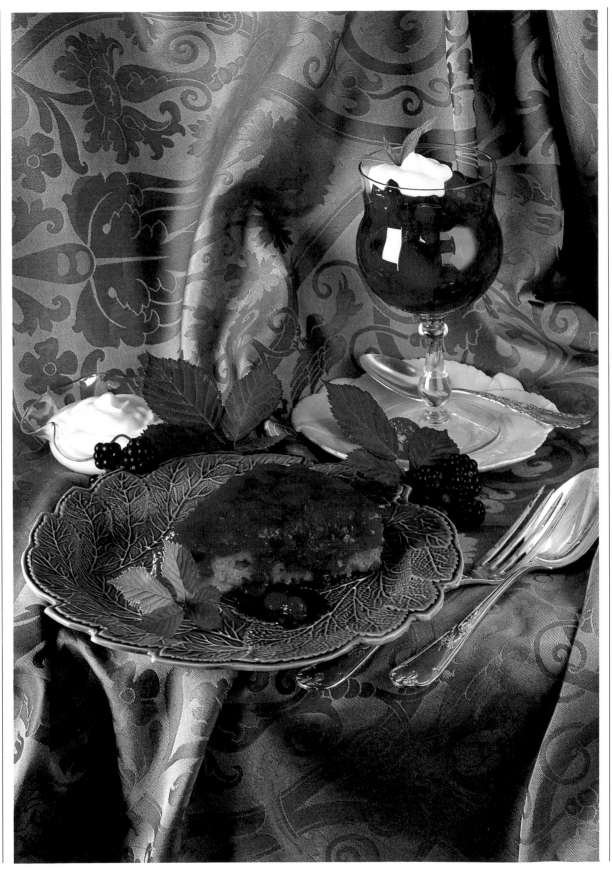

Sparkling Melon and Lime Soup

SERVES 4

A light, refreshing dessert to serve on a hot summer evening. Use Galia, Ogen, Honeydew or Charentais melons.

50 g (2 oz) granulated sugar
pared rind and juice of 1 lime
350 g (12 oz) melon flesh, diced
90 ml (6 tbsp) champagne or sparkling white wine, chilled

FOR THE DECORATION
julienne strips of mango
raspberries or strawberry slices
tiny mint sprigs, scented geranium or lemon balm leaves

1. Dissolve the sugar in 150 ml ($\frac{1}{4}$ pint) water in a saucepan over gentle heat. Add the lime rind, bring to the boil, then simmer for 2–3 minutes. (Alternatively, microwave the sugar and water on HIGH for 5 minutes or until dissolved, stirring occasionally. Add the lime rind and continue cooking for 1 minute.) Leave to cool.
2. When cold, strain the syrup into a blender or food processor. Add the lime juice and melon and purée until smooth. Chill until required.
3. Just before serving, stir in the champagne and decorate with the prepared fruit and leaves.

Not suitable for freezing.

Raspberry Dessert Soup

SERVES 4–6

A light and refreshing end to a meal on a hot summer's day, this dessert can be made from any soft berries, including redcurrants and even strawberries.

700 g (1½ lb) fresh raspberries, hulled, or frozen, thawed
1 bottle sweet wine, such as Sauternes, Vouvray or German Auslese
finely grated rind and juice of 1 lime (optional)
icing sugar, to taste
225 g (8 oz) crème fraîche, fromage frais or Greek yogurt
60 ml (4 tbsp) raspberry-flavoured liqueur (optional)

FOR THE DECORATION
mint leaves
edible flowers

1. Pick over the raspberries and discard any damaged fruit. Purée half in a blender or food processor until smooth. Keep the remainder in the refrigerator until needed. Stir the wine, lime rind and juice and icing sugar to taste into the purée. Cover and chill for 3–4 hours to allow the flavours to develop.

2. Spoon the crème fraîche into a bowl and add a few spoonfuls of fruit and wine purée. Beat well, then gradually stir in the remaining fruit and wine purée. Add the liqueur, if using.
3. Pour or ladle the soup into chilled soup plates and scatter the remaining raspberries over the top. Decorate with the mint leaves and edible flowers.

To freeze: freeze in a rigid container. Thaw in the refrigerator overnight.

Frudités

SERVES 6

A light, pretty dessert. Use other fruits in season to ring the changes.

2 crisp eating apples
2 bananas
225 g (8 oz) apricots, stoned
175 g (6 oz) black or green grapes, seeded
225 g (8 oz) strawberries
juice of 1 lemon

FOR THE DIP
150 ml (¼ pint) double cream
150 ml (¼ pint) soured cream
30 ml (2 tbsp) icing sugar, sifted

1. To make the dip, whip the two creams and icing sugar together in a bowl until standing in soft peaks. Pipe or spoon into six individual dishes.
2. Quarter and core the apples, but do not peel them. Peel the bananas and cut into 4 cm (1½ inch) chunks.
3. Arrange the fruit on individual serving plates and sprinkle immediately with lemon juice to prevent discoloration.
4. Place the dishes of cream dip next to the fruit and serve immediately. Use fingers or small fondue forks to dunk the fruit into the cream dip.

Not suitable for freezing.

WILD STRAWBERRY AND CHAMPAGNE JELLY

SERVES 6

The Alpine strawberry is a version of the rare wild strawberry, that is now cultivated in France. Also known as frais du bois, these deliciously flavoured baby strawberries do not need to be hulled before they are eaten.

100 g (4 oz) caster sugar
pared rind and juice of 1 lemon
20 ml (4 tsp) powdered gelatine
450 ml (¾ pint) pink champagne
175 g (6 oz) Alpine strawberries or frais du bois
edible flowers or sprigs of mint, to decorate

1. Put the sugar, lemon rind and 300 ml (½ pint) water in a saucepan. Heat gently until the sugar has dissolved.

(Alternatively, microwave on HIGH for 3 minutes or until dissolved, stirring occasionally.) Leave to cool.
2. Sprinkle the gelatine over the lemon juice in a small bowl and leave to soak for 2–3 minutes. Place the bowl over a pan of simmering water and stir until dissolved. (Alternatively, microwave on HIGH for 30 seconds or until dissolved.)
3. Mix the sugar syrup with the dissolved gelatine and the champagne. Divide most of the strawberries between six champagne flutes. Carefully pour over a little of the jelly and chill until set. When the jelly has set, pour over the remaining jelly. Chill until set.
4. Decorate with the reserved strawberries and edible flowers or mint sprigs.

Not suitable for freezing.

Above: WILD STRAWBERRY AND CHAMPAGNE JELLY.

LAYERED FRUIT TERRINE

SERVES 6

This luscious-looking terrine is easier to make than you think, but avoid lime fruit and pineapple because they prevent the jelly setting. Do not be restricted by the fruits used here, use any combination in season.

FOR THE JELLY

30 ml (6 tsp) powdered gelatine
450 ml (¾ pint) clear grape or apple juice (or half juice and rosé or white wine)
275 g (10 oz) small even-sized strawberries, hulled
200 g (7 oz) small black seedless grapes
4 large oranges, peeled, segmented and well drained
200 g (7 oz) small green seedless grapes

FOR THE SAUCE

225 g (8 oz) fresh raspberries, hulled, or frozen, thawed
icing sugar, to taste
lemon juice
dash of fruit liqueur or kirsch (optional)

FOR THE DECORATION

few extra strawberries or raspberries
sprigs of mint or strawberry leaves

1. To make the jelly, sprinkle the gelatine over 150 ml (¼ pint) of the grape juice in a small bowl and leave to soak for 2–3 minutes. Place the bowl over a pan of simmering water and stir until dissolved. (Alternatively, microwave on HIGH for 30 seconds or until dissolved.) Stir the dissolved gelatine into the remaining juice and mix well.

2. Pour a 0.5 cm (¼ inch) layer of jelly into the base of a 750 ml (1¼ pint) non-stick (or non-corrosive) loaf tin or mould. Chill until set.

3. Arrange the whole strawberries in a tightly packed layer over the set jelly. Arrange the black grapes in a thick layer over the strawberries, followed by the oranges, then the green grapes. Make sure the fruit is overlapping or tightly packed.

4. Slowly pour the fruit jelly over the fruit until it just covers the final layer. Tap the mould very lightly on the work surface to remove any air bubbles. Chill for at least 4 hours or until completely set.

5. To make the sauce, purée the raspberries in a blender or food processor until smooth. Press through a sieve if liked, and add sugar and lemon juice to taste. Stir in the liqueur, if using. Cover and chill.

6. To serve, dip the tin or mould in a bowl of lukewarm water for about 10 seconds and invert on to a flat surface. Remove the tin and, using a serrated or electric knife, cut the terrine into thick slices. Transfer each slice carefully on to individual chilled plates.

7. To decorate, pour a little sauce over a corner of each slice and arrange strawberries and mint sprigs on each plate. Serve immediately, with the remaining sauce handed separately.

Not suitable for freezing.

Illustrated on pages 8–9.

STRAWBERRY AND LOGANBERRY JELLY

SERVES 8

The subtle taste of puréed strawberries and loganberries combine to make this flavourful jelly. Other fruits can be used in the same way.

225 g (8 oz) granulated sugar
450 g (1 lb) strawberries, hulled
450 g (1 lb) loganberries or raspberries, hulled
30 ml (2 tbsp) powdered gelatine

FOR THE DECORATION

225 ml (8 fl oz) double cream, whipped
strawberries

1. Put the sugar and 300 ml (½ pint) water into a saucepan and heat gently until the sugar has dissolved. Bring to the boil and boil for 1 minute. (Alternatively, put the water and sugar in a bowl and microwave on HIGH for 3 minutes or until dissolved. Microwave on HIGH for a further minute.) Remove from the heat and leave to cool.

2. Purée the fruits in a blender or food processor, then sieve to remove the seeds.

3. Sprinkle the gelatine over 90 ml (6 tbsp) water in a small bowl and leave to soak for 2–3 minutes. Place the bowl over a pan of simmering water and stir until dissolved. (Alternatively, microwave on HIGH for 30 seconds or until dissolved.)

4. Stir the dissolved gelatine into the sugar syrup, then stir into the fruit purée until well blended. Pour the jelly mixture into a 1.4 litre (2½ pint) mould and chill until set.

5. To unmould, dip the mould up to the rim briefly in hot water, then place a plate upside down over the mould. Invert the two, giving them a good shake. Lift off the mould. Decorate the jelly with whipped cream and strawberries. Chill until ready to serve.

Not suitable for freezing.

GERMAN RUMTOPF

A rumtopf is a ceramic pot made especially for preserving fresh summer fruits in rum. Rumtopfs came into being as a result of German seafarers trying to take exotic fruits from the West Indies to Germany about 200 years ago.

Start to make a rumtopf when the first fruits of summer appear, usually strawberries, and continue through the summer months, until the rumtopf is full.

Most fruit can be put into a rumtopf but those with a high water content, such as melon and apple, should be avoided as they can cause fermentation. Also, avoid blackberries, rhubarb and gooseberries, as their sharpness can impart a bitter flavour. All fruits used must be ripe, sound, and very clean.

450 g (1 lb) caster sugar to every 450 g (1 lb) ripe strawberries, hulled
1 bottle of rum, no less than 40% alcoholic volume
225 g (8 oz) caster sugar to every 450 g (1 lb) of fruit, such as:
raspberries, hulled
loganberries, hulled
redcurrants and blackcurrants, stalks removed
peaches, skinned, halved and stoned
nectarines, skinned, halved and stoned
apricots, skinned, halved and stoned
plums, skinned, halved and stoned
greengages, skinned, halved and stoned
black and green grapes, seeded
cherries, stoned
pineapple, skinned, core removed and cut into small pieces
mango, skinned and cut into dice or slices
pawpaw, skinned, seeds removed and cut into small slices
kiwi fruits, peeled and sliced
pears, peeled, cored and sliced

1. Wash and thoroughly dry the rumtopf.

2. Put the strawberries into a large bowl, sprinkle with the caster sugar and mix lightly together. Cover and leave to stand for 1 hour.

3. Put the strawberries, sugar and any juices into the rumtopf and cover with rum to a depth of 1 cm (½ inch).

4. Cover the surface with clingfilm, then place a saucer on top of the clingfilm to keep the fruit submerged. Cover with more clingfilm, then the rumtopf lid. Put the rumtopf in a cool, airy cupboard.

5. Continue to add fruits to the rumtopf, soaking them with the stated amount of sugar and rum. When full, cover the rumtopf and store in a cool place for 2–3 months to mature. Serve with cream, ice cream or yogurt.

Not suitable for freezing.

AMARETTI STUFFED PEACHES

SERVES 4

Amaretti are almond macaroons made in Italy. They are available at Italian delicatessens, both in boxes and individually wrapped in tissue paper. Amaretti are delicious served with coffee and liqueurs at the end of a meal. If you cannot find them, use shop bought or home-made macaroons instead.

4 yellow peaches, skinned
50 g (2 oz) Amaretti or macaroons
1 egg yolk
25 g (1 oz) butter
25 g (1 oz) sugar
150 ml (¼ pint) dry white wine

1. Lightly grease an ovenproof dish.

2. Cut the peaches in half and carefully ease out the stones. Make the hollows in the peaches a little deeper with a sharp-edged teaspoon and reserve the removed flesh.

3. Crush the macaroons and mix them with the reserved peach flesh, the egg yolk, butter and 15 g (½ oz) of the sugar.

4. Use this mixture to stuff the hollows of the peach halves, mounding the filling slightly. Place the peaches in the prepared ovenproof dish and sprinkle with the rest of the sugar. Pour the white wine over and around the peaches.

5. Bake in the oven at 180°C (350°F) mark 4 for 25–30 minutes or until tender. (Alternatively, arrange around the edge of a large shallow dish, cover and microwave on HIGH for 3–5 minutes or until tender. Leave to stand, covered, for 5 minutes.) Serve hot or cold.

Not suitable for freezing.

BRANDIED STUFFED APRICOTS

SERVES 4

Smaller and more unusual than its relations the nectarine and peach, the apricot is highly prized for its unique flavour and aroma. Fresh apricots do not keep well and their season is short. If fresh apricots are not available, this recipe can be made with small peaches or nectarines, but as these are always larger than apricots you will only need half the quantity.

16 small apricots
120 ml (8 tbsp) apricot brandy
30 ml (2 tbsp) caster sugar
finely grated rind and juice of 1 lemon
150 g (5 oz) cottage cheese
50 g (2 oz) full fat soft cheese
15 ml (1 tbsp) icing sugar, sifted
chopped toasted hazelnuts, to decorate

1. Place the apricots, brandy, caster sugar, 15 ml (1 tbsp) lemon juice and 150 ml ($\frac{1}{4}$ pint) water in a saucepan. Poach gently for about 15 minutes until just tender. Remove the apricots and leave to cool for 30 minutes.

2. Boil the poaching liquid for 2–3 minutes until well reduced and syrupy. Leave to cool for 20 minutes.

3. Using a sharp knife, skin the apricots. Slice almost in half and remove the kernel.

4. Sieve the cottage cheese into a bowl, add the full fat soft cheese, icing sugar and grated lemon rind, then beat together until well mixed.

5. Sandwich the apricots together with a little of the cheese mixture. Divide the apricots between four individual glass dishes.

6. Spoon a little of the cooled syrup over the apricots. Chill for 2–3 hours, then decorate with chopped nuts before serving.

Not suitable for freezing.

ORANGES IN CARAMEL

SERVES 6

For a sweet, crunchy topping to this classic orange dessert, make caramel chips: dissolve 75 g (3 oz) granulated sugar very gently in 75 ml (3 fl oz) water. Increase the heat and boil rapidly without stirring until the syrup turns a rich brown caramel colour. Pour at once into a greased shallow tin (a Swiss roll tin is ideal), then leave until cold and set. Crush with a rolling pin or mallet into fine pieces and sprinkle over the oranges just before serving (not earlier or the caramel will soften).

225 g (8 oz) granulated sugar
6 large oranges
30–45 ml (2–3 tbsp) orange-flavoured liqueur

1. Put the sugar and 50 ml (2 fl oz) water in a saucepan and heat gently until the sugar has dissolved, brushing down the sides of the pan with hot water. Bring to the boil, then boil until the syrup turns a golden caramel colour.

2. Immediately, plunge the base of the pan into cold water to prevent the caramel darkening further. Carefully, pour 300 ml ($\frac{1}{2}$ pint) boiling water into the pan. Return the caramel to the heat and heat gently until it has completely dissolved into the water.

3. Meanwhile, thinly pare the rind from two of the oranges, taking care not to remove the white pith. Cut the rind into very fine shreds and set aside. Using a very sharp knife, remove the skin and white pith from all the oranges.

4. Put the oranges and shredded rinds into the caramel, cover and cook them very gently for 25–30 minutes until the oranges are tender, but do not allow to overcook—they must retain a good shape. Turn the oranges frequently during cooking.

5. Transfer the oranges and syrup to a large serving dish. Add the liqueur and leave to cool. Cover and chill. Serve with Crème Chantilly (see page 248).

Not suitable for freezing.

Opposite: ORANGES IN CARAMEL.

BARNSTAPLE FAIR PEARS

SERVES 4

The pear orchards of Devon used to supply stalls at the annual Barnstaple Fair. Originally these pears would have been simmered in local cider or scrumpy.

4 large firm Comice pears
25 g (1 oz) blanched almonds, split in half
50 g (2 oz) caster sugar
300 ml (½ pint) red wine
2 cloves

1. Peel the pears, leaving the stalks on. Spike the pears with the almond halves.
2. Put the sugar, wine and cloves in a saucepan just large enough to hold the pears and heat gently until the sugar has dissolved. Add the pears, standing them upright in the pan. Cover and simmer gently for about 15 minutes until the pears are just tender. Baste them from time to time with the liquid. (Alternatively, put the sugar, wine and cloves in a bowl and microwave on HIGH for 3–4 minutes until boiling, stirring occasionally. Add the pears, cover and microwave on HIGH for 8–10 minutes until the pears are tender.)
3. Using a slotted spoon, transfer the pears to a serving dish. Boil the syrup in the pan until the liquid is reduced by half. (If cooking in the microwave, uncover and cook on HIGH for 10 minutes or until reduced by half.)
4. Pour the wine syrup over the pears. Serve hot or cold with thick natural yogurt or clotted cream.

To freeze: pack in the cooled syrup.

Left: RASPBERRY AND WALNUT SHORTBREAD (PAGE 39).
Right: BARNSTABLE FAIR PEARS.

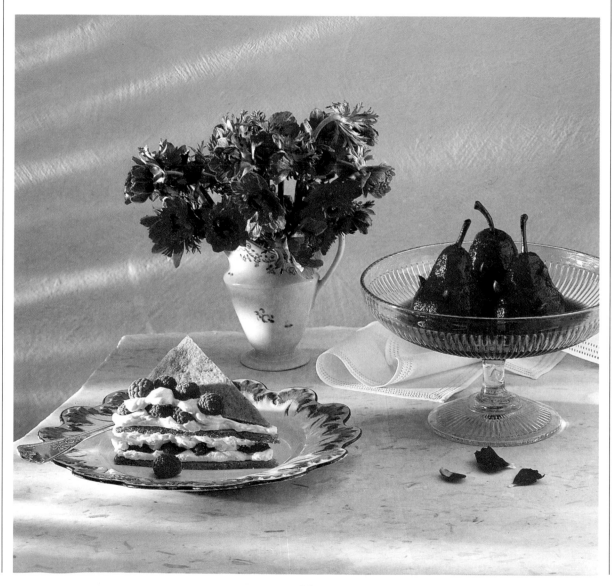

Pears Poached in Ginger Syrup

SERVES 4

Use firm Conference or slightly underripe Comice pears for this recipe.

150 ml (¼ pint) dry white wine
75 ml (5 tbsp) ginger wine
75 g (3 oz) light brown soft sugar
1 strip lemon rind
1 cinnamon stick
4 firm pears
30 ml (2 tbsp) preserved ginger in syrup, thinly sliced

1. Pour the white wine into a large heavy-based pan. Add 300 ml (½ pint) water, the ginger wine, sugar, lemon rind and cinnamon. Heat gently until sugar has dissolved, then remove from the heat. (Alternatively, put the ingredients in a bowl and microwave on HIGH for 3—4 minutes until boiling, stirring occasionally.)
2. Using a vegetable peeler or canelle knife, peel the pears from top to bottom in a spiral pattern. Leave the stalks on.
3. Put the pears in the wine and simmer gently for 30 minutes. Transfer to a serving bowl. (If cooking in the microwave, add to the syrup, cover and microwave on HIGH for 8—10 minutes or until the pears are tender.)
4. Boil the liquid in the pan until reduced by half, then strain and stir in the preserved ginger. (Alternatively, microwave on HIGH for 10 minutes or until reduced by half.) Pour over the pears in the bowl.
5. Leave the pears for 1—2 hours until completely cold, then chill overnight, spooning the syrup over them occasionally. Serve chilled, with cream.

To freeze: pack in the syrup at the end of step 5.

Almond Baked Apples

SERVES 4

The almond coating makes these baked apples with a difference.

75 g (3 oz) dried figs, rinsed and chopped
grated rind of 1 lime or ½ lemon
4 cooking apples, each about 225 g (8 oz)
50 g (2 oz) ground almonds
15 ml (1 tbsp) light brown soft sugar
15 ml (1 tbsp) butter or margarine, melted

1. Put the figs in a bowl, cover with boiling water and leave to soak for 5 minutes. Drain, then mix in the grated lime rind.
2. Peel and core the apples. Fill with the fig mixture, packing down firmly.
3. Mix the ground almonds and sugar together. Brush

each apple with the melted butter, then roll the apples in the ground almond mixture. Place the apples in a shallow 1.1 litre (2 pint) ovenproof dish.
4. Bake in the oven at 180°C (350°F) mark 4 for about 45—50 minutes or until the apples are cooked through and tender when pricked with a skewer. Serve hot.

Not suitable for freezing.

Flambéed Apples Triberg-Style

SERVES 4—6

This wonderful way of cooking apples comes from Triberg, a small picturesque town in the Black Forest— famous for its kirsch and its clocks! The apples are cooked with honey and lemon, then flambéed with kirsch, and may be cooked on a spirit burner at the dining table.

6 large dessert apples, such as Golden Delicious, Cox or Russet
40 g (1½ oz) unsalted butter
25 g (1 oz) caster sugar
thinly pared rind of 1 lemon, taken in one continuous spiral if possible
juice of 1 lemon
45 ml (3 tbsp) clear honey
60 ml (4 tbsp) kirsch
150 ml (¼ pint) double cream, lightly whipped with 15 ml (1 tbsp) kirsch

1. Peel, quarter and core the apples. Cut each quarter into half again.
2. Put the butter, sugar, lemon rind and juice and honey in a large shallow saucepan. Heat gently, stirring, until slightly thickened.
3. Add the apples to the pan and cook gently, turning the pieces frequently, for 10—15 minutes until the apples are just tender when pierced with the tip of a knife. Spoon the juices into a serving jug and set aside.
4. Add the kirsch to the apples, heat for 10 seconds, then set alight. Flambé the apples until the flames begin to subside. Spoon the apples, still slightly flaming, on to warmed serving plates. Serve immediately with the juices and flavoured whipped cream.

Not suitable for freezing.

COMPOTES

Compotes are mixtures of fruits cooked in sugar syrup, which can be served hot or cold. The syrup may be flavoured with spices or with orange and lemon rind, but the fruits, being quite highly flavoured themselves, require little or no extra flavouring. Hot compotes make perfect desserts for the winter, not only because they are warming, but also because they are full of vitamins. Chilled compotes will keep well for up to a week in the refrigerator.

Compotes can be made with a single fruit, but it is more interesting to have a mixture. So that the cooked fruits retain their shape as much as is possible, they should be added to the sugar syrup in the order of cooking time—those that need the longest time first, and so on. Small quantities can be made in the microwave but larger quantities cook better in a large saucepan. Always select ripe, but firm fruits. A little liqueur may be added to a compote, just enough to enhance the flavour, not to overpower it.

FOR THE BASIC SUGAR SYRUP

225 g (8 oz) granulated sugar

1. To make the sugar syrup, put the sugar and 300 ml ($\frac{1}{2}$ pint) cold water in a saucepan. Heat very gently until the sugar has completely dissolved.
2. Bring to the boil and boil the syrup for 1 minute.

SPRING COMPOTE

SERVES 6

Spring rhubarb needs careful cooking. It is very delicate and can easily break up.

1 quantity Basic sugar syrup (see above)
40 g (1$\frac{1}{2}$ oz) fresh ginger root, peeled and finely shredded
1.4 kg (3 lb) rhubarb, cut into 5 cm (2 inch) pieces

1. Make the sugar syrup in a shallow, wide saucepan. Add the ginger and cook gently for 2–3 minutes.
2. Add just enough rhubarb to make a single layer. Cook gently for 5–6 minutes until just tender, turning the pieces frequently. Transfer to a serving dish. Continue cooking the rhubarb in batches.
3. Boil the syrup until reduced and slightly thickened, then pour over the rhubarb. Serve the compote hot or cold, with Orange sabayon sauce (see page 248).

To freeze: cool then pack in a rigid container. Thaw overnight at cool room temperature. Serve cold.

Opposite: SUMMER CURRANT COMPOTE. REDCURRANT HAZELNUT GÂTEAU (PAGE 37).

SUMMER COMPOTE

SERVES 6–8

Serve this compote well chilled on bright, hot, sunny days with Crème Chantilly (see page 248). Or, cheer up a gloomy rainy day by serving it hot.

1 quantity Basic sugar syrup (see left).
450 g (1 lb) ripe peaches or nectarines, halved, stoned, skinned and cut into thick slices
450 g (1 lb) ripe apricots, skinned, halved and stoned
450 g (1 lb) dark cherries, stoned

1. Make the sugar syrup in a large, wide saucepan. Add the peach slices and cook gently for 10–15 minutes until barely tender.
2. Add the apricots and cook for a further 5 minutes until the apricots just begin to soften.
3. Add the cherries and cook just long enough to soften them without losing their colour, about 3 minutes.
4. Carefully transfer the fruits and syrup to a serving bowl. Leave to cool, then chill.

To freeze: pack in a rigid container. Thaw overnight at cool room temperature.

SUMMER CURRANT COMPOTE

SERVES 6

Add sugar to taste—with 50 g (2 oz) the compote will be quite tart.

50–75 g (2–3 oz) granulated sugar
225 g (8 oz) blackcurrants, stalks removed
450 g (1 lb) redcurrants, stalks removed
pared rind and juice of 1 medium orange
30 ml (2 tbsp) honey
350 g (12 oz) strawberries, hulled and sliced

1. Dissolve the sugar in 150 ml ($\frac{1}{4}$ pint) water in a pan. Boil for 1 minute. (Alternatively, microwave on HIGH for 3 minutes, stirring frequently. Continue to microwave on HIGH for 1 minute.)
2. Add the currants and orange rind and simmer until the fruits are just beginning to soften—about 1 minute only. (If cooking in the microwave, microwave on HIGH for 1–2 minutes or until beginning to soften.)
3. Carefully transfer the fruits and syrup to a serving bowl. Stir in the honey and leave to cool.
4. Mix in the orange juice, cover and chill well.
5. Just before serving, stir the strawberries into the compote. Serve with Baked custard (see page 165).

Not suitable for freezing.

23

AUTUMN COMPOTE

SERVES 6–8

Select very small pears for this compote. Lemon juice added to the syrup prevents the pears and apples discolouring, and adds a tangy flavour.

1 quantity Basic sugar syrup (see page 23)
juice of 1 lemon
450 g (1 lb) small ripe, but firm pears
450 g (1 lb) dessert apples, such as Cox or Russet
450 g (1 lb) Victoria plums, skinned and stoned

1. Make the sugar syrup in a large saucepan, adding the lemon juice. Thinly peel the pears, cut into half and remove the centre core (if only large pears are available, cut the pears into quarters). Add the pears to the syrup and cook very gently for about 10–15 minutes until barely tender.
2. Meanwhile, core the apples. Cut the apples into halves, then cut into slices across the halves.
3. Add the apple slices to the pan and cook for about 5 minutes until the apple slices are just tender. Add the plums and cook for a further 5 minutes.
4. Carefully transfer the fruits and syrup to a serving bowl, taking care not to break up the fruit. Serve hot or cold.

To freeze: cool then pack in a rigid container. Thaw overnight at cool room temperature. Serve cold.

Illustrated on page 31

WINTER COMPOTE

SERVES 6–8

A compote with a bitter sweet flavour, tangy and refreshing.

1 quantity Basic sugar syrup (see page 23)
450 g (1 lb) kumquats, thickly sliced
450 g (1 lb) clementines, peeled and segmented
175 g (6 oz) black grapes, seeded
175 g (6 oz) green grapes, seeded
175 g (6 oz) cranberries

1. Make the sugar syrup in a wide saucepan. Add the kumquats, cover and cook gently for about 15–20 minutes until barely tender.
2. Add the clementines and grapes, then cook for a further 5 minutes, gently turning the fruits in the syrup and taking care not to break them up. Add the cranberries and cook the compote for about 5 minutes until softened.
3. Carefully transfer the fruits and syrup to a serving bowl. Serve hot or cold.

To freeze: cool and pack in a rigid container. Thaw at cool room temperature.

STICKY PEAR UPSIDE DOWN PUDDING

SERVES 6–8

A hearty pudding that is quickly put together from storecupboard ingredients, yet is hard to resist. Ideal to serve at short notice. The canned pears in natural juice combine perfectly with the rich, dark, spicy sponge.

FOR THE PEAR LAYER
75 g (3 oz) butter or margarine
100 g (4 oz) light brown soft sugar
two 415 g (14½ oz) cans of pear halves in natural juice
FOR THE SPONGE
225 g (8 oz) plain flour
175 g (6 oz) light brown soft sugar
5 ml (1 tsp) bicarbonate of soda
pinch of salt
10 ml (2 tsp) ground ginger
2.5 ml (½ tsp) grated nutmeg
15 ml (1 tbsp) ground cinnamon
finely grated rind and juice of 1 large lemon
175 g (6 oz) black treacle
75 g (3 oz) butter or margarine
200 ml (7 fl oz) milk
2 eggs, beaten

1. To make the pear layer, warm the butter and sugar together. Spoon into a 2.3–2.6 litre (4–4½ pint) shallow ovenproof dish. Drain the pears and arrange cut side down around the base of the dish.
2. To make the sponge, mix the flour, sugar, bicarbonate of soda, salt and spices together in a bowl. Add the finely grated lemon rind, then make a well in the centre of the dry ingredients.
3. Warm the treacle and butter together. When evenly blended, pour into the well with the milk and 45 ml (3 tbsp) lemon juice. Add the eggs and beat well until evenly mixed.
4. Spoon the sponge over the pears. Stand the dish on an edged baking sheet.
5. Bake in the oven at 200°C (400°F) mark 6 for about 25 minutes. Reduce the oven temperature to 190°C (375°F) mark 5 and continue to cook for about a further 50 minutes, covering lightly if necessary. The pudding should be firm to the touch and a skewer inserted into the centre should come out clean.
6. Leave the pudding to stand for about 5 minutes. Run a blunt edged knife around the edge of the pudding. Invert on to an edged platter. Serve warm with custard, natural yogurt or single cream.

To freeze: pack and freeze the cooled pudding. Thaw at cool room temperature, then reheat at 190°C (375°F) mark 5 for about 30 minutes.

DANISH 'PEASANT GIRL IN A VEIL'

SERVES 4

This simple but delicious pudding of stewed apples layered with fried breadcrumbs and sugar is very similar to an apple charlotte. In Denmark, where it is called *bondepige med slør*, it takes its name from the fact that the apple and crumbs are 'veiled' or covered with cream.

50 g (2 oz) butter or margarine
175 g (6 oz) fresh rye or brown breadcrumbs
75 g (3 oz) light brown soft sugar
700 g (1½ lb) cooking apples
juice of ½ lemon
sugar, to taste
150 ml (¼ pint) double or whipping cream
50 g (2 oz) grated chocolate, to decorate

1. Melt the butter in a frying pan. Mix the breadcrumbs and sugar together. Add to the pan and fry until crisp, stirring frequently with a wooden spoon to prevent the crumbs from catching and burning.
2. Peel, core and slice the apples. Put them in a saucepan with 30 ml (2 tbsp) water, the lemon juice and sugar to taste. Cover and cook gently for 10–15 minutes until they form a purée. (Alternatively, put the apples, lemon juice and sugar in a bowl. Cover and microwave on HIGH for 7–10 minutes until they form a pulp, stirring frequently.) Leave to cool, then taste for sweetness and add more sugar if required.
3. Put alternate layers of the fried crumb mixture and apple purée into a glass serving dish, finishing with a layer of crumbs. Chill for 2–3 hours.
4. Whip the cream until stiff. Pipe over the top of the crumb mixture and decorate with grated chocolate. Serve chilled.

Not suitable for freezing.

ALMOND EVE'S PUDDING

SERVES 4

If liked, add 50 g (2 oz) sultanas, currants or raisins to the apple mixture in the base of this delicious family pudding. Grated orange or lemon rind added to the sponge topping also adds extra flavour.

FOR THE FILLING
700 g (1½ lb) cooking apples
5 ml (1 tsp) ground cinnamon
50 g (2 oz) demerara sugar

FOR THE TOPPING
100 g (4 oz) butter, softened
100 g (4 oz) demerara sugar
2 eggs, beaten
100 g (4 oz) self raising flour
25 g (1 oz) ground almonds
2.5 ml (½ tsp) almond flavouring
30 ml (2 tbsp) milk
25 g (1 oz) flaked almonds
icing sugar, for dredging

1. To make the filling, peel, quarter and core the cooking apples, then slice thickly. Place in a 1.4 litre (2½ pint) ovenproof dish. Combine the cinnamon and demerara sugar and scatter over the apples. Cover tightly with clingfilm while preparing the topping.
2. To make the topping, cream the butter and sugar together in a bowl until fluffy. Gradually beat in eggs. Fold in the flour, ground almonds, almond flavouring and milk.
3. Spread the mixture over the apples. Place the flaked almonds on top in six squares to form a chequerboard.
4. Bake in the oven at 180°C (350°F) mark 4 for 50–60 minutes until the apples are tender and the sponge risen and golden brown. Dredge icing sugar between the flaked nut squares. Serve with cream.

Not suitable for freezing.

SPICED APPLE AND PLUM CRUMBLE

SERVES 6

All plums can be cooked, but dessert varieties tend to be more expensive, so it makes good sense to look for cooking plums. Whether you cook with red or yellow plums is entirely a matter of personal choice but cooking plums worth looking for are Czars, small red cherry plums, Pershore Yellow Egg, Purple Pershore and Belle de Loutain. Greengages and damsons come from the plum family and can be used in any recipe for plums, although extra sugar may be required.

450 g (1 lb) plums
700 g (1½ lb) cooking apples
100 g (4 oz) butter or margarine
100 g (4 oz) sugar
7.5 ml (1½ tsp) ground mixed spice
175 g (6 oz) plain wholemeal flour
50 g (2 oz) blanched hazelnuts, toasted and chopped

1. Using a sharp knife, cut the plums in half, then carefully remove the stones.
2. Peel, quarter, core and slice the apples. Place the apples in a medium saucepan with 25 g (1 oz) of the butter, 50 g (2 oz) of the sugar and about 5 ml (1 tsp) of the mixed spice. Cover and cook gently for 15 minutes until the apples begin to soften.
3. Stir in the plums. Transfer the fruit mixture to a 1.1 litre (2 pint) shallow ovenproof dish. Leave to cool for about 30 minutes.
4. Stir the flour and remaining mixed spice well together. Rub in the remaining butter until the mixture resembles fine breadcrumbs. Stir in the rest of the sugar with the hazelnuts. Spoon the crumble over the fruit.
5. Bake in the oven at 180°C (350°F) mark 4 for about 40 minutes or until the top is golden, crisp and crumbly.

To freeze: cool and freeze in the dish at the end of step 4.

BLUEBERRY OAT CRUMBLE

SERVES 6–8

Originally a wild fruit of the heaths and woodlands of the USA and Canada, blueberries have been grown commercially since the early part of this century. Because of the similarity in name, the blueberry, blackberry and bilberry are often thought to be the same fruit. In fact, they are different varieties of the same family of berries, which also includes whortle-berries and huckleberries.

FOR THE FILLING
900 g (2 lb) blueberries
45 ml (3 tbsp) light brown soft sugar
30 ml (2 tbsp) plain flour
15 ml (1 tbsp) lemon juice

FOR THE CRUMBLE TOPPING
100 g (4 oz) butter
100 g (4 oz) plain flour
100 g (4 oz) light brown soft sugar
75 g (3 oz) rolled oats
50 g (2 oz) pecan or walnut halves, chopped and toasted
grated nutmeg (optional)

1. To make the filling, mix the blueberries with the sugar, flour and lemon juice in a 1.4 litre (2½ pint) pie dish.
2. To make the crumble topping, rub the butter into the flour in a bowl. Stir in the sugar, oats and nuts. Flavour with grated nutmeg, if liked. Spoon the crumble mixture on top of the berries and lightly press down.
3. Bake in the oven at 190°C (375°F) mark 5 for about 30–35 minutes or until golden brown. Serve warm or cold with custard or cream.

To freeze: wrap and freeze in the pie dish before baking. Bake from frozen at 200°C (400°F) mark 6 for 30 minutes, then at 190°C (375°F) mark 5 for 40–50 minutes.

Opposite: BLUEBERRY OAT CRUMBLE.

BLACKBERRY AND PEAR COBBLER

SERVES 4

Recipes with the strange-sounding title of 'cobbler' are invariably American in origin, although very little is known for certain about the meaning behind the word in culinary terms. Cobblers always have a scone dough topping which is stamped into small rounds.

FOR THE FILLING

| 450 g (1 lb) blackberries |
| 450 g (1 lb) ripe cooking pears, such as Conference |
| finely grated rind and juice of 1 lemon |
| 2.5 ml ($\frac{1}{2}$ tsp) ground cinnamon |

FOR THE TOPPING

| 225 g (8 oz) self raising flour |
| pinch of salt |
| 50 g (2 oz) butter or margarine |
| 25 g (1 oz) caster sugar |
| about 150 ml ($\frac{1}{4}$ pint) milk, plus extra to glaze |

1. To make the filling, pick over the blackberries and wash them. Peel and core the pears, slice thickly.

2. Put the blackberries and pears into a saucepan with the lemon rind and juice and the cinnamon. Poach for 15–20 minutes until the fruit is tender. Cool.

3. To make the topping, place the flour and salt in a bowl. Rub in the butter until the mixture resembles fine breadcrumbs, then stir in the sugar. Gradually add the milk to mix to a fairly soft dough.

4. Roll out the dough on a floured work surface until 1 cm ($\frac{1}{2}$ inch) thick. Cut out rounds using a fluted 5 cm (2 inch) pastry cutter.

5. Put the fruit in a pie dish and top with overlapping pastry rounds, leaving a gap in the centre.

6. Brush the top of the pastry rounds with milk. Bake in the oven at 220°C (425°F) mark 7 for 10–15 minutes until the pastry is golden brown. Serve hot.

To freeze: wrap and freeze at the end of step 5. Thaw and cook as above.

LEMON AND YOGURT MOUSSE

SERVES 8

Beautifully smooth, tangy and light, this mousse is delicious served with crisp biscuits. If possible, make your own yogurt (page 180) for this recipe.

| 50 ml (2 fl oz) milk |
| 4 eggs, separated |
| 100 g (4 oz) caster sugar |
| 2 drops of vanilla essence |
| 25 ml (5 tsp) powdered gelatine |
| 450 ml ($\frac{3}{4}$ pint) natural yogurt |
| juice of 1 lemon |
| 150 ml ($\frac{1}{4}$ pint) double cream |

1. Put the milk in a small saucepan and bring almost to the boil. Beat the egg yolks and 25 g (1 oz) of the sugar together in a small bowl until pale in colour. Gradually add the milk, mixing well. Return to the pan and stir constantly over a low heat until the mixture begins to thicken and just coats the back of a spoon. Do not boil. Pour out the mixture into a large bowl and add the vanilla essence.

2. Sprinkle the gelatine over 75 ml (5 tbsp) water in a small bowl and leave to soak for 2–3 minutes. Place the bowl over a pan of simmering water and stir until dissolved. (Alternatively, microwave on HIGH for 30 seconds until dissolved.) Cool slightly and add to the custard. Stir to mix.

3. Whisk in the yogurt and lemon juice, about 45 ml (3 tbsp), whisking the mixture until smooth. Leave until cool, beginning to thicken but not set.

4. Whisk the egg whites until stiff but not dry and fold in the remaining sugar. Lightly whip the cream and fold into the yogurt mixture with the whites. Pour into a large glass serving dish. Cover and chill to set—about 3 hours.

5. Remove from the refrigerator about 15 minutes before serving.

Not suitable for freezing.

STRAWBERRY YOGURT MOULD

SERVES 6

A light mousse made in a ring mould always looks pretty filled with fresh fruit, and strawberries are probably the most decorative of all the soft summer berries. The delicately flavoured mould has a very light set, just firm enough to turn it out. Substitute buttermilk for the yogurt, if preferred.

3 eggs
50 g (2 oz) caster sugar
finely grated rind and juice of 1 large lemon
450 g (1 lb) strawberries
20 ml (4 tsp) powdered gelatine
150 ml ($\frac{1}{4}$ pint) natural yogurt
150 ml ($\frac{1}{4}$ pint) strawberry yogurt

1. Whisk the eggs, sugar and lemon rind together in a large bowl, using an electric mixer, until the mixture is pale, thick and creamy and leaves a trail when the whisk is lifted from the bowl.

2. Hull 225 g (8 oz) of the strawberries and place in a blender or food processor with half of the lemon juice. Purée until smooth.

3. Gradually whisk the purée into the mousse mixture, whisking well to keep the bulk.

4. Sprinkle the gelatine over the remaining lemon juice in a small bowl and leave to soak for 2—3 minutes. Place the bowl over a pan of simmering water and stir until dissolved. (Alternatively, microwave on HIGH for 30 seconds or until dissolved.) Leave until cool.

5. Gradually add the dissolved gelatine to the mousse mixture with the natural and strawberry yogurts. Stir carefully but thoroughly to mix. Pour into a greased 1.7 litre (3 pint) ring mould and chill for 4—5 hours or until set.

6. To serve, dip the mould briefly in hot water, then invert on to a serving plate. Hull most of the remaining strawberries, but leave a few of the green hulls on for decoration. Fill the centre of the ring with the fruit. Serve with extra natural yogurt.

Not suitable for freezing.

Below: STRAWBERRY YOGURT MOULD.

PRICKLY PEAR AND LIME MOUSSE

SERVES 6–8

Available from late summer to late autumn, prickly pears come mainly from Brazil, Italy and Mexico. Choose those which look firm, fresh and plump. Take great care to avoid the prickles when handling the fruit as they will irritate the skin badly.

6–8 prickly pears, about 700 g (1½ lb)
4 eggs, separated
50 g (2 oz) caster sugar
grated rind and juice of 1 lime
15 ml (1 tbsp) powdered gelatine
150 ml (¼ pint) whipping cream

1. Carefully peel the prickly pears. Roughly chop the flesh, place in a food processor or blender and purée until smooth. Rub through a nylon sieve to remove the seeds, yielding about 300 ml (½ pint) purée.
2. Whisk the egg yolks, sugar, grated lime rind and juice together in a bowl, using an electric mixer, until thick and mousse-like. Stir in the pear purée.
3. Sprinkle the gelatine over 45 ml (3 tbsp) water in a small bowl and leave to soak for 2–3 minutes. Place the bowl over a saucepan of simmering water and stir until dissolved. (Alternatively, microwave on HIGH for 30 seconds or until dissolved.)
4. Whip the cream until it just holds its shape. Whisk the egg whites until stiff but not dry.
5. Carefully add the dissolved gelatine to the mousse mixture, stir in the cream, then fold in the egg whites.
6. Pour gently into six to eight individual glass dishes or a large glass serving bowl. Chill until set.

Not suitable for freezing.

MANDARIN AND LYCHEE MOUSSE

SERVES 6

Canned lychees are more widely available than the fresh fruit, and they have a good flavour.

3 eggs, separated
2 egg yolks
75 g (3 oz) caster sugar
298 g (10½ oz) can mandarin oranges in natural juice
310 g (11 oz) can lychees in syrup
15 ml (1 tbsp) powdered gelatine
150 ml (¼ pint) double cream

1. Whisk the five egg yolks and sugar in a large bowl standing over a saucepan of gently simmering water until the mixture is thick and holds a ribbon trail.

Remove the bowl from the pan. Leave to cool for 30 minutes, whisking occasionally.
2. Reserve 60 ml (4 tbsp) of the mandarin juice. Purée half the oranges and the remaining juice in a blender or food processor with the lychees and half the syrup.
3. Sprinkle the gelatine over the reserved mandarin syrup in a small bowl and leave to soak for 2–3 minutes. Place the bowl over a saucepan of simmering water and stir until dissolved. (Alternatively, microwave on HIGH for 30 seconds or until dissolved.) Cool slightly.
4. Stir the mandarin purée into the cooled egg yolk mixture, then stir in the dissolved gelatine until evenly mixed.
5. Whip the cream until standing in soft peaks. Whisk the egg whites until stiff. Fold first the cream, then the egg whites into the mousse until evenly blended. Turn into a glass serving bowl and chill for at least 2 hours until set.
6. When the mousse is set, serve decorated with the reserved mandarin oranges and extra whipped cream.

Not suitable for freezing.

PRUNE AND PORT FOOL

SERVES 4

Because the flavours in this fool are so strong, you can get away with using canned custard instead of home-made.

100 g (4 oz) stoned prunes, soaked overnight
50 g (2 oz) caster sugar
60 ml (4 tbsp) port
finely grated rind and juice of 1 medium orange
150 ml (¼ pint) thick custard, cooled
150 ml (¼ pint) double cream

1. Drain the prunes, then put in a saucepan with the sugar, port, orange rind and juice. Simmer for about 15 minutes until soft. (Alternatively, microwave, covered, on HIGH for 8 minutes or until soft.)
2. Leave to cool slightly, then purée in a blender or food processor. Leave to cool completely.
3. Fold the cooled custard into the puréed prunes. Whip the cream until standing in soft peaks, then fold into the prune custard until evenly blended.
4. Divide the mixture between four individual glasses. Chill for about 2 hours until firm. Serve chilled, with sweet biscuits.

To freeze: pour into a rigid container at the end of step 3 and freeze. Thaw in the refrigerator overnight.

Above: AUTUMN COMPOTE (PAGE 24).
Below: PRUNE AND PORT FOOL.

PASKHA

This traditional Russian Easter speciality is normally made in a special tall paskha mould, but you can use a clay flower pot instead. The flower pot should have a hole in the bottom, and be scrupulously clean—it is a good idea to buy one especially for making paskha, and keep it with your other kitchen equipment. For the following recipe you will need a 16.5 cm (6½ inch) wide flower pot that is about 12.5 cm (5 inches) deep. You will also need some clean white muslin. Make the paskha the day before it is to be served.

175 g (6 oz) unsalted butter
finely grated rind of 1 lemon
finely grated rind of 1 orange
175 g (6 oz) caster sugar
2 eggs
5 ml (1 tsp) vanilla essence
900 g (2 lb) curd cheese
150 ml (¼ pint) double cream
25 g (1 oz) citron peel, chopped
25 g (1 oz) candied lemon peel, chopped
25 g (1 oz) candied orange peel, chopped
100 g (4 oz) raisins, chopped
50 g (2 oz) blanched almonds, chopped
50 g (2 oz) natural colour glacé cherries, chopped
50 g (2 oz) glacé pineapple, chopped
FOR THE DECORATION
citron peel
glacé cherries
glacé pineapple
blanched almonds, halved and lightly toasted
fresh violets or primroses (optional)

1. Beat the butter with the lemon and orange rind and the caster sugar in a bowl until very light and fluffy. Beat in the eggs, one at a time, beating well after each addition. Add the vanilla essence and curd cheese and beat well together until very smooth.
2. Beat in the cream, then mix in the citron and candied peels, raisins, nuts, cherries and pineapple. Set aside.
3. Place the flower pot in the centre of a large square of muslin, then make a diagonal cut to the centre of the muslin. Line the flower pot smoothly with the muslin; the cut will enable the muslin to be overlapped for a smoother lining. If there are too many bumps in the muslin, these will mark the paskha and spoil its finished appearance.
4. Fill the flower pot with the paskha mixture, then bring the overhanging muslin up and over the mixture to enclose it completely. Place a small flat plate on top of the paskha, then place some heavy weight, or cans of food, on top of the plate, to compress the mixture. Stand the flower pot on a plate, then refrigerate overnight. (It is important

to stand the pot on a plate as a certain amount of liquid will drain away from the paskha as it is compressed.)
5. To unmould the paskha, open out the muslin on the top, then place a flat serving plate on top of the paskha. Invert the plate and the flower pot together. Remove the flower pot, then very carefully peel away the muslin.
6. Decorate the paskha attractively with strips of citron peel, cherries, pineapple, almonds—and violets and primroses, if liked. Keep the paskha refrigerated until ready to serve.

Not suitable for freezing.

RHUBARB AND ORANGE FOOL

SERVES 6

Serve this fool well chilled with sponge fingers or crisp biscuits. Follow the basic recipe to make other fruit fools of your choice.

450 g (1 lb) rhubarb
grated rind and juice of 1 orange
pinch of ground cinnamon
25—50 g (1—2 oz) sugar
300 ml (½ pint) whipping cream
5 ml (1 tsp) orange flower water
shredded orange rind, to decorate

1. Chop the rhubarb into 2.5 cm (1 inch) pieces, discarding the leaves and the white ends of the stalks.
2. Put the rhubarb, orange rind, juice, cinnamon and sugar into a pan. Cover and cook gently for about 15 minutes.
3. Uncover and boil rapidly for 10 minutes, stirring frequently, until the mixture becomes a thick purée. Leave to cool for 1 hour.
4. When cool, whip the cream until stiff. Fold into the mixture with the orange flower water to taste.
5. Spoon the fool into glasses and chill for 1—2 hours until required. Decorate with orange rind and serve with Sponge fingers (see page 174).

To freeze: pour into a rigid container at the end of step 4. Thaw overnight in the refrigerator.

Opposite: PASKHA.

MEETHE CHAWAL

SERVES 4–6

Meethe Chawal is a sweet Indian rice pudding with
almonds, raisins and coconut.

175 g (6 oz) long grain rice
2.5 ml ($\frac{1}{2}$ tsp) salt
100 g (4 oz) sugar
2.5 cm (1 inch) cinnamon stick
100 g (4 oz) ghee or melted butter
seeds of 4 green cardamom pods
1.25 ml ($\frac{1}{4}$ tsp) grated nutmeg
pinch of saffron threads
100 g (4 oz) slivered blanched almonds, toasted
100 g (4 oz) raisins
50 g (2 oz) desiccated coconut

1. Bring a large saucepan of water to the boil. Add the
rice and salt and bring back to the boil. Stir once, then
simmer, uncovered, for 10 minutes.

2. Meanwhile, put the sugar and cinnamon stick in a
separate heavy based pan. Add 300 ml ($\frac{1}{2}$ pint) water
and heat gently until the sugar has dissolved. Bring to
the boil, then boil rapidly for 1 minute. Remove from
the heat.

3. Drain the rice. Heat the ghee in a flameproof casserole, add the rice, cardamom and nutmeg and cook
gently, stirring, for 1–2 minutes until the rice glistens.

4. Add the sugar syrup (with the cinnamon stick) to the
rice and stir gently to mix. Sprinkle in the saffron and
stir again. Cover the pan tightly with a lid.

5. Bake in the oven at 180°C (350°F) mark 4 for 40
minutes. Discard the cinnamon stick and cover the
casserole tightly again. Leave to stand for 5 minutes,
then stir in the nuts, raisins and coconut. Spoon into
individual dishes and serve immediately with single
cream.

Not suitable for freezing.

LOCKSHEN PUDDING

SERVES 4

This Jewish recipe was originally made on a Friday and cooked slowly overnight for serving hot on Saturday.

100 g (4 oz) broad egg noodles (lockshen)
pinch of salt
1 egg
50 g (2 oz) sugar
1.25 ml (¼ tsp) ground cinnamon
finely grated rind of ½ lemon
50 g (2 oz) currants
50 g (2 oz) chopped almonds (optional)
25 g (1 oz) margarine

1. Put the noodles into a pan of rapidly boiling salted water and cook for about 10 minutes until tender.
2. Drain into a sieve and rinse with plenty of hot water to remove excess starch. Drain well.
3. Whisk the egg and sugar together in a bowl. Stir in the cinnamon, lemon rind, currants and nuts, if using. Stir in the noodles.
4. Melt the margarine in a 5 cm (2 inch) deep, flame-proof baking dish until hot but not smoking. Swirl around the dish to coat the sides and pour the excess into the noodle mixture. Stir well and pour the mixture into the baking dish.
5. Bake in the oven at 190°C (375°F) mark 5 for 45 minutes until set, crisp and brown on top. Serve hot.

Not suitable for freezing.

STEAMED FRUIT PUDDINGS

Steamed fruit puddings are made by a very gentle method of cooking in a bowl in a steamer or saucepan of boiling water. Follow the rules below and the result will always be soft and moist. These puddings are turned out and often served with a sauce.

GENERAL RULES FOR STEAMING

● Half-fill the steamer with water and heat so that it is boiling by the time the pudding is made. If you have no steamer, fill a large saucepan with water to come halfway up the pudding basin. Cover and bring to the boil.
● Grease the pudding basin well.
● Cut double greaseproof paper or a piece of foil to cover the pudding basin and grease well. Put a pleat in the paper or foil to allow the pudding to rise.
● Fill the basin not more than two-thirds.
● Cover the basin tightly with paper or foil to prevent steam or water entering. Secure with string and make a string handle to lift the basin in and out of the pan.
● Keep the water in the steamer boiling rapidly all the time and have a kettle of boiling water ready to top it up regularly, or the steamer will boil dry. If using a saucepan, put an old saucer or metal pastry cutter in the base to keep the basin off the bottom.

STEAMED FRUIT PUDDING

SERVES 4

450 g (1 lb) fruit, prepared and stewed, or drained canned fruit
100 g (4 oz) butter or margarine
100 g (4 oz) caster sugar
2 eggs, beaten
few drops of vanilla essence
175 g (6 oz) self raising flour
little milk, to mix

1. Half-fill a steamer or large saucepan with water and put it on to boil. Grease a 900 ml (1½ pint) pudding basin and spoon the fruit into the bottom.
2. Cream the butter and sugar together in a bowl until pale and fluffy. Add the eggs and vanilla essence, a little at a time, beating well after each addition.
3. Using a metal spoon, fold in half the flour, then fold in the rest, with enough milk to give a dropping consistency.
4. Pour the mixture into the prepared pudding basin. Cover with greased greaseproof paper or foil and secure with string. Steam for 1½ hours. Serve with custard.

VARIATIONS

Suet Pudding   Put 30 ml (2 tbsp) jam in the bottom of the basin. Mix together 175 g (6 oz) self raising flour, pinch of salt, 75 g (3 oz) shredded suet, 50 g (2 oz) caster sugar and 150 ml (¼ pint) milk. Cook as above for 1½–2 hours.

Syrup or Jam Pudding   Put 30 ml (2 tbsp) golden syrup or jam into the bottom of the basin instead of the fruit.

Individual Dried Fruit Puddings   Add 75 g (3 oz) dried mixed fruit to the basic mixture. Omit the stewed fruit. Spoon into greased dariole moulds and steam as for Steamed castle puddings (see below). *Illustrated opposite*

Mincemeat Pudding   Line the bottom and sides of the basin with a thin layer of mincemeat and fill with the sponge mixture. When the pudding is cooked, turn it out carefully so that the outside remains completely covered with the mincemeat.

Chocolate Pudding   See Steamed chocolate pudding on page 103.

Steamed Castle Puddings   Spoon a little jam in the bottom of greased dariole moulds and divide the sponge between them, filling them two-thirds full. Cover each mould with greased foil and secure with string. Steam for 30–45 minutes (depending on size).

Microwave Sponge Pudding   Halve the ingredients but use 100 g (4 oz) flour. Mix to a very soft consistency with 45–60 ml (3–4 tbsp) milk. Cover and cook on HIGH for 5–7 minutes or until just moist on the surface. Stand for 5 minutes.

Not suitable for freezing.

COMPOTE OF FRUIT WITH ELDERFLOWER CREAM

SERVES 4

The mixture of fruit, which can include any varieties in season, is here poached in fruit juice rather than the sugary syrup preferred by the Victorians. Elderflowers are beautifully aromatic and grow abundantly in the hedgerows. You can find dried elderflowers in health food shops.

25 g (1 oz) sugar
6 large heads of fresh elderflowers or 25 g (1 oz) dried elderflowers
150 ml (5 fl oz) fresh double cream
900 g (2 lb) mixed fresh fruit, such as gooseberries, rhubarb, pears, strawberries, cherries, prepared
300 ml (½ pint) unsweetened orange or apple juice
1 cinnamon stick
2 strips of lemon rind
clear honey, to taste (optional)

1. To make the elderflower cream, put the sugar and 150 ml (¼ pint) water in a saucepan and heat gently until the sugar has dissolved, then boil rapidly until the liquid is reduced by half. Take off the heat and submerge the fresh or dried flowers in the syrup.

2. Leave to infuse for at least 2 hours, then press the syrup through a sieve, discarding the elderflowers. Whip the cream until it just holds its shape, then fold in the elderflower syrup. Chill until ready to serve.

3. Put the fruit, fruit juice, cinnamon and lemon rind in a large saucepan and simmer gently for 3–5 minutes until the fruits are softened, but still retain their shape. Serve the compôte warm or cold with the elderflower cream.

Below: INDIVIDUAL DRIED FRUIT PUDDINGS.

CHRISTMAS PUDDING

SERVES 8

Plum pudding only took on its connections with Christmas when it was introduced to the Victorians by Prince Albert. Burying a silver coin in the mixture is said to bring good fortune to whoever finds it in their portion. All the family should make a wish while stirring the mixture on Stir Up Sunday, the Sunday before Advent.

100 g (4 oz) prunes, stoned and chopped
175 g (6 oz) currants
175 g (6 oz) raisins
175 g (6 oz) sultanas
25 g (1 oz) blanched almonds, chopped
finely grated rind and juice of 1 lemon
100 g (4 oz) plain flour
2.5 ml (½ tsp) grated nutmeg
2.5 ml (½ tsp) ground cinnamon
2.5 ml (½ tsp) salt
75 g (3 oz) fresh breadcrumbs
100 g (4 oz) shredded suet
100 g (4 oz) soft dark brown sugar
2 eggs, beaten
30 ml (2 tbsp) Lyle's black treacle
150 ml (¼ pint) brown ale
150 ml (¼ pint) brandy, rum or sherry
75 ml (5 tbsp) brandy, to flame

1. Grease a 1.7 litre (3 pint) pudding basin.
2. Place the dried fruits, nuts, lemon rind and juice in a large bowl. Mix well.
3. In a separate bowl, sift the flour, nutmeg, cinnamon and salt together. Add the breadcrumbs, suet and sugar and mix.
4. Pour in the beaten egg, black treacle and brown ale, and beat well. Stir in the dried fruit mixture until evenly incorporated. Cover with clingfilm and leave to stand in a cool place for 24 hours.
5. The next day, add the brandy, stirring well. Pack the mixture into the prepared pudding basin, pressing it down well.
6. Cover with pleated greaseproof paper and foil. Secure with string. Steam for 4–5 hours.
7. Remove the pudding from the pan and leave to cool completely for 1–2 hours. Unwrap the pudding, then rewrap in fresh greaseproof paper and foil.
8. Store in a cool, dry place for at least 1 month (or up to 1 year) before serving.
9. To serve, steam for 2–3 hours. Turn out on to a warmed serving dish and decorate with holly. Serve the pudding with Brandy or rum butter (see page 253), cream or custard.
10. To flame the pudding, warm the brandy gently in a small saucepan, pour over the pudding and light carefully with a match.

To freeze: wrap and freeze after maturing for 1 month.

TO COOK CHRISTMAS PUDDING IN THE MICROWAVE

A Christmas pudding can be cooked in a microwave. However, because the traditional Christmas pudding recipe contains a high proportion of sugar, dried fruits, fat and alcohol, all of which attract microwave energy and quickly reach a high temperature, it means great care must be taken not to overcook and possibly burn the pudding. As it is potentially dangerous, Christmas pudding should be watched during cooking in a microwave.

However, a Christmas pudding can be cooked in only 45 minutes in the microwave instead of 2½ hours by conventional cooking, and you do not need a saucepan of boiling water that has to be continually replenished. If, therefore, you are adapting your favourite Christmas pudding recipe, only add 30 ml (2 tbsp) of the alcohol suggested and replace the remaining liquid with milk or orange juice. Additional liquid should also be added to keep the pudding moist; allow an extra 15 ml (1 tbsp) milk for each egg added. A microwaved Christmas pudding should be eaten fairly soon after making. Store for up to 2–3 weeks in a cool place.

TO REHEAT CHRISTMAS PUDDING IN THE MICROWAVE

Remove all the wrappings and basin from the pudding. Put the pudding on an ovenproof serving plate, cut into the required number of portions and pull apart so that there is a space in the centre. Place a small tumbler of water in the centre. This introduces steam and helps to keep the pudding moist. Cover with a large upturned bowl. Cook on HIGH for 2–3 minutes, depending on the size of the pudding, or until hot. Remove the cover and glass and reshape the pudding with the hands. Decorate with a sprig of holly and serve.

To reheat an individual portion of Christmas pudding, put on a plate and cook, uncovered, for 1–1½ minutes until hot.

UPSIDE DOWN GUAVA AND ALMOND CAKE

SERVES 4–6

A fragrant sponge suitable for a family lunch or an elegant dinner party. Serve warm to enjoy at its best.

45 ml (3 tbsp) Lyle's golden syrup
5 ml (1 tsp) lemon juice
2 small ripe guavas, about 350 g (12 oz) total weight
100 g (4 oz) softened butter or margarine
100 g (4 oz) caster sugar
2 eggs
25 g (1 oz) self raising flour
75 g (3 oz) ground almonds

1. Place a round of non-stick baking paper in the base of a greased 20.5 cm (8 inch) sandwich tin.

2. Heat the golden syrup and lemon juice together in a pan and pour into the tin.

3. Peel and quarter the guavas and remove the seeds. Arrange, rounded side down, on top of the syrup.

4. Beat the butter and sugar together in a bowl until very pale and fluffy. Gradually beat in the eggs, then fold in the flour and ground almonds. Spoon the mixture on top of the guavas and carefully level the surface, without disturbing the guavas.

5. Bake in the oven at 180°C (350°F) mark 4 for 45–50 minutes or until the sponge is golden, well risen and springs back to the touch; covering lightly if necessary.

6. Cool the sponge in the tin for 3–4 minutes, loosen the edges of the cake with a palette knife and turn out on to a serving plate. Serve warm with cream.

Not suitable for freezing.

CRANBERRY AND ORANGE UPSIDE DOWN CAKE

SERVES 8

A moist sponge topped with a layer of tart cranberries. Best served warm.

FOR THE TOPPING
25 g (1 oz) butter, melted
350 g (12 oz) cranberries
75 g (3 oz) caster sugar
60 ml (4 tbsp) cranberry sauce

FOR THE CAKE
225 g (8 oz) self raising flour
5 ml (1 tsp) baking powder
large pinch of salt
1 egg
finely grated rind and juice of 1 large orange
50 ml (2 fl oz) milk
100 g (4 oz) butter or margarine, softened
100 g (4 oz) caster sugar

1. Grease a 23 cm (9 inch) round spring-release cake tin.

2. To make the topping, pour the melted butter into the prepared cake tin. Mix the cranberries, sugar and cranberry sauce together. Spoon the cranberry mixture evenly over the base of the cake tin.

3. To make the cake, put all the ingredients into a large bowl and beat until smooth and glossy. Carefully pour over the cranberries and level the surface.

4. Bake in the oven at 180°C (350°F) mark 4 for about 1 hour or until well risen and firm to the touch. Cover the top with a double sheet of greaseproof paper after 40 minutes to prevent overbrowning.

5. Leave to cool in the tin for 5 minutes, then turn the cake out on to a serving plate. Serve while warm with Fruit ice cream (see page 217) or whipped cream.

Not suitable for freezing.

Illustrated on page 13

REDCURRANT HAZELNUT GÂTEAU

SERVES 8–10

Cardamom adds a fragrant lemon taste to this light sponge. The hazelnuts are toasted first to bring out their flavour. This elegant summer dessert will impress dinner party guests.

FOR THE SPONGE
40 g (1½ oz) hazelnuts
6 green cardamom pods
2 eggs
150 g (5 oz) caster sugar
50 g (2 oz) plain flour

FOR THE FILLING
225 g (8 oz) redcurrants, stalks removed
15 ml (1 tbsp) arrowroot
15 ml (1 tbsp) lemon juice
150 ml (¼ pint) double cream
60 ml (4 tbsp) natural yogurt
icing sugar, for dusting

1. Grease a 20.5 cm (8 inch) sandwich tin and line the base with greaseproof paper. Dust with caster sugar and flour.

2. To make the sponge, first toast the hazelnuts under the grill until well browned. Rub off the skins. Cool, then coarsely grind.

3. Split open the cardamom pods and remove the seeds. Crush to a fine powder.

4. Using an electric whisk, beat the eggs, 75 g (3 oz) of the sugar and the ground cardamom together in a bowl until really thick. When the whisk is lifted the mixture should be thick enough to leave a trail.

5. Lightly fold in the flour and ground hazelnuts. Spoon the mixture into the prepared tin.

6. Bake in the oven at 180°C (350°F) mark 4 for about 25 minutes or until well risen but browned. Leave to cool in the tin for 10 minutes then turn out on to a wire rack to finish cooling.

7. Meanwhile to make the filling, place the redcurrants in a small pan with the remaining sugar and 100 ml (4 fl oz) water. Heat gently until the fruit softens and the sugar dissolves.

8. Mix the arrowroot to a smooth paste with a little water. Stir into the fruit, then bring to the boil, stirring all the time. Boil for 1 minute. Add the lemon juice, then cool, cover and chill.

9. To complete the gâteau, cut the sponge into two layers. Whip the cream until it just holds its shape and stir in the yogurt. Sandwich the sponge layers with the cream and fruit. Chill until required. Dust with icing sugar before serving.

To freeze: wrap and freeze the cakes at the end of step 6. Thaw at cool room temperature, then finish as above.

Illustrated on page 22

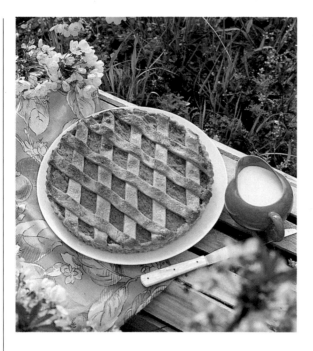

5. Quickly lattice the pastry strips over the fruit mixture. Brush with beaten egg and dust with caster sugar. Bake at 200°C (400°F) mark 6 for about 20 minutes, or until golden brown and crisp.

BLUEBERRY BUCKLE

SERVES 12

Serve this satisfying dessert with tangy crème fraîche or natural yogurt.

FOR THE CAKE
700 g (1½ lb) blueberries
350 g (12 oz) plus 30 ml (2 tbsp) self raising flour
5 ml (1 tsp) baking powder
50 g (2 oz) butter or margarine
150 g (5 oz) caster sugar
1 egg
300 ml (½ pint) milk
almond flavouring

FOR THE TOPPING
50 g (2 oz) butter or margarine
50 g (2 oz) plain flour
50 g (2 oz) caster sugar

1. Grease a 23 cm (9 inch) round baking dish.
2. To make the cake, toss the blueberries in the 30 ml (2 tbsp) flour and set aside.
3. Cream the butter and sugar in a bowl until pale and fluffy. Beat in the egg, then gradually add the milk, almond flavouring to taste and the remaining flour. Stir in the blueberries. Pour into the prepared dish.
4. To make the topping, rub the butter into the flour until the mixture resembles fine breadcrumbs. Stir in the sugar. Sprinkle over the cake mixture.
5. Bake in the oven at 190°C (375°F) mark 5 for 1–1¼ hours or until a skewer inserted into the centre comes out clean. Leave to cool for 15 minutes, then serve warm.

To freeze: wrap and freeze after cooling. Thaw at cool room temperature. Reheat, covered with foil, at 200°C (400°F) mark 6 for 30 minutes, removing the foil for the last 5 minutes.

PANADE

SERVES 6–8

The *boulangeries* of Provence provide wonderful fruit tarts but there are local specialities to make at home too. *Panade* is unusual: apples and pears are grated, cooked together with orange juice, then enclosed in pastry or dough. The origins of this recipe are not hard to trace, with so many fruit trees covering the valleys.

175 g (6 oz) butter or margarine
225 g (8 oz) plain flour
large pinch ground cinnamon
700 g (1½ lb) sweet eating apples
700 g (1½ lb) ripe pears
grated rind and juice of 1 large orange
beaten egg and caster sugar, for glazing

1. Rub 125 g (4 oz) butter into the flour and cinnamon until the mixture resembles fine breadcrumbs. Add enough chilled water, about 90 ml (6 tbsp), to bind to a soft paste. Wrap in cling film and refrigerate for 10 minutes.
2. On a lightly floured surface, roll the dough out thinly and line a 24 cm (9½ inch) loose-based fluted flan tin. Re-roll the excess pastry and cut into 1 cm (½ inch) wide strips. Cover and refrigerate until required. Bake the flan blind in the oven at 200°C (400°F) mark 6 for about 20 minutes.
3. Meanwhile, melt the remaining butter in a large non-stick frying pan. Stir in the peeled, cored and grated apples and pears, the grated orange rind and 45 ml (3 tbsp) orange juice.
4. Cook over a high heat, stirring constantly, until all excess moisture has evaporated and the mixture is quite dry. Spoon into the warm flan case.

Above: PANADE.

RASPBERRY AND WALNUT SHORTBREAD

SERVES 8

Two of Scotland's most celebrated foods—shortbread and raspberries—come together in this recipe to make a truly mouthwatering dessert that tastes even better than it looks. The walnuts are ground and added to the shortbread mixture for a subtle nutty flavour.

100 g (4 oz) walnut pieces
100 g (4 oz) butter
75 g (3 oz) caster sugar
175 g (6 oz) plain flour
450 g (1 lb) raspberries, hulled
50 g (2 oz) icing sugar
30 ml (2 tbsp) raspberry-flavoured liqueur or kirsch (optional)
300 ml (½ pint) whipping cream

1. Draw three 20.5 cm (8 inch) circles on non-stick baking paper. Place the circles on baking sheets.
2. Grind the walnuts finely in a blender or food processor.
3. Cream the butter and sugar together in a bowl until pale and fluffy. Beat in the walnuts and flour until a dough is formed. Divide the dough into three shortbread portions.
4. Put a portion of shortbread dough in the centre of each paper circle and press out with the heel of the hand until the dough is the same size as the circle.
5. Cut one of the circles into eight triangles with a sharp knife and ease them slightly apart. Refrigerate the circles and triangles for 30 minutes.
6. Bake in the oven at 190°C (375°F) mark 5 for 15–20 minutes, swapping over the sheets to ensure the shortbread browns evenly. Leave to cool and harden for 10 minutes on the paper, then transfer to wire racks to cool completely.
7. Meanwhile, reserve a third of the raspberries for decoration. Put the rest in a bowl with the icing sugar and liqueur, if using. Crush the raspberries with a fork, then leave them to macerate while the pastry rounds are cooling.
8. Assemble the shortbread just before serving, to ensure that the pastry remains crisp. Whip the cream until thick, then fold in the crushed raspberries and juice. Stand one round of pastry on a flat serving plate and spread with half of the cream mixture. Top with the remaining round of pastry, then the remaining cream mixture.
9. Arrange the triangles of pastry on top of the cream, wedging them in at an angle. Scatter the reserved whole raspberries in between. Serve the shortbread as soon as possible.

To freeze: wrap the cooled shortbread at the end of step 6. Thaw at cool room temperature, then finish as above.

Illustrated on page 20

APPLE AND BLACKBERRY CHARLOTTE

SERVES 4

A charlotte mould is a large round mould with sloping sides and is used for making the classic Charlotte Russe (see page 170) as well as a hot charlotte like this. A deep round cake tin works just as well if you do not have the special tin.

450 g (1 lb) cooking apples
450 g (1 lb) blackberries
grated rind and juice of ½ lemon
1.25 ml (¼ tsp) ground cinnamon
175–225 g (6–8 oz) sugar
30 ml (2 tbsp) bread or cake crumbs
6 large bread slices
50 g (2 oz) butter or margarine, melted

1. Grease a 1.4 litre (2½ pint) charlotte mould or a 15 cm (6 inch) round cake tin.
2. Peel, core and thickly slice the apples. Put in a saucepan with the blackberries, lemon rind and juice and cinnamon and cook gently for 10 minutes until the apples have softened slightly. Add the sugar and crumbs.
3. Cut the crusts off the bread. Trim one piece to a round the same size as the base of the tin, dip it into the melted butter and fit into the tin. Dip the remaining slices of bread in the butter and arrange closely around the side of the tin, reserving one piece for the top.
4. Spoon in the stewed fruit mixture and cover with the remaining slice of bread, trimmed to fit the top of the mould.
5. Bake in the oven at 190°C (375°F) mark 5 for about 1 hour. Turn out and serve with custard.

To freeze: wrap and freeze at the end of step 5.

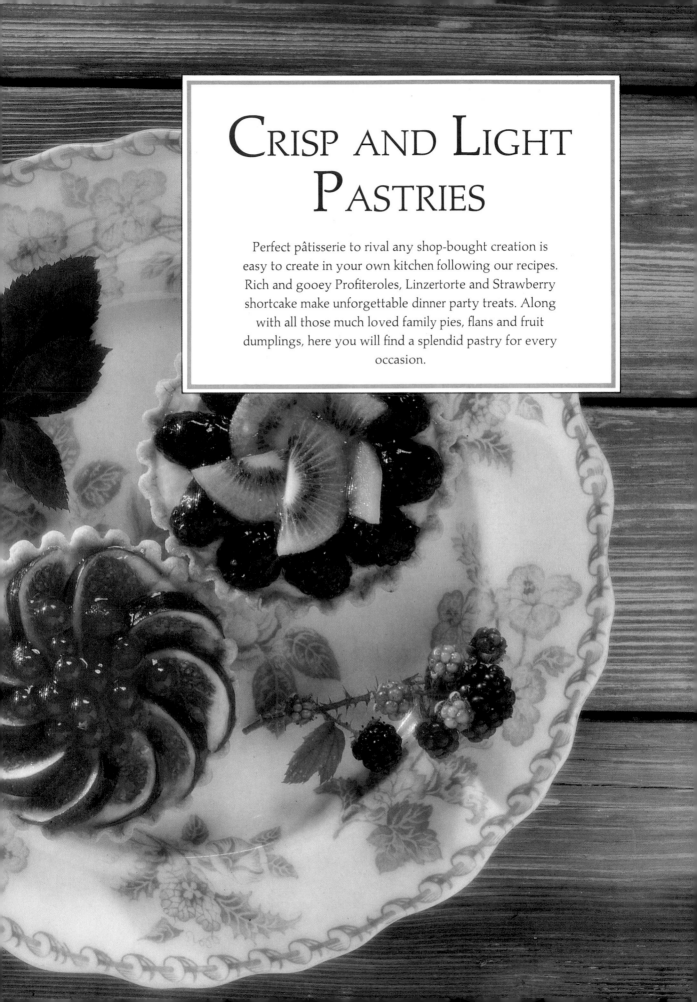

CRISP AND LIGHT PASTRIES

Perfect pâtisserie to rival any shop-bought creation is
easy to create in your own kitchen following our recipes.
Rich and gooey Profiteroles, Linzertorte and Strawberry
shortcake make unforgettable dinner party treats. Along
with all those much loved family pies, flans and fruit
dumplings, here you will find a splendid pastry for every
occasion.

Despite the mystique attached to making pastry, the only secrets to success are patience, practice and care. Unless making choux or phyllo (strudel) pastry, the golden rule is keep everything cool—kitchen, work surface, utensils, ingredients and yourself.

The perfect pastry is 'short'—light, crumbly and crisp, but not hard. The amount of fat and water added to the flour and the way the pastry is handled all govern the shortness. Even pastries with a little fat in them only require a little water. The more water you add, the harder and tougher the pastry will be. A very soft, easy to roll pastry will probably have too much water in it. It will shrink badly in the oven and have a tough, hard texture. Always add water a little at a time, remembering that the amount needed can vary from day to day depending on the absorbency of the flour and the humidity in your kitchen.

When rolling out pastry, dust the work surface and the rolling pin, never the pastry, with as little flour as possible. Roll the dough lightly and evenly in one direction only. Always roll away from you, rotating the pastry frequently to keep an even shape. Use light but firm strokes. Overrolled pastry will shrink dramatically when baked.

Baking Blind

Baking blind is the term used to describe the cooking of pastry cases without any filling. The pastry may be partially prebaked to be cooked for a further period when filled, or completely cooked if the filling requires no further cooking.

1. Make the pastry and line the flan case or tartlet tins. Chill for 30 minutes to 'rest' the pastry.
2. Cut out a piece of greaseproof paper or foil larger than the pastry case. Remove the pastry case from the fridge and prick the base.
3. Lay the paper or foil in the pastry case and fill with baking beans.
4. For partially prebaked cases, bake in the oven at 200°C (400°F) mark 6 for 10–15 minutes until the pastry is just 'set'. Remove the paper and beans, then bake for a further 5 minutes until lightly coloured. Pastry cases which need complete baking should be returned to the oven for a further 15 minutes or until pale golden brown.

Pastry cases which have been baked blind will keep for several days in an airtight tin or may be frozen.

Shortcrust Pastry Quantity Guide for Flans, Tartlets and Pies

Dish size	Pastry (flour weight)
15 cm (6 inch) plain or fluted flan ring	100 g (4 oz)
18 cm (7 inch) plain or fluted flan ring	150 g (5 oz)
20.5 cm (8 inch) plain or fluted flan ring	175 g (6 oz)
23 cm (9 inch) plain or fluted flan ring	200 g (7 oz)
18 × 6.5 cm (2½ inch) tartlets	225 g (8 oz) (pastry lid)
12 × 7.5 cm (3 inch) tartlets	225 g (8 oz)
900 ml (1½ pint) pie dish	175 g (6 oz) (pastry lid only)
1 litre (2 pint) pie dish	225 g (8 oz) (pastry lid)
20.5 cm (8 inch) pie plate	250 g (9 oz) (line and lid)

Apricot Glaze

Apricot glaze is used for glazing pastries and flans to make them look more attractive. The addition of a little liqueur gives extra flavour.

---

350 g (12 oz) jar apricot conserve

15–30 ml (1–2 tbsp) liqueur; kirsch, brandy, orange or almond-flavoured liqueur (optional)

---

1. Put the conserve into a small saucepan and heat gently, stirring all the time, until melted.
2. Press through a nylon sieve into another small, clean saucepan. Add the liqueur, or a little water, then bring to the boil, stirring. The glaze should always be at boiling point when used to ensure that it sets well.
3. Keep made up apricot glaze in a jar in the refrigerator, ready to be heated when required for glazing.

Shortcrust Pastry

MAKES 225 g (8 oz) PASTRY

This plain short pastry is probably the most widely used of all pastries. For shortcrust pastry, the proportion of flour to fat is 2:1, or twice the quantity. Therefore, for a recipe using quantities of shortcrust pastry other than 225 g (8 oz), simply use half the quantity of fat to the flour weight specified.

---

225 g (8 oz) plain flour

pinch of salt

50 g (2 oz) butter or margarine, chilled and diced

50 g (2 oz) lard, chilled and diced

---

1. Mix the flour and salt together in a bowl. Add the fat to the flour.
2. Using your fingertips, rub the fat lightly into the flour until the mixture resembles fine breadcrumbs.
3. Add 45–60 ml (3–4 tbsp) chilled water, sprinkling it evenly over the surface. (Uneven addition may cause blistering when the pastry is cooked.)
4. Stir in with a round-bladed knife until the mixture begins to stick together in large lumps. With one hand, collect the dough mixture together to form a ball.
5. Knead lightly for a few seconds to give a firm, smooth dough. Do not overhandle the dough.
6. To roll out, sprinkle a very little flour on a working surface and the rolling pin (not on the pastry) and roll out the dough evenly in one direction only, turning it occasionally. The usual thickness is 0.3 cm (⅛ inch). Do not pull or stretch the pastry.
7. The pastry can be baked straight away, but it is better if allowed to 'rest' for about 30 minutes in the tin or dish, covered in foil or clingfilm, in the refrigerator.
8. Bake in the oven at 200–220°C (400–425°F) mark 6–7, except where otherwise specified, until lightly browned (see individual recipes).

VARIATIONS

Wholemeal pastry Follow the recipe and method for Shortcrust pastry but use plain wholemeal flour instead of white. You may need a little extra water due to the absorbency of wholemeal flour.

Nut pastry Follow the recipe and method for Shortcrust pastry but stir in 25 g (1 oz) very finely chopped, shelled walnuts, cashew nuts, hazelnuts or almonds before adding the water.

To freeze: wrap tightly and freeze. Thaw at cool room temperature or overnight in the refrigerator.

SHORTCRUST PASTRY MADE IN A FOOD PROCESSOR

MAKES 225 g (8 oz) PASTRY

A food processor makes shortcrust pastry very quickly and gives good results. It is most important not to overmix the dough as a food processor works in seconds not minutes. For even 'rubbing in', turn the machine on in short bursts rather than letting it run continuously. Make sure you know the capacity of your food processor and never overload the processor bowl. If making a large quantity of pastry, make it in two batches.

225 g (8 oz) plain flour
pinch of salt
50 g (2 oz) butter or margarine, chilled and diced
50 g (2 oz) lard, chilled and diced

1. Mix the flour and salt together in the bowl of the food processor.
2. Add the fat to the flour. Mix for a few seconds until the mixture resembles fine breadcrumbs.
3. Add 45–60 ml (3–4 tbsp) chilled water and switch on until the mixture forms a smooth dough. Roll out and use as for shortcrust pastry.

Freeze as shortcrust pastry.

Previous Page: LAVENDER-SCENTED TARTLETS (PAGE 59).

FLAN PASTRY

MAKES 100 g (4 oz) PASTRY

Flan pastry is made by the same rubbing-in method as shortcrust, but the liquid used is beaten egg instead of water. It is usually sweetened with caster sugar which improves the flavour and is ideal for flan cases, small tarts and other sweet pastries. Quick and easy to prepare, flan pastry benefits from being chilled for at least 30 minutes before use.

100 g (4 oz) plain flour
pinch of salt
75 g (3 oz) butter or margarine and lard, chilled and diced
5 ml (1 tsp) caster sugar
1 egg, beaten

1. Mix the flour and salt together in a bowl. Rub the fat into the flour as for shortcrust pastry, until the mixture resembles fine breadcrumbs. Stir in the sugar.
2. Add the egg, stirring with a round-bladed knife until the ingredients begin to stick together in large lumps.
3. With one hand, collect the mixture together and knead lightly for a few seconds to give a firm, smooth dough. Roll out as for shortcrust pastry.
4. Bake in the oven at 200°C (400°F) mark 6, unless otherwise stated, until lightly browned.

Freeze as shortcrust pastry.

PÂTE SUCRÉE

MAKES 100 g (4 oz) PASTRY

This French, rich, sweet, short pastry is the best choice for Continental pâtisserie. Pâte sucrée is thin, crisp yet melting in texture. It keeps its shape, shrinks very little and does not spread during baking. Pâte sucrée is fairly quick and easy to make. Although it can be made in a bowl, the classic way to make this pastry is on a flat, cold surface such as marble.

100 g (4 oz) plain flour
pinch of salt
50 g (2 oz) caster sugar
50 g (2 oz) butter (at room temperature)
2 egg yolks

1. Sift the flour and salt on to a work surface. Make a well in the centre and add the sugar, butter and yolks.
2. Using the fingertips of one hand, pinch and work the sugar, butter and egg yolks together until well blended.
3. Gradually work in all the flour to bind the mixture together. Knead lightly until smooth.
4. Wrap the pastry in foil or clingfilm and leave to 'rest' in the refrigerator or a cool place for about 30 minutes, or overnight if possible.
5. Bake in the oven at 190°C (375°F) mark 5, unless otherwise stated, until lightly browned.

Freeze as shortcrust pastry.

SUETCRUST PASTRY

MAKES 225 g (8 oz) PASTRY

This pastry may be used for sweet basin puddings, roly-poly puddings and dumplings. It can be steamed, boiled or baked; the first two methods are the most satisfactory, as baked suetcrust pastry is inclined to be hard. Suetcrust pastry is quick and easy to make, and should be light and spongy in texture—the correct mixing, quick light handling and long, slow cooking will achieve this. For a lighter texture or if using wholemeal flour, replace 50 g (2 oz) of the flour with 50 g (2 oz) fresh breadcrumbs.

225 g (8 oz) self raising flour
2.5 ml (½ tsp) salt
100 g (4 oz) shredded suet

1. Mix the flour, salt and suet together in a bowl.
2. Using a round-bladed knife, stir in enough chilled water, about 150 ml (¼ pint), to give a light, elastic dough. Knead very lightly until smooth.
3. Roll out to 0.5 cm (¼ inch) thick and use as required.
4. Steaming or boiling basin and roly-poly puddings takes about 2–4 hours, depending on filling and size. Roly-poly puddings can also be wrapped in foil and baked in the oven at 200°C (400°F) mark 6 for about 45 minutes, unless otherwise stated. Dumplings cooked in simmering liquid take about 25 minutes.

Freeze as shortcrust pastry.

FLAKY PASTRY

This pastry can be used instead of puff pastry where a great rise is not needed. The fat should be of about the same consistency as the dough with which it is to be combined, which is why it is worked on a plate beforehand. This quantity is equivalent to one 368 g (13 oz) packet.

225 g (8 oz) plain flour
pinch of salt
175 g (6 oz) butter or a mixture of butter and lard
a squeeze of lemon juice

1. Mix the flour and salt together in a bowl. Soften the fat by working it with a knife on a plate, then divide into four equal portions.
2. Add one quarter of the fat to the flour and rub it in until the mixture resembles fine breadcrumbs.
3. Stirring with a round-bladed knife, add a squeeze of lemon juice and about 120 ml (8 tbsp) chilled water or sufficient to make a soft, elastic dough. Turn the dough on to a lightly floured work surface and knead until smooth. Roll out into an oblong three times as long as it is wide.
4. Using a round-bladed knife, dot a second quarter of the fat over the top two thirds of the pastry in flakes, so that it looks like buttons on a card.

5. Fold the bottom third of the pastry up and the top third down, then turn it so that the folded edges are at the sides.
6. Seal the edges of the pastry by pressing with a rolling pin. Wrap the pastry and leave in the refrigerator to 'rest' for 15 minutes. Re-roll as before and repeat twice more until the remaining fat has been used up.
7. Wrap the pastry loosely and leave to 'rest' in the refrigerator for at least 30 minutes before using.
8. Roll out on a lightly floured work surface to 0.3 cm (⅛ inch) thick and use as required. Leave to rest in the refrigerator for 30 minutes before baking. Brush with beaten egg before baking to give the characteristic glaze.
9. Bake in the oven at 200°C (400°F) mark 6, unless otherwise stated.

Freeze as shortcrust pastry.

CHOUX PASTRY

This light, crisp-textured pastry is used for making sweet and savoury eclairs, cream puffs, airgrettes and gougère. As long as the recipe instructions are strictly adhered to, choux pastry will always give good results. Always collect the ingredients together before starting to make choux pastry as all the flour needs to be added quickly as soon as the mixture has come to the boil. Raw choux paste is too soft and sticky to be rolled out and is, therefore, piped or spooned on to a dampened baking sheet for baking. During baking, the moisture in the dough turns to steam and puffs up the mixture leaving the centre hollow. Thorough cooking is important; if insufficiently cooked, the choux may collapse when taken from the oven and there will be uncooked pastry in the centre to scoop out. When the cooked choux has cooled and dried out, it can be filled with whipped cream or a savoury filling. Choux pastry can also be deep fried—pipe or spoon it directly into hot oil.

65 g (2½ oz) plain or strong plain flour
50 g (2 oz) butter or margarine
2 eggs, lightly beaten

1. Sift the flour on to a plate or piece of paper. Put the butter and 150 ml (¼ pint) water in a saucepan. Heat gently until the butter has melted, then bring to the boil. Remove the pan from the heat. Tip the flour at once into the hot liquid. Beat thoroughly with a wooden spoon.
2. Continue beating the mixture over the heat until smooth and forms a ball in the centre of the pan (take care not to overbeat or the mixture will become fatty). Remove from the heat and leave the mixture to cool for 1–2 minutes.
3. Beat in the eggs, a little at a time, adding only just enough to give a piping consistency.
4. It is important to beat the mixture vigorously at this stage to trap in as much air as possible. A hand held electric mixer is ideal for this purpose. Continue beating until the mixture develops an obvious sheen. Use as required.

5. Bake in the oven at 200°C (400°F) mark 6. Immediately after the choux pastry is removed from the oven, it should be pierced to allow steam to escape.

To freeze: freeze cooked choux pastry in a rigid container. Thaw at cool room temperature. Refresh in a hot oven.

PIPING CHOUX PASTRY

1. To fill a piping bag, usually fitted with a plain 1 cm (½ inch) nozzle, place it in a tall jug and turn back the open end over the jug rim. Spoon the pastry mixture into the bag and squeeze it down to eliminate air bubbles.
2. When making eclairs, it may help to mark evenly spaced lines on the baking sheet with the end of a wooden spoon as a guide for piping.
3. Hold the piping bag in one hand and, with the thumb and one finger of your other hand on the nozzle to guide it, press out the pastry. When the required length is reached, cut off the paste with a wet knife. Choux puffs and profiteroles can be piped or spooned into mounds.

PUFF PASTRY

The richest of all the pastries, puff requires patience, practice and very light handling. Whenever possible it should be made the day before use. It is not practical to make in a quantity with less than 450 g (1 lb) flour weight. This quantity is equivalent to two 368 g (13 oz) packets.

450 g (1 lb) strong plain flour
pinch of salt
450 g (1 lb) butter or margarine, chilled
15 ml (1 tbsp) lemon juice

1. Mix the flour and salt together in a bowl. Cut off 50 g (2 oz) of the butter and flatten the remaining butter with a rolling pin to a slab 2 cm (¾ inch) thick.
2. Cut the 50 g (2 oz) butter into small pieces, add to the flour and rub in. Using a round-bladed knife, stir in the lemon juice and about 300 ml (½ pint) chilled water or sufficient to make a soft, elastic dough.
3. Quickly knead the dough until smooth and shape into a round. Cut through half the depth in the shape of a cross. Open out to form a star.
4. Roll out, keeping the centre four times as thick as the flaps. Place the slab of butter in the centre of the dough and fold the flaps envelope-style.
5. Press gently with a rolling pin and roll out into a rectangle measuring about 40.5 × 20.5 cm (16 × 8 inches).
6. Fold the bottom third up and the top third down, keeping the edges straight. Seal the edges.
7. Wrap the pastry in greaseproof paper and leave to 'rest' in the refrigerator for 30 minutes. Put the pastry on a lightly floured work surface with the folded edges to the sides, then repeat the rolling, folding and resting sequence five times.
8. Shape the pastry as required, then leave to 'rest' in the refrigerator for 30 minutes before baking. Brush with beaten egg before baking.
9. Bake in the oven at 220°C (425°F) mark 7, for about 15 minutes on its own or longer if filled, unless otherwise stated.

Freeze as shortcrust pastry.

MILLE-FEUILLES

Roll out ¼ quantity Puff pastry or a 212 g (7½ oz) packet frozen puff pastry, thawed, into a rectangle measuring 25.5 × 23 cm (10 × 9 inches) and place on a dampened baking sheet. Prick all over. Bake as above for 10 minutes until golden brown. Cool, then trim the edges. Cut in half lengthways and cut each half across into six slices. Spread each half with raspberry jam then whipped cream. Sandwich together. Ice the tops with white glacé icing, reserving 30 ml (2 tbsp). Colour the reserved icing pink, then pipe fine lines of pink glacé icing across each pastry. Draw a skewer through the length of the Mille-feuilles to make a 'feather' pattern. Leave to set. Serves 6.

ROUGH PUFF PASTRY

Similar in texture to flaky pastry, rough puff can be used instead of flaky, except when even rising and appearance are particularly important. Rough puff is quicker and easier to make than puff or flaky pastry. This quantity is equivalent to one 368 g (13 oz) packet.

225 g (8 oz) plain flour
pinch of salt
75 g (3 oz) butter or margarine, chilled
75 g (3 oz) lard, chilled
lemon juice

1. Mix the flour and salt together in a bowl. Cut the butter and lard into 2 cm (¾ inch) cubes. Stir into the flour, without breaking up the pieces.
2. Add a squeeze of lemon juice and about 150 ml (¼ pint) chilled water or sufficient to mix to a fairly stiff dough, using a rounded-bladed knife.
3. On a lightly floured work surface, roll out into an oblong three times as long as it is wide. Fold the bottom third up and the top third down, then turn the pastry so that the folded edges are at the sides. Seal the ends of the pastry with a rolling pin. Wrap the pastry in greaseproof and 'rest' in refrigerator for 15 minutes.
4. Repeat this rolling and folding process three more times, turning the dough so that the folded edge is on the left-hand side each time. Wrap and 'rest' for 30 minutes.
5. Roll out the pastry to 0.3 cm (⅛ inch) thick and use as required. Leave to 'rest' in the refrigerator for 30 minutes before baking. Brush with beaten egg before baking to give the characteristic glaze.
6. Bake in the oven at 220°C (425°F) mark 7, unless otherwise stated.

Freeze as shortcrust pastry.

PHYLLO (FILO) OR STRÜDEL PASTRY

MAKES 225 g (8 oz) PASTRY

Phyllo is a pastry of water-like thinness from the Middle East which is used for both savoury and sweet pastries, such as Baklava. It is identical to strüdel pastry which originated in Europe and is used for the popular Apfel strüdel. Phyllo or strüdel pastry is fairly difficult and time-consuming to make. Unlike most pastries, it requires warm ingredients and, instead of light handling, it has to be kneaded and beaten. The dough is kneaded vigorously to enable the gluten in the flour to develop strength so the pastry can be stretched into a very thin, resilient sheet. For the same reason, strong plain flour is used as it yields more gluten to help produce an elastic dough. The thin sheet is either spread with a filling and rolled or folded, or it is cut into rectangles and stacked with a filling in between. Ready-made phyllo or strüdel pastry is available in sheets from continental shops and delicatessens.

225 g (8 oz) strong plain flour
2.5 ml (½ tsp) salt
1 egg, lightly beaten
30 ml (2 tbsp) vegetable oil
1.25 ml (¼ tsp) lemon juice
25 g (1 oz) butter, melted

1. Mix the flour and salt together in a large bowl. Make a well in the centre and pour in the egg, oil and lemon juice. Stirring with a fork, gradually add 75 ml (5 tbsp) lukewarm water or sufficient to make a soft, sticky dough.
2. Work the dough in the bowl until it leaves the sides. Turn out on to a lightly floured work surface and knead for 15 minutes. The dough should feel smooth.
3. Form it into a ball, place on a cloth and cover with a warmed bowl. Leave to 'rest' in a warm place for 30 minutes.
4. Lightly flour a clean cotton cloth. Place the ball of dough on the cloth and roll out into a rectangle about 0.3 cm (⅛ inch) thick, lifting and turning to prevent it sticking to the cloth.
5. Brush the top of the dough with little melted butter. Gently stretch the dough by carefully lifting it on the backs of the hands and fingertips, and pulling it from the centre to the outside, trying to keep it in a rectangle.
6. Continue lifting and stretching the dough until it becomes paper thin and the rectangle measures no less than 75 × 50 cm (30 × 20 inches). Trim off uneven thick edges with scissors or a sharp knife.

7. Leave the dough on the cloth to dry and 'rest' for about 15 minutes before lifting off carefully.
8. Bake in the oven at 190°C (375°F) mark 5, unless otherwise stated, until lightly browned.

Freeze as shortcrust pastry.

PEACH PIE

SERVES 6

Nectarines work equally well. Choose firm, but ripe fruit.

FOR THE PASTRY
225 g (8 oz) plain flour
50 g (2 oz) walnuts, finely chopped
100 g (4 oz) softened butter or margarine, cut into pieces
75 g (3 oz) caster sugar
2 egg yolks

FOR THE FILLING
900 g (2 lb) peaches
1 egg white, for glazing
caster sugar, for dredging

1. To make the pastry, place the flour on a work surface and sprinkle the walnuts over the top. Make a well in the centre and add the butter, sugar, egg yolks and 30 ml (2 tbsp) water.
2. Using the fingertips of one hand only, work the well ingredients together until evenly blended. Using a palette knife, gradually draw in the flour, then knead lightly until just smooth.
3. Roll out two thirds of the pastry on a floured work surface and use to line a 23 cm (9 inch) loose-based fluted flan tin. Chill for 30 minutes.
4. To make the filling, quarter the peaches and easy away from the stone. Peel off the skins carefully and divide each quarter in two lengthways.
5. Arrange the peaches in the pastry case. Roll out the remaining pastry and use to cover the pie, sealing well. Make a small hole in the centre to let steam escape.
6. Bake in the oven at 200°C (400°F) mark 6 for about 20–25 minutes or until just beginning to brown.
7. Brush the top of the pie with lightly beaten egg white and dredge with caster sugar. Return to the oven for a further 10 minutes or until well browned and crisp. Cool for 15 minutes in the tin before removing. Serve while still slightly warm, with cream.

Not suitable for freezing.

PAWPAW PIE

SERVES 8

Choose pawpaws, or papayas, that are firm yet ripe. If too soft, they will be difficult to slice evenly.

FOR THE PASTRY

275 g (10 oz) plain flour
5 ml (1 tsp) ground cinnamon
150 g (5 oz) softened butter
65 g (2½ oz) caster sugar
2 egg yolks
grated rind and juice of 1 large orange

FOR THE FILLING

2 medium ripe pawpaws
1 egg white, lightly beaten, for glazing
caster sugar, for dredging
300 ml (½ pint) double or whipping cream

1. To make the pastry, sift the flour and cinnamon on to a work surface. Make a well in the centre and add the butter, cut in small pieces, sugar, egg yolks and grated orange rind with 45 ml (3 tbsp) juice (reserve the remaining juice).

2. Using the fingertips of one hand only, work the well ingredients together until evenly blended. Using a palette knife, gradually draw in the flour, then knead lightly until just smooth. Wrap and chill for about 20 minutes.

3. Roll out two-thirds of the pastry on a floured work surface and use to line a 24 cm (9½ inch) loose-based fluted flan tin.

4. To make the filling, peel the pawpaws, halve, scoop out the seeds and thinly slice the flesh. Arrange in the pastry case.

5. Roll out the remaining pastry and use to cover the pie, sealing well.

6. Bake in the oven at 180°C (350°F) mark 4 for about 25 minutes or until just set but not browned.

7. Brush the top of the pie with egg white and dredge with caster sugar. Return to the oven for a further 20–25 minutes until well browned. Serve warm.

8. Lightly whip the cream. Stir in about 45 ml (3 tbsp) of the remaining orange juice. Serve with the pie.

Not suitable for freezing.

Above: PAWPAW PIE.

PECAN PIE

SERVES 8–10

Do not overcook or it will not have the sticky qualities essential for a good pecan pie. It works equally well with walnut halves.

200 g (7 oz) Shortcrust pastry (see page 42)

FOR THE FILLING
3 eggs
200 g (7 oz) dark brown soft sugar
225 ml (8 fl oz) maple syrup
large pinch of salt
5 ml (1 tsp) vanilla essence
50 g (2 oz) butter, melted
100 g (4 oz) pecan halves

1. Roll out the pastry and use to line a 23 cm (9 inch) fluted flan dish. Chill for 30 minutes. Bake blind in the oven at 200°C (400°F) mark 6 for 15 minutes.

2. To make the filling, put all of the remaining ingredients, except the pecan nuts, into a bowl and beat together until smooth. Stir in the pecan nuts. Pour the pecan mixture into the pastry case.

3. Bake in the oven at 180°C (350°F) mark 4 for 1 hour or until just set. Serve warm or cold with cream or vanilla ice cream.

Not suitable for freezing.

PUMPKIN PIE

SERVES 4–6

Increase or decrease the spices according to your own taste.

1 quantity Shortcrust pastry (see page 42)

FOR THE FILLING
450 g (1 lb) pumpkin
2 eggs
100 g (4 oz) caster sugar
60 ml (4 tbsp) milk
pinch of grated nutmeg
pinch of ground ginger
10 ml (2 tsp) ground cinnamon

1. Roll out the pastry on a floured work surface and use to line a 20.5 cm (8 inch) flan tin or deep pie plate. Trim and decorate the edges. Chill for about 30 minutes.

2. To make the filling, cut the pumpkin into pieces, remove any seeds and 'cotton-woolly' inside part and cut off the outside skin.

3. Steam the pieces of pumpkin between two plates over a pan of boiling water for 15–20 minutes until tender. Drain thoroughly, then mash well with a fork or purée in a blender or food processor.

4. Beat the eggs and sugar together in a bowl. Add the pumpkin purée, the milk and spices. Blend well and pour into the pastry case.

5. Bake in the oven at 220°C (425°F) mark 7 for 15 minutes, then reduce the oven temperature to 180°C (350°F) mark 4 and bake for a further 30 minutes or until the filling is set. Serve this pie warm, with whipped cream.

Not suitable for freezing.

ANGOSTURA PIE

SERVES 6–8

Normally associated with pink gin and hangovers, Angostura bitters is surprisingly good when it is sweetened and mixed with cream—as it is in this creamy pie.

1½ quantity Pâte sucrée (see page 43)

FOR THE FILLING
15 ml (1 tbsp) powdered gelatine
2 eggs, separated
50 g (2 oz) caster sugar
22.5 ml (1½ tbsp) Angostura bitters
300 ml (½ pint) double cream

FOR THE DECORATION
150 ml (¼ pint) double cream
15 ml (1 tbsp) icing sugar, sifted
14–16 pistachio nuts, skinned

1. Roll out the pastry on a lightly floured work surface and use to line a deep 20.5 cm (8 inch) pie plate or flan dish. Trim and decorate the edges. Prick the pastry all over with a fork. Chill the pastry in the refrigerator for at least 30 minutes.

2. Bake blind in the oven at 220°C (425°F) mark 7 for 20–25 minutes until the pastry is cooked. Leave to cool.

3. To make the filling, sprinkle the gelatine over 45 ml (3 tbsp) water in a small bowl and leave to soak for 2–3 minutes. Place the bowl over a pan of simmering water and stir until dissolved. (Alternatively, microwave on HIGH for 30 seconds or until dissolved.)

4. Whisk the egg yolks and sugar together in a bowl until very thick, then whisk in the Angostura bitters.

5. Whip the cream until it will hold soft peaks. Whisk the egg whites in a bowl until quite foamy, but not too stiff.

6. Whisk the dissolved gelatine into the Angostura mixture, then carefully fold in the cream and egg whites. Immediately pour the mixture into the pastry case. Chill until set.

7. To make the decoration, whip the cream with the icing sugar until thick enough to pipe, then fill a piping bag fitted with a large star nozzle. Pipe rosettes or stars of cream on top of the pie, then decorate with pistachio nuts. Chill until ready to serve.

Not suitable for freezing.

ALL SEASONS FRUIT SALAD PIE

SERVES 6

For convenience, use a packet of dried ready mixed fruit salad, or mix your own.

1 quantity Rough puff pastry (see page 45)

FOR THE FILLING
450 g (1 lb) dried mixed fruits, such as prunes, pears, peaches, apricots, apple rings, soaked overnight
75 g (3 oz) granulated sugar
beaten egg white, for glazing
caster sugar, for dredging
30 ml (2 tbsp) orange-flavoured liqueur
150 ml (¼ pint) double cream

1. To make the filling, drain the dried fruit, reserving 90 ml (6 tbsp) of the liquid. Layer the fruit in a 1.1 litre (2 pint) pie dish with the sugar and the reserved liquid. Place a pie funnel in the centre.

2. Roll out the pastry and use to cover the pie. Glaze with egg white and dredge with caster sugar.

3. Bake in the oven at 220°C (425°F) mark 7 for 25 minutes. Cover with foil, reduce the oven temperature to 190°C (375°F) mark 5 and bake for about 20 minutes.

4. Pour the liqueur, then the cream through the pie funnel to serve.

Not suitable for freezing.

OLD ENGLISH APPLE PIE

SERVES 6

A traditional apple pie flavoured with brown sugar, nutmeg, cinnamon and orange rind.

1½ quantity Shortcrust pastry (see page 42)

FOR THE FILLING
700 g (1½ lb) cooking apples
finely grated rind and juice of ½ lemon
50 g (2 oz) granulated sugar
50 g (2 oz) soft dark brown sugar
15 ml (1 tbsp) plain flour
pinch of grated nutmeg
1.25 ml (¼ tsp) ground cinnamon
finely grated rind and juice of ½ orange
50 g (2 oz) sultanas
15–25 g (½–1 oz) butter or margarine
caster sugar, for dredging

1. Roll out two thirds of the pastry on a floured work surface and use to line a 23 cm (9 inch) pie dish. Chill for

30 minutes with the remaining dough, wrapped in clingfilm.

2. Meanwhile to make the filling, peel and core the apples, then slice them thickly into a bowl of cold water to which the lemon juice has been added.

3. Mix the sugars, flour, nutmeg, cinnamon, lemon and orange rinds together and sprinkle a little of this on to the pastry lining.

4. Cover the base of the pastry lining with half of the sliced apples, then sprinkle with 25 g (1 oz) of the sultanas and half of the remaining sugar mixture. Repeat, using all the apples, sultanas and sugar. Sprinkle the fruit with the orange juice and dot with the butter.

5. Roll out the remaining pastry and use to cover the pie, sealing the edges well. Slash the top twice to let steam escape.

6. Use the pastry trimmings to make decorations for the pie. Brush the top of the pie with water and place on the decorations. Dredge with caster sugar.

7. Bake in the oven at 190°C (375°F) mark 5 for 35–40 minutes until the fruit is tender and the top is golden brown. Serve warm, with custard or cream.

To freeze: wrap and freeze at the end of step 7 and thaw at room temperature. Reheat in a hot oven if required. Alternatively, freeze the uncooked pie. Bake from frozen at 220°C (425°F) mark 7 for about 1 hour.

FRENCH APPLE FLAN

SERVES 8

Because it is attributed to the apple growing region of France, this flan is sometimes called Normandy Apple Flan. This recipe, which is just one of many versions, uses two types of apples, cooked in different ways, each one contrasting with the other. If you do not have apple brandy, use ordinary brandy.

double quantity Pâte sucrée (see page 43)

FOR THE FILLING
900 g (2 lb) cooking apples
175 g (6 oz) granulated sugar
50 g (2 oz) raisins
60 ml (4 tbsp) apple brandy
4–5 large dessert apples, such as Golden Delicious, Russet or Cox's
50 g (2 oz) caster sugar
½ quantity Apricot glaze (see page 42)

1. To make the filling, peel, quarter, core and slice the cooking apples. Put into a large saucepan with the granulated sugar and 30 ml (2 tbsp) water. Cover and cook gently for about 20 minutes until the apples become soft and fluffy.

2. Pour the cooked apples into a nylon sieve placed over a bowl. Leave to drain and cool. (The apple juice will not be needed.)

3. Put the raisins into a small saucepan with the apple brandy and cook gently for 2–3 minutes to soften the raisins. Leave to cool.

4. Roll out the pastry on a lightly floured work surface to a round, 2.5 cm (1 inch) larger than a 25.5 cm (10 inch) fluted flan tin. Line the tin with the pastry, pressing it well into the flutes. Trim the edges.

5. Beat the cooked apples until fairly smooth, then fold in the raisins and apple brandy. Spread the apple mixture evenly over the base of the pastry case.

6. Peel and core the dessert apples. Cut each apple in half, then cut each half into thin slices. Arrange the apple slices in concentric circles on top of the cooked apple mixture. Sprinkle the apple slices with the caster sugar.

7. Bake in the oven at 220°C (425°F) mark 7 for 30–35 minutes until the pastry is cooked and the apple slices are tender and very lightly browned.

8. Heat the apricot glaze until boiling. Immediately the flan is removed from the oven, brush the apricot glaze evenly over the apple slices. Leave the flan to cool to room temperature before serving. Serve with lightly whipped cream.

To freeze: freeze the flan before glazing. Thaw at cool room temperature, then reheat and glaze.

FRUIT AND CRÈME PÂTISSIÈRE PIE

SERVES 8–10

A delicious rich, sweet pastry enclosing a filling bursting with fruit and creamy pastry cream.

FOR THE PASTRY
275 g (10 oz) plain flour
finely grated rind of ½ lemon
45 ml (3 tbsp) icing sugar, sifted
pinch of salt
1 egg
2 egg yolks
200 g (7 oz) butter, cut into small pieces
milk, for glazing

FOR THE FILLING
450 g (1 lb) mixed fruit, such as cherries, blueberries, loganberries or blackberries
30 ml (2 tbsp) rum
300 ml (½ pint) Crème pâtissière (see page 248)
icing sugar, for dusting

1. Grease and line a 24 cm (9½ inch) sandwich tin.

2. To make the pastry, mix together the flour, lemon rind, icing sugar and salt in a bowl. Make a well in the centre. Beat the egg and egg yolks together and pour into the well. Add the butter. Using your fingertips, gradually work the eggs and butter into the flour.

3. Turn the pastry on to a floured work surface and knead lightly until smooth. Shape into a ball, wrap and chill for 30 minutes.

4. Take two-thirds of the dough and spread it over the base and the sides of the prepared tin. Make sure that there are no holes or the filling will leak out.

5. To make the filling, put the fruit in a single layer in the pastry case. Stir the rum into the crème patissière and spread on top of the fruit. Fold the pastry sides down over the filling. Brush the pastry with milk.

6. Roll out the remaining pastry and use to cover the pie. Seal the edges.

7. Bake in the oven at 190°C (375°F) mark 5 for 30 minutes, then reduce the oven temperature to 160°C (325°F) mark 3 and cook for 30–45 minutes until golden brown and shrinking away from the edges. Leave to cool in the tin. When cold, carefully turn out and dust with icing sugar.

Not suitable for freezing.

TARTE TATIN

SERVES 8

Correctly called Tarte des Demoiselles Tatin in French, this famous upside-down apple tart is named after the sisters Tatin, hoteliers in the nineteenth century who originated the recipe.

FOR THE PASTRY

100 g (4 oz) butter or margarine
175 g (6 oz) plain flour
15 g (½ oz) caster sugar
1 egg yolk

FOR THE FILLING

25 g (1 oz) butter or margarine
50 g (2 oz) caster sugar
450 g (1 lb) crisp eating apples

1. To make the pastry, rub the butter into the flour in a bowl until the mixture resembles fine breadcrumbs. Add the sugar. Blend the egg yolk with 15 ml (1 tbsp) water and stir into the mixture. Knead the dough lightly. Chill while making the filling.

2. To make the filling, melt the butter in a saucepan and add the sugar. Heat until caramelized and golden brown. Remove from the heat and pour into a 20.5 cm (8 inch) round sandwich tin.

3. Peel, core and halve the apples. Slice into 1 cm (½ inch) pieces. Pack them tightly to fill the bottom of the tin, leaving no gaps.

4. Roll out the pastry on a floured work surface to a round slightly larger than the tin. Place on top of the apples and tuck in around the edges of the tin. Chill for 30 minutes. Place the tin on a baking sheet.

5. Bake in the oven at 200°C (400°F) mark 6 for 30–35 minutes until the pastry is golden. Turn out, apple side uppermost, on to a warmed serving dish. Serve hot, with crème fraîche or soured cream.

Not suitable for freezing.

Below: TARTE TATIN.

DEEP-DISH APPLE FLAN

SERVES 8

A pretty pie covered with a lid of interlocking pastry leaves.

1½ quantity Flan pastry (see page 43)

FOR THE FILLING
1.4 kg (3 lb) cooking apples
3 cloves
50 g (2 oz) butter
5 ml (1 tsp) ground mixed spice
1 cinnamon stick
75 g (3 oz) caster sugar
beaten egg, for glazing
flaked almonds
demerara sugar
icing sugar, for dusting

1. Roll out the pastry and use to line a deep 22 cm (8½ inch) loose-based fluted flan tin. Chill the pastry trimmings, wrapped in clingfilm.
2. To make the filling, peel, quarter, core and thickly slice the apples. Put half of them in a medium saucepan. Add the cloves, butter, mixed spice, cinnamon and caster sugar. Cook, stirring, over a high heat until the apples are soft. Off the heat, remove the cloves and cinnamon stick, then add the remaining apples. Leave to cool slightly.
3. Spoon the apple mixture into the pastry case. Make pastry leaves from the trimmings. Arrange attractively interlocking over the apple filling and brush the pastry lightly with beaten egg. Sprinkle with flaked almonds and demerara sugar.
4. Bake in the oven at 180°C (350°F) mark 4 for about 35 minutes or until golden brown and crisp. Leave to cool for 10 minutes before removing from the tin. Serve warm dusted with icing sugar.

Not suitable for freezing.

APRICOT AND CARDAMOM FLAN

SERVES 6

Soaking the apricots with cardamoms and bay leaves gives them a delicious aromatic flavour.

100 g (4 oz) no-soak dried apricots
6 green cardamom pods, split
2 bay leaves
1½ quantity Pâte sucrée (see page 43)
150 ml (¼ pint) single cream
1 egg
1 egg yolk
25 g (1 oz) caster sugar
60 ml (4 tbsp) apricot jam

1. Place the apricots, cardamoms and bay leaves in a medium bowl. Completely cover with cold water and leave to soak overnight in the refrigerator.
2. Roll out the pastry on a lightly floured work surface and use to line a 34 × 11 cm (13½ × 4½ inch) loose-based fluted tranche tin. Chill for 10–15 minutes. Place on a flat baking sheet.
3. Bake blind in the oven at 190°C (375°F) mark 5 for about 20 minutes.
4. Drain the apricots, discard the bay leaves and cardamoms. Cut the apricots in half and pat dry with absorbent kitchen paper.
5. Whisk the cream, eggs and sugar together. Arrange the apricots, cut-side down, in the pastry case. Pour over the cream mixture.
6. Reduce the oven temperature to 180°C (350°F) mark 4 and bake for 35 minutes or until just set. Brown under the grill. Cool before removing the flan case.
7. Melt the apricot jam with 15 ml (1 tbsp) water over a gentle heat in a pan. Bring to the boil. Brush evenly over the warm flan. Serve warm or cold.

Not suitable for freezing.

Above left: APRICOT AND CARDAMOM FLAN. *Above right:* GLAZED NUT FLAN (PAGE 56). *Below:* DEEP-DISH APPLE FLAN.

LINZERTORTE

SERVES 12–16

Linzertorte, another Austrian speciality, is really more of a jam tart than a gâteau. However one classifies Linzertorte, it is a delicious and quickly made cake. The pastry acquires its distinctive colouring from the fact that the almonds are ground with their skins on. Linzertorte is best eaten when it has cooled to room temperature, but is still excellent cold.

FOR THE PASTRY

225 g (8 oz) plain flour
175 g (6 oz) unblanched almonds, finely ground
pinch of salt
5 ml (1 tsp) ground cinnamon
100 g (4 oz) icing sugar, sifted
finely grated rind of 1 lemon
225 g (8 oz) unsalted butter, at room temperature
2 egg yolks

FOR THE FILLING

350 g (12 oz) raspberry conserve

FOR THE GLAZE

1 small egg, beaten with 15 ml (1 tbsp) milk
5 ml (1 tsp) caster sugar
15 g (½ oz) flaked almonds, for sprinkling (optional)
icing sugar, for dusting

1. Place a square of foil on a baking sheet, then place a 28.5 cm (11 inch), 3 cm (1¼ inch) deep, flan ring in the centre. Butter the ring, then bring the foil up smoothly around the side of the ring to seal the bottom edge and prevent the pastry seeping out at the beginning of baking.

2. To make the pastry, mix the flour, almonds, salt, cinnamon, icing sugar and lemon rind together in a bowl. Cut the butter into pieces and add to the mixture with the egg yolks. Work all the ingredients together until they form a smooth ball of pastry. Wrap in clingfilm and chill for about 40 minutes until the pastry is firm.

3. Roll out just a little more than half of the pastry on a lightly floured work surface to a round 2.5 cm (1 inch) larger than the prepared flan ring. Line the flan ring with the pastry, pressing it smoothly around the side. Trim the pastry level with the top of the flan ring.

4. Add the pastry trimmings to the remaining pastry and roll out to an oblong about 28.5 × 15 cm (11 × 6 inches), the same thickness as the pastry in the flan ring. Trim the edges neatly, then cut into 10 long strips, about 1 cm (½ inch) wide.

5. Spread the raspberry conserve evenly over the base of the pastry in the flan ring. Lay the pastry strips flat, on top of the jam (the sides of the pastry will be above them) in a lattice pattern, cutting them to fit exactly. Loosen the sides of the pastry from the flan ring with a small palette knife, then bring them down over the pastry strips to form a neat border.

6. To make the glaze, lightly whisk the egg, milk and sugar together, then brush evenly over the pastry. Sprinkle the torte with flaked almonds, if wished.

7. Bake in the oven at 200°C (400°F) mark 6 for 10 minutes, then reduce the oven temperature to 180°C (350°F) mark 4 and continue cooking for 35 minutes until the pastry is golden brown. Leave to cool on the baking sheet without removing the flan ring.

8. When the pastry begins to firm, run a palette knife carefully around the sides to loosen the flan ring—but do not remove the ring until the torte has cooled to room temperature. Remove the flan ring, dust the icing sugar over the torte and transfer to a doily-lined plate.

To freeze: pack carefully and freeze the cooled torte. To thaw, unwrap and thaw at room temperature.

RICH PEAR SPONGE FLAN

SERVES 12

Make sure you use ripe even-sized pears or the appearance of the finished flan will be spoilt.

1¼ quantity Shortcrust pastry (see page 42)

FOR THE FILLING

150 g (5 oz) butter or margarine
150 g (5 oz) caster sugar
few drops of almond flavouring
3 eggs
100 g (4 oz) self raising flour
75 g (3 oz) cornflour
5 ml (1 tsp) baking powder
75 g (3 oz) ground almonds
30 ml (2 tbsp) milk
3 small ripe, even-sized pears
icing sugar, for dusting

1. Grease a 24 cm (9½ inch) round spring-release cake tin.

2. Roll out the pastry and use to line the tin. Chill.

3. To make the filling, cream the butter and sugar together in a bowl until pale and fluffy. Beat in a few drops of almond flavouring, then add the eggs, one at a time. Fold in the flours, baking powder and ground almonds, then fold in the milk. Spoon the mixture into the pastry case and level the surface.

4. Peel, core and halve the pears. Make a series of parallel cuts across the width of each pear half, but do not cut right through. Arrange the pear halves, rounded sides up, on top of the filling.

5. Bake in the oven at 190°C (375°F) mark 5 for 1¼ hours or until a skewer inserted into the centre comes out clean. Cool in the tin for 15 minutes, then carefully remove the sides of the tin. Serve warm or cold, dusted with icing sugar.

Not suitable for freezing.

Opposite: RICH PEAR SPONGE FLAN.

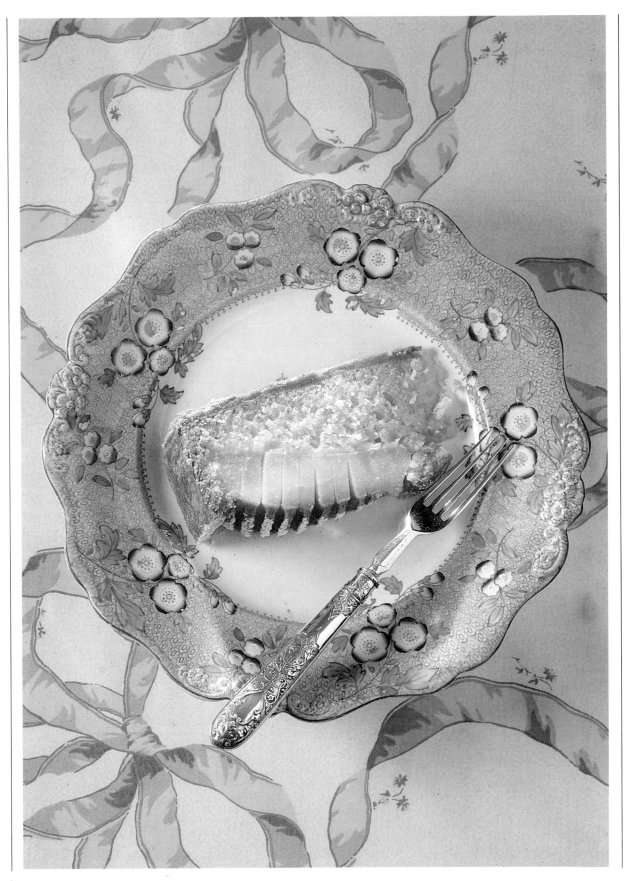

STRAWBERRY FLANS WITH SPUN SUGAR

SERVES 8–10

This pretty flan is decorated with a nest of spun sugar; it is not difficult to make but requires plenty of time.

1½ quantity Pâte sucrée (see page 43)
½ quantity Choux pastry (see page 44)

FOR THE FILLING
100 g (4 oz) blanched almonds
100 g (4 oz) caster sugar
600 ml (1 pint) double cream
450 g (1 lb) strawberries, hulled

FOR THE SPUN SUGAR
100 g (4 oz) granulated sugar
45 ml (3 tbsp) water
7.5 ml (1½ tsp) liquid glucose

1. Roll out the pâte sucrée on an upturned baking sheet to a 28.5 cm (11 inch) round. Prick the pastry well with a fork. Chill.

2. Put the choux pastry into a piping bag fitted with a 1 cm (½ inch) plain nozzle. Pipe a single ring of choux pastry round the edge of the pastry base, piping it 5 mm (¼ inch) in from the edge.

3. Bake in the oven at 200°C (400°F) mark 6 for 25–30 minutes or until the choux pastry is well risen and golden brown. Remove from the oven and pierce the choux pastry in several places to allow the steam to escape. Return to the oven for 2–3 minutes to dry out completely. Leave to cool on a wire rack.

4. To make the filling, put the almonds and sugar into a small, heavy-based saucepan and heat gently until the sugar dissolves and turns a rich caramel colour. Immediately pour on to an oiled baking sheet and allow to cool and set hard. Grind the nut mixture in an electric grinder, or crush finely with a rolling pin. Whisk the cream until it just holds soft peaks, then gently fold in the praline.

5. Place the pastry case on a large flat serving plate and fill with the praline cream. Cut the strawberries in half, or slices, and arrange them neatly on top of the cream.

6. To make the spun sugar, lightly oil a rolling pin. Cover the work surface with newspaper, and also cover the floor immediately below. Cover the newspaper on the work surface with greaseproof paper.

7. Put the sugar, water and liquid glucose into a heavy-based saucepan and heat gently until every granule of sugar dissolves, brushing down the sides of the pan with a little hot water. Boil the sugar syrup to a temperature of 160°C (320°F). Immediately plunge the base of the pan into cold water to prevent further cooking.

8. Dip two forks, held together, into the syrup, then hold them up high until a fine thread starts to fall. Gently spin the sugar threads around the rolling pin until a good quantity of threads accumulate. Remove from the rolling pin and set aside. Repeat until all the syrup has been used.

9. Pile the sugar nest on top of the strawberry flan and serve within 1 hour.

To freeze: wrap and freeze the flan case. Thaw at cool room temperature, then finish as above.

GLAZED NUT FLAN

SERVES 6–8

A light, crisp flan full to bursting with mixed nuts.

1 quantity Pâte sucrée (see page 43)

FOR THE FILLING
50 g (2 oz) hazelnuts
25 g (1 oz) pistachio nuts
1 egg
25 g (1 oz) caster sugar
25 g (1 oz) butter, melted
grated rind and juice of 1 lemon
pinch of grated nutmeg
60 ml (4 tbsp) Lyle's golden syrup
15 ml (1 tbsp) plain flour
75 g (3 oz) walnut pieces
75 g (3 oz) Brazil nuts
50 g (2 oz) pecan nuts

1. Roll out the pastry and use to line a 22 cm (8½ inch) loose-based fluted flan tin. Chill for 15 minutes.

2. Bake blind in the oven at 200°C (400°F) mark 6 for 10–12 minutes. Remove the beans and paper, then reduce the oven temperature to 180°C (350°F) mark 4 and bake for a further 10 minutes until pale golden.

3. Meanwhile to make the filling, brown the hazelnuts under a hot grill. Place in a clean tea towel and rub well to remove the skins. Dip the shelled pistachio nuts in boiling water for 1 minute. Drain and remove the skins.

4. Using an electric whisk, beat the egg and sugar together in a bowl until very thick and pale—about 5 minutes. Quickly stir in the melted butter, lemon rind, nutmeg and 30 ml (2 tbsp) of the golden syrup. Fold in the flour and finally all the nuts.

5. Spoon the nut mixture into the pastry case. Bake in the oven at 180°C (350°F) mark 4 for about 35 minutes or until golden brown and firm to the touch. Leave to cool for 10–15 minutes.

6. Heat the remaining golden syrup and 30 ml (2 tbsp) lemon juice together in a pan. Boil for 2–3 minutes until syrupy. Brush over the warm flan. Leave in the tin for 10–15 minutes before removing to a wire rack to cool. Serve warm or cold.

Not suitable for freezing.

Illustrated on page 53

TREACLE TART

SERVES 4–6

You may wonder why recipes for treacle tart always contain golden syrup rather than treacle. The explanation is quite simple. Treacle is the syrup which is left in the sugar refining process when the sugar has been crystallized. In the seventeenth century, when West Indian sugar cane was first refined to make sugar, treacle was unrefined and recipes for treacle tart such as this one would have used black treacle rather than syrup. It was not until the late nineteenth century that treacle itself was refined to make the golden syrup which is so popular today. As tastes changed, recipes which had originally used treacle began to specify syrup instead.

¾ quantity Shortcrust pastry (see page 42)

FOR THE FILLING
350 g (12 oz) Lyle's golden syrup
25 g (1 oz) butter or margarine
finely grated rind and juice of 1 lemon
75 g (3 oz) fresh white breadcrumbs
little beaten egg or milk, for glazing

1. Roll out the pastry on a floured work surface and use to line a 20.5 cm (8 inch) loose-based flan tin. Reserve the pastry trimmings. Chill while making the filling.
2. To make the filling, warm the golden syrup in a heavy-based pan with the butter and lemon rind and juice.
3. Sprinkle the breadcrumbs evenly over the base of the pastry case, then slowly pour in the melted syrup.
4. Make strips from the reserved pastry trimmings and place these over the tart in a lattice pattern, brushing the ends with water to stick them to the pastry case. Brush with a little beaten egg or milk.
5. Bake in the oven at 190°C (375°F) mark 5 for about 25–30 minutes until the filling is just set. Serve warm with whipped cream.

Not suitable for freezing.

FIG AND ALMOND TART

SERVES 4–6

Depending on the juiciness of the figs, the ground almond and semolina filling can be quite dry and crumbly, or moist: either way, it's delicious!

FOR THE PASTRY
75 g (3 oz) plain flour
40 g (1½ oz) ground almonds
40 g (1½ oz) caster sugar
100 g (4 oz) butter or margarine, softened
1 egg yolk
1–2 drops of vanilla essence

FOR THE FILLING
6–8 ripe figs
30 ml (2 tbsp) brandy
30 ml (2 tbsp) ground almonds
30 ml (2 tbsp) semolina
30 ml (2 tbsp) soft brown sugar
45 ml (3 tbsp) apricot jam
15 ml (1 tbsp) lemon juice

1. To make the pastry, place the flour on a work surface or pastry board and make a large well in the centre. Sift the ground almonds on to the flour.
2. In the well, place the caster sugar, butter, egg yolk and vanilla essence. Using the fingertips of one hand only, pinch and work these ingredients together until evenly blended. Gradually draw in the flour and ground almonds, using a palette knife, then form the mixture, with your hand, into a smooth, pliable dough. Wrap and chill well for at least 30 minutes.
3. Meanwhile to make the filling, peel the figs, slice thinly and place them in layers in a dish. Pour over the brandy and leave to soak.
4. Roll out the pastry and use to line an 18 cm (7 inch) fluted loose based flan tin. Prick the base.
5. Bake blind in the oven at 190°C (375°F) mark 5 for about 10–15 minutes or until dry and beginning to colour.
6. Mix the ground almonds, semolina and brown sugar together. Spoon evenly over the base of the flan. Arrange the figs on top. Return to the oven for 15–20 minutes.
7. Meanwhile, sieve the jam into a small pan. Add the lemon juice and heat until the jam has melted. Brush over the baked tart to glaze. Leave to cool slightly before serving with single cream or Greek yogurt.

Not suitable for freezing.

LAVENDER-SCENTED TARTLETS

SERVES 2

Lavender sugar gives the pastry a delicious flavour and it is really simple to make. Place 10 ml (2 tsp) dried lavender blossom in a screw-top jar with 30 ml (2 tbsp) caster sugar. Shake well and leave overnight. Sieve and discard the lavender.

FOR THE PASTRY
40 g (1½ oz) butter
90 g (3½ oz) plain flour
5 ml (1 tsp) lavender sugar (see above)
1 egg

FOR THE FILLING
15 ml (1 tbsp) plus 10 ml (2 tsp) lavender sugar
1 egg
50 ml (2 fl oz) single cream
selection of seasonal fruits
25 ml (1 fl oz) dry vermouth
5 ml (1 tsp) powdered gelatine

1. To make the pastry, rub the butter into the flour in a bowl until the mixture resembles breadcrumbs. Stir in the sugar and egg. Knead lightly to form a smooth dough. Wrap in clingfilm and chill for 10 minutes.
2. Roll out the pastry thinly on a lightly floured work surface and use to line two shallow, fluted flan dishes, about 9 cm (3½ inch) in diameter. Chill for 20 minutes.
3. Bake blind in the oven at 200°C (400°F) mark 6 for about 20 minutes. Reduce the oven temperature to 150°C (300°F) mark 2.
4. To make the filling, whisk 15 ml (1 tbsp) of the sugar, the egg and cream together. Pour into the pastry cases and bake for 20 minutes or until lightly set. Leave to cool completely.
5. Arrange a selection of fruits, some whole, some sliced, over the surface of the tartlets.
6. In a small bowl, stir the remaining sugar into the vermouth and 50 ml (2 fl oz) water. Sprinkle the gelatine over the liquid and leave to soak for 2—3 minutes. Place the bowl over a saucepan of simmering water and stir until dissolved. Cool slightly, then spoon evenly over the fruits to cover. Chill until set, about 5 minutes.

To freeze: wrap and freeze the baked tartlet cases. Unwrap and thaw at cool room temperature.

Illustrated on pages 40—41

CARAMELIZED APPLE WAFER

SERVES 6

Do not worry if the tops of the apple slices or the pastry edges look very dark—this is how it should be.

225 g (8 oz) frozen puff pastry, thawed
6 small Granny Smith apples, total weight about 450—700 g (1—1½ lb)
75 g (3 oz) butter or margarine, melted
60 ml (4 tbsp) demerara sugar

1. Cut the pastry into two equal pieces. Roll out each half very thinly on a lightly floured work surface to a rectangle measuring about 20.5 × 11.5 cm (8 × 4½ inches). Trim the edges. Place on a baking sheet.
2. Peel, halve and core the apples. Thinly slice the apple halves but not quite through to the base. The apples should still keep their shape.
3. Evenly space six halves flat side down on each pastry base. Cut each pastry base into three.
4. Brush the apple with the butter and sprinkle over the sugar.
5. Bake in the oven at 240°C (475°F) mark 9 for about 20 minutes or until the pastry is risen and golden. The apples should be quite soft and caramelized. Serve immediately with soured cream, Greek yogurt or crème fraîche.

Not suitable for freezing.

Opposite: CARAMELIZED APPLE WAFER.

APFEL STRÜDEL

SERVES 6

Although an apple filling has become synonymous with strüdel, it is equally good filled with fresh cherries or pears.

1 quantity Strüdel pastry (see page 46)

FOR THE FILLING
900 g (2 lb) cooking apples, peeled, cored and roughly chopped
finely grated rind and juice of 1 lemon
50 g (2 oz) sultanas
50 g (2 oz) almonds, chopped
75 g (3 oz) caster sugar
5 ml (1 tsp) ground cinnamon
40 g (1½ oz) butter, melted
100 g (4 oz) ground almonds
icing sugar, for dredging

1. Grease a baking sheet. Leave the dough to 'rest' in a warm place for 1 hour.
2. Spread a clean cotton cloth on a large surface and sprinkle lightly with flour. Place the dough on the cloth and roll out into a rectangle about 0.3 cm (⅛ inch) thick, lifting and turning it to prevent it sticking to the cloth.
3. Gently stretch the dough, working from the centre to the outside and using the backs of the hand until it is paper-thin. Trim the edges to form a rectangle measuring about 68 × 51 cm (27 × 20 inches). Leave the strüdel dough on the cloth to dry and 'rest' at room temperature for about 15 minutes before filling and rolling.
4. Meanwhile to make the filling, mix the apples, lemon rind and juice, sultanas, chopped almonds, sugar and cinnamon together.
5. Position the dough with one of the long sides towards you, brush with half the melted butter and sprinkle with the ground almonds. Spread the apple mixture over the dough, leaving a 5 cm (2 inch) border all round the edge.
6. Fold the pastry edges over the apple mixture, towards the centre. Lift the corners of the cloth nearest to you over the pastry, causing the strüdel to roll up, but stop after each turn in order to pat it into shape and to keep the roll even. Form the roll into a horseshoe shape. Brush with the rest of the melted butter and slide it on to the prepared baking sheet.
7. Bake in the oven at 190°C (375°F) mark 5 for about 40 minutes or until golden brown. Dredge thickly with icing sugar. Serve warm or cold.

To freeze: wrap and freeze the cold strüdel. Thaw at cool room temperature. Dredge with icing sugar and serve cold.

GALATABOUREGO

SERVES 12

This Cypriot dessert is similar to the Greek Baklava, but with a creamy custard filling.

5 sheets of phyllo or strüdel pastry
75 g (3 oz) butter, melted

FOR THE FILLING
568 ml (1 pint) milk
75 g (3 oz) caster sugar
75 g (3 oz) semolina
finely grated rind of 1 orange
100 g (4 oz) butter
4 eggs
150 ml (¼ pint) double cream

FOR THE SYRUP
350 g (12 oz) caster sugar
juice of 1 orange
30 ml (2 tbsp) orange blossom water

1. To make the filling, put the milk, sugar and semolina in a saucepan and heat gently, stirring all the time, until the sugar dissolves. Increase the heat, bring to the boil and cook until thickened. (Alternatively, put all of the ingredients in a large bowl and microwave on HIGH for 10–12 minutes or until boiling and thickened, stirring every minute.) Leave to cool slightly.
2. Stir in the orange rind, butter, a knob at a time, the eggs and cream. Cover the surface with a piece of greaseproof paper to prevent a skin forming and cool.
3. When the filling is cold, fold one sheet of phyllo pastry in half and trim to fit a roasting tin, measuring about 28.5 × 20.5 cm (11 × 8 inches). Brush with a little melted butter. Repeat with two more sheets of pastry.
4. Pour the custard filling on top of the pastry. Top with one folded sheet of pastry, brush with butter, then top with the remaining folded sheet of pastry. Brush the top generously with butter and mark the pastry into 12 squares with a sharp knife.
5. Bake in the oven at 190°C (375°F) mark 5 for 45–50 minutes or until golden brown.
6. Meanwhile to make the syrup, put the sugar, 200 ml (7 fl oz) water and the orange juice in a pan. Heat gently until the sugar has dissolved, then simmer for 10 minutes. (Alternatively, put the ingredients in a large bowl and microwave on HIGH for 8 minutes, stirring occasionally.) Stir in the orange blossom water.
7. Pour the hot syrup evenly over the hot Galatabourego. Cool. Chill before serving cut into squares.

Not suitable for freezing.

PAWPAW WONTONS WITH GINGER AND HONEY

SERVES 6

In Chinese cookery, wontons are usually filled with a savoury mixture. Here we adapt the recipe to use a sweet filling of pawpaw and lime.

FOR THE PASTRY
100 g (4 oz) plain flour
large pinch of salt
1 egg

FOR THE FILLING
1 ripe pawpaw
finely grated rind of 1 lime

FOR THE DIP
75 ml (5 tbsp) clear honey
juice of 2 limes
5 ml (1 tsp) finely chopped crystallized ginger
oil, for deep frying

1. To make the pastry, mix the flour and salt together in a bowl. Make a well in the centre, then add the egg. Beat well to make a smooth dough. Knead for about 5 minutes until elastic. Cover with a damp cloth and leave to 'rest' for 30 minutes.

2. Meanwhile to make the filling, halve the pawpaw and scoop out the seeds. Cut the flesh into twenty-four small chunks, then remove the skin. Mix with the lime rind.

3. Cut the pastry in half. Roll out one half on a lightly floured work surface until paper thin. Cut into twelve 7.5 cm (3 inch) squares. Cover with a damp tea towel. Repeat with the remaining pastry.

4. Place a piece of pawpaw on a piece of pastry. Wet the edges of the pastry with water, then fold diagonally in half to enclose the filling. Repeat with the remaining pastry and pawpaw.

5. To make the dip, mix the honey with the lime juice and ginger. Transfer to a small bowl or individual bowls for dipping.

6. Heat the oil in a deep fat fryer to 190°C (375°F). Fry the wontons in batches for about 4 minutes or until golden brown. Drain on absorbent kitchen paper and keep warm while frying the remainder. Serve with the ginger and honey dip.

Not suitable for freezing.

BAKLAVA

MAKES 20 SQUARES

If you have difficulty in obtaining phyllo pastry, you can replace it with a 368 g (13 oz) packet bought puff pastry. Cut into six equal pieces and roll out very thinly to a 24 × 18 cm (9½ × 7 inch) rectangle. Layer the pastry with the walnut mixture as below, using only 50 g (2 oz) melted butter. Bake and finish as below.

225 g (8 oz) walnuts, ground
50 g (2 oz) light brown soft sugar
2.5 ml (½ tsp) ground cinnamon
450 g (1 lb) packet phyllo or strüdel pastry
150 g (5 oz) butter, melted
175 g (6 oz) clear honey, warmed

1. Grease a 24 × 18 cm (9½ × 7 inch) roasting tin.

2. Mix the walnuts, sugar and cinnamon together in a bowl. Halve each sheet of pastry to measure a 25.5 cm (10 inch) square.

3. Fit one sheet of pastry into the bottom of the prepared tin, allowing it to come up the sides, and brush with melted butter. Repeat with five more pastry sheets. Sprinkle with 50 g (2 oz) of the nut mixture.

4. Repeat step 3 four more times to produce five layers of walnut mixture. Top with the remaining pastry and trim the sheets to fit the tin. Mark the surface of the pastry into 20 squares with the tip of a sharp knife.

5. Bake in the oven at 220°C (425°F) mark 7 for 15 minutes. Reduce the oven temperature to 180°C (350°F) mark 4 and bake for a further 10—15 minutes until golden brown.

6. Meanwhile, warm the honey in a saucepan over a low heat. Spoon over the cooked Baklava and leave to cool in the tin for 1—2 hours. Cut out the marked squares.

Not suitable for freezing.

CLEMENTINE BISCUITS WITH APRICOT SAUCE

SERVES 6

These make a convenient dinner party dessert because both the biscuits and filling can be made a day or two ahead. Store the biscuits in an airtight tin, and apricot sauce in a covered container in the refrigerator. Tangerines may be used instead of clementines.

FOR THE BISCUITS

75 g (3 oz) plain flour
pinch of salt
2 egg whites, very lightly whisked
75 g (3 oz) icing sugar, sifted
57 g (2¼ oz) unsalted butter, melted
icing sugar, for dusting

FOR THE FILLING

65 ml (2½ fl oz) milk
2.5 ml (½ tsp) cornflour
1 egg yolk
20–25 g (¾–1 oz) caster sugar
drop of vanilla essence
10 ml (2 tsp) brandy
30 ml (2 tbsp) ground almonds
150 ml (¼ pint) double cream, whipped
6–9 clementines or tangerines, peeled, pips removed and segmented

FOR THE APRICOT SAUCE

50 g (2 oz) sugar
225 g (8 oz) dried apricots, soaked overnight
squeeze of lemon juice

1. Line two baking sheets with greased greaseproof paper.
2. To make the biscuits, mix the flour, salt, egg whites and icing sugar together in a bowl. Stir in the melted butter. Spoon the mixture in 12 equal rounds, spaced a little way apart on the prepared baking sheets.
3. Bake in the oven at 180°C (350°F) mark 4 for about 10 minutes until a light golden colour. Leave to cool on a wire rack.
4. To make the filling, heat the milk to boiling point in a pan. Blend the cornflour with the egg yolk, then stir in the hot milk. Pour into a clean pan and cook over a low heat, stirring constantly until the sauce thickens. Remove from the heat and stir in the sugar, vanilla essence, brandy and ground almonds.
5. Cover the surface of the filling closely with clingfilm and leave to cool. When cold, fold in the whipped cream.
6. To make the sauce, dissolve the sugar in about 60 ml (4 tbsp) water in a pan. Add the drained apricots and lemon juice, then cover and simmer until soft.
7. Purée the sauce in a blender or food processor, or press through a sieve. Boil down further if the purée is too liquid, then leave to cool. Chill.
8. To assemble the dessert, place six of the biscuits on six cold plates. Cover with the filling, then top with clementine segments. Place the remaining biscuits on top and dust with icing sugar.
9. A decorative pattern can be created in the icing sugar by placing a red hot skewer briefly on it a number of times. Brush any surplus icing sugar from the plates.
10. Spoon the apricot sauce around the biscuits.

To freeze: pack the cooled biscuits and sauce separately. Thaw at cool room temperature.

BAKEWELL PUDDING

SERVES 6

A buttery mixture, flavoured with ground almonds and baked in a light, flaky pastry case, is the basis of this traditional British recipe, also known as Bakewell tart.

212 g (7½ oz) packet frozen puff pastry, thawed, or ¼ quantity Puff or ½ quantity Flaky pastry (see pages 45 and 44)
60 ml (4 tbsp) strawberry or raspberry jam

FOR THE FILLING

100 g (4 oz) ground almonds
100 g (4 oz) caster sugar
50 g (2 oz) butter
3 eggs, beaten
1.25 ml (¼ tsp) almond flavouring

1. Roll out the pastry on a floured work surface and use to line a 900 ml (1½ pint) shallow pie dish.
2. 'Knock up' the edge of the pastry with the back of a knife and mark the rim with the prongs of a fork. Spread the jam over the base. Chill while making the filling.
3. To make the filling, beat the almonds, sugar, butter, eggs and almond flavouring together in a bowl. Pour the filling over the jam and spread evenly.
4. Bake in the oven at 200°C (400°F) mark 6 for 30 minutes or until the filling is set. Serve warm or cold with cream or custard.

To freeze: wrap and freeze the cooled baked pudding. Thaw at cool room temperature. Serve cold.

Opposite: CLEMENTINE BISCUITS WITH APRICOT SAUCE.

CITRUS CURD TARTLETS

SERVES 6

Pretty individual tartlets filled with a three citrus curd.
Serve warm or cold.

double quantity Pâte sucrée (see page 43)
FOR THE FILLING
finely grated rind and juice of 2 limes
finely grated rind and juice of 1 lemon
finely grated rind and juice of 1 orange
3 eggs, beaten
225 g (8 oz) caster sugar
75 g (3 oz) butter, diced

1. Roll out the pastry on a lightly floured work surface and use to line six 10 cm (4 inch) fluted flan cases. Cover and chill while making the curd filling.
2. To make the filling, put all the ingredients in the top of a double saucepan or in a bowl standing over a pan of simmering water. Stir until the sugar has dissolved. Continue to cook over a low heat for about 20 minutes, stirring all the time, until the curd thickens. (Alternatively, put all of the ingredients in a large bowl and microwave on HIGH for 6–8 minutes until thickened, whisking every minute.)
3. Remove the curd from the heat and continue whisking for 3–4 minutes until the curd is very thick. Cover the surface with a piece of greaseproof paper and leave to cool while baking the pastry cases.
4. Place the flan cases on a baking sheet. Bake blind in the oven at 200°C (400°F) mark 6 for 10–15 minutes until set. Remove the paper and beans, then bake for a further 5–10 minutes until pale golden brown.
5. Fill the warm pastry cases with the warm curd and serve warm. Alternatively, cool both the curd and pastry cases before filling and serve cold.

To freeze: pack and freeze the empty pastry cases. Thaw at cool room temperature, then finish as above.

PROFITEROLES

SERVES 4

If you do not wish to use a piping bag to fill the buns with cream, the choux buns can be split in half, then sandwiched with the cream.

1 quantity Choux pastry (see page 44)
FOR THE CHOCOLATE SAUCE AND FILLING
100 g (4 oz) plain chocolate
15 g (½ oz) butter or margarine
30 ml (2 tbsp) golden syrup
2–3 drops of vanilla essence
150 ml (¼ pint) double cream
icing sugar, for dusting

1. Put the choux pastry in a piping bag fitted with a 1 cm (½ inch) plain nozzle. Pipe about 20 small bun shapes on two damp baking sheets.
2. Bake in the oven at 220°C (425°F) mark 7 for about 20–25 minutes until well risen and golden brown. Reduce the oven temperature to 180°C (350°F) mark 4. Remove the choux buns from the oven and make a hole in the side of each bun with a skewer or knife. Return to the oven for 5 minutes to dry out completely. Leave to cool on a wire rack.
3. For the chocolate sauce, melt the chocolate, butter, 30 ml (2 tbsp) water, the golden syrup and vanilla essence in a small saucepan over a very low heat. Stir well until smooth and well blended.
4. Whip the cream until it just holds its shape. Spoon into a piping bag, fitted with a medium plain nozzle and use to fill the choux buns through the hole in the sides.
5. Dust with icing sugar and serve with the chocolate sauce spooned over or served separately.

To freeze: pack the choux buns and chocolate sauce in separate rigid containers and freeze. Thaw at cool room temperature, then finish as above.

VARIATION

Chocolate eclairs Make the choux paste as page 44, then pipe 6.5 cm (2½ inch) long strips on damp baking sheets. Bake as above and cool on a wire rack. Fill with cream and dip the tops in melted chocolate or glacé icing made with 100 g (4 oz) icing sugar and 10 ml (2 tsp) cocoa powder blended with a little hot water.

Opposite: PROFITEROLES.

CROQUEMBOUCHE

SERVES 25–30

The Croquembouche is a traditional French wedding cake, made up of lots of choux buns piled into a pyramid. The buns are filled with crème pâtissière and coated in caramel. It may also be decorated with spun sugar (see page 56).

treble quantity Choux pastry (see page 44)
1 quantity Pâte sucrée (see page 43)
quadruple quantity Easy crème pâtissière (see page 248) or 900 ml (1½ pints) double cream, 300 ml (½ pint) single cream and 90 ml (6 tbsp) caster sugar
1.1 kg (2½ lb) granulated sugar
FOR THE DECORATION
crystallized rose petals
crystallized violets

1. Dampen three baking sheets with water.

2. Put the choux pastry into a piping bag fitted with a medium plain nozzle and pipe about sixty 2 cm (¾ inch) buns on to the baking sheets.

3. Bake in the oven at 200°C (400°F) mark 6 for 20–25 minutes until well risen and golden brown. Make a small slit in the side of each bun to release the steam, then transfer to a wire rack and leave to cool for 30 minutes.

4. Roll out the pâte sucrée on a lightly floured work surface to a 22 cm (8½ inch) round. Place on a baking sheet, crimp the edge and prick all over with a fork.

5. Bake in the oven at 180°C (350°F) mark 4 for 20 minutes until light golden brown. Cool for 30 minutes on a wire rack then transfer to a cake stand; use a highly ornamental one for a very special occasion.

6. Fill each choux bun with a little crème pâtissière. Or whip the double and single cream together until stiff, fold in the caster sugar and use to fill the buns.

7. To make the caramel, put one third of the granulated sugar with 300 ml (½ pint) water into a heavy based saucepan. Heat gently to dissolve the sugar and then bring to the boil and boil to 143°C–154°C (290°F–310°F) on a sugar thermometer or until the mixture reaches the hard crack stage. Remove from the heat and place the pan on a mat so it is tilted.

8. Dip one side of the filled choux buns into the caramel. Arrange around the edge of the pâte sucrée base, sticking the edges together.

9. Fill the centre with more caramel choux buns. When the first layer is completed, make another on top. Continue in this way, building up into a cone shape and packing the buns loosely. Make more caramel as necessary, using a second third of the sugar and 300 ml (½ pint) water.

10. When the cone is completed, make up more caramel using the remaining sugar and water and drizzle over the Croquembouche. Decorate with crystallized rose petals and violets.

To freeze: pack the choux buns in an airtight container at the end of step 3. Wrap and pack the pâte sucrée base separately. Thaw at cool room temperature, then finish as above.

PARIS-BREST

SERVES 8–10

This speciality of Paris is a large choux ring, split and filled with praline-flavoured cream. It could also be filled with crème Chantilly and fresh fruits, such as strawberries and raspberries. The top is strewn with slivered almonds, giving it a very attractive appearance.

double quantity Choux pastry (see page 44)
25 g (1 oz) almonds, blanched and cut into fine slivers
FOR THE FILLING
100 g (4 oz) unblanched almonds
100 g (4 oz) caster sugar
8 sponge fingers
45–60 ml (3–4 tbsp) orange-flavoured liqueur
600 ml (1 pint) double cream
icing sugar, for dusting

1. Line a large baking sheet with non-stick baking paper, then draw a 20.5 cm (8 inch) circle on the paper, using a plate as a guide.

2. Put the choux pastry into a large piping bag fitted with a large star nozzle. Following the drawn circle, pipe two rings of choux closely together on the baking sheet, then pipe two more rings on the top. Scatter the slivered almonds evenly over the top.

3. Bake in the oven at 220°C (425°F) mark 7 for 40–45 minutes until well risen and crispy. Remove the choux ring from the oven and pierce it in several places to allow the steam to escape. Return to the oven for 5–10 minutes to dry out completely. Transfer the choux ring to a wire rack and allow to cool for a few minutes.

4. Slice horizontally into two, cutting evenly around the centre. Separate the two halves, then scoop out any uncooked pastry from the centre. Leave to cool completely.

5. To make the filling, put the unblanched almonds and sugar into a heavy-based saucepan and heat very gently until the sugar dissolves and turns a rich caramel colour—do not let it become too dark as this will make the praline bitter. Pour the nuts on to a lightly oiled baking sheet and leave to cool. Finely crush or grind.

6. Cut the sponge fingers in half and lay them in a shallow dish. Sprinkle the liqueur over them, cover and leave to stand until the sponge fingers have absorbed the liqueur.

7. Whip the cream until it just holds its shape, then carefully fold in the praline.

8. Place the bottom half of the choux ring on a plate and fill with half the praline cream. Break up the soaked sponge fingers with a fork, then spoon over the praline cream. Spread the remaining praline cream evenly on top of the sponge fingers. Replace the top of the choux ring, then dust lightly with icing sugar. Chill until ready to serve.

To freeze: wrap and freeze at the end of step 4. Thaw at cool room temperature, then finish as above.

PITHIVIERS

SERVES 8

This decorative puff pastry cake is a speciality of Pithiviers, a town just south of Paris. It is filled with a rum-flavoured almond cream, and the top is scored in a distinctive spiral pattern.

---

368 g (13 oz) packet puff pastry or
½ quantity Puff pastry (see page 45)

FOR THE FILLING

50 g (2 oz) unsalted butter

100 g (4 oz) icing sugar, sifted

2 egg yolks

30 ml (2 tbsp) rum

100 g (4 oz) ground almonds

FOR THE GLAZE

1 egg

10 ml (2 tsp) icing sugar, sifted

---

1. Cut the pastry into two equal pieces. Roll out each piece on a lightly floured work surface to a square, a little larger than 25.5 cm (10 inches). Cut a 25.5 cm (10 inch) round from each piece of pastry, using a large plate or saucepan lid as a guide. Place one of the rounds on a baking sheet.

2. To make the filling, beat the butter until very soft in a bowl. Beat in the icing sugar, egg yolks and rum. Mix in the ground almonds until well combined.

3. Spread the almond filling in the centre of the pastry round on the baking sheet, leaving a border of about 2.5 cm (1 inch) all round.

4. Brush the pastry border with a little cold water, then place the second pastry round on top to enclose the filling. Press the edges firmly together to seal. Chill for at least 30 minutes.

5. To make the glaze, light beat the egg and icing sugar together.

6. Lightly flake the edge of the pastry by tapping it gently with a small knife, then decorate the edge by fluting it all the way round with the back of a knife.

7. Brush the top of the pastry with beaten egg glaze— do not allow the glaze to run down the side of the pastry as this will prevent it rising evenly. Using a small sharp knife, mark the top of the pastry with long curved lines, scoring about halfway through the pastry, starting at the centre of the pastry and ending at the edge. The lines should be about 0.5 cm (¼ inch) apart and should look like a spiral pattern when finished. Make a small hole in the centre to allow the steam to escape.

8. Bake in the oven at 230°C (450°F) mark 8 for about 20–25 minutes until well risen and golden brown. Leave to cool on the baking sheet. Serve at room temperature.

Not suitable for freezing.

RELIGIEUSE

SERVES 12

These two-tiered choux puffs acquired their name from the fact that they look like nuns. These are filled with a coffee-flavoured crème pâtissière, and iced with a coffee glacé icing. They may also be filled with cream and coated with chocolate icing, if preferred.

---

double quantity Choux pastry (see page 44)

1½ quantity Crème pâtissière (see page 248) with 15 ml (1 tbsp) coffee granules added to the milk when making the custard

½ quantity Crème Chantilly (see page 248)

FOR THE ICING

225 g (8 oz) icing sugar, sifted

5 ml (1 tsp) coffee granules

---

1. Line several baking sheets with non-stick baking paper.

2. Put the choux pastry into a piping bag fitted with a 1 cm (½ inch) plain nozzle. Pipe 12 buns, 5 cm (2 inches) in diameter, on to the prepared baking sheets, spacing them well apart. Then pipe another 12 smaller buns, about 4 cm (1½ inches) in diameter.

3. Bake the buns, with the small ones placed below the larger ones, at 220°C (425°F) mark 7 for about 35 minutes until well risen, golden brown and crisp. Remove the buns from the oven and pierce underneath to allow the steam to escape. Return to the oven for 5 minutes to dry out completely. Transfer to a wire rack to cool.

4. Put the coffee-flavoured crème pâtissière into a piping bag fitted with a 0.5 cm (¼ inch) plain nozzle. Fill all the buns with the crème pâtissière, piping it in through the hole made in the bottom. Place the buns, spaced well apart, on a wire rack. Place the rack over a tray or large plate.

5. To make the icing, put the icing sugar into a bowl and make a well in the centre. Dissolve the coffee granules in 45 ml (3 tbsp) boiling water, then add to the icing sugar and mix together to form a smooth, shiny icing that will coat the back of the spoon.

6. Spoon the icing evenly over each choux bun, then leave until completely set before fitting together.

7. Whip the crème Chantilly until thick enough to pipe, then fill a piping bag fitted with a large star nozzle. Pipe a rosette on top of each large choux bun, then carefully place the smaller buns on top of the cream, pressing gently into the cream to secure.

To freeze: pack and freeze the cooled buns. Thaw at cool room temperature, then finish as above.

PISTACHIO AND HAZELNUT GALETTE

SERVES 12

This simple cake is made with two rounds of pistachio and hazelnut pastry, filled with an orange liqueur-flavoured cream, mangoes and mandarin orange segments.

FOR THE PASTRY

200 g (7 oz) plain flour
pinch of salt
50 g (2 oz) icing sugar
50 g (2 oz) pistachio nuts, skinned and ground fairly finely
25 g (1 oz) hazelnuts, skinned, toasted, and ground fairly finely
200 g (7 oz) unsalted butter, cut into pieces

FOR THE FILLING

600 ml (1 pint) double cream
finely grated rind of 1 orange
30 ml (2 tbsp) orange-flavoured liqueur
15 ml (1 tbsp) icing sugar, sifted
1 large ripe mango
425 g (15 oz) can mandarin orange segments
icing sugar, for sifting
chopped pistachio nuts, for sprinkling

1. To make the pastry, sift the flour, salt and icing sugar into a bowl, add the nuts and mix well together. Rub the butter into the flour and nut mixture, working the ingredients together gently until they form a ball.

2. Cut the pastry into two equal pieces. Roll out each piece on a lightly floured surface to a round a little smaller than 25 cm (10 inches).

3. Place each pastry round in a 25 cm (10 inch) fluted flan tin, then press the pastry gently over the base of the tins until it fits exactly. Smooth the pastry with the back of a spoon, but do not stretch it. Prick with a fork.

4. Bake blind in the oven at 180°C (350°F) mark 4 for 30–35 minutes until the pastry is cooked and very lightly browned (if you have only one flan tin, bake the pastry rounds one at a time, keeping the one not being baked refrigerated until needed.)

5. Remove the cooked pastry rounds from the oven and immediately cut one of the rounds into 12 triangle-shaped pieces. Leave to cool slightly, then transfer to wire racks to cool completely.

6. To make the filling, whip the cream with the orange rind, liqueur and icing sugar until it will hold soft peaks.

7. Peel the mango, then cut the flesh from the stone in long thin slices. Drain the orange segments well, putting about 12 of the best ones aside for decoration.

8. Carefully place the whole pastry round on a large plate. Spread a generous layer of cream over the pastry, then arrange the mango slices and orange segments evenly over the cream.

9. Whip the remaining cream until thick enough to pipe and fill a piping bag fitted with a large star nozzle.

Pipe 12 large rosettes on top of the fruits, about 2.5 cm (1 inch) in from the edge.

10. Arrange the triangle-shaped pieces of pastry on top of the galette, placing them at an angle, each one supported by a rosette of cream. Sift icing sugar lightly over the galette. Decorate the galette with the remaining cream and reserved mandarin orange segments, then sprinkle over the nuts.

To freeze: wrap and freeze the unfilled pastry. Thaw at cool room temperature, then finish as above.

CENCI

MAKES 50

The Italians eat Cenci at any time of day, whenever they feel like a snack or something sweet to nibble. However, they make a delicious dessert served warm with Fruit purée sauce using raspberries (see page 244) or stewed fruit.

300 g (11 oz) plain flour
2 eggs, beaten
45 ml (3 tbsp) rum
60 ml (4 tbsp) caster sugar
5 ml (1 tsp) baking powder
pinch of salt
oil, for deep frying
icing or caster sugar, for sprinkling

1. Sift 250 g (9 oz) of the flour into a bowl. Make a well in the centre and add the eggs, rum, sugar, baking powder and salt. Mix the ingredients well together with a fork until they form a dough.

2. Sprinkle a work surface with some of the remaining flour. Turn out the dough on to the floured surface and gather into a ball with your fingers. Knead until smooth. Cut the dough into quarters. Roll out one quarter of the dough until almost paper thin, adding more flour to the work surface as necessary.

3. Cut into strips about 15 cm (6 inches) long and 2.5 cm (1 inch) wide. Tie the strips into loose knots. Repeat rolling, cutting and tying with the remaining three quarters of dough.

4. Heat the oil in a deep-fat fryer to 190°C (375°F). Fry four or five pastry twists for 1–2 minutes until golden. Drain on absorbent kitchen paper while frying the remainder. Sift icing sugar over the twists while hot. Serve warm or cold.

To freeze: pack the cooled Cenci in a rigid container. Thaw at cool room temperature. Dust with icing sugar.

Illustrated on page 149

Opposite: PISTACHIO AND HAZELNUT GALETTE.

APPLE AND HAZELNUT LAYER

SERVES 8

75 g (3 oz) hazelnuts, shelled
75 g (3 oz) butter
45 ml (3 tbsp) caster sugar
115 g (4½ oz) plain flour
pinch of salt
450 g (1 lb) Cox's apples, peeled, cored and sliced
15 ml (1 tbsp) apricot jam or marmalade
grated rind of 1 lemon
15 ml (1 tbsp) candied peel, chopped
30 ml (2 tbsp) currants
30 ml (2 tbsp) sultanas
icing sugar, whipped cream and hazelnuts, to decorate

1. Cut out two 20.5 cm (8 inch) circles of greaseproof paper. Grease two baking sheets.

2. Reserve 8 nuts and finely chop the remainder. Cream the butter and sugar until pale and fluffy. Stir in the flour, salt and chopped nuts, then form into a ball and chill for 30 minutes.

3. Put the apple in a saucepan with the jam and lemon rind and cook over a low heat for 5 minutes, until soft. Add the candied peel and dried fruit and simmer for 5 minutes.

4. Divide the pastry in half, place on the sheets of greaseproof paper and roll out into two circles. Transfer to the prepared baking sheets.

5. Bake in the oven at 190°C (375°F) mark 5 for 7–10 minutes, until light brown. Cut one circle into 8 triangles while warm. Leave to cool.

6. Just before serving, place the complete circle on a serving plate and cover with the apple mixture. Arrange the triangles on top. Dust with icing sugar, pipe cream on top and decorate the apple layer with hazelnuts.

To freeze: pack and freeze the pastry rounds and the filling separately. Thaw at cool room temperature, then finish as above.

GÂTEAU SAINT-HONORÉ

SERVES 12

This gâteau is named after Saint-Honoré, who was a Bishop of Amiens and is considered the patron saint of bakers. It is a wonderful gâteau, that combines two types of pastry, pâte sucrée and choux, to form a case that may be filled with an endless variety of fillings. This recipe uses the traditional crème Saint-Honoré, topped with a chocolate-flavoured cream.

1½ quantity Pâte sucrée (see page 43)

double quantity Choux pastry (see page 44)

FOR THE CRÈME SAINT-HONORÉ

double quantity Crème pâtissière (see page 248)

15 ml (1 tbsp) powdered gelatine

30 ml (2 tbsp) orange-flavoured liqueur

FOR THE CARAMEL

225 g (8 oz) granulated sugar

FOR THE TOPPING

75 g (3 oz) plain chocolate, broken into small pieces

300 ml (½ pint) double cream

chopped pistachio nuts, for sprinkling

---

1. Line a large baking sheet with non-stick baking paper.

2. Roll out the pâte sucrée on a flat, or upturned, baking sheet to a round a little larger than 28.5 cm (11 inches) in diameter. Using a flan ring or saucepan lid as a guide, cut the pastry into a 28.5 cm (11 inch) round. Remove the trimmings, then prick the pastry all over with a fork. Chill for 30 minutes.

3. Put the choux pastry into a piping bag fitted with a 1 cm (½ inch) plain nozzle. Pipe a single ring of choux pastry around the edge of the pâte sucrée, about 0.5 cm (¼ inch) in from the edge.

4. Bake in the oven at 200°C (400°F) mark 6 for 25–30 minutes until the choux pastry is well risen, golden brown and crisp. Remove from the oven and pierce the choux ring at intervals to allow the steam to escape. Return to the oven for 2–3 minutes to dry out completely. Transfer to a wire rack to cool.

5. Pipe the remaining choux in whirls, about 4 cm (1½ inches) in diameter, on the prepared baking sheet, spacing them well apart (only 14–15 buns are needed for the gâteau but it is best to make extra buns because all those used have to be perfect).

6. Bake in the oven at 220°C (425°F) mark 7 for 25–30 minutes until well risen, golden brown and crisp. Remove from the oven and pierce each bun underneath to allow the steam to escape. Return to the oven for about 5 minutes to dry out completely. Transfer to a wire rack to cool.

7. To make the crème Saint-Honoré, prepare the crème pâtissière to the stage where the custard is cooled, ready for adding the egg whites and cream.

8. Sprinkle the gelatine over 45 ml (3 tbsp) water in a small bowl and leave to soak for 2–3 minutes. Place the bowl over a saucepan of simmering water and stir until dissolved. (Alternatively, microwave on HIGH for 30 seconds or until dissolved.)

9. Whisk the egg whites until stiff, then fold into the cooled custard. Whip the cream, adding the liqueur, until it just holds its shape, then quickly whisk in the dissolved gelatine. Fold the cream into the custard. Keep at room temperature while completing the gâteau.

10. Spoon some of the crème Saint-Honoré into a piping bag fitted with a 0.5 cm (¼ inch) plain nozzle, and fill 14–15 of the best choux buns, piping it in through the hole made in the bottom. Scrape any cream from the base of the buns with a small palette knife. Put the buns aside while making the caramel.

11. To make the caramel, put the sugar into a saucepan with 75 ml (3 fl oz) water. Heat gently until the sugar has dissolved, brushing down the sides of the pan with the hot water from time to time. Bring the syrup to the boil and boil until it turns a golden caramel colour. Immediately, plunge the base of the pan into cold water to prevent the caramel darkening further. Place the pan in a large bowl and fill the bowl to halfway up the side of the pan with boiling water—this will keep the caramel fluid.

12. Place the pâte sucrée base on a plate. Take one of the choux buns and dip the base in the caramel, then place it on the choux ring, holding it in position for a few seconds to secure. Continue with the remaining buns, placing them close together. Spoon the remaining caramel over each bun to coat evenly. Spoon the remaining crème Saint-Honoré into the choux case. Chill while making the topping.

13. For the topping, put the chocolate into a small bowl with 45 ml (3 tbsp) water. Stand the bowl over a pan of simmering water then heat until the chocolate melts, stirring frequently until smooth. Remove from the heat and leave to cool. Whip the cream until thick but not buttery, then carefully fold in the cooled chocolate.

14. Put the chocolate cream into a piping bag fitted with a medium star nozzle and pipe the cream decoratively over the top of the crème Saint-Honoré. Sprinkle with pistachio nuts and serve. If not serving immediately, keep in a cool place—the gâteau will stand quite well for 1–2 hours.

To freeze: pack and freeze the choux buns and the base separately. Thaw at cool room temperature, then finish as above.

Opposite: GÂTEAU SAINT-HONORÉ.

STRAWBERRY SHORTCAKES

SERVES 6

Any other soft fruits such as raspberries, loganberries, blackberries, bilberries or redcurrants can be used as an alternative filling for these delicious shortcakes. Skinned and roughly chopped peaches and nectarines would also be delicious. The tart flavour of berries or currants can be counteracted by adding a little more sugar.

FOR THE SHORTCAKE

275 g (10 oz) self raising flour
7.5 ml (1½ tsp) baking powder
good pinch of salt
75 g (3 oz) butter, cut into pieces
50 g (2 oz) caster sugar
1 egg, beaten
few drops of vanilla essence
75–90 ml (5–6 tbsp) milk

FOR THE FILLING

450 g (1 lb) strawberries, 6 set aside, the remainder hulled
30 ml (2 tbsp) orange-flavoured liqueur
30 ml (2 tbsp) icing sugar
300 ml (½ pint) double or whipping cream
45 ml (3 tbsp) redcurrant jelly

1. Grease and flour a baking sheet.
2. To make the shortcake, sift the flour, baking powder and salt into a bowl. Rub in the butter until the mixture resembles breadcrumbs. Stir in the caster sugar.
3. Make a well in the centre of the dry ingredients and add the egg, vanilla essence and milk. Using a palette knife, cut through the dry ingredients until evenly blended, then quickly and lightly bring the mixture together using the fingertips of one hand.
4. Gently knead the dough on a lightly floured work surface until just smooth. Roll out to a thickness of 1 cm (½ inch) and cut out six 9 cm (3½ inch) fluted rounds.
5. Gather up the scraps, knead lightly and roll out again. Place the rounds on the prepared baking sheet. Brush the tops of the rounds with milk—do not let it trickle down the sides.
6. Bake in the oven at 230°C (450°F) mark 8 for about 11 minutes or until the shortcakes are well risen and golden brown. Remove from the oven and keep warm.
7. To make the filling, thickly slice half the strawberries. Put into a bowl and add the liqueur. Sift in 15 ml (1 tbsp) of the icing sugar.
8. With a fork, lightly crush the remaining strawberries and sift in the rest of the icing sugar. Whip the cream until it just holds its shape and stir in the crushed strawberries.
9. Cut the shortcakes in half while still warm. Carefully run the point of a sharp knife from the side of the shortcake into the centre. Rotate the shortcake and saw with the sharp knife until the cake is cut in two.
10. Spoon half the cream on to the shortcake bases and cover with the sliced strawberries. Spoon over the remaining cream and replace the shortcake tops.
11. Put the redcurrant jelly into a small pan and heat gently until liquid. (Alternatively, place in a small bowl and microwave on HIGH for 1–2 minutes.) Leave to cool for 5–10 minutes, then brush over the shortcakes. Decorate with whole strawberries.

To freeze: wrap and freeze the cooled shortbread at the end of step 6. Thaw at cool room temperature. Warm in a hot oven for 5 minutes, then finish as above.

ROLY-POLY WITH HOT JAM SAUCE

SERVES 4

If you prefer a baked roly-poly, wrap in foil and bake at 200°C (400°F) mark 6 for 45 minutes. (1 hour if cooking from frozen.)

¾ quantity Suetcrust pastry (see page 44)
90 ml (6 tbsp) red jam
little milk, for brushing

FOR THE SAUCE

45 ml (3 tbsp) red jam
finely grated rind of 1 orange
10 ml (2 tsp) arrowroot
150 ml (¼ pint) fresh orange juice

1. Roll out the pastry on a floured work surface to a 25.5 × 20 cm (10 × 8 inch) oblong. Spread the 90 ml (6 tbsp) jam over the pastry to 0.5 cm (¼ inch) of the edges. Brush the edges with milk.
2. Roll up the pastry evenly like a Swiss roll, starting from one short side.
3. Place the roll, seam side down, on a sheet of greased foil measuring at least 30.5 × 23 cm (12 × 9 inches). Wrap the foil loosely around the roll to allow room for expansion during cooking. Seal well.
4. Place the roly-poly in the top of a steamer over a pan of boiling water and steam for 1½–2 hours, topping up the water as necessary.
5. Just before serving, make the sauce. Put the jam and orange rind in a heavy-based saucepan. Mix the arrowroot to a paste with a little of the orange juice, then stir the remaining orange juice into the pan. Heat gently until the jam has melted, then stir in the arrowroot paste and bring to the boil. Simmer until thickened, stirring constantly.
6. Unwrap the roly-poly and place on a warmed serving plate. Pour over the hot jam sauce and serve immediately.

To freeze: wrap the roly-poly at the end of step 3. Steam from frozen, allowing an extra 30 minutes.

Opposite: ROLY-POLY WITH HOT JAM SAUCE.

SUSSEX POND PUDDING

SERVES 6

An old-fashioned recipe from the south of England, Sussex pond pudding takes its name from the fact that during cooking the whole lemon inside bursts, and the resulting juice combines with the other ingredients of butter and sugar to produce a delicious pool or 'pond' of lemon sauce. Be sure to prick the fruit thoroughly all over with a skewer before placing it inside the suet crust pastry case, otherwise the lemon will remain whole and spoil the finished effect.

1½ quantity Suetcrust pastry (see page 44)
100 g (4 oz) butter, cut into pieces
100 g (4 oz) demerara sugar
1 large lemon

1. Roll out two-thirds of the pastry on a floured work surface to a circle, 2.5 cm (1 inch) larger all round than the top of a 1.4 litre (2½ pint) pudding basin. Use to line the pudding basin.
2. Put 50 g (2 oz) of the butter into the centre with 50 g (2 oz) of the sugar. Prick the lemon all over with a skewer. Put the whole lemon on top of the butter and sugar. Add the remaining butter and sugar.
3. Roll out the remaining pastry and use to cover the pudding. Dampen the edges and seal the lid. Cover with greaseproof and foil. Secure with string.
4. Place over a pan of boiling water and steam for about 4 hours, topping up the water as necessary.
5. Remove the foil and paper and turn out on to a warmed serving dish. During cooking the lemon inside the pudding bursts and produces a delicious lemon sauce. Each serving should have a piece of the lemon, which will be much softened by the cooking.

Not suitable for freezing.

PEAR AND APPLE DUMPLINGS

SERVES 4

Delicious, lightly cooked pears or apples, filled with apple brandy-soaked fruit and encased in crisp pastry. If preferred, the dumplings can be filled with a more everyday mixture of cinnamon, sugar and butter.

1 quantity Suetcrust pastry (see page 44) or 1 quantity Rough puff pastry (see page 45) or a 368 g (13 oz) packet, thawed
beaten egg, for glazing
FOR THE FILLING
50 g (2 oz) sultanas
30 ml (2 tbsp) apple brandy
4 ripe, firm pears or eating apples

1. For the filling, put the sultanas and apple brandy in a small bowl and leave to soak for 30 minutes.
2. Peel the fruit, leaving the stalks on the pears. Remove the cores from the bottom and fill with the soaked sultanas. Reserve any remaining apple brandy.
3. Divide the pastry into four. Roll out each piece on a lightly floured work surface to an 18 cm (7 inch) square if making pear dumplings or a 15 cm (6 inch) square if making apple dumplings. Cut each square into a large cross. Cut leaves from the pastry trimmings.
4. Brush the fruit with any remaining apple brandy, then place a fruit on the centre of each pastry cross. Bring the edges of the pastry together to completely enclose the fruit.
5. Brush the edges with beaten egg and seal together. Brush the pastry leaves with beaten egg and stick on to the dumplings to decorate. Transfer the dumplings to a baking sheet, then brush with beaten egg to glaze.
6. Bake in the oven at 200°C (400°F) mark 6 for 25 minutes until golden brown. Serve warm with whipped cream flavoured with a little apple brandy and icing sugar.

Not suitable for freezing.

PEAR AND GINGER ROLL

SERVES 6

1 quantity Suetcrust pastry (see page 44)
FOR THE FILLING
450 g (1 lb) firm, but ripe pears, peeled, cored and sliced
50 g (2 oz) sultanas
2.5 ml (½ tsp) ground ginger
50 g (2 oz) demerara sugar
icing sugar, for dusting

1. Roll out the pastry on a lightly floured work surface to a 28 × 23 cm (11 × 9 inch) rectangle.
2. Mix the pears with the sultanas, ginger and demerara sugar.
3. Spread evenly over the pastry to within 1 cm (½ inch) of the edges. Turn in the edges to contain the filling and brush them lightly with water. Roll up the pastry from the longest side, like a Swiss roll.
4. Place the roll, seam side down, on a large sheet of greased foil. Wrap the foil loosely around the roll to allow room for expansion during cooking. Seal well.
5. Place the roll in the top of a steamer over a pan of boiling water and steam for about 1½ hours, topping up the water as necessary.
6. Lift the roll carefully from the saucepan. Allow it to stand for a minute or two, then unwrap and place on a hot serving dish. Dredge with sugar and serve with Walnut Rum Sauce (see page 247).

Not suitable for freezing.

Opposite: PEAR AND APPLE DUMPLINGS.

CHOCOLATE CREATIONS

Wonderfully wicked, sinfully rich, these chocolate
desserts take your eye and tempt your palate. Such very
special melt-in-the-mouth concoctions are pure
pleasure—resist them if you can.

Passionate chocolate lovers know that there is nothing quite like the rich, dark, smooth sensation of chocolate. It is rarely out of favour or fashion; it is still the most luxurious and versatile of ingredients when you want to produce a sensational dessert. The following recipes will take you from a simple but delicious Chocolate lime mousse to the most wonderful Squidgy chocolate mousse cake.

A variety of chocolate has been used in the recipes: plain, milk, white and cocoa powder. As each one has different cooking properties, it is not really advisable to substitute one for another, unless stated.

Melting Chocolate

Many of the recipes require melted chocolate and it is important to do this gently. Stand the bowl containing the chocolate over a saucepan of just simmering water and stir until the chocolate becomes smooth and creamy. Extra care should be taken when melting white chocolate because it has a tendency to separate on heating. Stir it all the time to ensure that one area does not get particularly hot. Alternatively, melt plain or white chocolate in the microwave on LOW, stirring frequently.

If chocolate is overheated, it will become very granular and can easily scorch. Overheated chocolate can sometimes be rectified by adding a small knob of blended white vegetable fat.

Decorating with Chocolate

Chocolate flavour cake covering is useful for scrolls and curls because it is more pliable, but the flavour is not so good. Crumbled chocolate flake makes a useful last minute decoration.

Handle chocolate decorations as little as possible since body heat will melt them and leave fingerprints on the surface.

Chocolate caraque   Melt at least 100 g (4 oz) chocolate in a bowl over a pan of simmering water. Pour it in a thin layer on to a marble slab or cold baking sheet and leave to set until it no longer sticks to your hand when you touch it. Holding a large knife with both hands, push the blade across the surface of the chocolate to roll pieces off in long curls. Adjust the angle of the blade to get the best curls.

Chocolate shapes   Make a sheet of chocolate as above and cut into neat triangles, squares or shapes with a sharp knife, or stamp out circles with a small round cutter.

Leaves   Using a small paintbrush, thinly spread melted chocolate on the undersides of clean, dry, undamaged rose leaves. Leave to set. Gently peel off chocolate.

Chocolate curls   Using a potato peeler, pare thin curls from the edge of a thick block of chocolate.

Lacy chocolate shapes   Drizzle melted chocolate in irregular shapes on to a sheet of foil. Chill until set. Peel off carefully to use.

Chocolate caraque, shapes, leaves and curls can be stored in an airtight container in the refrigerator or frozen.

CHOCOLATE FUDGE CAKE

SERVES 12–14

This gooey, triple-layered chocolate cake is best cut with a large, sharp, wetted knife.

FOR THE CAKE
275 g (10 oz) plain flour
45 ml (3 tbsp) cocoa powder
6.25 ml (1¼ tsp) baking powder
2.5 ml (½ tsp) bicarbonate of soda
large pinch of salt
100 g (4 oz) plain chocolate
150 g (5 oz) butter
225 g (8 oz) light brown soft sugar
2 eggs, beaten
150 ml (¼ pint) natural yogurt
2.5 ml (½ tsp) vanilla essence

FOR THE FUDGE ICING
450 g (1 lb) icing sugar
100 g (4 oz) cocoa powder
100 g (4 oz) butter
90 ml (6 tbsp) milk

1. Grease three 18 cm (7 inch) sandwich tins, line the bases with greaseproof paper and grease the paper.
2. To make the cake, sift the flour, cocoa powder, baking powder, bicarbonate of soda and salt together.
3. Break the chocolate into small pieces. Place in a heatproof bowl over a pan of simmering water and heat gently until the chocolate melts. (Alternatively, microwave on LOW for 4–5 minutes or until melted, stirring occasionally.) Leave to cool for 30 minutes.
4. Cream the butter and brown sugar together in a bowl until light and fluffy. Beat in the eggs, then fold in the chocolate, the sifted ingredients, yogurt and vanilla essence. Turn the mixture into the prepared tins and level the surface.
5. Bake in the oven at 190°C (375°F) mark 5 for 25–30 minutes until risen and firm to the touch. Turn out on to a wire rack and leave to cool.
6. To make the fudge icing, sift the icing sugar and cocoa powder together. Put into a heavy-based saucepan with the butter and milk. Heat gently until the butter has melted, then beat until smooth. Remove from the heat.
7. Use some of the fudge icing to sandwich the three cakes together. Cover the sides and top of the cake with the remaining icing.

To freeze: open freeze until firm, then place in a rigid container or wrap in foil.

Previous Page: DARK CHOCOLATE TRUFFLE CAKE (PAGE 87)
Opposite: CHOCOLATE ROULADE.

CHOCOLATE ROULADE

SERVES 8–10

Do not worry if the roulade cracks as you roll it, the cracks are part of its charm.

FOR THE ROULADE

100 g (4 oz) plain chocolate
4 eggs, separated
100 g (4 oz) caster sugar

FOR THE FILLING

150 ml ($\frac{1}{4}$ pint) double cream
15 ml (1 tbsp) icing sugar
150 ml ($\frac{1}{4}$ pint) Greek yogurt
few drops of rose water (optional)
225 g (8 oz) raspberries

FOR THE DECORATION

icing sugar, for dusting
150 ml ($\frac{1}{4}$ pint) double cream
100 g (4 oz) raspberries, hulled
few small rose, geranium or mint leaves

1. Grease a 23 × 33 cm (9 × 13 inch) Swiss roll tin, line with greaseproof paper and grease the paper.
2. To make the roulade, break the chocolate into small pieces. Place in a heatproof bowl standing over a pan of simmering water and heat gently until the chocolate melts. (Alternatively, microwave on LOW for 4–5 minutes or until melted, stirring occasionally.)
3. Whisk the egg yolks and sugar together in a bowl until very thick and pale in colour. Beat in the chocolate. Whisk the egg whites until stiff, then fold carefully into the chocolate mixture. Pour the mixture into the prepared tin and spread out evenly.
4. Bake in the oven at 180°C (350°F) mark 4 for 20–25 minutes until well risen and firm to the touch.
5. While the roulade is cooking, lay a piece of grease-proof paper on a flat work surface and sprinkle generously with caster sugar. When the roulade is cooked, turn it out on to the paper. Carefully peel off the lining paper. Cover the roulade with a warm, damp tea towel and leave to cool.
6. To make the filling, whip the cream with the icing sugar until it forms soft peaks. Fold in the yogurt with a few drops of rose water. Spread the cream over the roulade. Sprinkle with the raspberries. Starting from one of the narrow ends, carefully roll it up, using the paper to help. Transfer the roulade to a serving plate and dust generously with icing sugar.
7. To make the decoration, whip the remaining cream until it forms soft peaks and spoon into a piping bag fitted with a star nozzle. Pipe the cream down the centre of the roulade and the sides. Decorate with raspberries and rose, geranium or mint leaves.

To freeze: roll the cooled roulade with the paper inside it, then overwrap. Thaw at cool room temperature, then finish as above.

DEVIL'S FOOD CAKE

SERVES 16–18

This classic cake comes from the United States. This authentic version makes a cake of huge proportions in true American style!

FOR THE CAKES

450 g (1 lb) plain flour
15 ml (1 tbsp) bicarbonate of soda
pinch of salt
75 g (3 oz) cocoa powder
345 ml (½ pint, plus 3 tbsp) milk
10 ml (2 tsp) vanilla essence
150 g (5 oz) butter or margarine
400 g (14 oz) dark brown soft sugar
4 eggs

FOR THE AMERICAN FROSTING AND DECORATION

700 g (1½ lb) caster sugar
3 egg whites
50 g (2 oz) plain chocolate (optional)

1. Grease three 22 cm (8½ inch) sandwich tins and line the bases with greaseproof paper.

2. To make the cakes, sift the flour, bicarbonate of soda and salt together. Mix the cocoa, milk and vanilla essence together until smooth.

3. Using an electric hand-held mixer, cream the butter in a bowl until pale and fluffy, then gradually beat in the sugar. Add the eggs, one at a time, beating very thoroughly after each addition. Beat in the flour and cocoa mixtures alternately. Divide the mixture between the prepared tins.

4. Bake in the oven at 180°C (350°F) mark 4 for about 35 minutes until firm to the touch. Turn out on to a wire rack and cool.

5. To make the American frosting, put the sugar and 180 ml (¼ pint, plus 2 tbsp) water in a heavy-based saucepan and heat gently until the sugar has dissolved. When completely dissolved, boil rapidly to 115°C (240°F)—use a sugar thermometer to check the temperature.

6. Meanwhile, whisk the egg whites until stiff in a large deep bowl. Allow the bubbles to settle, then slowly pour the hot syrup on to the egg whites, whisking constantly. When all the sugar syrup is added, continue whisking until the mixture stands in peaks and just starts to become matt around the edges. The icing sets quickly, so work rapidly.

7. Sandwich the three cakes together with a little of the frosting. Spread the remaining frosting over the top and sides of the cake with a palette knife. Pull the icing up into peaks all over. Leave the cake on a wire rack for 30 minutes to allow the icing to set slightly.

8. Break the chocolate into small pieces. Place in a heatproof bowl standing over a pan of simmering water and heat gently until the chocolate melts. (Alternatively, microwave on LOW for 2–3 minutes or until melted, stirring occasionally.) Spoon the chocolate into a greaseproof paper piping bag and drizzle over the top of the cake. Leave to set completely.

To freeze: wrap and freeze at the end of step 4. Thaw, then finish as before.

CINNAMON CHOCOLATE TORTE

SERVES 6–8

Most supermarkets and delicatessens sell French, Swiss or Belgian chocolate that is suitable for baking—they are not oversweet and have excellent melting properties. For this cake, do not use the block or chips labelled 'cooking chocolate'—their flavour could ruin the finished cake.

FOR THE CAKE

175 g (6 oz) plain chocolate
175 g (6 oz) butter
200 g (7 oz) caster sugar
5 eggs, separated
150 g (5 oz) plain flour
15 ml (3 tsp) ground cinnamon
75 g (3 oz) ground almonds

FOR THE FILLING

90 ml (6 tbsp) apricot jam
30 ml (2 tbsp) lemon juice
300 ml (½ pint) whipping cream, whipped
icing sugar, for dusting

1. Grease and line two 19 cm (7½ inch) sandwich tins.

2. To make the cake, first break the chocolate into small pieces. Place in a heatproof bowl with 45 ml (3 tbsp) water. Stand the bowl over a pan of simmering water and heat gently until the chocolate melts. (Alternatively, microwave on LOW for 6 minutes or until melted, stirring occasionally.) Leave to cool.

3. Cream the butter and sugar together in a bowl until light. Beat in the egg yolks. Add the cooled chocolate, mixing well.

4. Whisk the egg whites. Sift the flour with 10 ml (2 tsp) of the cinnamon and fold into the creamed mixture with the ground almonds and egg whites. Spoon the mixture into the prepared tins.

5. Bake in the oven at 190°C (375°F) mark 5 for 35–40 minutes or until a skewer inserted into the centre comes out clean. Turn out the cake on to a wire rack and leave to cool for about 2 hours. Cut each cake into two layers.

6. To make the filling, put the apricot jam in a small pan with the lemon juice and remaining cinnamon, then heat gently. Cool and spread on the cakes. Layer up with cream and dust the top with icing sugar just before serving.

To freeze: wrap and freeze at the end of step 5. Thaw, unwrapped, at cool room temperature.

SQUIDGY CHOCOLATE MOUSSE CAKE

SERVES 8

This delicious combination of rich chocolate sponge and soft, squidgy chocolate mousse topping is perfect for a dinner party dessert.

450 g (1 lb) plain chocolate
45 ml (3 tbsp) orange-flavoured liqueur
9 eggs, 5 of them separated
150 g (5 oz) caster sugar
100 g (4 oz) unsalted butter, softened

FOR THE DECORATION

blanched julienne strips of orange rind
grated chocolate

1. Grease a 20.5 cm (8 inch) spring-release cake tin, line with greaseproof paper and grease the paper.
2. Break 225 g (8 oz) of the chocolate into small pieces. Place in a heatproof bowl standing over a pan of simmering water and heat gently until the chocolate melts. (Alternatively, microwave on LOW for 4–5 minutes or until melted, stirring occasionally.) Stir in 15 ml (1 tbsp) of the liqueur, then remove from the heat.
3. Using an electric whisk, whisk 5 egg yolks and the sugar together in a bowl until thick and creamy. Beat in the butter, a little at a time, until smooth. Beat in the melted chocolate until smooth.
4. Whisk the 5 egg whites until stiff, then fold into the chocolate mixture. Turn into the prepared tin.
5. Bake in the oven at 180°C (350°F) mark 4 for 40 minutes until risen and firm. Leave the cake to cool in the tin for 1 hour.
6. To make the top layer, melt the remaining chocolate as before, then stir in the remaining liqueur. Remove from the heat and cool for 1–2 minutes. Separate the remaining eggs and beat the egg yolks into the chocolate mixture. Whisk the egg whites until stiff, then fold into the chocolate mixture.
7. Press the crust down on the baked cake with your fingers and pour the top layer over it. Chill overnight.
8. The next day, remove the cake carefully from the tin and put on to a serving plate. Arrange strips of orange rind around the outside edge and decorate with grated chocolate.

To freeze: wrap and freeze at the end of step 7. Thaw overnight at cool room temperature, then finish as above.

CHOCOLATE COFFEE REFRIGERATOR SLICE

SERVES 6

This luxurious chilled entertaining dessert requires no cooking.

30 ml (2 tbsp) instant coffee granules
45 ml (3 tbsp) brandy
100 g (4 oz) plain chocolate
50 g (2 oz) icing sugar
100 g (4 oz) unsalted butter, softened
2 egg yolks
300 ml ($\frac{1}{2}$ pint) whipping cream
50 g (2 oz) chopped almonds, toasted
about 30 sponge fingers
coffee beans, to decorate

1. Grease a 22 × 11.5 cm ($8\frac{1}{2}$ × $4\frac{1}{2}$ inch) top measurement loaf tin and line the base with greaseproof paper. Grease the paper.
2. Make up the coffee granules with 250 ml (8 fl oz) boiling water and stir in the brandy. Set aside to cool for 15 minutes.
3. Break the chocolate into small pieces. Place in a heatproof bowl with 15 ml (1 tbsp) water. Stand the bowl over a pan of simmering water and heat gently until the chocolate melts. (Alternatively microwave on LOW for 4–5 minutes or until melted, stirring occasionally.) Remove from the heat and leave to cool for about 5 minutes.
4. Sift the icing sugar into a bowl. Add the butter and beat together until pale and fluffy. Add the egg yolks, beating well.
5. Lightly whip the cream and chill half of it. Stir the remaining cream, the cooled chocolate and the nuts into the butter and egg yolk mixture.
6. Line the bottom of the prepared tin with sponge fingers, cutting to fit if necessary. Spoon over one third of the coffee and brandy mixture.
7. Layer the chocolate mixture and sponge fingers in the tin, soaking each layer with coffee and ending with soaked sponge fingers. Weight down lightly and chill for 3–4 hours until set.
8. Turn out, remove the paper and decorate with the reserved whipped cream and the coffee beans.

To freeze: turn out and open freeze until firm. Wrap and freeze. Thaw overnight in the refrigerator.

CHOCOLATE BOX GÂTEAU

SERVES 9

The sides of this cake are covered with neat home-made squares of chocolate. If you do not have time to make them yourself, buy ready made chocolate squares from good sweet shops or delicatessens.

FOR THE SPONGE
3 eggs
100 g (4 oz) caster sugar
75 g (3 oz) plain flour
30 ml (2 tbsp) cocoa powder

FOR THE FILLING AND DECORATION
150 g (5 oz) plain chocolate
300 ml (½ pint) double cream
700 g (1½ lb) mandarin oranges or tangerines, peeled and segmented
1 quantity Apricot glaze (see page 42)

1. Grease and flour an 18 cm (7 inch) square cake tin, then line the base with greaseproof paper.
2. To make the sponge, using an electric whisk, whisk the eggs and sugar together in a bowl until very thick and pale, and the mixture leaves a trail when the whisk is lifted. Sift the flour and cocoa powder over the mixture, then fold in using a large metal spoon. Transfer to the prepared tin.
3. Bake in the oven at 190°C (375°F) mark 5 for 30—35 minutes or until firm to the touch and shrunken from the sides of the tin. Turn out and cool on a wire rack.
4. Break the chocolate into small pieces. Place in a heatproof bowl standing over a pan of simmering water and heat gently until the chocolate melts. (Alternatively, microwave on LOW for 4—5 minutes or until melted.)
5. Meanwhile, spread a sheet of foil on a baking sheet and mark a 22 cm (8½ inch) square. Spread the chocolate evenly over the square marked on the foil. Leave until set. When set, trim the edges and cut into 24 squares, measuring about 5 cm (2 inches).
6. Whip the cream until it just holds its shape. Cut the cake in half horizontally, then sandwich together with a little of the cream and a few of the mandarins.
7. Arrange the rest of the fruit evenly all over the top of the cake and brush with warm apricot glaze.
8. Spread a little of the remaining cream round the sides of the cake. Press on the chocolate squares, over-lapping each one slightly. Spoon the remaining cream into a piping bag fitted with a star nozzle and pipe around the top of the cake.

To freeze: wrap and freeze at the end of step 3. Thaw at cool room temperature, then finish as above.

Left: CHOCOLATE AND LIME MOUSSE *(PAGE 98).*
Right: CHOCOLATE BOX GÂTEAU.

BLACK FOREST GÂTEAU

SERVES 10

This famous and much loved cake from Germany is perfect for any grand occasion, or as a dessert for a dinner party. The cherries should really be fresh morello cherries, but as these are not always easy to come by, canned cherries are used instead. When fresh morello cherries are available, poach them in a sugar syrup and carefully remove their stones before using in the gâteau.

FOR THE CAKE

100 g (4 oz) butter
6 eggs
225 g (8 oz) caster sugar
75 g (3 oz) plain flour
50 g (2 oz) cocoa powder
2.5 ml ($\frac{1}{2}$ tsp) vanilla essence

FOR THE FILLING AND DECORATION

two 425 g (15 oz) cans stoned black cherries, drained and syrup reserved
60 ml (4 tbsp) kirsch
600 ml (1 pint) whipping cream
100 g (4 oz) Chocolate caraque (see page 78)
5 ml (1 tsp) arrowroot

1. Grease a deep 23 cm (9 inch) round cake tin and line the base with greaseproof paper.
2. To make the cake, put the butter into a bowl, place over a pan of warm water and beat until really soft but not melted.
3. Whisk the eggs and sugar together in a large bowl standing over a pan of simmering water until pale and creamy, and thick enough to leave a trail on the surface when the whisk is lifted. Remove from the heat and whisk until cool.
4. Sift the flour and cocoa together, then lightly fold into the mixture with a metal spoon. Fold in the vanilla essence and softened butter. Turn the mixture into the prepared tin and tilt the tin to spread the mixture evenly.
5. Bake in the oven at 180°C (350°F) mark 4 for about 40 minutes until well risen, firm to the touch and beginning to shrink away from the sides of the tin. Turn out of the tin on to a wire rack, covered with grease-proof paper, and leave to cool for 30 minutes. Cut the cake into three horizontally.
6. Place one layer on a flat plate. To make the filling, mix 75 ml (5 tbsp) of the cherry syrup and the kirsch together. Spoon 45 ml (3 tbsp) over the cake layer.
7. Whip the cream until it just holds its shape, then spread a little thinly over the soaked sponge. Reserve a quarter of the cherries for decoration and scatter half the remainder over the cream.
8. Repeat the layers of sponge, syrup, cream and cherries. Top with the third cake round and spoon over the remaining kirsch-flavoured syrup.
9. Spread a thin layer of the remaining cream around the sides of the cake, reserving a third to decorate. Press on the chocolate caraque, reserving a few to decorate the top.
10. Spoon the remaining cream into a piping bag fitted with a large star nozzle and pipe whirls of cream around the edge of the cake. Top each whirl with a chocolate curl.
11. Fill the centre with the reserved cherries. Blend the arrowroot with 45 ml (3 tbsp) cherry syrup. Place in a small saucepan, bring to the boil and boil, stirring, for a few minutes until the mixture is clear. Brush the glaze over the cherries.

To freeze: wrap the cooled cake at the end of step 5. Thaw, unwrapped, at room temperature, then finish as above.

CHOCOLATE AND CHESTNUT GÂTEAU

SERVES 12

Thin layers of chocolate sponge are sandwiched together with a rich, gooey chestnut cream. The easiest way to cut the cake into four is to use a large knife with a long, sharp blade. Lay the cake flat on a board, then slice through horizontally. When sandwiching the pieces back together, make sure they are replaced in their original position, or you may end up with a lop-sided cake. Try to obtain unsweetened chestnut purée for best results.

23 cm (9 inch) chocolate Genoese (see page 124)
425 g (15 oz) can natural chestnut purée
300 ml ($\frac{1}{2}$ pint) double cream
30 ml (2 tbsp) brandy
canned whole chestnuts, drained
grated chocolate
icing sugar, for dusting

1. To make the filling, break the chocolate into small pieces. Place in a heatproof bowl standing over a pan of simmering water and heat gently until the chocolate melts. (Alternatively, microwave on LOW for 4 minutes or until melted, stirring occasionally.) Pour the chocolate into a food processor with the chestnut purée, cream and brandy and blend until smooth. Leave to cool and thicken slightly.
2. Carefully slice the cake into four horizontally and sandwich together with a little of the chestnut cream. Cover the top and sides with the remaining cream and mark in a decorative pattern with a palette knife. Decorate with chestnuts dipped in grated chocolate, plain chocolate preferably. Dust the gâteau lightly with a little icing sugar.

To freeze: wrap and freeze before decorating. Thaw, then finish as above.

WHISKY MOCHA FLAN

SERVES 6–8

This flan is made with a coffee-flavoured bavarois mixture and topped with whisky cream.

1 quantity Shortcrust pastry (see page 42)

FOR THE FILLING
75 g (3 oz) plain chocolate
10 ml (2 tsp) powdered gelatine
150 ml ($\frac{1}{4}$ pint) milk
15 ml (1 tbsp) instant coffee granules
3 egg yolks
15 ml (1 tbsp) caster sugar
150 ml ($\frac{1}{4}$ pint) double cream

FOR THE TOPPING
200 ml (7 fl oz) double cream
15–30 ml (1–2 tbsp) whisky
15 ml (1 tbsp) caster sugar
Chocolate caraque (see page 78), to decorate

1. Roll out the pastry on a lightly floured work surface and use to line a 23 cm (9 inch) fluted flan tin. Trim the edges, then prick with a fork. Chill for 30 minutes.

2. Bake blind in the oven at 220°C (425°F) mark 7 for 20–25 minutes until the pastry is cooked and very lightly browned. Leave to cool.

3. To make the filling, break the chocolate into small pieces. Place in a heatproof bowl standing over a pan of simmering water and heat until the chocolate melts. Stir until smooth. (Alternatively, microwave on LOW for 3–4 minutes or until melted, stirring occasionally.)

4. Remove the pastry case from the flan tin and place it, upside down, on a sheet of greaseproof paper. Using a pastry brush, brush half of the melted chocolate evenly all over the pastry case. Leave in a cool place until the chocolate sets. Turn the flan case over and brush the inside with the remaining chocolate and leave to set.

5. Sprinkle the gelatine over 30 ml (2 tbsp) water in a small bowl and leave to soak for 2–3 minutes. Place the bowl over a pan of simmering water and stir until dissolved. (Alternatively, microwave on HIGH for 30 seconds or until dissolved.)

6. Put the milk and coffee granules into a small saucepan. Heat gently until the coffee dissolves completely and the milk comes almost to the boil. Very lightly whisk the egg yolks and sugar together in a bowl. Pour in the coffee-flavoured milk and mix well.

7. Place the bowl over a pan of hot water and cook the custard, stirring continuously, until thick enough to coat the back of the spoon. (Alternatively, microwave the custard on HIGH for 2–2$\frac{1}{2}$ minutes, stirring every 30 seconds.)

8. As soon as the custard thickens, strain it through a nylon sieve into a clean bowl. Stir in the dissolved gelatine. Leave the custard to cool, stirring frequently to prevent a skin forming.

9. Whip the cream until it will just hold soft peaks, then gently fold into the coffee custard. Place the chocolate coated flan case on a flat serving plate, fill with the coffee cream mixture. Chill until set.

10. To make the topping, whip the cream with the whisky and sugar until it will just hold soft peaks. Spread an even layer of cream over the top of the flan. Whip the remaining cream until thick enough to pipe and fill a piping bag fitted with a medium star nozzle. Pipe whirls of cream around the top of the flan, then decorate with chocolate caraque. Chill.

To freeze: freeze at the end of step 9. Thaw in the refrigerator overnight, then finish as above.

FROZEN CHOCOLATE, RUM AND RAISIN CAKE

SERVES 12

A delicious, mousse-like ice cream cake with a crisp, dark chocolate base. Serve with cream.

FOR THE FILLING
50 g (2 oz) raisins
60 ml (4 tbsp) dark rum
50 g (2 oz) caster sugar
3 egg yolks
175 g (6 oz) plain chocolate
300 ml ($\frac{1}{2}$ pint) double cream

FOR THE BISCUIT CRUST
100 g (4 oz) butter or margarine, melted
225 g (8 oz) plain chocolate biscuits, crushed

1. Put the raisins and rum in a small bowl and leave to soak for several hours or overnight.

2. To make the biscuit crust, mix the butter and biscuits together. Press into the base of a 20.5 cm (8 inch) spring-release cake tin. Chill for 30 minutes or overnight.

3. To make the filling, put the sugar and 75 ml (5 tbsp) water in a small saucepan and heat gently until dissolved. When the sugar is completely dissolved, increase the heat and boil the mixture rapidly for 4 minutes to make a syrup.

4. Meanwhile, lightly whisk the egg yolks with any excess rum from the soaked raisins. Gradually pour the sugar syrup on to the egg yolks, whisking all the time.

5. Break the chocolate into small pieces. Place in a heatproof bowl standing over a pan of simmering water and heat gently until the chocolate melts. (Alternatively, microwave on LOW for 4–5 minutes or until melted, stirring occasionally.) Stir into the egg yolk mixture. Leave to cool.

6. When cold, whip the cream until stiff, then fold into the chocolate mixture. Fold in the raisins. Pour the mixture into the tin on top of the biscuit base.

7. Cover tightly with clingfilm and foil, then freeze for at least 3–4 hours or until firm. Remove from the freezer for 5 minutes before serving. Serve cut into wedges.

Opposite: WHISKY MOCHA FLAN.

CHOCOLATE MACAROON LOG

SERVES 10

To make the hazelnut flavour more pronounced in this recipe, substitute ground, unblanched hazelnuts for the almonds when making the macaroons and omit the almond flavouring.

FOR THE MACAROONS

3 egg whites, size 6
175 g (6 oz) ground almonds
275 g (10 oz) caster sugar
7.5 ml (1½ tsp) almond flavouring

FOR THE FILLING AND DECORATION

100 g (4 oz) hazelnuts
100 g (4 oz) plain chocolate
300 ml (½ pint) double cream
45 ml (3 tbsp) almond-flavoured liqueur

FOR THE DECORATION

icing sugar, for dusting
cocoa powder, for dusting
Chocolate leaves (see page 78)
hazelnuts

1. To make the macaroons, line two baking sheets with non-stick baking paper. Whisk the egg whites in a bowl until stiff, then fold in the ground almonds, sugar and almond flavouring.

2. Spoon the mixture into a piping bag fitted with a 1 cm (½ inch) plain nozzle and pipe 30 small rounds on to the prepared baking sheets, allowing room between each for the mixture to spread.

3. Bake in the oven at 180°C (350°F) mark 4 for about 20 minutes. Transfer to a wire rack to cool for 20 minutes.

4. To make the filling, spread the nuts out on a baking sheet. Brown in the oven at 200°C (400°F) mark 6 for 5–10 minutes. Tip on to a tea towel and rub off the skins. Chop finely.

5. Break the chocolate into small pieces. Place in a heatproof bowl standing over a pan of simmering water and heat gently until the chocolate melts. (Alternatively, microwave on LOW for 4–5 minutes or until melted, stirring occasionally.) Leave to cool for 5 minutes.

6. Whip the cream until it holds its shape. Gradually beat in the cooled chocolate, nuts and liqueur.

7. Use some of the chocolate cream to sandwich the macaroons together. Place them side by side on a serving plate to form a double log. Spread chocolate cream on top and add a further layer of macaroons. Spread the remaining chocolate cream over the top and sides. Chill overnight.

8. To serve, dust with icing sugar and cocoa, then decorate with chocolate leaves and whole hazelnuts.

Not suitable for freezing.

CHOCOLATE CINNAMON FLAN

SERVES 6–8

When sliced, this flan reveals its layers of creamy chocolate and cinnamon custard.

1 quantity Shortcrust pastry (see page 42)

FOR THE FILLING

300 ml (½ pint) milk
1 vanilla pod
15 ml (1 tbsp) powdered gelatine
3 eggs, separated
100 g (4 oz) caster sugar
50 g (2 oz) plain or milk chocolate
5 ml (1 tsp) ground cinnamon

FOR THE DECORATION

Chocolate curls (see page 78)
icing sugar, for dusting

1. Roll out the pastry and use to line a deep 24 cm (9½ inch) fluted flan ring.

2. Bake blind in the oven at 200°C (400°F) mark 6 for 20–25 minutes or until golden brown and cooked through. Leave to cool.

3. To make the filling, place the milk and vanilla pod in a small saucepan and bring to the boil. Cover and leave to infuse for about 30 minutes.

4. Sprinkle the gelatine over 45 ml (3 tbsp) water in a small bowl and leave to soak for 2–3 minutes. Place the bowl over a pan of simmering water and stir until dissolved. (Alternatively microwave on HIGH for 30 seconds or until dissolved.)

5. Whisk the egg yolks and 75 g (3 oz) of the caster sugar together in a bowl until very pale and thick. Remove the vanilla pod from the milk. Return the milk to the boil and pour on to the egg mixture, whisking.

6. Return the mixture to the pan and heat gently until it thickens enough to coat the back of a wooden spoon. Do not boil.

7. Remove from the heat, add the dissolved gelatine and stir.

8. Divide the mixture between two bowls. Break the chocolate into one bowl and stir until melted. Cool until beginning to set. Whisk the cinnamon into the other bowl. Cool until beginning to set.

9. Whisk the egg whites until stiff but not dry. Add the remaining sugar and whisk again until stiff. Fold half the meringue mixture into each custard.

10. Pour half the chocolate custard into the pastry case. Freeze for a few minutes to set. Add the cinnamon custard and freeze quickly to set. Finish with the remaining chocolate mixture. Decorate with chocolate curls and dust with icing sugar. Chill until ready to serve.

To freeze: pack and freeze. Thaw overnight in the refrigerator. (The pastry will be slightly softer but still acceptable.)

DARK CHOCOLATE TRUFFLE CAKE

SERVES 24

A very rich chocolate cake with a brandy truffle filling. If you have time, make extra filling, chill until firm enough to shape, then roll into small truffle balls. Roll in cocoa powder and use to decorate the top of the cake.

FOR THE CAKE

225 g (8 oz) plain chocolate
100 g (4 oz) butter
350 g (12 oz) caster sugar
2.5 ml (½ tsp) vanilla essence
2 eggs, separated
150 ml (¼ pint) soured cream
350 g (12 oz) self raising flour
5 ml (1 tsp) bicarbonate of soda

FOR THE FILLING

350 g (12 oz) plain chocolate
175 g (6 oz) butter
75 ml (5 tbsp) brandy

FOR THE ICING

200 g (7 oz) plain chocolate
200 ml (7 fl oz) double cream

1. Grease a 25.5 cm (10 inch) spring-release cake tin and line the base with greaseproof paper.
2. To make the cake, break the chocolate into small pieces. Place in a large heatproof bowl with the butter and 150 ml (¼ pint) water. Stand the bowl over a pan of simmering water and heat gently until the chocolate melts. (Alternatively, microwave on HIGH for 2–3 minutes or until melted, stirring occasionally.) Beat in the sugar and vanilla essence, then leave to cool.
3. Beat in the egg yolks, then fold in the soured cream, flour and bicarbonate of soda. Whisk the egg whites until stiff, then fold into the mixture. Pour the mixture into the prepared tin.
4. Bake in the oven at 180°C (350°F) mark 4 for 1 hour or until risen and just firm to the touch. Turn out on to a wire rack and leave to cool.
5. To make the filling, break the chocolate into small pieces. Place in a large heatproof bowl with the butter. Stand the bowl over a pan of simmering water and heat gently until the chocolate melts, stirring. (Alternatively, microwave on HIGH for 2–3 minutes or until the chocolate melts, stirring occasionally.) Stir in 45 ml (3 tbsp) of the brandy. Leave until slightly thickened.
6. Cut the cake into two layers and sprinkle the remaining brandy on each cut half. Place the top half in the base of the tin, cut side up. Pour in the truffle filling. Place the second half of sponge on top. Chill until set.
7. When the cake is set, unmould and stand on a wire rack placed over a baking sheet.
8. To make the icing, break the chocolate into pieces.

Place in a large heatproof bowl with the cream. Stand the bowl over a pan of simmering water and heat gently until the chocolate melts. (Alternatively, microwave on LOW for 3–4 minutes or until melted, stirring occasionally.)
9. Cool until the icing coats the back of a spoon. Pour the icing over the cake, using a palette knife to cover the sides. Leave until set.

To freeze: wrap and freeze at the end of step 6. Thaw in the refrigerator overnight, then finish as above.

Illustrated on pages 76–77

CHOCOLATE FUDGE SAUCE CAKE

SERVES 8–10

A sticky rich chocolate cake with its own delicious sauce topping. Serve with ice cream or chilled whipped cream.

FOR THE CAKE

175 g (6 oz) self raising flour
2.5 ml (½ tsp) baking powder
pinch of salt
25 g (1 oz) cocoa powder
100 g (4 oz) dark brown soft sugar
200 ml (7 fl oz) milk
25 g (1 oz) butter or margarine, melted
2.5 ml (½ tsp) vanilla essence
50 g (2 oz) walnuts, almonds or pecan nuts, chopped

FOR THE SAUCE

100 g (4 oz) dark brown soft sugar
2.5 ml (½ tsp) instant coffee powder
25 g (1 oz) cocoa powder

1. Grease an 18 cm (7 inch) square cake tin.
2. To make the cake, put all the ingredients, except the nuts, in a bowl and beat until smooth and glossy. Stir in the nuts. Pour the mixture into the prepared tin and level the surface.
3. To make the sauce, put all the ingredients and 150 ml (¼ pint) water in a saucepan. Heat gently until the sugar dissolves, stirring all the time, then increase the heat and bring to a rapid boil. Carefully pour over the cake mixture.
4. Bake in the oven at 180°C (350°F) mark 4 for 35–40 minutes or until the cake is risen and firm to the touch. Leave to cool in the tin.
5. When the cake is cold, turn it out on to a serving plate. Some of the fudge topping will be left in the tin, simply scrape it out with a spatula and spread on top of the cake. Serve the cake cut into squares, on its own or with vanilla ice cream.

To freeze: pack in a rigid container. Thaw overnight at cool room temperature.

Exceedingly Gooey Chocolate Brownies

MAKES 24 SQUARES

As the name suggests, this makes very rich, gooey brownies.

550 g (1¼ lb) plain chocolate
225 g (8 oz) butter, cut into pieces
3 eggs
30 ml (2 tbsp) freshly made strong coffee
225 g (8 oz) caster sugar
75 g (3 oz) self raising flour
2.5 ml (½ tsp) salt
175 g (6 oz) walnut halves, chopped
5 ml (1 tsp) vanilla essence

1. Grease and line a baking tin measuring 22 × 29.5 cm (8½ × 11½ inches) across the top and 19 × 26.5 cm (7½ × 10½ inches) across the base.
2. Using a very sharp knife, roughly chop 225 g (8 oz) of the chocolate. Break the remaining chocolate into small pieces. Place in a heatproof bowl with the butter. Stand the bowl over a pan of simmering water and heat gently until the chocolate melts, stirring. (Alternatively, microwave on LOW for 10 minutes or until melted, stirring occasionally.) Leave to cool.
3. Mix the eggs, coffee and sugar together in a bowl, then gradually beat in the chocolate mixture. Fold in the flour, salt, walnuts, vanilla essence and chopped chocolate. Pour the mixture into the prepared tin.
4. Bake in the oven at 190°C (375°F) mark 5 for 45 minutes or until just firm to the touch in the centre. Leave to cool in the tin.
5. When the cake is completely cold, turn out on to a board and trim the edges. Cut into 24 squares. Serve on their own or with Cinnamon or Chocolate flake ice cream (see page 217).

To freeze: pack and freeze the cooled brownies, interleaved with greaseproof paper. Thaw at cool room temperature.

Hazelnut and Chocolate Gâteau

SERVES 14

Chocolate and hazelnut spread is sold in tubs in good supermarkets and delicatessens.

FOR THE CAKE
225 g (8 oz) butter
225 g (8 oz) light brown soft sugar
4 eggs, separated
100 g (4 oz) self raising flour
pinch of salt
100 g (4 oz) ground hazelnuts
100 g (4 oz) plain chocolate, finely grated
FOR THE FILLING
600 ml (1 pint) double cream
150 ml (10 tbsp) chocolate and hazelnut spread
50 g (2 oz) hazelnuts, toasted and finely chopped
FOR THE DECORATION
cocoa powder, sifted
whole hazelnuts

1. Grease and line a 23 cm (9 inch) round spring-release cake tin.
2. To make the cake, cream the butter and sugar together in a bowl until pale and fluffy. Beat in the egg yolks, one at a time, then fold in the flour and salt. Stir in the hazelnuts and chocolate. Whisk the egg whites until stiff and fold into the cake mixture. Pour the mixture into the prepared tin.
3. Bake in the oven at 170°C (325°F) mark 3 for 1–1¼ hours or until a skewer inserted into the centre comes out clean. Leave to cool in the tin.
4. To make the filling, whip the cream until it holds its shape. Mix with the chocolate and hazelnut spread.
5. Cut the cake into three layers and sandwich together with some of the hazelnut cream. Spread more cream around the sides of the cake and coat in the nuts.
6. Spread more of the hazelnut cream over the top of the cake. Spoon the remaining hazelnut cream into a piping bag fitted with a large star nozzle and pipe around the edge of the cake. Decorate with a little cocoa powder and whole hazelnuts.

To freeze: omit the hazelnut and cocoa decoration. Open freeze until firm then wrap. Thaw at cool room temperature or overnight in the refrigerator. Complete the decoration.

Above: EXCEEDINGLY GOOEY CHOCOLATE BROWNIES.
Below: MISSISSIPPI MUD PIE *(PAGE 92).*

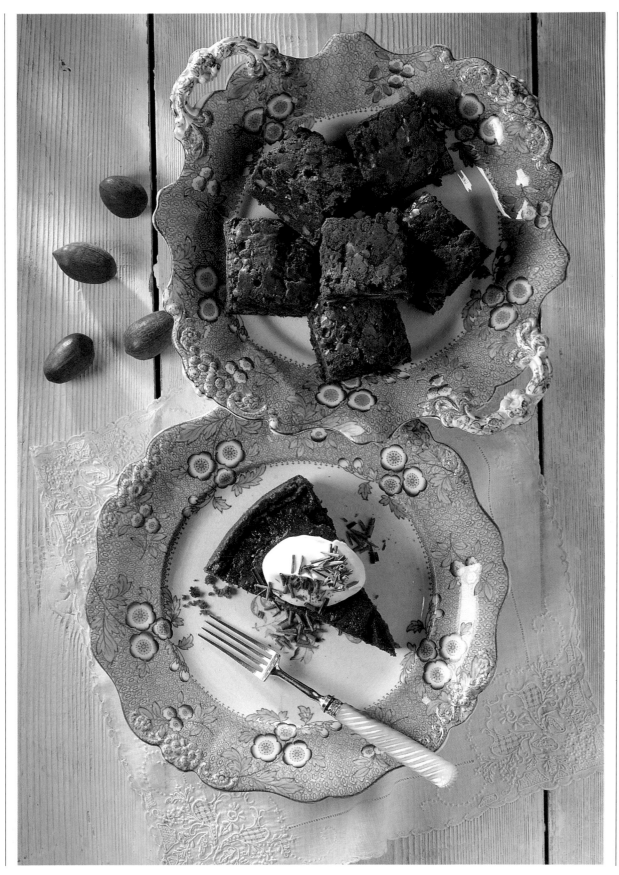

RIGO JACSI

MAKES 24 SQUARES

Absolute temptation! These rich squares of chocolate gâteau, classic in their make-up of chocolate flavoured Genoese and ganache, were named after a gypsy violinist, who was said to have broken the heart of many a princess.

½ quantity chocolate Genoese (see page 124)

FOR THE GANACHE
425 g (15 oz) plain chocolate
600 ml (1 pint) double cream
45 ml (3 tbsp) brandy

FOR THE ICING
100 g (4 oz) plain chocolate
30 ml (2 tbsp) brandy
100 g (4 oz) icing sugar, sifted

1. Grease a 23 × 33 cm (9 × 13 inch) Swiss roll tin and line the base with greaseproof paper. Spread the cake mixture evenly in the prepared tin.
2. Bake in the oven at 180°C (350°F) mark 4 for 20–25 minutes until well risen, firm to the touch and beginning to shrink away from the sides of the tin. Leave to cool in the tin.
3. To make the ganache, break the chocolate into small pieces. Place the chocolate and cream in a large saucepan and heat gently, stirring, until the chocolate melts and blends smoothly with the cream. Do not boil. (Alternatively, put the ingredients in a bowl and microwave on LOW for 8–10 minutes or until melted. Do not allow the mixture to boil.)
4. Pour the ganache into a bowl if necessary and leave to cool, but not set hard, stirring the cream frequently to prevent a skin forming. When cold, whip the ganache with the brandy until very light and fluffy, taking care not to overwhip.
5. Cut the chocolate sponge into two layers. Place one piece on a flat board or baking sheet. Cut a length of card, or several thicknesses of foil, long enough to fit around the sponge cake, and about 7.5 cm (3 inches) deep. Fit the card snugly around the sponge, forming square corners as you do so, and secure with sticky tape. Alternatively, place the sponge cake in a deep square cake tin, placing it against two sides of the tin, then form a false 'wall' for the other side, with several thicknesses of foil.
6. Spoon the whipped ganache on top of the layer of chocolate sponge to a depth of about 5 cm (2 inches) and spread evenly. Place the second layer of sponge on top. Chill for at least 1 hour.
7. To make the icing, break the chocolate into small pieces. Place in a small saucepan with 15 ml (1 tbsp) water, the brandy and icing sugar. Stir over a gentle heat until the chocolate melts and blends with the icing sugar to make a smooth icing. (Alternatively, put the ingredients in a bowl and microwave on LOW for 5 minutes or until melted, stirring frequently.) Spread the chocolate icing over the top layer and leave to set.

8. Carefully remove the 'wall' from around the cake. Cut the gâteau into twenty-four 4 cm (1½ inch) squares, using a sharp knife dipped in hot water and dried each time before cutting. Chill until 20–30 minutes before serving.

To freeze: open freeze the completed cakes. Thaw overnight in the refrigerator.

CAPPUCINO CAKE

SERVES 16–18

A dark chocolate and coffee cake with a frothy cream and cocoa topping, reminiscent of a good cappucino. Use freshly made coffee, not instant.

FOR THE CAKE
225 g (8 oz) plain chocolate
15 ml (1 tbsp) instant coffee granules
225 g (8 oz) butter or margarine
225 g (8 oz) dark brown soft sugar
5 eggs
100 g (4 oz) ground almonds
100 g (4 oz) cornflour
30 ml (2 tbsp) strong coffee, cooled
30 ml (2 tbsp) dark rum

FOR THE TOPPING
300 ml (½ pint) whipping cream
15 ml (1 tbsp) dark rum
cocoa powder

1. Grease a 23 cm (9 inch) round spring-release cake tin and line the base with greaseproof paper.
2. To make the cake, break the chocolate into small pieces. Place in a heatproof bowl with the instant coffee. Stand the bowl over a pan of simmering water and heat gently until the chocolate melts, stirring. (Alternatively, microwave on LOW for 6–7 minutes or until melted.)
3. Cream the butter and sugar together in a bowl until pale and fluffy. Beat in the eggs, one at a time, beating well after each addition. Fold in the almonds, cornflour and chocolate. Pour the mixture into the prepared tin and level the surface.
4. Bake in the oven at 180°C (350°F) mark 4 for 1 hour 15–20 minutes or until risen and just firm to the touch. Cover the cake with greaseproof paper to prevent it becoming too brown, if necessary. Leave the cake to cool in the tin.
5. When cold, prick the cake all over with a fine skewer. Mix the coffee and rum together, then pour evenly over the cake. Leave for at least 30 minutes.
6. To make the topping, whip the cream with the rum until it just holds its shape. Remove the cake from the tin and transfer to a serving plate. Spoon the cream on top and spread evenly with a palette knife. Sift a little cocoa over the cream to decorate.

To freeze: wrap and freeze at the end of step 5. Thaw at cool room temperature, then finish as above.

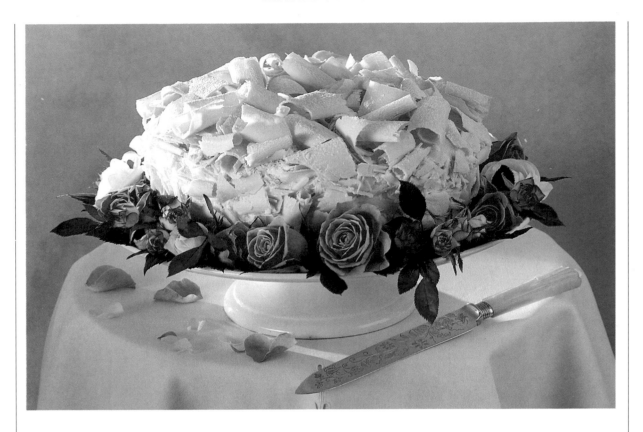

WHITE CHOCOLATE GÂTEAU

SERVES 18–20

This rich gâteau, covered in a mass of white chocolate curls, is delicious enough to be served as an alternative wedding cake. If doing so, place the cake on a large cake stand and surround with fresh flowers.

23 cm (9 inch) Genoese cake (see page 124)
FOR THE FILLING
175 g (6 oz) plain chocolate
30 ml (2 tbsp) brandy
2 eggs, separated
300 ml (½ pint) double cream
5 ml (1 tsp) powdered gelatine
FOR THE DECORATION
275 g (10 oz) white chocolate
150 ml (¼ pint) double cream
icing sugar, for dusting

1. To make the filling, break the chocolate into small pieces. Place in a heatproof bowl standing over a pan of simmering water and heat gently until the chocolate melts. (Alternatively, microwave on LOW for 5—7 minutes or until melted, stirring occasionally.) Remove from the heat and stir in the brandy and egg yolks. Whip the cream until it just stands in soft peaks, then fold into the chocolate mixture.

2. Sprinkle the gelatine over 15 ml (1 tbsp) water in a small bowl and leave to soak for 2—3 minutes. Place the bowl over a pan of simmering water and stir until dissolved. (Alternatively, microwave on HIGH for 30 seconds or until dissolved.) Cool, then stir into the chocolate mixture. Whisk the egg whites until stiff, then fold in.

3. Cut the cake into two layers. Put one piece of sponge back in the tin. Pour the mousse filling on top. Put the second piece of sponge on top. Leave to set.

4. While the filling is setting, make the decoration. Melt the white chocolate as in step 1. Spread out thinly on a marble slab or a clean, smooth work surface. Leave until set. When the chocolate is set, push a clean stripping knife (see Note below) across the chocolate at an angle of about 25 degrees to roll off large thick chocolate curls. Chill until ready for decorating.

5. When the mousse is set, whip the cream until it holds its shape. Ease the cake out of the tin and cover with the cream. Cover completely with the chocolate curls and dust lightly with a little icing sugar.

Note: A stripping knife is a decorator's tool used for scraping off wallpaper! It has a sharp flexible blade and is ideal for making large chocolate curls. Buy one and keep it specifically for this purpose.

Not suitable for freezing.

Above: WHITE CHOCOLATE GÂTEAU.

CHOCOLATE CUSTARD PIE
SERVES 8

1 quantity Shortcrust pastry (see page 42)

FOR THE FILLING
100 g (4 oz) sugar
50 g (2 oz) plain flour
pinch of salt
450 ml (¾ pint) milk
50 g (2 oz) plain chocolate
3 egg yolks
40 g (1½ oz) butter or margarine
5 ml (1 tsp) vanilla essence
225 ml (8 fl oz) double or whipping cream
Chocolate curls (see page 78) or grated chocolate, to decorate

1. Roll out the pastry on a lightly floured work surface and use to line a 23 cm (9 inch) loose-based fluted flan tin or ring placed on a baking sheet. Crimp the edges of the pastry and chill for 30 minutes. Prick the base of the pastry case.
2. Bake blind in the oven at 200°C (400°F) mark 6 for 10–15 minutes until set. Remove the paper and beans and bake for a further 5–10 minutes until lightly coloured. Leave to cool.
3. To make the filling, mix the sugar, flour and salt in a large saucepan and stir in the milk.
4. Break the chocolate into small pieces and add to the pan. Heat gently until the chocolate has melted, stirring continuously.
5. Whisk until the chocolate and milk are blended, then increase the heat and cook for about 10 minutes, stirring constantly. Remove the pan from the heat.
6. Beat the egg yolks and whisk in a small amount of the hot chocolate sauce. Slowly pour the egg mixture into the saucepan, stirring rapidly. Cook over low heat stirring, for 10–15 minutes, until the mixture is very thick and creamy. Do not allow to boil.
7. Remove from the heat. Stir in the butter and vanilla essence, then pour into the cold pastry case. Cover to prevent a skin forming and chill for about 4 hours until set.
8. Just before serving, whip the cream lightly and spread evenly over the chocolate filling. Decorate the top with chocolate curls or grated chocolate. Serve chilled.

To freeze: open freeze the set pie at the end of step 7 until firm, then wrap and freeze. Thaw overnight in the refrigerator.

MISSISSIPPI MUD PIE
SERVES 16
This rich and sticky pie originated in the United States, where it is served warm with hot fudge sauce or cold topped with whipped cream and grated chocolate. Either way, a small portion is all that is needed.

FOR THE BASE
100 g (4 oz) ginger biscuits, crushed
100 g (4 oz) digestive biscuits, crushed
75 g (3 oz) butter, melted
25 g (1 oz) light brown soft sugar

FOR THE FILLING
225 g (8 oz) butter or margarine
175 g (6 oz) plain chocolate
120 ml (8 tbsp) golden syrup
4 eggs, beaten
50 g (2 oz) pecan nuts, chopped

1. Grease a 23 cm (9 inch) loose-based cake tin.
2. To make the base, mix the biscuits with the butter and sugar. Press into the bottom and 4 cm (1½ inches) up the sides of the prepared tin. Chill while making the filling.
3. To make the filling, put the butter, chocolate and syrup in a saucepan and heat very gently until melted, stirring all the time. (Alternatively, put the ingredients in a bowl and microwave on LOW for 4–6 minutes or until melted, stirring frequently.) Cool, then beat in the eggs and pecans. Pour the mixture into the biscuit crust.
4. Bake in the oven at 180°C (350°F) mark 4 for 1¼ hours or until just firm to the touch but still soft in the centre. Serve warm or cold.

To freeze: wrap and freeze the cold pie. Thaw overnight in the refrigerator. Serve cold.

Illustrated on page 89

MAGIC CHOCOLATE PUDDING

SERVES 4–6

This delicious chocolate pudding, which is a great hit with children, is called 'magic' because it separates magically during baking into a rich chocolate sauce at the bottom and a sponge cake on top.

50 g (2 oz) butter or margarine
75 g (3 oz) caster sugar
2 eggs, separated
350 ml (12 fl oz) milk
40 g (1½ oz) self raising flour
25 ml (5 tsp) cocoa powder

1. Grease a 1 litre (1¾ pint) ovenproof dish.
2. Cream the butter and sugar together in a bowl until light and fluffy. Beat in the egg yolks and stir in the milk.
3. Sift the flour and cocoa powder together over the creamed mixture, then beat in until evenly mixed. Whisk the egg whites until stiff and fold into the mixture. Pour into the prepared dish.
4. Bake in the oven at 180°C (350°F) mark 4 for 35–45 minutes until the top is set and spongy to the touch. This pudding will separate into a custard layer with a sponge topping. Serve hot.

Not suitable for freezing.

Below: MAGIC CHOCOLATE PUDDING.

CHOCOLATE FILO PIE

SERVES 9–12

An unusual way to use up stale cake crumbs.

4 sheets of filo pastry (see page 46)
50 g (2 oz) melted butter

FOR THE FILLING

75 g (3 oz) butter, softened
75 g (3 oz) icing sugar
4 eggs, separated
75 g (3 oz) ground almonds
100 g (4 oz) plain or chocolate cake crumbs
100 g (4 oz) dried mixed fruit
100 g (4 oz) plain chocolate, grated
15 ml (1 tbsp) cocoa powder, sifted
150 ml (¼ pint) double cream

FOR THE DECORATION

50 g (2 oz) flaked almonds
15 ml (1 tbsp) icing sugar, sifted

1. To make the filling, cream the butter and icing sugar together in a bowl until pale and fluffy. Gradually beat in the egg yolks, then the almonds, cake crumbs, mixed fruit, chocolate, cocoa powder and cream. Whisk the egg whites until stiff, then fold into the chocolate mixture.

2. Fold one sheet of filo pastry in half and trim to fit a 22 × 28.5 cm (8½ × 11½ inch) baking dish. Repeat with the remaining sheets of pastry, reserving the trimmings.

3. Lay one of the folded sheets of pastry in the dish and spread with one third of the chocolate filling. Cover with a second folded sheet of pastry. Repeat the layers twice more ending with a pastry layer. Brush the top with the melted butter. Cut the pastry trimmings into neat strips and sprinkle on top. Brush with more melted butter. Sprinkle with the almonds and icing sugar.

4. Bake in the oven at 190°C (375°F) mark 5 for 40 minutes or until golden brown. Serve hot or cold, cut into squares, with vanilla ice cream.

Not suitable for freezing.

ZUCCOTTO

SERVES 6

A rich, Italian version of tipsy cake.

45 ml (3 tbsp) brandy
30 ml (2 tbsp) orange-flavoured liqueur
30 ml (2 tbsp) cherry or almond-flavoured liqueur
350 g (12 oz) trifle sponges or Madeira cake
150 g (5 oz) plain chocolate
450 ml (¾ pint) double cream
100 g (4 oz) icing sugar
50 g (2 oz) blanched almonds, toasted and chopped
50 g (2 oz) hazelnuts, toasted and chopped

FOR THE DECORATION

icing sugar
cocoa powder

1. Line a 1.4 litre (2½ pint) pudding basin or round-bottomed bowl with damp muslin.

2. In a separate bowl, mix together the brandy and liqueurs and set aside.

3. Split the trifle sponges in half through the centre (if using Madeira cake, cut into 1 cm (½ inch) slices). Sprinkle with the brandy and liqueurs. Line the basin with the moistened sponges, reserving enough to cover the top.

4. Using a sharp knife, chop 75 g (3 oz) of the chocolate into small pieces and set aside.

5. In a separate bowl, whip the cream and icing sugar together until stiff, then fold in the chopped chocolate and nuts.

6. Divide this mixture in two and use one half to spread over the sponge lining in an even layer.

7. Break the remaining chocolate into small pieces. Place in a small heatproof bowl standing over a pan of simmering water and heat gently until the chocolate melts. (Alternatively, microwave on LOW for 2–3 minutes or until melted, stirring occasionally.) Cool slightly, then fold into the remaining cream mixture. Use this to fill the centre of the pudding.

8. Level the top of the Zuccotto and cover with the remaining moistened sponge. Trim the edges. Cover and chill for at least 12 hours.

9. To serve, uncover, invert a flat serving plate over the basin and turn upside down. Lift off the bowl, and carefully remove the muslin. Serve cold, dusted with icing sugar and cocoa powder.

To freeze: open freeze the unmoulded Zuccotto until firm, then wrap and freeze. Thaw overnight in the refrigerator.

Opposite: PETITS POTS AU CHOCOLAT.

PETITS POTS AU CHOCOLAT

SERVES 6

These little chocolate pots rely heavily on the flavour of the chocolate used. So it is essential to use a good quality chocolate.

15 ml (1 tbsp) coffee beans
3 egg yolks
1 egg
75 g (3 oz) caster sugar
750 ml (1¼ pints) milk and single cream mixed
75 g (3 oz) plain chocolate

FOR THE DECORATION

150 ml (¼ pint) whipping cream
Chocolate shapes (see page 78) or coffee dragées

1. Toast the coffee beans under a moderate grill for a few minutes, then set aside.

2. Beat the egg yolks, egg and sugar together in a bowl until very pale.

3. Place the milk, cream and coffee beans in a saucepan and bring to the boil. Strain the hot milk on to the egg mixture, stirring all the time. Discard the coffee beans. Return the mixture to the saucepan.

4. Break up the chocolate and add to the pan. Stir over gentle heat (do not boil) for about 5 minutes until the chocolate has almost melted and the mixture is slightly thickened. Whisk lightly until the mixture is evenly blended.

5. Stand six individual 150 ml (¼ pint) ramekin dishes or custard pots in a roasting tin, then pour in enough hot water to come halfway up the sides of the dishes. Pour the custard mixture slowly into the dishes, dividing it equally between them. Cover.

6. Bake in the oven at 150°C (300°F) mark 2 for 1–1¼ hours or until the custard is lightly set. Leave to cool completely.

7. To serve, whip the cream and spoon into a piping bag fitted with a large star nozzle. Pipe a whirl on top of each dessert. Decorate with chocolate shapes or coffee dragées.

Not suitable for freezing.

POIRES BELLE HÉLÈNE
SERVES 6

100 g (4 oz) sugar
thinly pared rind and juice of 2 oranges
6 cooking pears (preferably Conference)
225 g (8 oz) plain chocolate
60 ml (4 tbsp) orange-flavoured liqueur
orange slices, to decorate

1. Put the sugar, 900 ml (1½ pints) water and half the orange rind in a large heavy-based saucepan and heat gently, without stirring, until the sugar has dissolved.
2. Meanwhile, peel the pears quickly (to prevent discoloration), leaving the stalks on. Cut out the cores from the bottom and level them so that the pears will stand upright.
3. Stand the pears in the syrup, cover the pan and simmer gently for 20 minutes or until tender. Remove from the heat and leave to cool, covered tightly. Spoon the syrup over the pears occasionally during cooling.
4. Cut the remaining orange rind into thin matchstick (julienne) strips. Blanch in boiling water for 2 minutes, then drain and immediately refresh under cold running water. Leave to drain on absorbent kitchen paper.
5. To make the chocolate sauce, break the chocolate into small pieces. Place in a heatproof bowl with the liqueur. Stand the bowl over a pan of simmering water and heat gently until the chocolate melts. (Alternatively, microwave on LOW for 7–8 minutes or until melted, stirring occasionally.)
6. Remove the pears from the syrup and stand them on a large serving dish or six dishes and chill for 2 hours.
7. Discard the orange rind from the syrup. Stir the melted chocolate into 150 ml (¼ pint) of the syrup with the orange juice, then slowly bring to the boil, stirring constantly. Simmer, stirring, until the sauce is thick and syrupy.
8. To serve, pour the hot chocolate sauce over the cold pears and sprinkle with the orange julienne. Decorate with orange slices and serve immediately.

Not suitable for freezing.

WHITE CHOCOLATE AND SHERRY MOUSSE
SERVES 8

The chocolate horns can be made in advance. The filled horns will keep in the refrigerator for up to two days. Pack them in a single layer in a rigid container. Serve with a refreshing red fruit salad.

100 g (4 oz) white chocolate
45 ml (3 tbsp) dry sherry or eau de vie
150 ml (¼ pint) double cream
2 eggs, separated
5 ml (1 tsp) powdered gelatine
15 ml (1 tbsp) milk
16 Chocolate horns, to serve (see page 98)
Chocolate shapes, to decorate (see page 78)

1. Break the chocolate into small pieces. Place in a medium heatproof bowl with the sherry and 30 ml (2 tbsp) water. Stand the bowl over a pan of simmering water and heat until the chocolate melts. (Alternatively, microwave on LOW for 2–3 minutes or until melted, stirring occasionally.) Stir well until the mixture is smooth.
2. Lightly whip the cream in a bowl until it just holds its shape. Fold in the egg yolks and chocolate mixture.
3. Sprinkle the gelatine over the milk in a small bowl and leave to soak for 2–3 minutes. Place the bowl over a pan of simmering water and stir until dissolved. (Alternatively, microwave on HIGH for 30 seconds or until dissolved.) Stir into the chocolate mixture. Chill until beginning to set.
4. Whisk the egg whites until stiff but not dry, then fold into the chocolate mixture. Leave to set until the consistency of whipped cream.
5. Stand the chocolate horns in tall glasses or mugs and spoon in the mousse. Chill the horns for at least 1 hour before serving decorated with chocolate shapes.

To freeze: pack and freeze the filled horns. Thaw in the refrigerator for 2 hours.

Opposite: WHITE CHOCOLATE AND SHERRY MOUSSE.

CHOCOLATE AND LIME MOUSSE

SERVES 2

Lime adds a refreshing tang to the chocolate flavour.

75 g (3 oz) plain chocolate
2 eggs, separated
15 ml (1 tbsp) caster sugar
finely grated rind and strained juice of 1 small lime
150 ml (¼ pint) double cream
2.5 ml (½ tsp) powdered gelatine
grated chocolate or twists of lime, to decorate

1. Break the chocolate into small pieces. Place in a small heatproof bowl standing over a pan of simmering water and heat gently until the chocolate melts. (Alternatively, microwave on LOW for 4–5 minutes or until melted, stirring occasionally.) Cool slightly.
2. Whisk the egg yolks, sugar and lime rind in a bowl, using an electric whisk, until thick and mousse-like. Whisk in the chocolate, then 30 ml (2 tbsp) of the cream.
3. Sprinkle the gelatine over the lime juice in a small bowl and leave to soak for 2–3 minutes. Place the bowl over a saucepan of simmering water and stir until dissolved. (Alternatively, microwave on HIGH for 30 seconds or until melted.) Whisk into the chocolate mixture.
4. Whisk the egg whites until stiff but not dry, then fold into the chocolate mixture.
5. Divide the mousse between two glasses and chill until set. Whip the remaining cream and use to decorate the desserts with grated chocolate or twists of lime. Leave at cool room temperature for about 30 minutes before serving.

Not suitable for freezing.

Illustrated on page 82

CHOCOLATE HORNS

MAKES 8

Start making chocolate horns the day before you intend to use them. Once made, they will keep in the refrigerator for two weeks or they can be frozen. Serve filled with mousses, fools, sorbets or ice creams. See the recipe for White chocolate and sherry mousse on page 96.

6 oz (175 g) plain chocolate

1. Line eight cream horn tins with non-stick baking paper.
2. Break the chocolate into small pieces. Place in a small heatproof bowl standing over a pan of simmering water and heat gently until the chocolate melts. (Alternatively, microwave on LOW for 3–4 minutes or until melted, stirring occasionally.)

3. Using a pastry brush, brush the inside of the paper with a thick layer of the chocolate, making sure it goes right down to the tip. Chill until set.
4. If necessary re-melt the remaining chocolate as above. (If using the microwave, cook on LOW for 1–2 minutes.) Repeat step 3.
5. Carefully remove the chocolate lined paper from the tins, then peel away the baking paper. Store the chocolate horns in the refrigerator until required.

To freeze: pack in a rigid container and freeze. Thaw overnight in the refrigerator.

CHOCOLATE MOUSSE GÂTEAU

SERVES 10–12

The richest of chocolate desserts, this gâteau will keep in the refrigerator for 3–4 days, where it will gradually become more fudge-like. It can be filled with chocolate ganache or served on its own with lightly whipped cream or a light vanilla custard.

250 g (9 oz) plain chocolate
15 ml (1 tbsp) instant coffee powder
30 ml (2 tbsp) brandy
4 eggs
5 ml (1 tsp) vanilla essence
50 g (2 oz) caster sugar
10 ml (2 tsp) cornflour
25 g (1 oz) cocoa powder, sifted
¼ quantity Ganache (see page 90)
cocoa powder, for dusting

1. Lightly oil a 25.5 × 12 cm (10 × 4¾ inch) ribbed Balmoral tin or 900 g (2 lb) loaf tin. Line the base and sides of the tin with non-stick baking paper.
2. Break the chocolate into small pieces. Place in a medium heatproof bowl with the coffee powder, brandy and 30 ml (2 tbsp) water. Stand the bowl over a pan of simmering water and heat gently until the chocolate melts. Stir until smooth and set aside to cool.
3. Using an electric whisk, whisk the eggs, vanilla essence, sugar and cornflour together in a bowl until very thick and pale. Fold in the cool, but not cold, chocolate mixture with the cocoa powder. Pour the mixture into the prepared tin.
4. Bake in the oven at 180°C (350°F) mark 4 for about 1 hour or until a skewer inserted into the centre comes out clean. (The cake may be cracked slightly.) Remove from the tin. Leave to cool.
5. Slice the cake at 2.5 cm (1 inch) intervals and sandwich together with two-thirds of the ganache. Spread the remaining mixture over the top and sides of the cake. Chill for 10 minutes. Dust with cocoa.

To freeze: pack and open freeze without the cocoa powder at the end of step 5. Cover tightly when solid. Thaw overnight in the refrigerator.

BLACK BREAD PUDDING

SERVES 6

This unlikely combination of flavours makes an unusual bread pudding. It works well with other tart fruits such as redcurrants and cranberries.

3 eggs, separated
100 g (4 oz) caster sugar
2.5 ml ($\frac{1}{2}$ tsp) ground cinnamon
pinch of salt
350 g (12 oz) dark rye breadcrumbs
100 g (4 oz) plain chocolate, grated
350 g (12 oz) blackcurrants, stalks removed
25 g (1 oz) light brown soft sugar
icing sugar, for dusting

1. Grease a 20.5 cm (8 inch) soufflé dish.
2. Whisk the egg yolks, caster sugar and cinnamon together in a bowl until pale and fluffy.
3. Whisk the egg whites and salt until stiff. Fold into the egg yolk mixture with the breadcrumbs and chocolate. Arrange the blackcurrants in the base of the prepared dish and sprinkle with the brown sugar. Pour the bread mixture over the fruit.
4. Bake in the oven at 180°C (350°F) mark 4 for 40 minutes or until firm to the touch. Dust with icing sugar and serve hot or cold with soured cream.

Not suitable for freezing.

CHOCOLATE SNOWBALL

SERVES 4–6

This luscious dessert should be left for at least 24 hours before eating. The outer layer forms a crust while the centre remains a soft fudge.

175 g (6 oz) plain chocolate
7.5 ml (1$\frac{1}{2}$ tsp) instant coffee granules
175 g (6 oz) caster sugar
175 g (6 oz) unsalted butter, diced
4 eggs
15 ml (1 tbsp) dark rum
FOR THE DECORATION
225 ml (8 fl oz) double cream
Frosted petals (see page 10)

1. Line a 750 ml (1$\frac{1}{4}$ pint) pudding basin with foil.
2. Break the chocolate into pieces and place in a saucepan. Dissolve the coffee in 45 ml (3 tbsp) water and add it to the pan with the sugar. Heat gently until the chocolate melts. (Alternatively, put the ingredients in a bowl and microwave on HIGH for 1–2 minutes or until the chocolate has melted.)

3. Transfer the chocolate mixture to a bowl, if necessary, and beat well with an electric hand-held mixer or a balloon whisk. Slowly whisk in the butter until evenly combined. Whisk in the eggs, one at a time. Stir in the rum. Pour the mixture into the prepared pudding basin.
4. Bake in the oven at 180°C (350°F) mark 4 for about 1$\frac{1}{4}$ hours or until risen and firm, but still slightly wobbly like a soufflé, with a thick, cracked crust.
5. Leave to cool at room temperature, then press down with your fingertips to level the surface. Cover and chill for at least 24 hours. Unmould on to a serving plate.
6. Whip the cream until it holds its shape. Fill a piping bag fitted with a star nozzle and pipe rosettes on the pudding until completely covered. Decorate with a sprinkling of frosted petals, if wished.

Not suitable for freezing.

CHOCOLATE BISCUIT CAKE

SERVES 8

Serve this easy dessert with mugs of strong coffee to round off an informal supper.

125 g (4 oz) plain chocolate
15 ml (1 tbsp) Lyle's golden syrup
125 g (4 oz) butter
30 ml (2 tbsp) double cream
125 g (4 oz) digestive biscuits, broken up
25 g (1 oz) raisins
25 g (1 oz) glacé cherries, halved
50 g (2 oz) flaked almonds, toasted

1. Butter a loose-bottomed 15–18 cm (6–7 inch) tin or ring.
2. Break the chocolate into pieces and place in a bowl over a pan of hot water. Add the syrup, butter and cream.
3. When the chocolate and butter have melted, remove the pan from the heat and cool slightly. (Alternatively, microwave on HIGH for 2–3 minutes or until melted, stirring occasionally.)
4. Mix the biscuits, fruit and nuts into the chocolate mixture.
5. Turn the mixture into the prepared tin, lightly level the top, then chill for at least 1 hour before serving.

To freeze: pack and freeze once the mixture is set. Thaw at cool room temperature.

CHOCOLATE AND PRALINE RING

SERVES 4–6

Before adding the cream and egg whites, the custard must be the right consistency. It should be cold and just beginning to thicken. Too runny, and the pudding separates into layers; too set, and the finished result will be lumpy.

50 g (2 oz) plain or milk chocolate
200 ml (7 fl oz) milk
15 ml (1 tbsp) powdered gelatine
75 ml (5 tbsp) cold black coffee
3 eggs, separated
50 g (2 oz) caster sugar
2.5 ml (½ tsp) cornflour
50 g (2 oz) praline powder (see page 104)
75 ml (5 tbsp) double cream

FOR THE DECORATION

whipped cream
marrons glacés (optional)

1. Lightly oil a 1.1 litre (2 pint) ring mould.
2. Break the chocolate into small pieces. Place in a medium saucepan and add the milk. Heat gently until the chocolate melts. Bring to the boil, stirring all the time, until the chocolate mixture is smooth—about 2–3 minutes.
3. Sprinkle the gelatine over the cold black coffee in a small bowl and leave to soak for 2–3 minutes. Place the bowl over a saucepan of simmering water and stir until dissolved. (Alternatively, microwave on HIGH for 30 seconds or until dissolved.)
4. Whisk the egg yolks, 25 g (1 oz) of the caster sugar and the cornflour together in a bowl until very thick and pale. Slowly add the hot chocolate mixture, whisking all the time.
5. Return the mixture to the rinsed-out pan and stir over a very gentle heat until it thickens enough to coat the back of a wooden spoon. Do not allow to boil. Pour the mixture into a bowl.
6. Stir the dissolved gelatine into the chocolate mixture with 30 ml (2 tbsp) of the praline powder. Leave to cool completely.
7. When the custard is cool and just beginning to set, whip the cream until it just begins to hold its shape. Fold into the mixture. Whisk the egg whites until stiff but not dry. Whisk in the remaining sugar, then fold into the custard.
8. Pour into the prepared ring mould and chill for about 3 hours to set.
9. To serve, dip the mould briefly into hot water and invert the ring on to a serving plate. Decorate with the remaining praline, whipped cream and marrons glacés, if using.

Not suitable for freezing.

CHOCOLATE MOUSSE CUPS

SERVES 6

This must be the most delicious chocolate mousse you can imagine, encased in crisp, sugar-dusted filo pastry.

3 large sheets filo pastry, about 25.5 × 51 cm (10 × 20 inches)
25 g (1 oz) butter
100 g (4 oz) plain chocolate
30 ml (2 tbsp) brandy
15 ml (1 tbsp) instant coffee powder
2 eggs, separated
150 ml (¼ pint) double cream, lightly whipped
toasted flaked almonds, to decorate
icing sugar, for dusting

1. Cut each filo pastry sheet into 12 squares. Line 12 deep bun tins with three overlapping squares, brushing with melted butter between each layer.
2. Bake blind in the oven at 200°C (400°F) mark 6 for 10–12 minutes or until the pastry is crisp, golden brown and cooked through. Turn out on to a wire rack and leave to cool.
3. Break the chocolate into small pieces. Place in a heatproof bowl with the brandy, coffee powder and 15 ml (1 tbsp) water. Stand the bowl over a pan of simmering water and heat gently until the chocolate melts. Stir the mixture until smooth. (Alternatively, microwave on LOW for 4–6 minutes or until melted, stirring occasionally.)
4. Stir in the egg yolks, cool slightly, then mix in the cream. Whisk the egg whites until stiff but not dry, then fold into the chocolate mixture. Leave to set until the consistency of thick cream. Spoon the mousse into the pastry cups and chill for 1 hour.
5. Sprinkle the mousse cups with the toasted flaked almonds and dust heavily with icing sugar before serving with single cream.

Not suitable for freezing.

Above: CHOCOLATE AND PRALINE RING.
Below: CHOCOLATE MOUSSE CUPS.

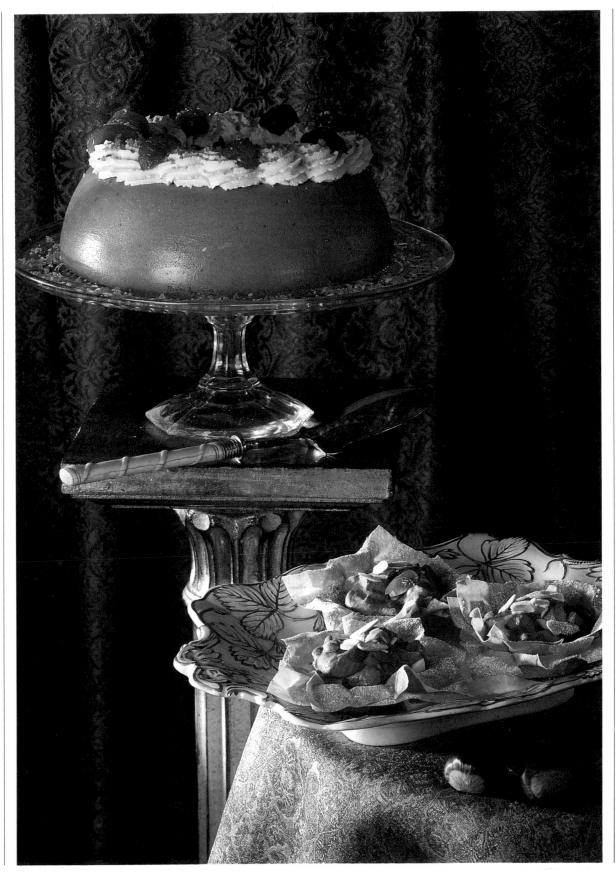

BANANA AND CHOCOLATE CHIP SPONGE

SERVES 4

A favourite with children. If you own a microwave, this dessert can be reheated successfully, a portion at a time, covered, on HIGH for 2 minutes.

100 g (4 oz) butter or margarine
100 g (4 oz) caster sugar
2 eggs, beaten
175 g (6 oz) self raising flour
about 45 ml (3 tbsp) milk
1 small banana, peeled and chopped
50 g (2 oz) chocolate chips

1. Grease a 900 ml (1½ pint) pudding basin.
2. Cream the butter and sugar together in a bowl until pale and fluffy. Gradually beat in the eggs.
3. Using a metal spoon, fold in the flour. Add enough milk to give a soft dropping consistency. Stir in the banana and chocolate.
4. Spoon the mixture into the prepared basin. Cover with greased greaseproof paper and foil, then secure with string. Steam for about 1½ hours or until firm to the touch. (Alternatively, cover with greaseproof paper only and microwave on HIGH for 5–6 minutes.) Turn out on to a warmed plate and serve with hot Chocolate sauce (see page 244).

Not suitable for freezing.

BAKED CHOCOLATE MARBLE SPONGE

SERVES 8

A delicious family pudding to serve on cold winter days.

75 g (3 oz) plain chocolate
175 g (6 oz) butter or margarine
175 g (6 oz) light brown soft sugar
3 eggs, beaten
200 g (7 oz) self raising flour
45 ml (3 tbsp) milk
50 g (2 oz) macaroons

1. Grease a 1.3 litre (2¼ pint) loaf dish.
2. Break the chocolate into small pieces. Place in a small heatproof bowl standing over a pan of simmering water and heat until the chocolate melts. (Alternatively, microwave on LOW for 3–4 minutes or until melted, stirring occasionally.) Leave to cool.
3. Cream the butter and sugar together in a bowl until pale and fluffy. Gradually beat in the eggs. Using a metal spoon, fold in the flour and milk.

4. Divide the mixture in two and flavour half with the cooled chocolate, folding it evenly through the mixture.
5. Place alternate spoonfuls of the mixtures in two layers in the prepared dish and zig-zag a knife through the mixture to make a marbled pattern. Roughly crush the macaroons and scatter over the top. Cover with foil.
6. Bake in the oven at 180°C (350°F) mark 4 for about 1¼ hours or until firm to the touch. Turn out and serve thickly sliced with hot Chocolate sauce (see page 244) or Chocolate fudge sauce (see page 253).

Not suitable for freezing.

Illustrated on page 252

CHOCOLATE AND CHESTNUT GINGER FLAN

SERVES 12

1½ quantity Pâte sucrée (see page 43)
FOR THE FILLING
50 g (2 oz) plain or bitter chocolate
75 ml (5 tbsp) stem ginger syrup
2 eggs
50 g (2 oz) caster sugar
150 ml (¼ pint) double or whipping cream
425 g (15 oz) can unsweetened chestnut purée
white and plain Chocolate curls (see page 78), to decorate

1. Roll out the pastry on a lightly floured work surface and use to line the base and sides of a 35.5 × 10 cm (14 × 4 inch) shallow rectangular flan frame or a 23 cm (9 inch) flan ring.
2. Bake blind in the oven at 190°C (375°F) mark 5 for 15 minutes, then remove the beans and continue to bake for 5–10 minutes or until golden brown and cooked through. Cool completely in the flan frame.
3. Meanwhile to make the filling, break the chocolate into small pieces. Place in a heatproof bowl with the ginger syrup. Stand the bowl over a pan of simmering water and heat gently until the chocolate melts. Stir only once or twice after the chocolate has started to melt. (Alternatively, microwave on LOW for 4 minutes, stirring occasionally.) Remove from the heat.
4. Whisk the eggs and sugar together in a bowl with an electric whisk, until very pale and thick. Whip the cream until it holds its shape and fold in the cool but not cold chocolate. Fold into the egg mixture.
5. Using an electric whisk, whip the chestnut purée with a quarter of the chocolate mixture until smooth. Gradually whisk in the remaining mixture. Cover and chill for at least 1 hour.
6. About 30 minutes before serving, spoon the mixture into the cold pastry case. Decorate.

To freeze: pack and freeze the filled flan case. Unwrap and thaw at cool room temperature. Decorate as above.

DOUBLE CHOCOLATE MUFFINS

SERVES 12

A classic recipe from the United States, muffins are becoming increasingly popular here. And no wonder too, as they are quick to make and taste delicious, especially if served fresh from the oven.

100 g (4 oz) plain chocolate
50 g (2 oz) cocoa powder
225 g (8 oz) self raising flour
5 ml (1 tsp) baking powder
50 g (2 oz) dark brown soft sugar
pinch of salt
100 g (4 oz) plain chocolate dots
225 ml (8 fl oz) milk
60 ml (4 tbsp) vegetable oil
5 ml (1 tsp) vanilla essence
1 egg

1. Thoroughly grease 12 deep muffin or bun tins. Place a large paper cake case in each.
2. Break the chocolate into small pieces. Place in a large heatproof bowl standing over a pan of simmering water and heat gently until the chocolate melts. (Alternatively, microwave on LOW for 3–4 minutes or until melted, stirring occasionally.)
3. Remove from the heat and stir in the remaining ingredients. Beat thoroughly together. Spoon the mixture into the paper cases.
4. Bake in the oven at 220°C (425°F) mark 7 for 15 minutes until well risen and firm to the touch. Serve warm.

To freeze: wrap and freeze the cooled muffins. Thaw at cool room temperature. Reheat at 180°C (350°F) mark 4 for 5–10 minutes.

STEAMED CHOCOLATE PUDDING

SERVES 4

Vary this favourite nursery pudding by adding 50 g (2 oz) chopped nuts, chocolate chips, sultanas, raisins or dried apricots to the basic mixture, or 25 g (1 oz) chopped stem ginger.

100 g (4 oz) butter or margarine
100 g (4 oz) caster sugar
60 ml (4 tbsp) cocoa powder
2 eggs, beaten
175 g (6 oz) self raising flour
about 45 ml (3 tbsp) milk

1. Grease a 900 ml (1½ pint) pudding basin.
2. Cream the butter and sugar together in a bowl until pale and fluffy. Blend the cocoa powder and 30 ml (2 tbsp) hot water to a smooth cream, then gradually add to the creamed mixture.
3. Add the beaten eggs, a little at a time, beating well after each addition. Using a metal spoon, fold in the flour. Add enough milk to give a soft dropping consistency.
4. Spoon the mixture into the prepared basin. Cover with greased greaseproof paper and secure with string. Steam for 1½ hours. (Alternatively, microwave on HIGH for 5–6 minutes.) Turn out on to a warmed plate and serve with Chocolate sauce (see page 244).

Not suitable for freezing.

CHOCOLATE AND ORANGE TRIFLE

SERVES 8

350 g (12 oz) chocolate cake
4 oranges
120 ml (8 tbsp) orange-flavoured liqueur
4 egg yolks
50 g (2 oz) caster sugar
45 ml (3 tbsp) cornflour
vanilla essence
568 ml (1 pint) milk
45 ml (3 tbsp) stem ginger syrup
300 ml (½ pint) double cream
toasted almonds and stem ginger, to decorate

1. Thinly slice the cake and use to line the base of a shallow serving dish.
2. Peel and segment the oranges. Place the segments on top of the cake. Spoon the liqueur evenly over the cake and orange.
3. In a saucepan, combine the egg yolks, sugar, cornflour and vanilla essence. Gradually stir in the milk and ginger syrup; bring the mixture almost to the boil and simmer for 4–5 minutes until thickened, stirring all the time.
4. Pour the custard evenly into the dish. Leave to cool.
5. Whip the cream until it just holds its shape then spoon on top of the custard. Decorate with almonds and stem ginger.

Not suitable for freezing.

DARK AND LIGHT CHOCOLATE TERRINE

SERVES 6–8

A wickedly delicious chocaholic's dream! Be careful when slicing, as the terrine softens very quickly.

FOR THE PRALINE
225 g (8 oz) blanched almonds or skinned hazelnuts
100 g (4 oz) granulated sugar

FOR THE DARK CHOCOLATE MOUSSE
175 g (6 oz) plain chocolate
75 g (3 oz) unsalted butter
75 g (3 oz) caster sugar
30 ml (2 tbsp) cocoa powder, sifted
3 egg yolks
30 ml (2 tbsp) rum or brandy
300 ml (½ pint) double or whipping cream

FOR THE WHITE CHOCOLATE MOUSSE
175 g (6 oz) white chocolate
50 g (2 oz) unsalted butter, softened
2 egg yolks
200 ml (⅓ pint) double or whipping cream

1. Grease and line a 750 ml (1¼ pint) loaf tin with clingfilm. Lightly oil a baking sheet.
2. To make the praline, toast the nuts in the oven at 180°C (350°F) mark 4 or until golden brown, stirring occasionally. Put the sugar with 15 ml (1 tbsp) water into a heavy-based saucepan. Melt over a gentle heat until the sugar has dissolved. Stir in the warm nuts and boil until the syrup starts to brown. Immediately pour on to the prepared baking sheet. Leave to cool completely, then roughly crush with a rolling pin or in a blender or food processor. Store in an airtight tin until needed.
3. To make the mousses, break both chocolates into small pieces. Place in two small heatproof bowls standing over pans of simmering water and heat gently until the chocolates melt. Stir until smooth. (Alternatively, microwave on LOW for 2–3 minutes or until melted, stirring occasionally.) Cool slightly.
4. To make the dark chocolate mousse, cream the butter and half the sugar together until pale and creamy. Beat in the cocoa powder. In another bowl, beat the egg yolks and the remaining sugar until pale. Stir in the rum. Whip the cream until it just holds its shape. Working quickly, beat the melted plain chocolate into the creamed butter. Stir this into the yolk mixture, then carefully fold in the cream. Set aside.
5. To make the white chocolate mousse, beat the butter into the melted white chocolate. Stir in the yolks and 30 ml (2 tbsp) crushed praline. Whip the cream until it just holds its shape and fold into the chocolate mixture.
6. Drop large spoonfuls of each mousse alternately into the prepared tin until full. Tap the tin on the work surface to level. Cover and chill for at least 4 hours (or overnight preferably) until very firm.

7. To serve, turn out the mousse on to a flat serving dish and peel off the clingfilm. With a palette knife, press the remaining praline over the top and sides. Chill for 30 minutes to firm, then serve cut into slices. This dessert is so rich it needs nothing extra to accompany it.

Not suitable for freezing.

CHOCOLATE LACE BASKETS

SERVES 6

These dainty lace baskets are made with chocolate-flavoured cake covering. When set, it is less brittle than plain chocolate and is therefore less likely to crack. Don't attempt these unless you have time to spare, as they require patience.

150 g (5 oz) plain chocolate-flavoured cake covering
1 small mango
¼ fresh pineapple
12 strawberries
1 passion fruit

1. Break the cake covering into small pieces. Place in a heatproof bowl standing over a pan of simmering water and heat gently until it melts. (Alternatively, microwave on LOW for 4–6 minutes or until melted, stirring occasionally.)
2. Invert six 8.5 cm (3½ inch) ring moulds and stretch clingfilm over the rounded bases to cover completely.
3. Spoon half the melted chocolate cake covering into a greaseproof paper piping bag and snip off the point. Pipe three of the ring moulds with a lacy pattern of cake covering.
4. Fill a second bag with melted cake covering and pipe the remaining three moulds. Chill until set.
5. Meanwhile, peel the mango and chop the flesh. Cut the pineapple flesh into pieces. Hull the strawberries. Halve the passion fruit and scoop out the pulp.
6. Carefully lift the chocolate baskets with the clingfilm, then remove the clingfilm from the shells. Fill the baskets with the fruit. Serve with whipped cream.

To freeze: pack the unfilled chocolate baskets in a rigid container. Thaw in the refrigerator overnight, then finish as above.

Opposite: CHOCOLATE LACE BASKETS.

LIGHT BATTERS AND OMELETTES

Luscious fillings and light, golden pancakes combine to
make truly sublime ensembles from classic Crêpes Suzette
to sensational Crêpes soufflés au framboise. For other
wonderful ways with batters such as beignets, fritters and
Clafoutis plus sweet soufflé omelettes, read on!

Batter is a liquid and flour mixture, with a consistency similar to single cream. Pouring batter is used to make pancakes or crêpes, waffles and scones, and a thicker, coating batter is used to give a crisp, protective coating to food to make fritters or beignets.

A blender or food processor takes the work out of batter making. Put the eggs and other liquid ingredients into the machine, spoon the flour on top of them and process for a second or two, just enough to blend the ingredients together. Not long enough to create lots of bubbles.

Alternatively, make the batter by hand. Put the dry ingredients in a large bowl, make a deep well in the centre, using a wooden spoon, then add the eggs and a little of the liquid. Blend the liquid ingredients together in the well, then gradually incorporate the surrounding flour. Do this slowly, keeping the central mixture smooth and free of lumps. As the mixture becomes thicker, add the remaining liquid, a little at a time and keep beating until all of the flour is incorporated. Once all the flour is added and the mixture is absolutely smooth, add the remaining liquid.

If you have time, 'rest' the batter for about 30 minutes to give the starch grains a chance to swell. This will give a lighter, less doughy batter. Re-mix the batter before cooling.

An essential for pancake and omelette making is a good heavy-based frying pan. Ideally it should be kept solely for pancake or omelette making and should never be scrubbed, just wiped out with absorbent kitchen paper after use. Store the pan wrapped, to prevent the surface being scratched. Choose a pan with a base area of about 20.5–23 cm (8–9 inches), with or without a non-stick coating. If available, follow the manufacturers instructions for use, otherwise, first heat a new pan with plenty of oil to 'season' or seal it. Repeat the process once or twice until it has a perfect surface. Then pour out the oil and start pancake making. Once you get in the swing and your confidence grows, make several batches of pancakes at once, freezing the extras for another day.

BASIC PANCAKE BATTER
MAKES 8 PANCAKES OR CRÊPES

100 g (4 oz) plain flour
pinch of salt
1 egg
300 ml ($\frac{1}{2}$ pint) milk
oil, for frying

1. Sift the flour and salt into a bowl and make a well in the centre. Break in the egg and beat well with a wooden spoon. Gradually beat in the milk, drawing in the flour from the sides to make a smooth batter.

2. Heat a little oil in an 18 cm (7 inch) heavy-based frying pan, running it around the base and sides of the pan, until hot. Pour off any surplus.

3. Pour in just enough batter to thinly coat the base of the pan. Cook for 1–2 minutes until golden brown. Turn or toss and cook the second side until golden.

4. Transfer the pancake to a plate and keep hot. Repeat with the remaining batter to make eight pancakes. Pile the cooked pancakes on top of each other with greaseproof paper in between each one and keep warm in the oven while cooking the remainder.

5. Serve as soon as they are all cooked, sprinkled with sugar and lemon juice.

VARIATIONS

Buckwheat Pancakes   Replace half the flour with buckwheat flour and add an extra egg white.

Orange, Lemon or Lime Pancakes   Add the finely grated rind of 1 lemon, $\frac{1}{2}$ an orange or 1 lime with the milk.

Chocolate Pancakes   Replace 15 g ($\frac{1}{2}$ oz) of the flour with sifted cocoa powder.

To freeze: interleave with greaseproof paper and wrap in foil. Thaw at room temperature for 2–3 hours or overnight in the refrigerator. To thaw quickly, spread out separately and leave at room temperature for about 20 minutes. Reheat the foil-wrapped pancakes in the oven at 190°C (375°F) mark 5 for 20–30 minutes. Alternatively, separate the pancakes and heat in an oiled frying pan for 30 seconds on each side.

Previous Page: PANCAKES WITH FRUIT AND CREAM.

FRITTER OR COATING BATTER

MAKES 200 ml (7 fl oz)

Fritter or coating batter is thicker than pancake batter, so it will cling to foods dipped into it, which can then be deep-fried.

100 g (4 oz) plain flour
pinch of salt
1 egg
150 ml (¼ pint) milk or milk and water mixed

1. Sift the flour and salt into a bowl and make a well in the centre. Break in the egg and beat well with a wooden spoon.
2. Gradually beat in the liquid, drawing in the flour from the sides to make a smooth batter.

VARIATION

To make a lighter batter, use 15 ml (1 tbsp) oil instead of the egg. Just before cooking, whisk two egg whites stiffly and fold them into the batter. Use the batter immediately.

APPLE FRITTERS

SERVES 4

These mouth watering apple fritters can be made successfully using pineapple or bananas. Serve them with cream.

3 medium cooking apples
oil, for deep-frying
1 quantity Fritter batter (see above)
FOR THE COATING
caster sugar
ground cinnamon

1. Peel and core the apples and cut into 0.5 cm (¼ inch) thick rings.
2. Heat the oil in a deep fat fryer to 180°C (350°F). Dip the apple rings in the fritter batter and deep fry for 2–3 minutes until golden.
3. Drain on absorbent kitchen paper. Toss in caster sugar and ground cinnamon, then serve.

VARIATIONS

Pineapple Fritters Use a well drained 226 g (8 oz) can pineapple rings instead of the apples.

Banana Fritters Use 4 small bananas, peeled and cut in half lengthways, instead of the apples.

Pear Fritters Use 3–4 medium pears, peeled, cored and cut into thick rings, instead of the apples.

Not suitable for freezing.

RICH PANCAKES

MAKES 12–14

These work equally well if you replace the brandy or rum with your favourite liqueur.

50 g (2 oz) icing sugar
100 g (4 oz) plain flour
pinch of salt
50 g (2 oz) butter, melted
15 ml (1 tbsp) brandy, rum or liqueur
1 egg, beaten

1. To make the batter, sift the icing sugar, flour and salt into a bowl. Make a well in the centre, then pour in the butter, brandy and egg.
2. Beat the mixture well, then gradually add about 150 ml (¼ pint) warm water. Continue beating and adding water until a thin batter is obtained.
3. Make 12–14 pancakes (see page 108). Serve with orange juice and sugar to taste.

To freeze: interleave with greaseproof paper and wrap in foil. To thaw and reheat, see page 108.

CRÊPES SUZETTE

SERVES 4–6

A classic French dessert; with its spectacular flambéed finish, Crêpes Suzette is just perfect for a special dinner party. Traditionally flambéed at the table in a copper chafing dish in restaurants specializing in haute cuisine, the crêpes can look just as good at home carried flaming to the table on a silver or china plate.

105 ml (7 tbsp) orange-flavoured liqueur
1 quantity Pancake batter (see page 108)
100 g (4 oz) unsalted butter
100 g (4 oz) caster sugar
finely grated rind and juice of 1 large orange

1. Stir 15 ml (1 tbsp) of the liqueur into the batter. Make 8–12 crêpes (see page 108). Stack with greaseproof paper in between and keep warm in the oven.
2. To serve, heat the butter and sugar together in a large, heavy-based frying pan until thick and syrupy. Add 30 ml (2 tbsp) of the liqueur and the orange rind and juice and heat through.
3. Fold the crêpes into triangle shapes by folding each one in half, then in half again. Place them in the frying pan and spoon over the sauce to coat evenly.
4. Heat the remaining liqueur gently in a ladle or separate small pan. Transfer the crêpes and sauce to a warmed serving dish, pour over the warmed liqueur and set alight. Carefully carry the crêpes to the table while still flaming.

To freeze: freeze and thaw the crêpes (see page 108). Finish as above.

BANANA PANCAKES

SERVES 4

These lightly spiced pancakes will be popular with all the family.

15 g (½ oz) caster sugar
large pinch of ground mixed spice
½ quantity Pancake batter (see page 108)
4 large ripe bananas
oil and butter, for frying
lemon juice, for sprinkling

1. Stir the sugar and mixed spice into the batter.
2. Peel and slice the bananas into 0.5 cm (¼ inch) pieces.
3. Heat a little oil and butter in a medium non-stick frying pan. Add the slices from one banana and brown on one side. Turn the slices over.
4. Pour in a thin layer of batter and fry over a moderate heat until browned. Slide out the pancake and keep warm, lightly covered, in a low oven.
5. Fry remaining three pancakes in the same way. Sprinkle the pancakes with lemon juice.

Not suitable for freezing.

CRÊPES ANNETTE

SERVES 6

Kirsch-flavoured pancakes filled with a rich mixture of cream cheese and cherries.

FOR THE CRÊPES
250 g (9 oz) plain flour
5 ml (1 tsp) baking powder
2.5 ml (½ tsp) bicarbonate of soda
pinch of salt
135 ml (9 tbsp) kirsch
568 ml (1 pint) milk
25 g (1 oz) butter, melted
2 eggs, beaten
oil, for frying
FOR THE FILLING
425 g (15 oz) can black cherries
175 g (6 oz) full fat soft cheese
50 g (2 oz) caster sugar

1. To make the crêpes, sift the flour, baking powder, bicarbonate of soda and salt into a bowl. Add 90 ml (6 tbsp) of the kirsch, the milk, butter and eggs, then beat until smooth.
2. Heat a little oil in a heavy-based frying pan. Pour in 30 ml (2 tbsp) batter. Swirl around the pan and cook until golden underneath. Turn over and cook on the other side. Make 12 crêpes.

3. Stack the crêpes with greaseproof paper in between and keep warm in the oven.
4. To make the filling, drain the cherries; reserve the juice and a few cherries. Stone the cherries, if necessary. Beat the soft cheese and sugar together until soft and fluffy. Chop the remaining cherries roughly and fold them into the cheese mixture.
5. Spread a little filling on each crêpe and fold into triangles; or put the filling in the centre and roll up the crêpes. Arrange in a serving dish and keep warm.
6. Heat the reserved cherries and syrup in a pan. Gently warm the remaining kirsch. Drizzle the cherries and syrup over the crêpes, then add the kirsch and set alight.

To freeze: freeze the crêpes (see page 108).

ORANGE AND NECTARINE CRÊPES

SERVES 4–6

Peaches can be used in place of the nectarines.

1 quantity Pancake batter (see page 108)
finely grated rind and juice of 2 oranges
50 g (2 oz) caster sugar
4 large ripe nectarines
30 ml (2 tbsp) orange-flavoured liqueur
45 ml (3 tbsp) brandy

1. Grease an ovenproof dish.
2. Make 8–12 crêpes (see page 108). Stack the crêpes with greaseproof paper in between and keep warm in the oven.
3. Make the orange juice up to 150 ml (¼ pint) with water. Place the rind and juice in a saucepan with the sugar. Warm gently until the sugar dissolves, then boil for 1 minute.
4. Meanwhile, quarter each nectarine, skin and roughly chop the flesh. Place the flesh in the syrup and simmer gently for 3–4 minutes.
5. Remove from the heat and stir in the liqueur. Strain off the syrup and reserve.
6. Fill the pancakes with the nectarines, then fold each pancake into a fan shape. Place, slightly overlapping, in the prepared ovenproof dish. Pour over the syrup and cover tightly with greased foil.
7. Bake in the oven at 190°C (375°F) mark 5 for about 25 minutes or until thoroughly hot.
8. Place the brandy in a small saucepan. Warm slightly, then set alight with a match and immediately pour over the crêpes. Serve straight away, with cream or yogurt.

To freeze: freeze the pancakes (see page 108).

Opposite: ORANGE AND NECTARINE CRÊPES.

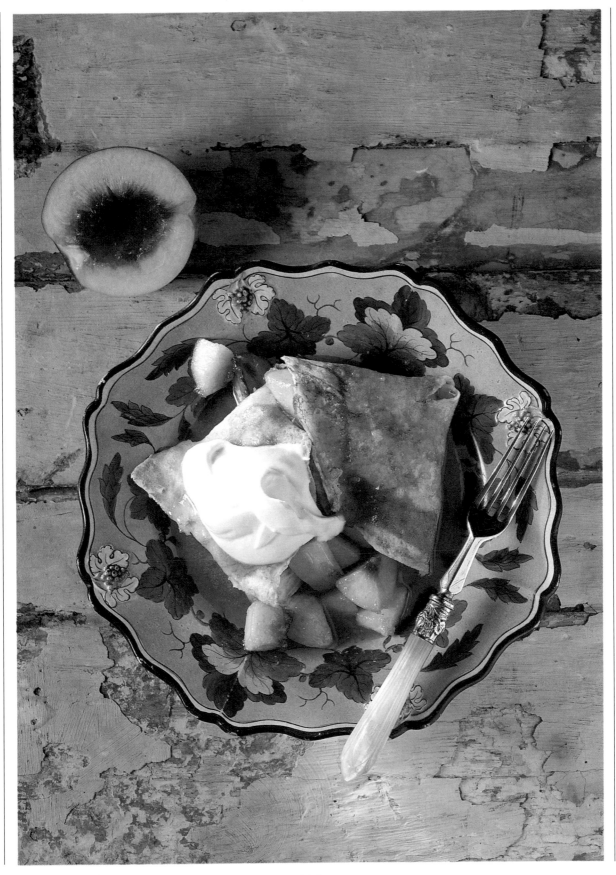

PANCAKES CREOLE

SERVES 4–6

All the best flavours of Creole cooking combine to make these mouthwatering pancakes.

1 quantity Pancake batter (see page 108)
finely grated rind and juice of 1 lime
50 g (2 oz) butter or margarine
50 g (2 oz) demerara sugar
60 ml (4 tbsp) dark rum
2.5 ml (½ tsp) ground cinnamon
3–4 bananas

FOR THE DECORATION

twists of orange
twists of lime

1. Make 8–12 pancakes (see page 108). Stack the pancakes with greaseproof paper in between and keep warm in the oven.
2. Put the lime rind and juice in a saucepan with the butter, sugar, rum and cinnamon. Heat gently until the butter has melted and the sugar dissolved, stirring occasionally.
3. Peel the bananas and slice thinly into the sauce. Cook gently for 5 minutes until tender.
4. Remove the banana slices from the sauce with a slotted spoon. Place a few slices in the centre of each pancake, then fold the pancakes into 'envelopes' around the cooked bananas.
5. Place in a warmed serving dish and pour over the hot sauce. Decorate with orange and lime twists. Serve with cream.

To freeze: freeze the pancakes (see page 108).

GINGER AND APPLE PANCAKE LAYER

SERVES 8

Using eating apples means that they retain their shape and you will not need to add much sugar.

5 ml (1 tsp) ground ginger
1 quantity Pancake batter (see page 108)
900 g (2 lb) eating apples
caster sugar, to taste
50 g (2 oz) sultanas
120 ml (8 tbsp) ginger preserve

1. Grease a shallow ovenproof dish.
2. Stir the ground ginger into the pancake batter. Make 8 pancakes (see page 108). Stack the pancakes with greaseproof paper in between and keep warm in the oven.

3. Peel, quarter and core the apples, then roughly chop. Place the apples in a medium saucepan with 30 ml (2 tbsp) water and sugar to taste. Cover and cook gently for about 5 minutes or until the apples soften. (Alternatively, put the ingredients in a bowl. Cover and microwave on HIGH for 6–8 minutes or until soft.) Add the sultanas.
4. Place one pancake in the prepared dish and spread with a little of the apple mixture. Repeat the layers until all of the pancakes and apple mixture are used, finishing with a pancake. Cover with buttered foil.
5. Bake in the oven at 200°C (400°F) mark 6 for about 30 minutes or until really hot.
6. Meanwhile, place the ginger preserve and 60 ml (4 tbsp) water in a pan and heat gently until melted. (Alternatively, put the ingredients in a bowl and microwave on HIGH for 2 minutes.) Sieve the mixture and pour over the pancake layer just before serving. Serve cut into wedges.

To freeze: pack and freeze at the end of step 4. To use, thaw overnight at cool room temperature, then finish as above.

APRICOT AND ALMOND CRÊPE GÂTEAU

SERVES 6–8

An unusual cold gâteau where the custard changes into a sauce when cooked. This would be very good served with extra stewed fruits and cream.

16 Orange crêpes (see page 108)

FOR THE FILLING

350 g (12 oz) dried apricots
300 ml (½ pint) orange juice
225 g (8 oz) ground almonds
30 ml (2 tbsp) caster sugar
30–60 ml (2–4 tbsp) double cream
100 g (4 oz) sultanas

FOR THE CUSTARD

5 egg yolks
75 g (3 oz) caster sugar
450 ml (¾ pint) milk or single cream, scalded

1. Grease a 1 litre (1¾ pint) charlotte mould or soufflé dish. The diameter of the dish should be a little wider than the diameter of the crêpes.
2. Make the crêpes (see page 108). Stack the crêpes with greaseproof paper in between and keep warm in the oven.
3. To make the filling, place the apricots and orange juice in a saucepan. Cover and simmer for about 10 minutes or until just tender. (Alternatively, microwave, covered, on HIGH for 5–7 minutes.) Strain off any liquid and reserve. Blend or sieve the apricots to make a thick purée.

4. Mix the ground almonds with the sugar and enough cream to bind to a spreadable paste.

5. Spread each crêpe with almond paste, then apricot purée. Layer the crêpes in the prepared dish, sprinkling with sultanas between each layer.

6. To make the custard, beat the egg yolks and caster sugar together in a bowl until pale and fluffy. Add the scalded milk or cream and stir well. Carefully ladle over the crêpes. Cover with buttered greaseproof paper.

7. Bake in the oven at 150°C (300°F) mark 2 for 30–40 minutes or until the custard is set. Leave to cool completely.

8. When cold, run a thin-bladed knife around the edge to loosen and turn out on to a serving plate. Serve the gâteau, cut into wedges with the reserved orange cooking liquid poured over.

Not suitable for freezing.

CHOCOLATE CINNAMON CRÊPES

SERVES 4–5

This makes ten generously filled crêpes, enough for five, allowing two each, or enough for four greedy people, allowing for second helpings.

15 ml (3 tsp) ground cinnamon
1 quantity Pancake batter (see page 108)
100 g (4 oz) plain flour
50 g (2 oz) caster sugar
300 ml (½ pint) milk
50 g (2 oz) plain chocolate, cut into pieces
grated rind of 1 lemon
4 eggs
grated white and plain chocolate, to decorate

1. Lightly grease a large shallow ovenproof dish.

2. Stir 10 ml (2 tsp) of the cinnamon into the batter. Make ten crêpes (see page 108). Stack the crêpes with greaseproof paper in between and keep warm in the oven.

3. Mix the flour, sugar and remaining cinnamon together in a bowl. Blend to a smooth paste with a little of the milk. Heat the remaining milk to boiling point and whisk in the flour mixture. Bring to the boil, whisking all the time; it should be very thick. Remove from the heat.

4. Stir the chocolate and lemon rind into the mixture until completely blended and smooth. Gradually beat the egg yolks into the chocolate mixture. Whisk the egg whites until stiff, then fold in the mixture.

5. Spoon about 60 ml (4 tbsp) mixture on to the centre of each crêpe. Fold in the sides to completely enclose. Place in one layer in the prepared dish, seam side downwards.

6. Bake in the oven at 220°C (425°F) mark 7 for 15–20 minutes until just set. Decorate with grated chocolate. Serve hot or cold.

To freeze: freeze the unfilled crêpes (see page 108).

CRÊPES SOUFFLÉES AU FRAMBOISE

SERVES 4

The delicious soufflé filling puffs up as the crêpes bake in the oven. Serve immediately before they collapse.

8 Orange crêpes (see page 108)
25 g (1 oz) caster sugar
15 g (½ oz) plain flour
150 ml (¼ pint) milk
2 eggs, separated
45 ml (3 tbsp) raspberry-flavoured liqueur
225 g (8 oz) raspberries, hulled
15 ml (1 tbsp) icing sugar, sifted

1. Grease an ovenproof dish.

2. Make the crêpes (see page 108). Stack the crêpes with greaseproof paper in between and keep warm in the oven.

3. Put the sugar, flour and milk in a heavy-based saucepan and bring to the boil, whisking all the time. Cool slightly, then stir in the egg yolks and liqueur. Whisk the egg whites until stiff, then fold lightly into the mixture.

4. Place a few raspberries on one half of each crêpe, reserving a few for decoration. Top the raspberries with the soufflé mixture, then fold the crêpes in half to enclose the raspberries and filling. As each one is filled, transfer it to the prepared dish, arranging them side by side.

5. Bake in the oven at 220°C (425°F) mark 7 for 5 minutes. Sprinkle with the icing sugar and bake for a further 5 minutes. Serve immediately, with raspberry fruit purée sauce (see page 244), decorated with the reserved raspberries.

Not suitable for freezing.

STRAWBERRY SAVARIN

SERVES 6

A savarin is an open-textured, spongy yeast cake. Once cooked, it is soaked in a sugar or liqueur syrup.

15 g (½ oz) fresh yeast or 7.5 ml (1½ tsp) dried
45 ml (3 tbsp) tepid milk
2 eggs, lightly beaten
50 g (2 oz) butter, melted and cooled
100 g (4 oz) plain flour
15 ml (1 tbsp) caster sugar
25 g (1 oz) desiccated coconut
90 ml (6 tbsp) redcurrant jelly or sieved strawberry jam
75 ml (5 tbsp) lemon juice
450 g (1 lb) strawberries, hulled

1. Lightly oil a 1.3 litre (2¼ pint) savarin tin or ring mould and turn it upside down on absorbent kitchen paper to drain off the excess oil.

2. Blend the fresh yeast with the milk. If using dried yeast, sprinkle it on to the milk and leave in a warm place for 15 minutes or until frothy. Gradually beat the eggs and butter into the yeast liquid.

3. Mix the flour, sugar and coconut together in a bowl. With a wooden spoon, gradually stir in the yeast mixture to form a thick smooth batter. Beat together.

4. Turn the batter into the prepared tin, cover with oiled clingfilm and leave in a warm place for about 30 minutes or until the savarin is nearly doubled in size.

5. Bake in the oven at 190°C (375°F) mark 5 for 35–40 minutes until golden. Turn out on to a wire rack placed over a large plate.

6. Put the jelly and lemon juice into a small pan over a low heat. (Alternatively, microwave on HIGH for 1–2 minutes.) When the jelly has melted, spoon over the warm savarin until well glazed, allowing any excess to collect on the plate under the wire rack. Transfer the savarin to a serving plate.

7. Return the excess jelly mixture to the pan and add the strawberries; stir to coat. Remove from heat and cool for 15–20 minutes or until almost set. Spoon into the centre of the savarin. Serve warm or cold.

VARIATIONS

Strawberry Babas Divide the yeast batter between six 9 cm (3½ inch) ring tins. Leave to rise until the moulds are nearly two-thirds full, then bake for 15–20 minutes. Replace the lemon juice with brandy or kirsch, soak each baba well and place on individual serving plates. Finish with strawberries and soured cream as above.

Rum Babas Make as strawberry babas but soak the warm babas in a rum syrup made with 120 ml (8 tbsp) clear honey, 120 ml (8 tbsp) water and rum or rum essence to taste. Serve filled with whipped cream.

To freeze: wrap and freeze the cooled savarin. Thaw overnight at cool room temperature, then warm gently, covered, in a low oven. Spoon over the warm jelly and finish as above.

FRUIT AND RUM SAVARIN

SERVES 6

Served filled with fresh fruits, this savarin is soaked in a rum syrup.

15 g (½ oz) fresh yeast
45 ml (3 tbsp) tepid milk
100 g (4 oz) strong plain flour, sifted with a pinch of salt
30 ml (2 tbsp) caster sugar
2 eggs, beaten
50 g (2 oz) unsalted butter, softened
225 g (8 oz) granulated sugar
120 ml (8 tbsp) dark rum
2 bananas, peeled and sliced
450 g (1 lb) black grapes, halved and seeded
2 kiwi fruit, peeled and sliced
2 small oranges, skinned and segmented

1. Grease and flour a 1.1 litre (2 pint) savarin or ring mould.

2. Put the yeast in a warmed small bowl and add the milk; cream together. Add 25 g (1 oz) of the flour and beat well with a fork. Leave in a warm place for 10–15 minutes until frothy.

3. Put the remaining flour in a warmed large bowl with 5 ml (1 tsp) of the caster sugar and the eggs. Add the frothy yeast mixture, then beat until an elastic dough is formed. Cover with a floured tea towel and leave in a warm place until doubled in size.

4. Beat the softened butter into the dough a little at a time until evenly incorporated.

5. Put the dough in the prepared mould. Cover with a floured tea towel and leave to prove in a warm place until it has risen to the top of the mould. Uncover the mould.

6. Bake in the oven at 200°C (400°F) mark 6 for 25–30 minutes until risen and golden brown.

7. Meanwhile, make the rum sugar syrup. Put the granulated sugar and 200 ml (7 fl oz) water in a heavy-based saucepan and heat gently until the sugar has dissolved. Bring to the boil and boil steadily, without stirring, for 5 minutes until syrupy. Remove from the heat and stir in 90 ml (6 tbsp) of the rum.

8. Turn the savarin out on to a wire rack placed over a large plate or tray. Prick all over the savarin with a fine skewer, then slowly spoon over the warm syrup. Collect any syrup that drips on to the plate or tray and spoon it back over the savarin. Leave until completely cold.

9. Toss the prepared fruits together with the remaining caster sugar and rum. Place the savarin on a serving plate and pile the fruits in the centre. Serve immediately with single cream.

To freeze: wrap and freeze the cooled savarin. Thaw overnight at cool room temperature, then warm gently, covered, in a low oven. Spoon over the warm syrup and finish as above.

Opposite: STRAWBERRY BABAS.

Waffles

SERVES 4

These crisp, light wafers, made from batter, are cooked in a special waffle iron. The cooking time varies with different kinds of waffle irons, but as a rule 2–3 minutes is sufficient. Follow the manufacturer's instructions.

100 g (4 oz) self raising flour
pinch of salt
15 ml (1 tbsp) caster sugar
1 egg, separated
30 ml (2 tbsp) butter or margarine, melted
150 ml (¼ pint) milk
2.5 ml (½ tsp) vanilla essence (optional)

1. Heat the waffle iron according to the manufacturer's instructions.
2. Mix the flour, salt and sugar together in a bowl. Add the egg yolk, melted butter, milk and vanilla essence. Beat to give a smooth coating batter. Whisk the egg white until stiff and fold into the batter.
3. Pour just enough batter into the iron to run over the surface. Close the iron and cook for 2–3 minutes, turning the iron if using a non-electric type.
4. When the waffle is cooked, it should be golden brown and crisp and easily removed from the iron—if it sticks, cook for 1 minute longer.
5. Serve immediately with butter and golden or maple syrup, or a fruit conserve of your choice.

To freeze: interleave with greaseproof paper and wrap in foil. Thaw at room temperature for 2–3 hours or overnight in the refrigerator. Reheat the foil-wrapped waffles in the oven at 190°C (375°F) mark 5 for 30 minutes.

Drop Scones

MAKES 16–18

Drop scones take their name from the fact that the mixture is 'dropped' from the mixing spoon on to a hot griddle. Made with storecupboard ingredients, they are ideal for an impromptu dessert. Serve with golden or maple syrup and lashings of whipped cream.

150 g (5 oz) self raising flour
pinch of salt
15 ml (1 tbsp) caster sugar
15 ml (1 tbsp) oil
1 egg, beaten
150 ml (¼ pint) milk
lard or oil, for greasing

1. Sift the flour, salt and sugar into a bowl. Add the oil, egg and milk. Stir with a wooden spoon to combine to a thick batter the consistency of double cream.
2. Grease a griddle or heavy frying pan with a little lard or oil and place over moderate heat until hot.

3. Drop spoonfuls of the mixture from the point of a spoon on to the griddle, keeping them well apart to allow for spreading.
4. Cook over moderate heat for 2–3 minutes until bubbles rise and burst all over the surface of the scones and the undersides are golden brown. Turn them over with a palette knife and cook for 2–3 minutes.
5. Transfer the cooked scones to a clean tea towel and fold the cloth over to enclose them while making the remaining scones. Serve hot.

To freeze: pack and freeze the cold scones. Thaw at cool room temperature. Reheat in the oven, wrapped in foil, at 190°C (375°F) mark 5 for 15–20 minutes.

Gulab Jamun

SERVES 4–6

Gulab Jamun are popular in India; they are very sweet and syrupy, with a wonderfully exotic aroma of rose water, which is worth adding at the end for an authentic Gulab Jamun. Rose water is available in bottles at chemists, delicatessens and herbalists.

225 g (8 oz) granulated sugar
6 green cardamom pods, lightly crushed
175 g (6 oz) dried skimmed milk with vegetable fat
10 ml (2 tsp) baking powder
50 g (2 oz) self raising flour
15 ml (1 tbsp) semolina
about 150 ml (¼ pint) milk
oil, for deep-frying
rose water, for sprinkling

1. Put the sugar and 450 ml (¾ pint) water in a saucepan. Bring slowly to the boil, stirring until the sugar has dissolved. Add the crushed cardamoms and boil rapidly for 4 minutes. Remove from the heat and cover.
2. Mix the dried milk, baking powder, flour, semolina and enough milk together in a bowl to mix to a stiff dough rather like shortcrust pastry.
3. Knead the dough on a work surface until smooth. Divide into 24 pieces. Keep covered with clingfilm to prevent the dough drying out. Roll each piece of dough into a completely smooth ball.
4. Heat the oil in a deep fat fryer to 170°C (325°F). Deep fry the dough pieces in batches for 2–3 minutes until golden brown on all sides, turning them with a slotted spoon to ensure even browning. They must not fry too quickly as they have to cook all the way through before becoming too brown on the outside. Remove with a slotted spoon, drain on absorbent kitchen paper and keep warm while frying the remainder.
5. While the Gulab Jamuns are still hot, transfer them to a warmed serving dish. Pour over the warm syrup and sprinkle with rose water. Serve warm or cold.

Not suitable for freezing.

Opposite: GULAB JAMUN.

LE CLAFOUTIS

SERVES 6

A Clafoutis is a baked batter pudding popular throughout France. It is usually made with black cherries. Traditionalists insist that the cherries must not be stoned; we found that with stoned cherries it was much easier and daintier to eat! The choice is yours.

45 ml (3 tbsp) kirsch
450 g (1 lb) black cherries, stoned
FOR THE BATTER
75 g (3 oz) plain flour
50 g (2 oz) icing sugar
pinch of salt
25 g (1 oz) butter, melted
300 ml (½ pint) creamy milk
3 eggs, beaten
icing sugar, for dusting

1. Generously grease a shallow ovenproof dish or tin.
2. Pour the kirsch over the cherries and leave to macerate for at least 30 minutes.
3. To make the batter, mix the flour, icing sugar and salt together in a bowl, then make a well in the centre. Pour in the butter, milk and eggs. Beat together to make a smooth batter. Pour a very thin layer of batter into the prepared dish.
4. Bake in the oven at 220°C (425°F) mark 7 for 5–10 minutes or until just set.
5. Drain the cherries, reserving the liquid, and arrange in a layer over the batter. Stir the reserved liquid into the remaining batter, pour evenly over the cherries. Return to the oven and bake for a further 40–45 minutes or until risen and golden brown.
6. Leave to cool for 5 minutes, then dust generously with icing sugar and serve while still warm with single cream.

Not suitable for freezing.

BEIGNETS DE FRUITS

SERVES 8

Most fruits make delicious beignets. Remember that soft fruits like apricots or peaches will require a much shorter cooking time than fruits such as apples and pears.

225 g (8 oz) plain flour
large pinch of salt
15 ml (1 tbsp) icing sugar
300 ml (½ pint) beer
2 eggs, separated
15 ml (1 tbsp) oil
oil, for deep-frying
2 large eating apples, peeled, cored and cut into rings
2 firm nectarines, stoned and cut into quarters
2 bananas, peeled and cut into chunks
caster sugar, for sprinkling

1. To make the batter, mix the flour, salt and sugar together in a bowl, then make a well in the centre. Add the beer and egg yolks. Beat together to make a smooth batter. Add the oil. Whisk the egg whites until stiff, then fold into the batter.
2. Heat the oil in a deep fat fryer to 190°C (375°F). Dip the prepared fruits in the batter and deep fry in batches. The apples will take about 4 minutes and the nectarines and banana about 3 minutes.
3. Drain on absorbent kitchen paper and keep warm while frying the remainder. Serve hot, sprinkled with caster sugar.

Not suitable for freezing.

Opposite: BEIGNETS DE FRUITS.

FRESH STRAWBERRY FRITTERS

SERVES 4

Serve with a mixture of Greek yogurt and cream flavoured with a little orange liqueur and orange rind.

350 g (12 oz) large firm, ripe strawberries
60 ml (4 tbsp) icing sugar
175 g (6 oz) plain flour
pinch of salt
oil, for deep-frying

1. Hull the strawberries and toss in 30 ml (2 tbsp) of the icing sugar.

2. To make the batter, mix the flour, salt and remaining icing sugar together in a bowl, then make a well in the centre. Add 175 ml (6 fl oz) water and beat vigorously with a wooden spoon to make a smooth batter. Chill.

3. Heat the oil in a deep fat fryer or a wok to 190°C (375°F). Dip the strawberries in the batter, then remove with a slotted spoon taking up plenty of the batter with the fruit.

4. Deep fry for 3–4 minutes until crisp. Remove with a slotted spoon and drain on absorbent kitchen paper. Keep warm in the oven while cooking the remainder.

Not suitable for freezing.

DAMSON AND APPLE TANSY

SERVES 4

Tansies originally included the bitter-sweet herb, tansy.

2 large Cox's apples, peeled, cored and thinly sliced
225 g (8 oz) damsons, halved, stoned and quartered
15 g (½ oz) butter
40 g (1½ oz) sugar
pinch of ground cloves
pinch of ground cinnamon
4 eggs, separated
45 ml (3 tbsp) soured cream

1. Put the apples, damsons, butter and half of the sugar in a large frying pan. Cook over a gentle heat until the fruit is softened, stirring continuously. Stir in the cloves and cinnamon, then remove from the heat.

2. Beat the egg yolks and cream together and stir into the fruit. Whisk the egg whites until stiff, then fold in.

3. Cook over a low heat until the mixture has set. Sprinkle the top with the remaining sugar, then brown under a hot grill. Serve immediately, straight from the pan, with soured cream.

Not suitable for freezing.

RUM SOUFFLÉ OMELETTE

SERVES 1

2 eggs, separated
5 ml (1 tsp) caster sugar
15 ml (1 tbsp) dark rum
15 g (½ oz) butter
15 ml (1 tbsp) apricot jam, warmed
30 ml (2 tbsp) icing sugar

1. Mix the egg yolks, caster sugar and rum together in a bowl.
2. Whisk the egg whites until stiff and standing in peaks.
3. Melt the butter in a heavy-based omelette pan until foaming. Fold the egg whites quickly into the egg yolk mixture, then pour into the foaming butter.
4. Cook over moderate heat for 2–3 minutes until the underside of the omelette is golden brown. Place the pan under a preheated hot grill and cook for a few minutes more until the top is golden brown.
5. Slide the omelette on to a sheet of foil placed on a warmed serving plate. Spread with the warmed jam, then tip the foil to fold over the omelette.
6. Sift the icing sugar thickly over the top of the omelette, then mark in a criss-cross pattern with hot metal skewers, if liked. Carefully remove the foil and serve immediately.

VARIATIONS

Fruit Soufflé Omelette Replace the jam with sliced fresh fruit or berries, such as raspberries or strawberries.
Chocolate Soufflé Omelette Omit the jam and drizzle the omelette with 40 g (1½ oz) melted chocolate (in step 5). Add a few chopped nuts. Sprinkle the omelette with a mixture of icing sugar and cinnamon.

Not suitable for freezing.

Opposite: DAMSON AND APPLE TANSY.
Above: RUM SOUFFLÉ OMELETTE.

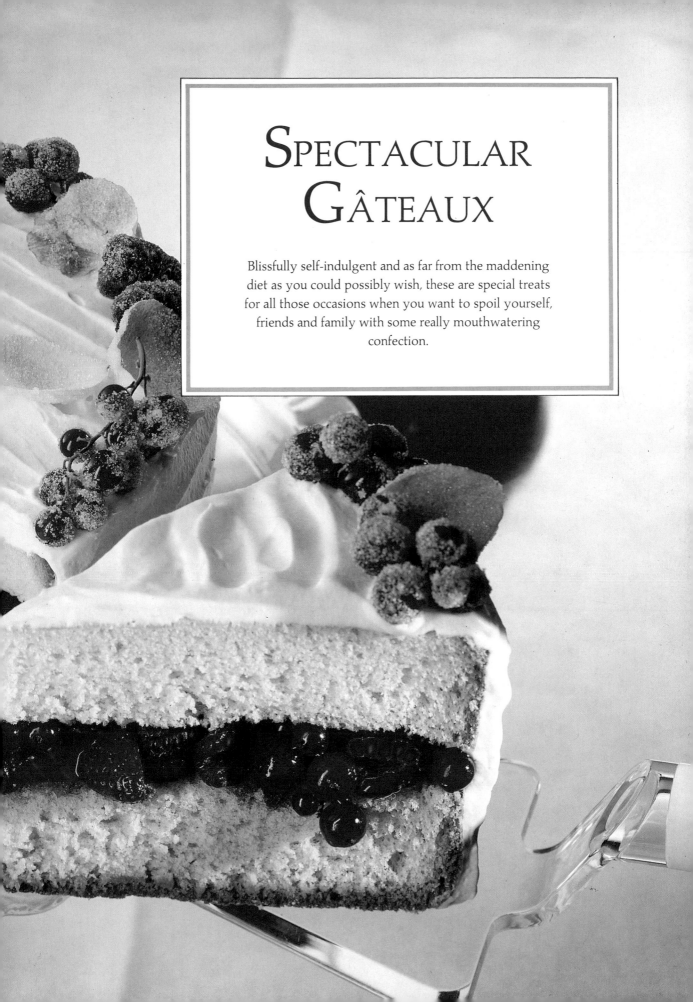

SPECTACULAR GÂTEAUX

Blissfully self-indulgent and as far from the maddening diet as you could possibly wish, these are special treats for all those occasions when you want to spoil yourself, friends and family with some really mouthwatering confection.

You can't beat a light-as-a-feather sponge to create a mouthwatering dessert. Lots of gâteaux are based on a basic Genoese or whisked sponge. These are delicious enough simply to split and fill with fruit and cream, or can be transformed into totally irresistible, decadent desserts with nuts, liqueurs and praline.

Lightness, the essence of a good sponge, comes from using the freshest eggs possible and whisking them with sugar until thick and creamy. There is no fat in the classic sponge and the cake rises simply because of the air incorporated during whisking.

A moister version of the whisked sponge is a Genoese cake. This is also made by the whisking method, but melted butter is added with the flour. This gives a delicate sponge with a moister texture than the plain whisked sponge and a more delicious rich and buttery taste.

When adding melted butter, make sure it is just liquid and pour into the mixture around the sides of the bowl and fold in very light. Do not try to substitute margarine for butter in this recipe or the flavour and texture will be lost. A Genoese cake keeps better than a plain whisked sponge.

To make a really good sponge

● The eggs and sugar must be whisked until thick enough to leave a trail when the whisk is lifted from the surface. If you use a balloon whisk or a hand-held electric mixer, place the bowl over a saucepan of hot water to speed the thickening process. When whisking in an electric table top mixer, additional heat is not required.

● Do not let the bottom of the bowl touch the water or the mixture will become too hot. When the mixture is really thick and double in volume, take the bowl off the heat and continue to whisk until it is cool.

● Add the flour carefully. Sift it first, then add a little at a time to the whisked mixture and fold it in with a metal spoon until evenly blended. Do not stir or the air bubbles will be broken and the cake will not rise.

● Once the tin is filled, give it a sharp bang on a work surface to release any large air bubbles that may be trapped. If left, they will give the sponge an uneven texture.

● Make a Genoese cake the day before filling, it will be easier to cut. Wrap and chill to firm it up.

● Preheat the oven before starting to make cakes so that it will be at the correct temperature by the time the cake is ready to go in. Check that the shelves are in the correct position—place in the centre of the oven where possible. To test whether a cake is cooked, press the centre top of the cake very lightly with your fingertip. The cake should be spongy and should give only very slightly to the pressure, then rise again immediately, retaining no impression.

● It should have shrunk slightly away from the sides of the tin. Allow the cake a few minutes to cool, then loosen the sides with a blunt edged knife and turn out on to a wire rack. Invert once turned out so that the delicate crust is not cut by the wire rack.

BASIC GENOESE CAKE

MAKES ONE 23 cm (9 inch) CAKE

A Genoese cake is the basis for many gâteaux. It is important to add the butter slowly, carefully and lightly, in step 5, or the cake will have a heavy texture.

75 g (3 oz) butter
6 eggs
175 g (6 oz) caster sugar
150 g (5 oz) plain flour
30 ml (2 tbsp) cornflour

1. Grease a 23 cm (9 inch) spring-release cake tin and line with greaseproof paper.
2. Put the butter into a saucepan and heat gently until melted, then remove from the heat and leave for a few minutes to cool slightly.
3. Put the eggs and sugar in a heatproof bowl standing over a pan of hot water. Whisk until pale and creamy and thick enough to leave a trail on the surface when the whisk is lifted. Remove from the heat and whisk until cool.
4. Sift the flours together into a bowl. Fold half the flour into the egg mixture with a metal spoon.
5. Pour half the cooled butter around the edge of the mixture. Gradually fold in the remaining butter and flour alternately. Fold in very lightly or the butter will sink and result in a heavy cake. Pour the mixture into the prepared tin.
6. Bake in the oven at 180°C (350°F) mark 4 for 35–40 minutes until well risen, firm to the touch and beginning to shrink away from the sides of the tin. Turn out on to a wire rack and leave to cool.

VARIATION

Chocolate Genoese Substitute 25 g (1 oz) of the plain flour with cocoa powder. Sift the cocoa with the flours and proceed as above.

To freeze: wrap and freeze after cooling. Thaw at cool room temperature.

Previous page: RED FRUIT GÂTEAU (PAGE 138).

Basic Whisked Sponge

MAKES TWO 18 cm (7 inch) SPONGES

This classic fatless sponge also forms the basis of gâteaux, however it does not keep as well as a Genoese cake and should be eaten on the day of making.

3 eggs
75 g (3 oz) caster sugar
75 g (3 oz) plain flour

1. Grease two 18 cm (7 inch) sandwich tins, line with greaseproof paper, then dust with a mixture of flour and caster sugar.
2. Put the eggs and sugar in a large heatproof bowl standing over a pan of hot water. Whisk until doubled in volume and thick enough to leave a thin trail on the surface when the whisk is lifted.
3. Remove from the heat and continue whisking for a further 5 minutes until the mixture is cool.
4. Sift half the flour over the mixture and fold in very lightly, using a large metal spoon. Sift and fold in the remaining flour in the same way.
5. Pour the mixture into the prepared tins, tilting the tins to spread the mixture evenly. Do not use a palette knife or spatula to smooth the mixture as this will crush out the air bubbles.
6. Bake in the oven at 190°C (375°F) mark 5 for 20–25 minutes until well risen, firm to the touch and beginning to shrink away from the sides of the tins. Turn out on to a wire rack and leave to cool.

To freeze: wrap and freeze after cooling. Thaw at cool room temperature.

VARIATIONS

To make two 20.5 cm (8 inch) sponges, use 4 eggs, 100 g (4 oz) caster sugar and 100 g (4 oz) plain flour.

Swiss Roll   **1.** Line a 33 × 23 cm (13 × 9 inch) Swiss roll tin with greaseproof paper.
2. Make the sponge as above but use 100 g (4 oz) plain flour and fold in with 15 ml (1 tbsp) hot water. Pour into the prepared tin. Tilt the tin backwards and forwards to spread the mixture in an even layer.
3. Bake in the oven at 200°C (400°F) mark 6 for 10–12 minutes until golden brown, well risen and firm.
4. Meanwhile, place a sheet of greaseproof paper over a damp tea towel. Dredge the paper with caster sugar.
5. Quickly turn out the cake on to the paper, trim off the crusty edges and spread with jam. Roll up the cake with the aid of the paper. Make the first turn firmly so that the whole cake will roll evenly and have a good shape when finished, but roll the cake more lightly after this turn.
6. Place seam-side down on a wire rack and dredge with caster sugar.

Chocolate Swiss Roll   Make the sponge as for Swiss roll, above, but replace 15 ml (1 tbsp) plain flour with 15 ml (1 tbsp) sifted cocoa powder. Turn out the cooked sponge and trim as above, then cover with a sheet of

greaseproof paper and roll with the paper inside. When cold, unroll and remove the paper. Spread with whipped cream and re-roll. Dust with icing sugar.

To freeze: roll up the cake with the greaseproof paper inside. Overwrap and freeze. Thaw at cool room temperature, unroll and finish as above.

Apple Hazelnut Genoese

SERVES 6

Home-made apple jelly or purée gives the best flavour, but do not add too much sugar; the seven-minute frosting is very sweet.

3 eggs
100 g (4 oz) caster sugar
50 g (2 oz) plain flour
15 ml (1 tbsp) cornflour
25 g (1 oz) ground hazelnuts
75 g (3 oz) butter, melted and cooled
90 ml (6 tbsp) apple jelly or purée
FOR THE FROSTING
1 egg white
175 g (6 oz) caster sugar
pinch of salt
pinch of cream of tartar
30 ml (2 tbsp) thick apple purée

1. Grease two 18 cm (7 inch) sandwich tins, line the bases with greaseproof paper and grease the paper.
2. Whisk the eggs and sugar together in a bowl until very thick. Sift in the flour and cornflour. Add the hazelnuts, then fold in the butter. Turn the mixture into the prepared tins.
3. Bake in the oven at 180°C (350°F) mark 4 for about 25 minutes or until the sponge springs back when pressed lightly with a finger and has shrunk away a little from the tins. Turn out on to a wire rack and leave to cool for 1–2 hours.
4. Sandwich the layers with apple jelly. To prepare the seven-minute frosting put all the ingredients into a bowl and whisk lightly. Place the bowl over a pan of hot water and heat, whisking continuously, until the mixture thickens sufficiently to stand in peaks. This will take about 7 minutes.
5. Cover the cake with the frosting, peaking up the surface. Leave for 2–3 hours before serving to allow the frosting to firm up.

To freeze: wrap and freeze the cakes at the end of step 3. Thaw at cool room temperature, then finish as above.

DOBOS TORTE

SERVES 8

The old Austro-Hungarian empire is the home of this elaborate 'drum cake'. Versions of the traditional sponge rounds, layered with chocolate cream and glazed with caramel, are still to be found in the best cafés and pastry shops from Vienna to Budapest. Be sure to mark the caramel into portions before it hardens or it will be extremely difficult to cut.

4 eggs
275 g (10 oz) caster sugar
150 g (5 oz) plain flour
100 g (4 oz) plain chocolate
100 g (4 oz) crushed biscuits or chopped nuts, for coating

FOR THE FILLING
3 egg whites
175 g (6 oz) icing sugar, sifted
225 g (8 oz) butter

1. Line two baking sheets with non-sticking baking paper.
2. Whisk the eggs and 175 g (6 oz) of the caster sugar in a bowl standing over a pan of hot water. Whisk until the mixture is thick enough to leave a trail on the surface when the whisk is lifted. Remove from the heat.
3. Sift half the flour over the mixture and fold in lightly with a metal spoon. Add the remaining flour in the same way. Carefully spread some of the mixture out on the prepared baking sheets in large rounds measuring about 20.5 cm (8 inches) in diameter.
4. Bake in the oven at 190°C (375°F) mark 5 for 7–10 minutes until golden brown. Loosen from the baking sheets and trim each round to a neat shape with a sharp knife, using a saucepan lid as a guide. Transfer them to wire racks and leave to cool for about 15 minutes.
5. Re-line the baking sheets, spread on more mixture. Bake, trim and cool as before. There will be enough mixture to make six or seven rounds.
6. Select the round with the best surface and lay it on an oiled baking sheet.
7. Put the remaining caster sugar in a small, heavy-based saucepan. Dissolve the sugar, without stirring, over a gentle heat and boil it steadily to a rich brown.
8. Pour it over the round on the baking sheet, spreading it with a knife brushed with oil. Mark into eight sections and trim round the edge.
9. Break the chocolate into small pieces. Place in a heatproof bowl standing over a pan of simmering water and heat gently until the chocolate melts. (Alternatively, microwave on LOW for 5–6 minutes, stirring occasionally until the chocolate melts.) Remove from the heat.
10. To make the filling, put the egg whites and icing sugar into a heatproof bowl standing over a pan of simmering water. Whisk until very thick, then remove from the heat.
11. Put the butter into a bowl and beat until pale and soft. Gradually beat in the egg and sugar mixture, then stir in the melted chocolate.

12. Sandwich the remaining biscuit rounds together with some of the filling and put the caramel-covered one on top.
13. Spread the sides of the torte with the remaining filling and press the crushed biscuit crumbs or chopped nuts round the sides.

To freeze: wrap and freeze the cooled cakes at the end of step 5. Thaw at cool room temperature, then finish as above.

RASPBERRY CINNAMON TORTE

SERVES 6

A crumbly almond cake with a soft centre surrounding moist raspberries. Serve just warm to enjoy the torte at its best.

150 g (5 oz) butter or margarine
150 g (5 oz) caster sugar
150 g (5 oz) ground almonds
150 g (5 oz) self raising flour
1 egg
5 ml (1 tsp) ground cinnamon
225 g (8 oz) raspberries, hulled
mixed icing sugar and cinnamon, for dusting

1. Grease a 22 cm (8½ inch) spring-release cake tin and line the base with greaseproof paper.
2. Place the butter, caster sugar, almonds, flour, egg and ground cinnamon in a bowl. Beat well.
3. Spread half the almond mixture into the prepared tin, using a fork to flatten lightly. Sprinkle over the raspberries, then dot over the remaining almond mixture so it almost covers the fruit. Stand the tin on a baking sheet.
4. Bake in the oven at 180°C (350°F) mark 4 for about 1 hour, covering lightly when well browned. The torte should feel just firm to the touch with a springy texture. Cool in the tin for about 1 hour.
5. Dust with mixed cinnamon and icing sugar and serve warm.

Not suitable for freezing.

Opposite: DOBOS TORTE.

ANGEL CAKE

SERVES 8–10

Angel cake is a classic American cake. It is baked in a special angel cake tin which has a hole in the centre. Look in your local kitchen shop for one or use a savarin tin. Angel cake is white in colour and very light. Cut it carefully with a serrated knife so that the delicate sponge is not crushed.

FOR THE CAKE

150 g (5 oz) caster sugar
75 g (3 oz) plain flour
2.5 ml (½ tsp) salt
6 egg whites
5 ml (1 tsp) cream of tartar
1.25 ml (¼ tsp) almond flavouring
1.25 ml (¼ tsp) vanilla essence
10 ml (2 tsp) lemon juice

FOR THE FILLING AND DECORATION

150 ml (¼ pint) double cream
2 fresh figs, sliced

1. Grease and flour a 2.3 litre (4 pint) angel cake tin or savarin mould.

2. To make the cake, sift half of the sugar, the flour and salt together three times.

3. Using an electric whisk, whisk the egg whites until foamy. Add the cream of tartar and continue whisking until the egg whites are stiff but not dry. Gradually add the remaining sugar, about 15 ml (1 tbsp) at a time, whisking well between each addition. Whisk in the almond flavouring, vanilla essence and the lemon juice.

4. Sift about a quarter of the flour and sugar mixture over the egg mixture and fold in very lightly using a metal spoon. Repeat until all of the mixture is added. Spoon into the prepared tin.

5. Bake in the oven at 180°C (350°F) mark 4 for about 35–40 minutes or until the cake is risen and springs back when pressed gently.

6. Invert the tin on to a wire rack and leave to cool with the tin covering the cake. When cold, carefully run a palette knife around the sides and centre of the tin, then remove the cake.

7. Transfer the cake to a serving plate. Whip the cream until it just holds its shape and use to fill a piping bag fitted with a star nozzle. Pipe around the bottom edge of the cake. Decorate with the figs.

To freeze: wrap and freeze the cake at the end of step 6. Thaw overnight, wrapped, at cool room temperature, then finish as above.

STRAWBERRY ALMOND LAYER GÂTEAU

SERVES 8

To make this gâteau, a basic Swiss roll mixture is cooked and, instead of being rolled up, it is cut into three and layered with strawberries and cream. Make a Swiss roll up to the end of step 3 (see page 125), then turn out on to a sheet of greaseproof paper dredged with caster sugar. Leave to cool on the paper.

1 Swiss roll (see page 125)

FOR THE FILLING AND DECORATION

700 g (1½ lb) small strawberries
15 ml (1 tbsp) icing sugar
30 ml (2 tbsp) strawberry liqueur
75 g (3 oz) plain chocolate
30 ml (2 tbsp) strawberry jam
450 ml (¾ pint) whipping cream
few drops of almond flavouring
75 g (3 oz) flaked almonds, toasted

1. Hull and slice 450 g (1 lb) of the strawberries and put in a bowl with the icing sugar and liqueur. Leave to stand for 20 minutes, stirring occasionally.

2. Trim the edges of the Swiss roll, then cut widthways into three even pieces.

3. Meanwhile, break the chocolate into small pieces. Place in a small heatproof bowl standing over a pan of simmering water and heat gently until the chocolate melts. (Alternatively, microwave on LOW for 2 minutes or until melted, stirring occasionally.)

4. Halve the remaining strawberries (leaving the stalks attached). Dip the base of each piece of strawberry in the melted chocolate. Place on a sheet of greaseproof paper and leave to set.

5. Drain the strawberry slices, reserving the juice. Stir the jam into the juice and mix together. Brush a little of the jam and juice mixture over two pieces of the cake. Top with the strawberry slices.

6. Whip the cream until it stands in soft peaks, then flavour to taste with a little almond flavouring. Spread a little cream on top of the strawberries.

7. Place the strawberry covered pieces of cake on top of one another, then cover with the remaining piece of cake. Spread the top and sides with the remaining jam mixture, then cover completely with the cream. Press the toasted nuts on the sides. Decorate the top with the chocolate dipped strawberries.

To freeze: cut the Swiss roll to size then wrap and freeze. Thaw at cool room temperature, then finish as above.

Above: ANGEL CAKE.
Below: STRAWBERRY ALMOND LAYER GÂTEAU.

SACHERTORTE

SERVES 8–10

Famous the world over, Sachertorte was the invention of Franz Sacher, a master sugar baker, in Vienna in 1832. It is a very rich, moist, chocolate cake. The traditional cake is covered with a chocolate fondant icing, but as this is rather sweet, a ganache icing is used here.

FOR THE CAKE

150 g (5 oz) plain chocolate
100 g (4 oz) unsalted butter or margarine, softened
100 g (4 oz) caster sugar
100 g (4 oz) ground almonds
4 eggs, separated
50 g (2 oz) fresh brown breadcrumbs
30 ml (2 tbsp) apricot jam, melted

FOR THE ICING

200 g (7 oz) plain chocolate
200 ml (7 fl oz) double cream

1. Grease a 23 cm (9 inch) spring-release cake tin, line with greaseproof paper and grease the paper.

2. To make the cake, break the chocolate into small pieces. Place in a heatproof bowl standing over a pan of simmering water and heat gently until the chocolate melts. (Alternatively, microwave on LOW for 4–5 minutes or until melted, stirring occasionally.) Remove from the heat.

3. Cream the butter and sugar together in a bowl until pale and fluffy. Stir in the almonds, egg yolks, breadcrumbs and melted chocolate, then beat until well combined.

4. Whisk the egg whites until stiff and fold half into the chocolate mixture, then fold in the other half. Pour the mixture into the prepared tin and level the surface.

5. Bake in the oven at 180°C (350°F) mark 4 for 40–45 minutes until firm to the touch.

6. Cover with a damp tea towel, leave for 5 minutes to cool slightly, then unclip the sides of the tin and invert on to a wire rack. Remove the base. Turn the cake the right way up, cover again and leave to cool. When cold, brush the top with the melted apricot jam.

7. To make the icing, break the chocolate into small pieces. Place in a heatproof bowl with the cream. Stand the bowl over a pan of simmering water and heat until the chocolate melts and blends with the cream. (Alternatively, microwave on LOW for 6–7 minutes, stirring

Above: SACHERTORTE.

occasionally until the chocolate melts.) Cool for a few minutes until the icing just coats the back of a spoon.

8. Stand the cake and the wire rack on a baking sheet and pour over the icing. Gently shake the cake to spread the icing evenly and use a palette knife, if necessary, to ensure that the sides are completely covered. Leave in a cool place to set, but do not put in the refrigerator or the icing will lose its shine.

To freeze: wrap and freeze the cake before icing. Thaw at cool room temperature, then finish as above.

CARAMEL BANANA TORTE
SERVES 8
In step 6, work quickly, so that the caramel does not set before you have a chance to spread it over the top of the gâteau.

FOR THE CAKE

175 g (6 oz) self raising flour
1.25 ml (¼ tsp) baking powder
1.25 ml (¼ tsp) bicarbonate of soda
50 g (2 oz) butter or margarine, cut into pieces
150 g (5 oz) caster sugar
175 g (6 oz) ripe bananas
2.5 ml (½ tsp) grated nutmeg
45 ml (3 tbsp) milk
1 egg, beaten

FOR THE CARAMEL

75 g (3 oz) sugar

FOR THE FILLING AND DECORATION

175 g (6 oz) full fat soft cheese
30 ml (2 tbsp) lemon juice
30 ml (2 tbsp) icing sugar
175 g (6 oz) ripe bananas
50 g (2 oz) flaked almonds, toasted

1. Grease a 20.5 cm (8 inch) round cake tin, line the base with greaseproof paper and grease the paper.

2. Sift the flour, baking powder and bicarbonate of soda into a bowl. Rub in the butter until the mixture resembles fine breadcrumbs, then stir in the sugar.

3. Peel the bananas and mash them in a bowl, then beat in the nutmeg, milk and egg. Stir the banana mixture into the dry ingredients. Turn the mixture into the prepared tin and level the surface.

4. Bake in the oven at 180°C (350°F) mark 4 for about 40 minutes. Cool in the tin for 5 minutes, then turn out on to a wire rack and leave to cool. Cut the cake into two layers.

5. To make the caramel, put the sugar into a small saucepan. Dissolve, without stirring, over gentle heat, then boil until a rich brown colour.

6. When the caramel is ready, immediately pour it on to the top of the cake. Use an oiled knife to spread the caramel so that it completely covers the top. Mark into eight portions with the point of a knife.

7. To make the filling, put the soft cheese, lemon juice and icing sugar into a bowl and beat together. Peel and chop the bananas and add to half of the cheese mixture. Use this mixture to sandwich the cakes together.

8. Spread a little of the remaining cheese mixture around the sides of the cake and cover with most of the almonds. Decorate the caramel top with the remaining cheese mixture and almonds.

To freeze: wrap and freeze at the end of step 4. Thaw at cool room temperature, then finish as above.

NUSSKUCHEN
SERVES 12
Nusskuchen comes in many forms, but is always made with nuts of some kind. This is a light cake filled with a hazelnut butter cream.

23 cm (9 inch) Genoese cake (see page 124)

FOR THE FILLING AND DECORATION

250 g (9 oz) hazelnuts
4 egg whites
225 g (8 oz) icing sugar, sifted
225 g (8 oz) unsalted butter
5 ml (1 tsp) vanilla essence

1. Put the hazelnuts on to a baking sheet. Bake in the oven at 180°C (350°F) mark 4 for 10–15 minutes until their skins become loose. Put the nuts in a clean tea towel and rub until the skins are removed. Put the skinned nuts on a baking sheet and return to the oven for 5–10 minutes until lightly browned. Remove from the oven and leave to cool. Put about 24 nuts aside for decoration, then chop the remainder finely.

2. To make the filling, put the egg whites and icing sugar in a large bowl standing over a pan of hot water. Whisk until they form a stiff shiny meringue—do not allow the meringue to become too hot. Remove from the heat and continue whisking until the meringue is cooled, and forms stiff peaks.

3. Beat the butter until very pale and fluffy, then beat in the vanilla essence. Gradually beat the meringue into the butter. Divide the butter cream in two and mix half the chopped nuts into one half.

4. Cut the cake into three even layers. Sandwich the sponge layers together with the hazelnut butter cream. Spread plain butter cream over the top and around the sides of the cake. Coat the sides with the remaining chopped hazelnuts. Place the gâteau on a plate.

5. Put the remaining butter cream into a piping bag fitted with a small star nozzle. Pipe a decorative edge around the top of the gâteau, then decorate with the reserved whole hazelnuts. Keep in a cool place until ready to serve.

To freeze: open freeze until firm, then pack and freeze. Thaw at cool room temperature.

TORTA DI MELE

SERVES 6

This recipe for a Genoese sponge, which is heavy with sweet dessert apples, is made in the classic way. If you are in a hurry, you can cut corners with this particular recipe, because the weight of the apples tends to disguise the texture of the cake! Simply beat the eggs and sugar together with a wooden spoon, then fold in the flour mixture, followed by the melted butter, milk, lemon rind and apples.

5–10 ml (1–2 tsp) oil
15–30 ml (1–2 tbsp) dried breadcrumbs
FOR THE CAKE
100 g (4 oz) butter, melted and cooled
4 eggs
150 g (5 oz) caster sugar
150 g (5 oz) plain flour, sifted with 5 ml (1 tsp) baking powder and pinch of salt
finely grated rind of 1 lemon
700 g (1½ lb) Golden Delicious apples, peeled, cored and thinly sliced
icing sugar, for dusting

1. Brush the inside of a 23 cm (9 inch) loose-based cake tin with oil. Sprinkle with breadcrumbs, then shake off the excess.
2. To make the cake (see page 124), adding the lemon rind and apples last. Pour the mixture into the tin.
3. Bake in the oven at 180°C (350°F) mark 4 for about 40 minutes until a skewer inserted into the centre comes out clean.
4. Leave the cake to rest in the tin for about 5 minutes, then turn out on to a wire rack and leave to cool completely for 2–3 hours. Dust icing sugar over the top of the cake just before serving.

To freeze: wrap and freeze the cake. Thaw overnight at cool room temperature.

BRANDY PRALINE RING

SERVES 8

Adding the brandy and coffee mixture to the warm cake ensures that it is absorbed.

50 g (2 oz) whole unblanched almonds
225 g (8 oz) caster sugar
4 eggs
100 g (4 oz) plain flour
60 ml (4 tbsp) strong black coffee
75 ml (5 tbsp) brandy
300 ml (½ pint) whipping cream

1. Grease a 1.6–1.7 litre (2¾–3 pint) ring mould. Oil a baking sheet.

2. Make the praline using the almonds and 50 g (2 oz) of the sugar (see page 133). Roughly crush half the praline and reserve. Finely crush the remainder.
3. Place the eggs and 100 g (4 oz) of the sugar in a bowl. Using an electric whisk, whisk until very thick and pale in colour—the mixture should leave a trail when the beaters are lifted from the bowl.
4. Using a metal spoon, carefully fold in the flour, finely crushed praline and 15 ml (1 tbsp) of the coffee. Gently pour the mixture into the prepared mould.
5. Bake in the oven at 190°C (375°F) mark 5 for about 30–40 minutes until well risen and just firm to the touch.
6. Meanwhile prepare the brandy syrup. Pour 350 ml (12 fl oz) water into a saucepan, add the remaining sugar and heat gently until the sugar dissolves. Bring to the boil then boil for 1 minute. Cool slightly and add 60 ml (4 tbsp) of the brandy with the remaining coffee.
7. Remove the cake from the oven and prick the surface with a fine skewer. Spoon over half the syrup and leave to soak for about 20 minutes. Invert the ring on to a plate and spoon over the remaining syrup. Cool.
8. Lightly whip the cream, stir in the remaining brandy and spoon into the centre of the ring. Decorate the cake as liked with the roughly crushed praline.

To freeze: wrap and freeze at the end of step 7. Thaw overnight, wrapped, at cool room temperature, then finish as above.

COFFEE PRALINE GÂTEAU

SERVES 6

Praline can be made in large quantities and stored in an airtight container for decorating cakes or flavouring mousses and ice creams.

FOR THE SPONGE
2 eggs
75 g (3 oz) caster sugar
50 g (2 oz) plain flour
15 ml (1 tbsp) coffee flavouring
FOR THE PRALINE
25 g (1 oz) caster sugar
25 g (1 oz) blanched almonds
FOR THE FILLING
150 ml (¼ pint) double cream
30 ml (2 tbsp) coffee-flavoured liqueur
icing sugar, for dusting

1. Grease a 20.5 cm (8 inch) round cake tin, line the base with greaseproof paper and grease the paper. Dust with caster sugar and flour.
2. To make the sponge, put the eggs and sugar in a large heatproof bowl standing over a pan of hot water. Whisk until pale and creamy and thick enough to leave a trail on the surface when the whisk is lifted. Remove from the heat and whisk until cool.

3. Sift the flour evenly over the surface of the mixture and fold in lightly, using a large metal spoon. Lightly fold in the coffee flavouring. Turn the mixture into the prepared tin.

4. Bake in the oven at 180°C (350°F) mark 4 for about 30 minutes or until the sponge springs back when pressed lightly with a finger and has shrunk away a little from the sides of the tin. Turn out on to a wire rack and leave to cool.

5. Meanwhile to make the praline, oil a baking sheet. Put the caster sugar and almonds into a small frying pan and heat gently, shaking the pan occasionally, until the sugar dissolves and caramelizes to a rich brown colour.

6. Pour the mixture on to the baking sheet and leave for 10–15 minutes to cool and harden. When cold, grind or crush with the end of a rolling pin in a strong bowl.

7. To make the filling, whip the cream until it holds its shape, then whisk in the liqueur and fold in three-quarters of the praline.

8. Cut the sponge into two layers and sandwich with the cream. Dust the top with icing sugar and decorate with the remaining praline. Chill for 1–2 hours.

To freeze: wrap and freeze the sponge at the end of step 4. Thaw overnight at cool room temperature, then finish as above.

Passion Fruit Gâteau

SERVES 8–10

This layered cake, with its exotic passion fruit filling, is ideal for a summer wedding buffet. (Make two cakes for about 20 guests.) If liked, make the cakes well in advance and freeze them. On the day, fill, ice and decorate.

FOR THE CAKE
4 eggs, separated
100 g (4 oz) caster sugar
100 g (4 oz) self raising flour
pinch of salt
25 g (1 oz) unsalted butter, melted

FOR THE PASSION FRUIT CREAM
350 g (12 oz) fromage blanc
75 ml (5 tbsp) thick natural yogurt
few drops of orange flower water
25 ml (1½ tbsp) icing sugar
5 ripe passion fruit, halved

FOR THE DECORATION
150 ml (¼ pint) double cream, lightly whipped
75–100 g (3–4 oz) pistachio nuts, chopped
shelled pistachio nuts

1. Grease a 23 cm (9 inch) loose-based cake tin and line the base with greaseproof paper.

2. To make the cake, whisk the egg yolks and sugar together in a bowl until thick and pale. Sift the flour and salt over and fold in lightly.

3. Whisk the egg whites until stiff but not dry, then lightly fold into the yolk mixture. Trickle the butter over and carefully fold in. Turn the mixture into the prepared tin.

4. Bake in the oven at 180°C (350°F) mark 4 for 25–35 minutes until risen and springy to the touch when lightly pressed in the centre. Leave to cool slightly in the tin, then turn out on to a wire rack covered with a tea towel. Remove the lining paper and leave to cool completely.

5. To make the passion fruit cream, mix the fromage blanc, yogurt, orange flower water and icing sugar together in a bowl. Stir in the passion fruit flesh.

6. Cut the cake into three equal layers. Spread about one-third of the passion fruit cream over the bottom layer. Place the second layer gently on top and cover with another third of the passion fruit cream, not taking it right to the edge. Spread the remaining passion fruit cream over the top cake layer, not taking it right to the edge, and gently place this on top of the cake.

7. For the decoration, reserving a little of the whipped cream for piping around the top of the cake, spread the remainder over the sides of the cake. Coat the sides with the chopped pistachio nuts.

8. Spoon the reserved cream into a piping bag fitted with a small star nozzle and pipe a border around the top edge of the cake. Decorate with the pistachio nuts.

To freeze: open freeze the completed gâteau until firm then overwrap. Thaw overnight in the refrigerator.

STRAWBERRY ROSE RING

SERVES 6–8

1 quantity Genoese cake, made in a 25.5 cm (10 inch) ring mould (see page 124)

FOR THE SYRUP

100 g (4 oz) granulated sugar

45 ml (3 tbsp) rose water

60 ml (4 tbsp) kirsch or orange-flavoured liqueur

FOR THE FILLING

450 g (1 lb) strawberries

30 ml (2 tbsp) rose water

30 ml (2 tbsp) icing sugar

50 g (2 oz) pistachios, chopped

FOR THE DECORATION

300 ml (½ pint) double cream

orange shreds

1. To make the syrup, put the sugar in a pan with 150 ml (¼ pint) water and heat gently, stirring occasionally until the sugar has dissolved. Bring to the boil and boil rapidly for 1 minute until slightly thickened. Cool completely, then stir in the rose water and liqueur.
2. Put the cake back into the washed mould and spoon over the syrup until it is all absorbed. Leave for 1–2 hours for the syrup to sink through.
3. To make the filling, hull the strawberries, keeping some unhulled ones for the decoration. Halve or quarter the remaining strawberries and toss them with the rose water and icing sugar.
4. Turn the cake out on to a serving plate and fill the centre with the strawberries. Whip the cream until just holding its shape and fill a piping bag fitted with a star nozzle. Pipe a decorative border around the ring. Scatter the pistachios over the strawberries. Scatter the orange shreds over the cake and decorate with the remaining whole strawberries and strawberry leaves, if liked.

To freeze: wrap and freeze the cake at the end of step 2. Thaw at cool room temperature, then finish as above.

MARZIPAN SURPRISE GÂTEAU

SERVES 6

Make the decoration for this gâteau as simple or elaborate as you like.

33 × 23 cm (13 × 9 inch) Swiss roll, filled with raspberry jam (see page 125)

FOR THE FILLING

350 g (12 oz) fresh or frozen raspberries, thawed

little icing sugar

30 ml (2 tbsp) kirsch (optional)

FOR THE DECORATION

350 g (12 oz) white marzipan

pink food colouring

60 ml (4 tbsp) warmed raspberry jam, sieved

150 ml (¼ pint) whipping cream

fresh flowers

1. Line a 1.1 litre (2 pint) pudding basin with clingfilm. Slice the Swiss roll and use to line the bottom and sides of the basin, reserving a few slices to cover the top.
2. To make the filling, mix the raspberries with icing sugar to taste and the kirsch, if using. Spoon into the centre of the sponge. Press down well and cover with the remaining slices of Swiss roll. Place the saucer on top and lightly weigh down. Chill in the refrigerator overnight.
3. Turn out the cake on to a board and remove the clingfilm. Colour the marzipan with a few drops of pink food colouring and roll out to a round just large enough to cover the cake. Paint the cake with the warmed jam and carefully drape over the marzipan, moulding it to fit the shape. Trim away any excess marzipan.
4. Stand the cake on a cake stand. Whip the cream until it just holds its shape and spoon into a piping bag fitted with a large star nozzle. Pipe around the base of the cake. Decorate with flowers.

Not suitable for freezing.

Opposite: MARZIPAN SURPRISE GÂTEAU.

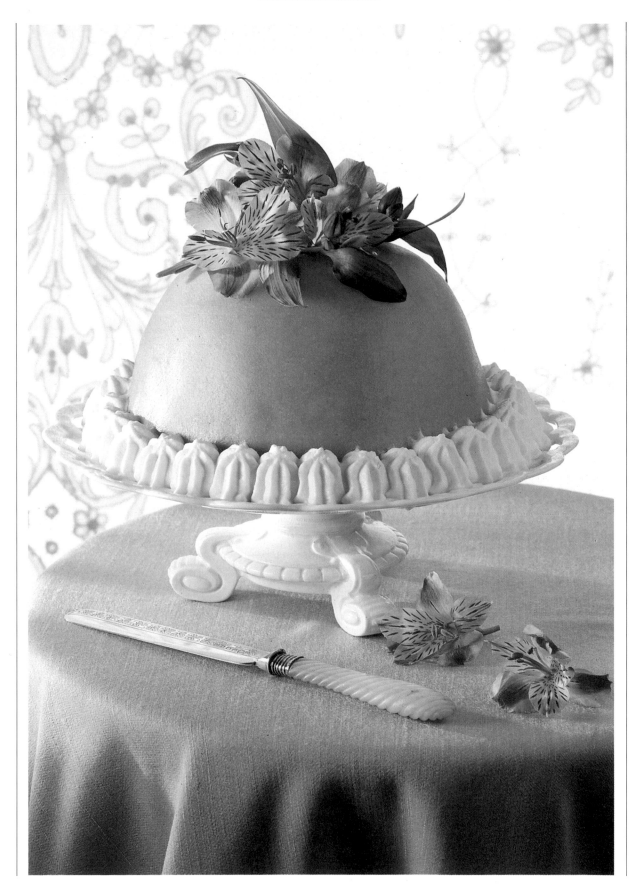

PRUNE AND WALNUT GÂTEAU WITH BRANDY BUTTER

SERVES 8

Prunes and nuts keep this gâteau moist.

FOR THE CAKES

175 g (6 oz) butter or margarine, softened
75 g (3 oz) self raising wholemeal flour
75 g (3 oz) self raising flour
175 g (6 oz) caster sugar
2 eggs
5 ml (1 tsp) ground mixed spice
30 ml (2 tbsp) milk
175 g (6 oz) stoned no-soak dried prunes, roughly chopped
75 g (3 oz) walnut halves, chopped

FOR THE FILLING AND DECORATION

100 g (4 oz) butter, softened
100 g (4 oz) icing sugar, sifted
30 ml (2 tbsp) brandy
icing sugar, for dusting

1. Grease three 18 cm (7 inch) sandwich tins and line the bases with greaseproof paper.
2. To make the cakes, put the butter, flours, sugar, eggs, mixed spice and milk in a blender or food processor and process until smooth. Stir in the prunes and nuts. Pour the mixture into the prepared tins.
3. Bake in the oven at 180°C (350°F) mark 4 for 30−35 minutes or until risen and firm to the touch. Turn out on to a wire rack and leave to cool.
4. To make the filling, cream the butter until very pale and soft, then beat in the icing sugar. Add the brandy, a little at a time, taking care not to allow it to curdle.
5. When the cakes are cool, sandwich them together with the brandy filling. Dust the cake with icing sugar to decorate.

To freeze: wrap and freeze before decorating with icing sugar. Thaw overnight, wrapped, at cool room temperature.

PARSNIP, APRICOT AND NUT GÂTEAU

SERVES 8

No one will guess that this gâteau contains parsnips. It is delicious and moist, and has the added bonus of being packed with fibre.

FOR THE CAKE

225 g (8 oz) light brown soft sugar
275 g (10 oz) self raising flour
5 ml (1 tsp) ground mixed spice
large pinch of salt
150 ml (¼ pint) walnut oil
50 g (2 oz) butter, melted and cooled
2 eggs
225 g (8 oz) parsnips, peeled and finely grated
100 g (4 oz) walnuts, finely chopped

FOR THE FILLING AND DECORATION

225 g (8 oz) no-soak dried apricots
150 ml (¼ pint) orange juice
200 g (7 oz) low fat soft cheese
15 ml (1 tbsp) clear honey
icing sugar, to decorate

1. Grease and line three 20.5 cm (8 inch) sandwich tins.
2. To make the cake, put all the ingredients except the parsnips and walnuts in a blender or food processor and process until smooth. Add the parsnips and walnuts. Divide the mixture evenly between the prepared tins.
3. Bake in the oven at 180°C (350°F) mark 4 for 30−40 minutes or until risen and firm to the touch. Swap the positions of the tins halfway through cooking so that they cook evenly. Turn out on to a wire rack and leave to cool.
4. Meanwhile to make the filling, put the apricots and orange juice in a saucepan. Cover and simmer until the apricots are tender. (Alternatively, put the apricots and orange juice in a bowl, cover and microwave on HIGH for 6−8 minutes or until tender.) Cool, then purée until smooth.
5. When the cakes are cold, spread two of them with the apricot purée. Beat the cheese with the honey and spread carefully on top of the apricot purée. Sandwich the cakes together, putting the unfilled one on top.
6. To decorate the cake, cut some 2.5 cm (1 inch) wide strips of greaseproof paper and lay across the top of the cake. Sift icing sugar over the top of the cake to cover completely. Carefully remove the paper to reveal a striped pattern.

Not suitable for freezing.

Opposite: ORANGE CHARLOTTE GÂTEAU.

ORANGE CHARLOTTE GÂTEAU

SERVES 6

A really special gâteau, a little bit like a trifle!

20–24 sponge fingers or boudoir biscuits

FOR THE FILLING

18 cm (7 inch) Whisked sponge (see page 125)

120 ml (8 tbsp) orange-flavoured liqueur

1 orange

150 ml (¼ pint) double or whipping cream

15 ml (1 tbsp) icing sugar

FOR THE DECORATION

150 ml (¼ pint) double or whipping cream

kumquats or orange shreds

orange segments

1. Line a 20.5 cm (8 inch) charlotte mould with non-stick baking paper. Line the base and sides of the mould with the sponge fingers.

2. Cut the whisked sponge into 1 cm (½ inch) cubes. Press one third of the sponge cubes into the base of the mould and sprinkle with one third of the liqueur.

3. Finely grate the rind of the orange and place in a bowl with the cream and icing sugar. Whip until very stiff.

4. Remove the pith from the orange like peeling an apple. Cut the orange into segments. Chop the segments roughly and fold into the cream. Spread half the cream over the soaked sponge.

5. Cover the cream with the second third of the sponge and sprinkle with half the remaining liqueur. Press down gently. Cover with the remaining cream and top with the remaining sponge. Sprinkle with the remaining liqueur and press down gently. Cover and chill for 2–3 hours.

6. To serve, turn out on to a serving plate, remove the paper and decorate with whipped cream, kumquats or orange shreds and segments.

Not suitable for freezing.

PEAR AND HAZELNUT GÂTEAU WITH CARAMEL LATTICE

SERVES 6

Do not add the caramel lattice more than 1 hour in advance of serving or it will start to dissolve.

23 cm (9 inch) Genoese cake (see page 124), made with 100 g (4 oz) toasted ground hazelnuts folded in with the flour

FOR THE FILLING

2 ripe pears, peeled, cored and chopped

little lemon juice

150 ml (¼ pint) double cream

150 ml (¼ pint) soured cream

pinch of grated nutmeg

FOR THE TOPPING

3 ripe pears, peeled, quartered and thinly sliced

little lemon juice

50 g (2 oz) skinned hazelnuts, toasted and roughly chopped

100 g (4 oz) granulated sugar

1. Cut the cake into two layers with a serrated knife. To make the filling, toss the pears in a little lemon juice to prevent discolouration. Pour the double cream, soured cream and nutmeg into a bowl. Whip until just holding its shape, then fold in the pears. Use to fill the cake.
2. To make the topping, toss the sliced pears in a little lemon juice and arrange in a wheel-like pattern on top of the cake. Scatter the hazelnuts over the pears.
3. Put the sugar in a small, heavy-based saucepan with 30 ml (2 tbsp) water. Dissolve the sugar over a gentle heat without boiling. When dissolved, bring to the boil and boil rapidly until the sugar turns amber. Working quickly, remove from the heat and dip the base of the pan in a bowl of cool water to prevent further cooking.
4. Once the bubbles have subsided, quickly pour the caramel in a thin steady stream over the top of the cake to form a zig-zag lattice pattern. Leave to set for 5 minutes, then serve.

To freeze: freeze the unfilled cake. Thaw at cool room temperature, then finish as above.

RED FRUIT GÂTEAU

SERVES 8–10

This is the cake to capture the spirit of summer. A melt-in-the-mouth sponge covered with a sauce made from fruits of the forest.

FOR THE CAKE

100 g (4 oz) plain flour

50 g (2 oz) unsalted butter

4 eggs, size 4

100 g (4 oz) caster sugar

few drops of vanilla essence (optional)

FOR THE SAUCE

700 g (1½ lb) mixed red summer fruit, such as raspberries, strawberries, redcurrants, loganberries

sugar, to taste

45 ml (3 tbsp) lemon juice

15 ml (1 tbsp) rose water (optional)

FOR THE DECORATION AND FILLING

1 egg white

450 g (1 lb) mixed red summer fruit

a few pink or red rose petals

caster sugar

300–450 ml (½–¾ pint) double cream

1. Line the base of a 25.5 cm (10 inch) spring-release cake tin with non-stick baking paper. Grease the tin and the paper. When set, dust out the tin with flour.
2. To make the cake (see page 124), adding the vanilla essence. Pour the mixture into the prepared tin.
3. Bake in the oven at 180°C (350°F) mark 4 for 35–40 minutes. When cooked, the cake will look evenly brown, will spring back when lightly pressed, and will have shrunk slightly from the sides of the tin. Cool for 5 minutes, then turn out on to a wire rack and cool.
4. To make the sauce, put all the ingredients into a pan and heat gently until the juice starts to run from the fruit and the sugar melts. Add a little water and press through a nylon sieve, or purée then sieve. Chill.
5. Prepare the frosted fruit for the decoration. Lightly beat the egg white. Brush a few berries or fruit and rose petals with a thin coating of egg white. Sprinkle with caster sugar and lay on non-stick paper to dry. Pick over the remaining fruit.
6. Whip the cream until it just holds its shape. Chill until ready to use.
7. To assemble the cake, using a long serrated knife, carefully cut the cake into two layers. Sandwich together with some of the fruit sauce and the prepared fruit. Spread the cream evenly over the top and sides of the cake. Decorate with the frosted fruit and petals. Serve the remaining fruit sauce separately in a jug.

To freeze: wrap and freeze the sponge at the end of step 3. Thaw at cool room temperature, then finish as above.

Illustrated on pages 122–123

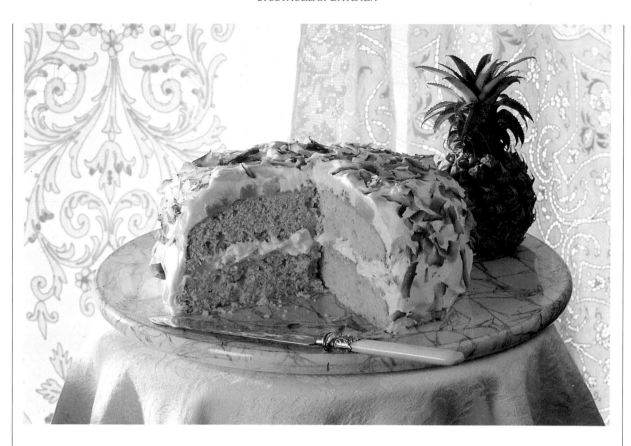

COCONUT MALIBU GÂTEAU

SERVES 20

A rich, coconut-flavoured gâteau, layered with pineapple and generously flavoured with Malibu, a coconut and rum liqueur.

FOR THE CAKES

225 g (8 oz) butter or margarine
225 g (8 oz) caster sugar
3 eggs, separated
450 g (1 lb) self raising flour
pinch of salt
5 ml (1 tsp) baking powder
200 ml (7 fl oz) coconut milk
100 g (4 oz) desiccated coconut

FOR THE FILLING AND DECORATION

90–120 ml (6–8 tbsp) Malibu
350 g (12 oz) fresh or canned pineapple
600 ml (1 pint) whipping cream
50 g (2 oz) shredded or flaked coconut, toasted

1. Grease and line two 23 cm (9 inch) round cake tins.
2. To make the cakes, cream the butter and sugar together in a bowl until pale and fluffy. Gradually beat in the egg yolks. Sift the flour, salt and baking powder together.
3. Add half of the coconut milk with half of the dry ingredients to the creamed mixture. Fold in the coconut, then add the remaining coconut milk and dry ingredients. Whisk the egg whites until stiff, then fold lightly into the mixture. Pour the mixture into the prepared tins.
4. Bake in the oven at 180°C (350°F) mark 4 for 40–45 minutes or until risen and firm to the touch. Turn out on to a wire rack and leave to cool.
5. When cold, prick the cakes with a fine skewer and sprinkle with 60 ml (4 tbsp) of the Malibu. Leave for at least 30 minutes.
6. To make the filling, cut the pineapple into small pieces. Whip the cream with the remaining Malibu to taste until it forms soft peaks. Spread a little cream over each cake. Sprinkle one cake with two thirds of the pineapple, place the other cake, cream side down, on top of the first cake. Press together with the flat of your hand.
7. Sprinkle the remaining pineapple pieces over the top of the cake. Spread the remaining cream all over the top and sides of the cake and sprinkle with the coconut. Chill until ready to serve.

To freeze: wrap and freeze the cake at the end of step 4. Thaw, wrapped, at cool room temperature, then finish as above.

Above: COCONUT MALIBU GÂTEAU.

CHOCOLATE-WRAPPED ORANGE LIQUEUR GÂTEAU

SERVES 12

The sponge is soaked in a liqueur syrup, and coated in an intriguing chocolate frill that is easy to make but never fails to impress.

FOR THE SPONGE

200 g (7 oz) self raising flour
50 g (2 oz) cornflour
7.5 ml (1½ tsp) baking powder
175 g (6 oz) caster sugar
3 eggs, separated
finely grated rind and juice of 1 small orange
105 ml (7 tbsp) oil
45 ml (3 tbsp) milk

FOR THE LIQUEUR SYRUP

100 g (4 oz) granulated sugar
finely grated rind and juice of 1 orange
45 ml (3 tbsp) orange-flavoured liqueur

FOR THE DECORATION

2 large oranges
300 ml (½ pint) double cream
225 g (8 oz) plain chocolate
cocoa powder, for dusting

1. Grease a deep 22 cm (8½ inch) spring-release cake tin and line the base with greaseproof paper.
2. To make the sponge, mix the flours, baking powder and sugar together in a bowl. Blend the egg yolks with the orange rind and juice, oil and milk, then mix into the dry ingredients. Beat thoroughly with a wooden spoon to make a smooth batter. Whisk the egg whites until stiff, then fold into the mixture. Pour into the tin.
3. Bake in the oven at 180°C (350°F) mark 4 for about 55 minutes or until well risen and firm to the touch.
4. Meanwhile to make the syrup, put the sugar, orange rind and juice and 60 ml (4 tbsp) water in a heavy-based saucepan and heat gently until the sugar has dissolved. Bring to the boil and boil rapidly for 2 minutes. Stir in the liqueur.
5. Prick the hot cake all over with a fork, then spoon over the hot syrup. Leave to cool.
6. To make the decoration, peel the oranges, discarding all of the white pith. Roughly chop the flesh. Whip the cream until it forms soft peaks.
7. Remove the cooled cake from the tin and place on a serving plate. Arrange the chopped orange on top. Spread the cream all over the top and sides.
8. Break the chocolate into small pieces. Place in a bowl standing over a saucepan of simmering water and heat until the chocolate melts. (Alternatively, microwave on LOW for 4–5 minutes, stirring occasionally.

9. Meanwhile, cut a strip of greaseproof paper long enough to go round the sides of the cake and wide enough to come 4 cm (1½ inches) above the cake. When the chocolate is melted, spread it evenly all over the paper with a palette knife. Leave to cool until no longer runny but still sticky when pressed with a finger.
10. Wrap the chocolate around the gâteau, pressing it gently on to the cream so that it sticks. Carefully pinch the chocolate and paper into pleats where it extends above the cake. Leave until set then carefully peel away the paper. Dust the top with a little cocoa powder.

To freeze: wrap and freeze at the end of step 5. Thaw overnight at cool room temperature, then finish as above.

SEMOLINA CAKE

SERVES 12

This cake is popular throughout Greece and Turkey.

FOR THE CAKE

225 g (8 oz) caster sugar
6 eggs
250 g (9 oz) fine semolina
finely grated rind of 1 lemon
75 g (3 oz) ground rice
7.5 ml (1½ tsp) baking powder
large pinch of salt
60 ml (4 tbsp) lemon juice
50 g (2 oz) blanched almonds

FOR THE SYRUP

10 green cardamom pods, crushed
2 bay leaves
1 cinnamon stick
1 strip of lemon rind
450 g (1 lb) caster sugar

1. Grease a 23 cm (9 inch) square cake tin.
2. To make the cake, put all the ingredients, except the almonds, in a bowl and whisk together with a hand held whisk until well mixed. Pour into the tin.
3. Bake in the oven at 180°C (350°F) mark 4 for 1–1¼ hours or until firm to the touch and golden brown. Arrange the almonds in a pattern on top of the cake halfway through the cooking time.
4. Meanwhile to make the syrup, put all the ingredients in a saucepan with 300 ml (½ pint) water. Heat gently until the sugar has dissolved, stirring all the time. Bring to the boil, then simmer for 10 minutes. Strain and cool.
5. When the cake is cooked, spoon over the syrup. Leave to cool in the tin. Turn out on to a work surface, then invert on to a serving plate. Serve, cut into squares or diamonds, with Greek yogurt.

To freeze: wrap and freeze the cooled, syrup soaked cake. Thaw overnight at cool room temperature.

Opposite: CHOCOLATE-WRAPPED ORANGE LIQUEUR GÂTEAU.

Fruit Salad Gâteau

SERVES 14

A hollowed-out cake filled with fruit and passion
fruit cream.

---

23 cm (9 inch) Genoese cake (see page 124)

FOR THE FILLING

1 small ripe mango

6 fresh lychees

225 g (8 oz) strawberries

few blueberries

finely grated rind of 1 lime

150 ml ($\frac{1}{4}$ pint) double cream

75 ml (5 tbsp) Greek yogurt

2 passion fruit

FOR THE DECORATION

150 ml ($\frac{1}{4}$ pint) double cream

100 g (4 oz) chopped mixed nuts

2 small ripe star fruit, sliced

few cape gooseberries

juice of 1 lime

15 ml (1 tbsp) caster sugar

10 ml (2 tsp) arrowroot

---

1. Using a serrated knife, make a cut around the cake
that is about 2.5 cm (1 inch) in from the edge and about
4 cm (1$\frac{1}{2}$ inches) deep.

2. Holding the knife almost horizontally and following
the first cut, cut through to the centre to remove a thin
layer of sponge. This will be the lid.

3. Scoop out the sponge in the centre of the cake, being
careful not to cut through to the bottom. Save the
scooped out sponge crumbs for making Truffles or
Chocolate filo pie (see page 94).

4. To make the filling, slice the mango each side of the
stone. Peel, then cut the flesh into small chunks. Peel the
lychees and stone. Hull the strawberries and halve. Mix
all the fruits with the blueberries and the lime rind.

5. Whip the cream until it holds its shape and mix with
the yogurt. Halve the passion fruit, scoop out the pulp
and mix with the cream and yogurt.

6. Spoon the passion fruit cream into the sponge case.
Top with the fruit salad. Replace the lid of the sponge
and push down firmly.

7. Whip the cream for the decoration until it just holds
its shape. Spread thinly over the top and around the
sides of the cake. Using a palette knife, press the nuts on

to the sides of the cake. Arrange the fruit on the top of
the cake.

8. Put the lime juice and caster sugar in a small saucepan and heat gently until the sugar dissolves. Blend the
arrowroot to a smooth paste with 90 ml (6 tbsp) cold
water.

9. When the sugar has dissolved, add the arrowroot
mixture to the saucepan. Bring to the boil, stirring all the
time. The mixture should be thick enough to coat the
back of a spoon. Cool slightly, stirring all the time, then
spoon the glaze over the fruit. Leave until set.

*To freeze: wrap and freeze at the end of step 3. Thaw
overnight at cool room temperature, then finish as above.*

Cherry and Kirsch Gâteau

SERVES 10

A dessert to make the most of ripe summer cherries.

---

two 20.5 cm (8 inch) Whisked sponges (see page 125)

FOR THE FILLING

900 g (2$\frac{1}{4}$ lb) cherries

30 ml (2 tbsp) sugar

30 ml (2 tbsp) kirsch

300 ml ($\frac{1}{2}$ pint) double cream

150 ml ($\frac{1}{4}$ pint) Greek yogurt

---

1. Reserve about 450 g (1 lb) of the best cherries for the
decoration. To make the filling, stone the remaining
cherries and put them in a saucepan with the sugar and
90 ml (6 tbsp) water. Cover and simmer gently until
tender, stirring occasionally. Drain, reserving the juice.
Cool, then purée the cherries in a blender or food
processor with the kirsch. Stir half the purée into the
reserved juice to make a sauce.

2. Whip the cream until stiff, then fold in the yogurt.
Spread one of the sponges with the cherry purée,
allowing it to run down the sides a little. Spread with
half of the cream. Place the second sponge on top.

3. For the decoration, spread the remaining cream on
top of the cake. Stone most of the reserved cherries,
leaving some whole with the stalks attached. Decorate
the top with the cherries. Serve with the cherry sauce
handed separately.

*To freeze: wrap and freeze the cooked sponges. Freeze the
cherry purée and sauce in rigid containers. Thaw overnight at
cool room temperature, then finish as above.*

Opposite: Fruit Salad Gâteau.

THE CHEESECAKE COLLECTION

Creamily rich, velvety smooth, these cheesecake recipes
will set your tastebuds tingling. From the traditional
European baked cheesecake to the sumptuous and
squidgy Marbled chocolate fudge cheesecake. Bake one
soon and treat yourself to a new taste experience.

Cheesecakes are always made from unripened cheeses. These may be full fat soft cheese, curd cheese or cottage cheese. Full fat soft cheese is creamy rich made from full milk, enriched with double cream to give a high fat content. This gives cheesecakes a superbly smooth texture. Low fat soft cheese is a low fat alternative, useful if you are counting calories, but will not give such a rich texture and flavour. Curd cheese is made from full milk and has the most pronounced (cheesy) flavour. Its texture is slightly grainy. Cottage cheese is lighter than either, made from skimmed milk. The texture of cottage cheese is lumpy and the flavour mild. There is often a good deal of whey left in the cheese, making it rather moist. Push it through a fine sieve and drain off any excess whey before adding to the mixture.

Bake cheesecakes in spring-release cake tins to make turning out easy. If you do not own a spring-release tin, a cake tin with a loose base works almost as well. Baked cheesecakes should be cooked on a low temperature to make sure that the eggs do not curdle.

When making chilled cheesecakes, set with gelatine. All the rules for using gelatine apply (see page 188). Once the cheesecake has set, remove it from the tin to prevent any reaction between the metal tin and the acid in the cheesecake causing discolouration.

Store leftover cheesecake, closely wrapped, in the refrigerator and serve within a day or two. Some cheesecakes freeze well (see the recipes). Freeze in the tin until solid, then turn out and wrap in freezer film or foil. Thaw slowly, overnight in the refrigerator.

TRADITIONAL BAKED CHEESECAKE

SERVES 8

Lemon and sultanas are the traditional flavourings for a European baked cheesecake.

FOR THE BASE

50 g (2 oz) self raising flour
2.5 ml (½ tsp) baking powder
50 g (2 oz) butter, softened
50 g (2 oz) caster sugar
1 egg

FOR THE FILLING

4 eggs, separated
225 g (8 oz) caster sugar
450 g (1 lb) full fat soft cheese
40 g (1½ oz) plain flour
grated rind and juice of 1 lemon
300 ml (½ pint) soured cream
75 g (3 oz) sultanas
pinch of grated nutmeg, for sprinkling

1. Grease a 20.5 cm (8 inch) round spring-release cake tin and line the base with greaseproof paper, then grease the paper.
2. To make the base, sift the self raising flour and baking powder into a bowl. Add the butter, sugar and egg. Mix well and beat for 2–3 minutes. Spread the mixture evenly over the bottom of the prepared tin.
3. To make the filling, whisk the egg yolks with the sugar until the mixture is thick and creamy.
4. Beat the soft cheese lightly in a bowl. Add the whisked egg mixture and mix until smooth. Sift in the plain flour and stir in. Add the lemon rind and juice, 150 ml (¼ pint) of the soured cream and the sultanas.
5. Whisk the egg whites until stiff, then fold into the mixture. Pour on to the mixture in the tin.
6. Bake in the oven at 170°C (325°F) mark 3 for 1 hour or until firm but still spongy to the touch. Turn off the heat and leave in the oven for 1 hour with the door ajar.
7. Remove from the oven and cool completely for 2–3 hours. Carefully remove the cheesecake from the tin. To serve, spread the remaining soured cream over the top and sprinkle with grated nutmeg.

To freeze: pack and freeze the cold cheesecake before covering with cream. Thaw in the refrigerator overnight, then finish as above.

Previous page: BAKED BLENDER CHEESECAKE WITH RED FRUIT SAUCE (PAGE 158). Above: TRADITIONAL BAKED CHEESECAKE. Below: CALCIONI ALL'ASCOLANA (PAGE 148).

RICOTTA CHEESECAKE

SERVES 8

This classic Italian cheesecake does not have a base and is flavoured with candied peel, rum and almonds.

450 g (1 lb) ricotta cheese
3 eggs, separated
100 g (4 oz) caster sugar
50 ml (2 fl oz) rum or brandy
50 g (2 oz) ground almonds
50 g (2 oz) chopped candied peel
finely grated rind of 1 lemon
caster sugar, for dredging

1. Grease and flour a 20.5 cm (8 inch) spring-release cake tin and line the base with greaseproof paper.
2. Beat the ricotta cheese with the egg yolks and 50 g (2 oz) of the sugar in a bowl. Fold in the rum, almonds, peel and lemon rind.
3. Whisk the egg whites with the remaining sugar until stiff. Fold into the cheese mixture. Spoon into the prepared tin.
4. Bake in the oven at 180°C (350°F) mark 4 for 45 minutes or until firm to the touch and slightly shrunk away from the sides of the tin.
5. Turn the oven off. Leave the cheesecake to cool in the oven, with the door ajar.
6. To serve, carefully remove the cheesecake from the tin and dredge with caster sugar.

Not suitable for freezing.

CALCIONI ALL'ASCOLANA

SERVES 16

Individual cheesecake turnovers filled with a delicious ricotta and candied peel mixture.

FOR THE PASTRY
225 g (8 oz) plain flour
pinch of salt
2 eggs, beaten
30 ml (2 tbsp) olive oil
FOR THE FILLING
225 g (8 oz) ricotta cheese
50 g (2 oz) ground almonds
25 g (1 oz) caster sugar
1 egg yolk
finely grated rind of 1 lemon
50 g (2 oz) candied peel, finely chopped
beaten egg, to glaze
icing sugar, for dusting

Above: RICOTTA CHEESECAKE. *Below:* CENCI (PAGE 68).

1. To make the pastry, put the flour and salt in a bowl. Make a well in the centre and stir in the eggs and olive oil. Using your fingertips, knead the mixture together to make a smooth dough.
2. Turn out on to a floured work surface and knead for about 5 minutes. Wrap and chill for 30 minutes.
3. To make the filling, mix the ingredients together.
4. Roll out the pastry on a lightly floured work surface until it is very thin. Cut out 10 cm (4 inch) rounds, using a plain cutter. Re-roll the pastry trimmings and use to make more rounds, making 16 rounds in total.
5. Divide the filling between the pastry rounds. Brush the edges with the beaten egg, then fold each round in half to enclose the filling. Brush with beaten egg to glaze. Transfer to baking sheets.
6. Bake in the oven at 190°C (375°F) mark 5 for 25–30 minutes or until golden brown. Serve cold, dusted with icing sugar.

To freeze: wrap and freeze the cold cheesecakes. Thaw overnight at cool room temperature.

Illustrated on page 147

BAKED BANANA CHEESECAKE

SERVES 8–10

FOR THE BASE
225 g (8 oz) chocolate-covered digestive biscuits, crushed
75 g (3 oz) butter, melted
FOR THE FILLING
50 g (2 oz) butter or margarine
50 g (2 oz) self raising flour
225 g (8 oz) low fat soft cheese
4 firm, ripe bananas, peeled and chopped
100 g (4 oz) caster sugar
4 eggs
100 g (4 oz) plain chocolate drops
FOR THE TOPPING
300 ml (½ pint) soured cream
1 chocolate flake, crumbled

1. Grease a 20.5 cm (8 inch) spring-release cake tin.
2. To make the base, mix the biscuits and butter together. Press into the base of the prepared tin and level the surface. Chill while making the filling.
3. To make the filling, put all the ingredients, except the chocolate drops, in a blender or food processor and purée until smooth and well mixed. Stir in the chocolate drops. Pour the filling over the base and level the surface.
4. Bake in the oven at 180°C (350°F) mark 4 for 1¼ hours or until just set. Leave to cool in the tin.
5. To serve, remove from the tin and spread the cream on top of the cheesecake. Sprinkle with the flake.

Not suitable for freezing.

BAKED LEMON AND BLACKCURRANT CHEESECAKE

SERVES 8

Use frozen blackcurrants straight from the freezer. Stir them quickly and lightly into the cheesecake mixture.

FOR THE BASE

75 g (3 oz) butter or margarine, melted
50 g (2 oz) caster sugar
175 g (6 oz) digestive biscuits, crushed

FOR THE FILLING

225 g (8 oz) low fat soft cheese
grated rind and juice of 1 lemon
3 eggs, separated
100 g (4 oz) caster sugar
25 g (1 oz) plain flour
100 g (4 oz) frozen or fresh blackcurrants
icing sugar, for dusting

1. Grease a loose-based 18–20.5 cm (7–8 inch) round cake tin.
2. To make the base, mix the butter, sugar and biscuits together. Press the mixture evenly over the base of the prepared tin. Chill to firm while preparing the filling.
3. To make the filling, beat the cheese with the grated lemon rind and juice, the egg yolks, 50 g (2 oz) of the sugar and the flour. Whisk the egg whites until stiff but not dry, then whisk in the remaining sugar. Carefully fold into the cheese mixture with the blackcurrants. Spoon on to the biscuit base and level the top.
4. Bake in the oven at 180°C (350°F) mark 4 for about 1¼ hours or until well risen and fairly firm to the touch. Reduce the oven temperature to 170°C (325°F) mark 3 and cook for about another 30 minutes or until quite firm to the touch. Cover loosely with foil during baking to prevent overbrowning. The cheesecake will sink slightly in the centre.
5. Leave the cheesecake to stand for a few minutes then, using a palette knife, ease the sides away from the tin. Carefully push the cake out of its tin base, then slide off the base. Cool, then dust with icing sugar.

To freeze: cool, pack and freeze. Thaw overnight in the refrigerator.

LEMON MUESLI CHEESECAKE

SERVES 6

If you are buying muesli specially to make the base for this cheesecake, select a sugar-free variety or at least one that is low in sugar.

FOR THE BASE

175 g (6 oz) muesli
75 g (3 oz) butter or margarine, melted

FOR THE FILLING

3 lemons
15 ml (1 tbsp) powdered gelatine
225 g (8 oz) low fat soft cheese
150 ml (¼ pint) natural yogurt
60 ml (4 tbsp) clear honey
2 egg whites

1. Grease a 20.5 cm (8 inch) spring-release cake tin.
2. To make the base, mix the muesli and melted butter together. Press the mixture over the base of the prepared tin, using the back of a metal spoon. Chill to set while making the filling.
3. To make the filling, finely grate the rind of 2 of the lemons. Set aside. Squeeze the juice from the 2 lemons and make up to 150 ml (¼ pint) with water.
4. Sprinkle the gelatine over the lemon juice and water in a bowl and leave to soak for 2–3 minutes. Place the bowl over a pan of simmering water and stir until dissolved. (Alternatively, microwave on HIGH for 30 seconds or until dissolved.) Leave to cool slightly.
5. Whisk the cheese, yogurt and honey together in a separate bowl. Stir in the grated lemon rind and dissolved gelatine until evenly incorporated. Whisk the egg whites until standing in stiff peaks. Fold into the cheesecake mixture until evenly incorporated. Spoon the mixture into the prepared tin and level the surface. Chill for at least 4 hours until set.
6. Coarsely grate the rind from the remaining lemon over the centre of the cheesecake, to decorate. Alternatively, slice the lemon thinly and arrange on top of the cheesecake. Remove the cheesecake from the tin and place on a serving plate. Serve chilled.

To freeze: wrap and freeze at the end of step 5. Thaw overnight in the refrigerator, then finish as above.

APPLE AND SULTANA CHEESECAKE

SERVES 8

This is rather like a cheesecake pie.

1 quantity Shortcrust pastry (see page 42)

FOR THE FILLING
100 g (4 oz) dried apple rings
100 g (4 oz) sultanas
grated rind and juice of 1 lemon
30 ml (2 tbsp) rum
25 g (1 oz) butter, softened
100 g (4 oz) low fat soft cheese
25 g (1 oz) self raising flour
caster sugar
100 g (4 oz) cottage cheese, sieved
30 ml (2 tbsp) milk
3 eggs

1. To make the filling, soak the apple rings overnight in cold water. Soak the sultanas overnight with the grated lemon rind, 45 ml (3 tbsp) lemon juice and the rum.
2. Line the base of a 1.4–1.7 litre (2½–3 pint) loaf tin with greaseproof paper.
3. Roll out three quarters of the pastry and use to line the base and sides of the prepared tin.
4. Beat the butter, soft cheese, flour, 25 g (1 oz) caster sugar and the cottage cheese together in a bowl. Whisk the milk, 2 eggs and 1 egg yolk together, then whisk into the cheese mixture.
5. Well drain and chop the apple. Stir the apple and sultanas into the cheese mixture. Spoon into the pastry base.
6. Roll out the remaining pastry and use to cover the filling, sealing the edges well. Beat the remaining egg white and brush over the pastry. Sprinkle with a little caster sugar.
7. Bake in the oven at 190°C (375°F) mark 5 for about 1½ hours. Leave to cool in the tin for 20 minutes before turning out. Cool for a further 1 hour. Serve cut into thick slices.

Not suitable for freezing.

MARBLED CHOCOLATE FUDGE CHEESECAKE

SERVES 16

The cold cheesecake has a much heavier, fudgier texture than when served hot.

FOR THE BASE
225 g (8 oz) chocolate chip cookies
50 g (2 oz) chocolate drops
75 g (3 oz) butter, melted

FOR THE FILLING
100 g (4 oz) plain chocolate
150 g (5 oz) butter or margarine
200 g (7 oz) caster sugar
3 eggs
100 g (4 oz) plain flour
vanilla essence
150 g (5 oz) low fat soft cheese

1. Grease a 20.5 cm (8 inch) loose-based cake tin.
2. To make the base, roughly crush the chocolate chip cookies and mix with the chocolate chips and butter. Spoon into the prepared tin and pack down with the back of a spoon. Chill while making the filling.
3. To make the filling, break the chocolate into small pieces. Place in a large bowl with the butter. Stand the bowl over a pan of simmering water and heat gently until the chocolate melts. (Alternatively, microwave on LOW for 4–5 minutes or until melted, stirring occasionally.)
4. Add half of the sugar, 2 of the eggs, the flour and a few drops of vanilla essence to the chocolate and beat together. Pour the mixture into the prepared tin.
5. Beat the cheese, remaining sugar and egg and a few drops of vanilla essence together. Spoon on top of the chocolate mixture. Pull a knife through the two mixtures to give a marbled effect.
6. Bake in the oven at 180°C (350°F) mark 4 for 1 hour 10–20 minutes or until firm to the touch. Leave to cool in the tin for 5 minutes. Serve hot with Greek yogurt or cold with vanilla ice cream.

To freeze: wrap and freeze after baking. Thaw overnight in the refrigerator.

Rum and Raisin Cheesecake

SERVES 8

A light, fluffy baked cheesecake with a pastry base.

FOR THE PASTRY

225 g (8 oz) self raising flour
5 ml (1 tsp) bicarbonate of soda
5 ml (1 tsp) cream of tartar
75 g (3 oz) butter
finely grated rind of 1 lemon
150 ml (¼ pint) soured cream

FOR THE FILLING

75 g (3 oz) raisins
75 ml (5 tbsp) dark rum
100 g (4 oz) cottage cheese
100 g (4 oz) full fat soft cheese
2 eggs, separated
50 g (2 oz) caster sugar
150 ml (¼ pint) double cream
15 ml (1 tbsp) icing sugar, for dusting

1. Grease a 25.5 cm (10 inch) flan dish.

2. To make the filling, put the raisins and rum in a saucepan and bring to the boil. Remove from the heat and leave to cool for 15 minutes.

3. Meanwhile, to make the pastry, sift the flour, bicarbonate of soda and cream of tartar into a bowl. Rub in the butter until the mixture resembles fine breadcrumbs. Add the lemon rind. Bind to a smooth dough with the soured cream. Roll out and use to line the prepared dish.

4. Beat the cottage and cream cheeses together in a bowl. Stir in the rum and raisins.

5. In a separate bowl, whisk the egg yolks and caster sugar together until pale and fluffy. Whisk in the double cream, and continue whisking until the mixture is the consistency of lightly whipped cream. Fold into the cheese, rum and raisin mixture. Whisk the egg whites until stiff, then fold into the mixture. Pour into the pastry case.

6. Bake in the oven at 180°C (350°F) mark 4 for about 1 hour. Turn off the heat and leave to cool in the oven for 15 minutes. Remove from the oven and cool for a further 45 minutes. Dust with icing sugar.

Not suitable for freezing.

Hot Chocolate Cheesecake

SERVES 10–12

This cheesecake has a rich, irresistible flavour. Unusually for a cheesecake, it is served straight from the oven; however, should there be any left it tastes good cold as well.

FOR THE CHOCOLATE PASTRY

150 g (5 oz) plain flour
75 g (3 oz) butter or margarine
30 ml (2 tbsp) cocoa powder, sifted
30 ml (2 tbsp) caster sugar
25 g (1 oz) ground hazelnuts
1 egg yolk

FOR THE FILLING

2 eggs, separated
75 g (3 oz) caster sugar
350 g (12 oz) curd cheese
40 g (1½ oz) ground hazelnuts
150 ml (¼ pint) double cream
25 g (1 oz) cocoa powder, sifted
10 ml (2 tsp) dark rum
icing sugar, for dusting

1. Grease a 20.5 cm (8 inch) round loose-based cake tin.

2. To make the chocolate pastry, put the flour in a bowl and rub in the butter until the mixture resembles fine breadcrumbs. Stir in the cocoa powder, sugar and hazelnuts. Add the egg yolk and sufficient water to give a soft dough.

3. Roll out the pastry on a lightly floured work surface and use to line the prepared tin. Chill while making the filling.

4. To make the filling, whisk the egg yolks and sugar together in a bowl until thick enough to leave a trail on the surface when the whisk is lifted. Whisk in the cheese, nuts, cream, cocoa powder and rum until blended.

5. Whisk the egg whites until stiff, then fold into the cheese mixture. Pour into the pastry case and fold the edges of the pastry over the filling.

6. Bake in the oven at 170°C (325°F) mark 3 for 1½ hours until risen and just firm to the touch. Remove carefully from the tin and dust icing sugar over the top. Serve while still hot.

Not suitable for freezing.

Opposite: Hot Chocolate Cheesecake.

GINGER AND BANANA CHEESECAKE

SERVES 6–8

The flavour of banana and ginger go very well together, but you can ring the changes by using chocolate digestive biscuits for the base of this cheesecake instead of ginger biscuits, and omitting the preserved ginger from the filling. Decorate the top with banana slices arranged alternately with chocolate buttons.

FOR THE BASE

225 g (8 oz) ginger biscuits, crushed
100 g (4 oz) unsalted butter, melted and cooled

FOR THE FILLING

225 g (8 oz) full fat soft cheese
150 ml (¼ pint) soured cream
3 bananas
30 ml (2 tbsp) clear honey
15 ml (1 tbsp) chopped preserved ginger (with syrup)
15 ml (1 tbsp) powdered gelatine
60 ml (4 tbsp) lemon juice

FOR THE DECORATION

banana slices
preserved ginger slices

1. To make the base, mix the biscuits and melted butter together. Press the mixture over the base of a 20.5 cm (8 inch) spring-release tin or deep cake tin with a removable base. Chill for about 30 minutes.
2. To make the filling, beat the cheese and cream together in a bowl until well mixed. Peel and mash the bananas, then beat into the cheese mixture with the honey and ginger.
3. Sprinkle the gelatine over the lemon juice in a small bowl and leave to soak for 2–3 minutes. Place the bowl over a pan of simmering water and stir until dissolved. (Alternatively, microwave on HIGH for 30 seconds or until dissolved.)
4. Stir the dissolved gelatine slowly into the cheesecake mixture. Spoon on to the biscuit base. Chill for about 3–4 hours until the cheesecake is set.
5. To serve, remove the cheesecake carefully from the tin and place on a serving plate. Decorate around the edge with banana and ginger slices. Serve as soon as possible or the banana will discolour.

To freeze: wrap and freeze at the end of step 4. Thaw overnight in the refrigerator, then finish as above.

RASPBERRY RIPPLE CHEESECAKE

SERVES 12

This cheesecake looks best made in a heart-shaped tin. Or use any other tin with a 2.3 litre (4 pint) capacity.

FOR THE BASE

25 g (1 oz) blanched almonds
225 g (8 oz) almond butter biscuits, crushed
100 g (4 oz) butter or margarine, melted
few drops of almond flavouring

FOR THE FILLING

450 g (1 lb) raspberries
300 ml (½ pint) Greek yogurt
150 g (5 oz) low fat soft cheese
15 ml (1 tbsp) powdered gelatine
2 egg whites
50 g (2 oz) icing sugar
mint leaves, to decorate

1. Grease a 2.3 litre (4 pint) loose-based cake tin or spring-release cake tin.
2. To make the base, lightly toast the almonds, then finely chop. Mix with the biscuits and butter. Add a few drops of almond flavouring. Spoon the mixture into the base of the prepared tin and pack down with the back of a metal spoon. Chill while making the filling.
3. To make the filling, purée 225 g (8 oz) of the raspberries in a blender or food processor, then press through a sieve. Pour three-quarters of the purée into a bowl and reserve. Add the yogurt and cheese to the purée remaining in the blender and process until well blended.
4. Sprinkle the gelatine over 30 ml (2 tbsp) water in a small bowl and leave to soak for 2–3 minutes. Place the bowl over a pan of simmering water and stir until dissolved. (Alternatively, microwave on HIGH for 30 seconds or until dissolved.) Leave to cool, then add to the cheese mixture.
5. Whisk the egg whites with the icing sugar until very thick and shiny. Fold into the cheese mixture.
6. Arrange 100 g (4 oz) of the reserved raspberries over the biscuit base. Pour the cheese mixture into the tin. Sprinkle with the remaining raspberries. Spoon in the reserved purée and mark in a swirl with a knife to make a marbled pattern. Chill for 3–4 hours or until set.
7. To serve, unmould and decorate with mint leaves.

Not suitable for freezing.

Opposite: RASPBERRY RIPPLE CHEESECAKE.

MINI GRAPE CHEESECAKES

SERVES 24

These creamy individual baked cheesecakes are
decorated with halved black grapes.

FOR THE PASTRY
275 g (10 oz) plain flour
pinch of salt
175 g (6 oz) butter or margarine, cut into pieces
50 g (2 oz) caster sugar

FOR THE FILLING
225 g (8 oz) full fat soft cheese
2 eggs, beaten
25 g (1 oz) caster sugar
10 ml (2 tsp) plain flour
finely grated rind and juice of $\frac{1}{2}$ lemon

FOR THE DECORATION
175 g (6 oz) black grapes, halved and seeded
150 ml ($\frac{1}{4}$ pint) whipping cream, whipped

1. To make the pastry, put the flour and salt into a
bowl. Rub in the butter until the mixture resembles
breadcrumbs. Stir in the sugar and add sufficient water,
about 60 ml (4 tbsp), to mix to a smooth dough.
2. Roll out the pastry on a lightly floured work surface
and cut out twelve 7.5 cm (3 inch) rounds, using a fluted
pastry cutter. Use to line 24 deep patty tins.
3. Bake blind in the oven at 200°C (400°F) mark 6
for 10 minutes. Remove the foil and baking beans, then
return to the oven for a further 5 minutes.
4. Meanwhile to make the filling, beat the soft cheese,
eggs, sugar, flour and lemon rind and juice together in a
bowl until evenly mixed. Pour the filling into the pastry
cases.
5. Lower the oven temperature to 150°C (300°F) mark
2 and bake the cheesecakes for 15 minutes until the
fillings are set. Leave to cool on a wire rack for 30
minutes, then refrigerate the cheesecakes for at least
1 hour before serving.
6. Just before serving, decorate the top of each cheesecake with the grapes and piped whipped cream.

*To freeze: wrap and freeze at the end of step 5. Thaw
overnight in the refrigerator, then finish as above.*

TROPICAL CHEESECAKE

SERVES 8

Sweet, aromatic and juicy mangoes are used in the
cheesecake filling, with kiwi fruit slices to decorate.

FOR THE BASE
75 g (3 oz) butter, melted
175 g (6 oz) plain chocolate digestive biscuits, finely crushed
50 g (2 oz) desiccated coconut

FOR THE FILLING
2 medium mangoes
30 ml (2 tbsp) powdered gelatine
150 ml ($\frac{1}{4}$ pint) orange juice
350 g (12 oz) full fat soft cheese
100 g (4 oz) caster sugar
2 eggs, separated
30 ml (2 tbsp) lemon juice
300 ml ($\frac{1}{2}$ pint) double cream
3 kiwi fruit, peeled and sliced, to decorate

1. Lightly oil a 22 cm ($8\frac{1}{2}$ inch) spring-release cake tin.
Line the base with greaseproof and grease the paper.
2. To make the base, stir the melted butter into the
biscuit crumbs and coconut. Mix well together. Press
into the prepared tin. Chill for 30 minutes.
3. To make the filling, peel the mangoes and cut the
flesh from the stone. Discard the stone. Roughly chop
or mash the flesh.
4. Sprinkle the gelatine over the orange juice in a bowl
and leave to soak for 2—3 minutes. Place the bowl over a
pan of simmering water and stir until dissolved. (Alternatively, microwave on HIGH for 30 seconds or until
dissolved.) Leave the gelatine to cool for 5 minutes.
5. Beat the soft cheese and sugar together in a bowl
until smooth, then beat in the egg yolks and lemon
juice. Stir in the mango flesh and dissolved gelatine.
Lightly whip the cream and fold into the mixture.
6. Whisk the egg whites until stiff, then carefully fold
into the cheese mixture. Pour on to the biscuit base.
Chill for 3—4 hours until firm. Carefully remove the
cheesecake from the tin. Decorate with the kiwi fruit.

*To freeze: wrap and freeze at the end of step 6. Thaw
overnight in the refrigerator, then finish as above.*

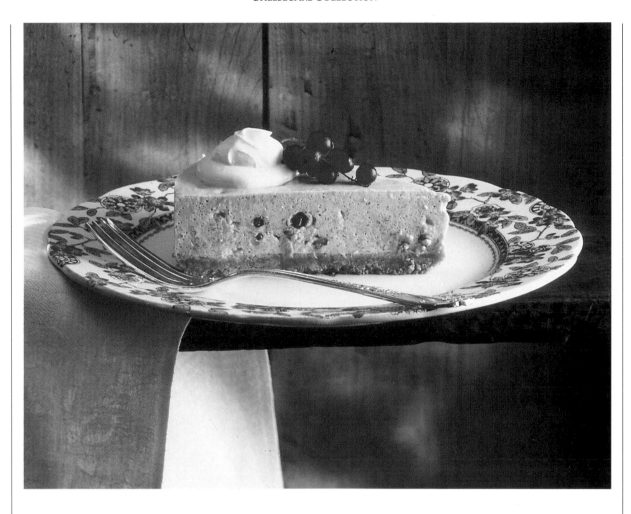

REDCURRANT CHEESECAKE

SERVES 4–6

Fresh redcurrants are only to be had during the height of summer but their sharpness does go very well with the sweet cheesecake base. Substituting a fruit-flavoured yogurt for natural gives more fruit flavour and a hint of extra colour.

FOR THE BASE

65 g (2½ oz) butter, melted
150 g (5 oz) digestive biscuits, finely crushed

FOR THE FILLING

175 g (6 oz) redcurrants
15 ml (1 tbsp) powdered gelatine
100 g (4 oz) cottage cheese
1 egg, separated
40 g (1½ oz) caster sugar
150 ml (¼ pint) natural yogurt
150 ml (¼ pint) double cream
15 ml (1 tbsp) redcurrant jelly
redcurrants, to decorate

1. To make the base, mix the butter and crushed biscuits together. Press the mixture into a loose-based 20.5 cm (8 inch) cake tin, lining the base and sides.

2. To make the filling, put the redcurrants in a medium saucepan with 45 ml (3 tbsp) water and simmer gently for 5–6 minutes until just soft. (Alternatively, cover and microwave on HIGH for 3–4 minutes.) Leave to cool.

3. Sprinkle the gelatine over 45 ml (3 tbsp) water in a small bowl and leave to soak for 2–3 minutes. Place the bowl over a pan of simmering water and stir until dissolved. (Alternatively, microwave on HIGH for 30 seconds or until dissolved.) Leave until lukewarm.

4. Put the cheese, egg yolk, sugar and yogurt in a food processor or blender and work until smooth. Whip the cream until it just holds its shape. Fold the cooked redcurrants, redcurrant jelly, dissolved gelatine and most of the cream into the cheese mixture. Whisk the egg white until stiff, then fold into the mixture.

5. Pour the mixture on to the biscuit base and chill until set. Remove from the tin and decorate with the remaining cream and redcurrants.

Not suitable for freezing.

Above: REDCURRANT CHEESECAKE.

BAKED BLENDER CHEESECAKE WITH RED FRUIT SAUCE

SERVES 8

The cheesecake will rise quite dramatically in the oven at first, then settle back down in the tin. If using a fan-assisted oven, reduce the temperature according to manufacturer's instructions.

FOR THE BASE

175 g (6 oz) digestive biscuits, crushed
50 g (2 oz) ground almonds
75 g (3 oz) butter, melted

FOR THE FILLING

225 g (8 oz) full fat soft cheese
225 g (8 oz) cottage cheese
60 ml (4 tbsp) double cream
2 eggs, separated
1 egg yolk
15 ml (1 tbsp) cornflour
grated rind and juice of 3 lemons
100 g (4 oz) caster sugar

FOR THE SAUCE

350 g (12 oz) strawberries, hulled
350 g (12 oz) raspberries, hulled
40 g (1½ oz) icing sugar
90 ml (6 tbsp) orange-flavoured liqueur or fresh orange juice

FOR THE DECORATION

whipped cream
halved strawberries
frosted rose petals (see page 10)
icing sugar, for dusting

1. Grease the base and sides of a 20.5 cm (8 inch) spring-release cake tin and line with greaseproof paper.
2. To make the base, stir the crushed biscuits and ground almonds into the melted butter and blend well. Press half the mixture into the base of the prepared tin.
3. To make the filling, blend the cheeses, double cream, egg yolks, cornflour, lemon rind and 60 ml (4 tbsp) lemon juice together in a blender or food processor.
4. Whisk the egg whites until stiff but not dry. Whisk in 30 ml (2 tbsp) of the caster sugar, then whisk again until stiff and shiny. Fold in the remaining caster sugar. Gently fold the egg whites into the cheese mixture. Spoon into the tin. Sprinkle the remaining biscuit mixture on top.
5. Bake in the oven at 200°C (400°F) mark 6 for 30 minutes. Reduce the oven temperature to 180°C (350°F) mark 4 and bake for a further 45 minutes or until a skewer inserted into the centre comes out clean. Cover with foil if necessary during cooking. Leave to cool in the tin. Chill for at least 1 hour.

6. To make the sauce, blend the strawberries, raspberries, icing sugar and liqueur together in a blender or food processor. Sieve to remove pips. Chill.
7. Carefully remove the tin from the sides of the cheesecake. Peel off the lining paper. Place a flat serving plate on top of the cheesecake and invert. Remove the base of the tin and lining paper. Decorate with whipped cream, halved strawberries and rose petals. Dust with icing sugar and serve with the chilled red fruit sauce.

To freeze: pack and freeze the undecorated cheesecake. Freeze the sauce separately. Thaw in the refrigerator overnight then decorate as above.

Illustrated on pages 144–145

COFFEE CHEESECAKE

SERVES 8

If you can find them, use sugar coffee beans, available from high class confectioners, to decorate.

FOR THE BASE

50 g (2 oz) butter, melted
175 g (6 oz) gingernut biscuits, finely crushed

FOR THE FILLING

15 ml (1 tbsp) powdered gelatine
15 ml (1 tbsp) instant coffee powder
30 ml (2 tbsp) coffee-flavoured liqueur
150 g (5 oz) light brown soft sugar
450 g (1 lb) curd cheese
300 ml (½ pint) whipping cream
coffee beans, to decorate

1. Lightly oil a 20.5 cm (8 inch) loose-based deep cake tin or spring-release cake tin.
2. To make the base, stir the butter and crushed biscuits together. Press firmly into the base of the prepared tin. Chill for 30 minutes until set.
3. To make the filling, sprinkle the gelatine over 45 ml (3 tbsp) water in a small bowl and leave to soak for 10 minutes. Place the bowl over a pan of simmering water and stir until dissolved. (Alternatively, microwave on HIGH for 30 seconds or until dissolved.)
4. Stir the coffee and coffee liqueur into 300 ml (½ pint) boiling water. Stir in the gelatine, then the sugar.
5. Put the coffee mixture and curd cheese into a blender or food processor and work until just smooth. Leave until beginning to set. Lightly whip the cream and fold half into the cheese mixture.
6. Turn the mixture into the prepared tin and chill for 2–3 hours or until set.
7. When set, remove from the tin. Pipe whirls of the remaining cream around the cheesecake and decorate.

To freeze: wrap and freeze at the end of step 6. Thaw overnight in the refrigerator, then decorate as above.

Opposite: COFFEE CHEESECAKE.

PUMPKIN CHEESECAKE

SERVES 20

This makes a very large cheesecake, suitable for a buffet party.

FOR THE PUMPKIN LAYER

700 g (1½ lb) peeled and seeded pumpkin, chopped
75 g (3 oz) granulated sugar
thinly pared rind and juice of 3 oranges
6 passion fruit
22.5 ml (4½ tsp) powdered gelatine

FOR THE BASE

100 g (4 oz) unsalted butter
45 ml (3 tbsp) golden syrup
350 g (12 oz) digestive biscuits, crushed

FOR THE CHEESE LAYER

4 eggs, separated
175 g (6 oz) caster sugar
finely grated rind of 3 lemons
60 ml (4 tbsp) lemon juice
700 g (1½ lb) full fat soft cheese
45 ml (3 tbsp) powdered gelatine
450 ml (¾ pint) double cream

FOR THE DECORATION

200 ml (7 fl oz) double cream, whipped
few skinned pistachio nuts

1. To make the pumpkin layer, put the pumpkin, sugar and orange rind and juice into a large saucepan. Cover and cook gently for about 45 minutes until very soft. Cool slightly, then purée in a blender or food processor.
2. Cut each passion fruit in half and scoop out the seeds into a nylon sieve placed over a small bowl. Work the seeds in the sieve with the back of a spoon until all of the juice is extracted into the bowl. Stir the juices into the pumpkin purée.
3. Sprinkle the gelatine over 45 ml (3 tbsp) water in a small bowl and leave to soak for 2—3 minutes. Place the bowl over a pan of simmering water and stir until dissolved. (Alternatively, microwave on HIGH for 30 seconds or until dissolved.) Stir the dissolved gelatine into the pumpkin purée, then put the purée aside to cool.
4. To make the base, put the butter and golden syrup in a large pan and heat gently until the butter melts. (Alternatively, microwave on HIGH for 2 minutes or until melted, stirring once.) Stir in the biscuits and mix well. Spread the biscuit mixture evenly over the base of a 30.5 cm (12 inch) spring-release cake tin, pressing gently to firm. Chill the biscuit base while making the cheese layer.
5. To make the cheese layer, whisk the egg yolks, caster sugar and lemon rind together in a bowl until the mixture is very thick and creamy, and leaves a trail when the whisk is lifted. Gradually, whisk in the lemon

juice. Beat the soft cheese until very soft, then gradually beat in the lemon mixture.
6. Dissolve the gelatine in 90 ml (6 tbsp) water, as above. Whip the cream until it holds soft peaks. Whisk the egg whites until stiff.
7. Mix the dissolved gelatine into the cheese and lemon mixture, then quickly fold in the cream, followed by the egg whites. Pour the mixture on to the biscuit base. Chill for at least 1 hour until set.
8. Very carefully pour the cold, but not yet set, pumpkin mixture on top of the set cheesecake. Smooth the surface. Chill for at least 3 hours, or preferably overnight, until well set.
9. To serve, carefully run a palette knife around the side of the cheesecake then gently remove the side of the tin. Place the cheesecake on a serving dish. Decorate with whipped cream and pistachios. Chill until serving.

Not suitable for freezing.

CRANBERRY CHEESECAKE

SERVES 10

Cranberry cheesecake looks good as part of a buffet party spread. Serve with a jug of pouring cream or soured cream, for those who like it.

FOR THE FILLING

225 g (8 oz) full fat soft cheese
2 eggs, separated
finely grated rind and juice of 2 lemons
225 g (8 oz) caster sugar
300 ml (½ pint) natural yogurt
300 ml (½ pint) double cream
15 ml (1 tbsp) powdered gelatine
225 g (8 oz) cranberries
10 ml (2 tsp) arrowroot

FOR THE BASE

175 g (6 oz) digestive biscuits, crushed
75 g (3 oz) butter, melted

1. Lightly oil a 25.5 cm (10 inch) fluted savarin spring-release tin.
2. For the filling, beat the cheese, egg yolks, lemon rind, 50 g (2 oz) of the sugar and the yogurt together in a bowl. Whip the cream lightly and fold into the cheese mixture.
3. In a small bowl, mix 75 ml (5 tbsp) lemon juice with 30 ml (2 tbsp) water. Sprinkle in the gelatine and leave to soak for 2—3 minutes. Place the bowl over a pan simmering water and stir until dissolved. (Alternatively, microwave on HIGH for 30 seconds or until dissolved.) Stir into the cheese mixture and leave to cool.
4. Whisk the egg whites until standing in soft peaks, then fold into the cheese mixture until evenly incorporated. Pour the mixture into the prepared tin. Chill for 3—4 hours until completely set.

5. To make the base, mix the biscuits and melted butter together. Spoon the mixture over the set cheesecake and pat down firmly. Chill again for 1 hour until set.

6. Cook the cranberries, remaining sugar and 150 ml (¼ pint) water in a pan for about 10 minutes until soft but still whole. Blend a little water with the arrowroot, stir into the cranberry mixture and slowly bring to boiling point. Cook for 2–3 minutes, then leave to cool for 30 minutes.

7. Invert the cheesecake on to a flat serving plate. Spoon the cranberry mixture into the centre before serving.

To freeze: invert the cheesecake on to the lid of a deep rigid container. Cover with the base. Thaw overnight in the refrigerator, then finish as above.

ORANGE LIQUEUR CHEESECAKE

SERVES 6

This is more like a cheesecake flan than a traditional cheesecake.

1 quantity Flan pastry (see page 43)

FOR THE FILLING
225 g (8 oz) full fat soft cheese
150 ml (¼ pint) natural yogurt
25 g (1 oz) caster sugar
finely grated rind and juice of 1 medium orange
10 ml (2 tsp) powdered gelatine
30 ml (2 tbsp) lemon juice
45 ml (3 tbsp) orange-flavoured liqueur
1 egg white
grated chocolate, to decorate

1. Roll out the pastry very thinly and use to line a 20.5 cm (8 inch) fluted flan tin.

2. Bake blind in the oven at 200°C (400°F) mark 6 for about 25 minutes.

3. To make the filling, beat the soft cheese, using a wooden spoon, in a bowl. Gradually beat in the yogurt, sugar, orange rind and 60 ml (4 tbsp) orange juice.

4. Sprinkle the gelatine over the lemon juice in a small bowl and leave to soak for 2–3 minutes. Place the bowl over a pan of simmering water and stir until dissolved. (Alternatively, microwave on HIGH for 30 seconds or until dissolved.) Stir the dissolved gelatine into the cheese mixture with the liqueur. Whisk the egg white until stiff, then fold in.

5. Turn the mixture into the cold pastry case and leave to set. Decorate with grated chocolate.

To freeze: leave to set, open freeze without chocolate and wrap when frozen. Thaw overnight in the refrigerator, then finish as above.

CARROT CHEESECAKE

SERVES 8–10

Ginger biscuits also make a good base for this unusual cheesecake.

FOR THE BASE
225 g (8 oz) digestive biscuits, crushed
100 g (4 oz) butter or margarine, melted

FOR THE FILLING
100 g (4 oz) butter or margarine
100 g (4 oz) light brown soft sugar
2 eggs, separated
225 g (8 oz) low fat soft cheese
225 g (8 oz) carrots, peeled and finely grated
5 ml (1 tsp) ground mixed spice
75 g (3 oz) self raising flour
50 g (2 oz) ground almonds
50 g (2 oz) raisins

FOR THE TOPPING
225 g (8 oz) low fat soft cheese
15 ml (1 tbsp) clear honey
10 ml (2 tsp) lemon juice
25 g (1 oz) blanched almonds, toasted and chopped

1. Grease an 18 cm (7 inch) square loose-based tin.

2. To make the base, mix the biscuits and butter together. Pack into the prepared tin. Chill.

3. To make the filling, cream the butter and sugar together in a bowl until pale and fluffy. Beat in the egg yolks, soft cheese, carrots, mixed spice, flour, almonds and raisins.

4. Whisk the egg whites until stiff, then fold into the mixture. Pour into the prepared tin and level the surface.

5. Bake in the oven at 180°C (350°F) mark 4 for about 1¼ hours or until firm to the touch. Leave to cool, then remove from the tin.

6. To make the topping, beat the cheese, honey and lemon juice together. Spread over the top of the cheesecake and mark into a pattern with a fork. Sprinkle with the chopped almonds.

Not suitable for freezing.

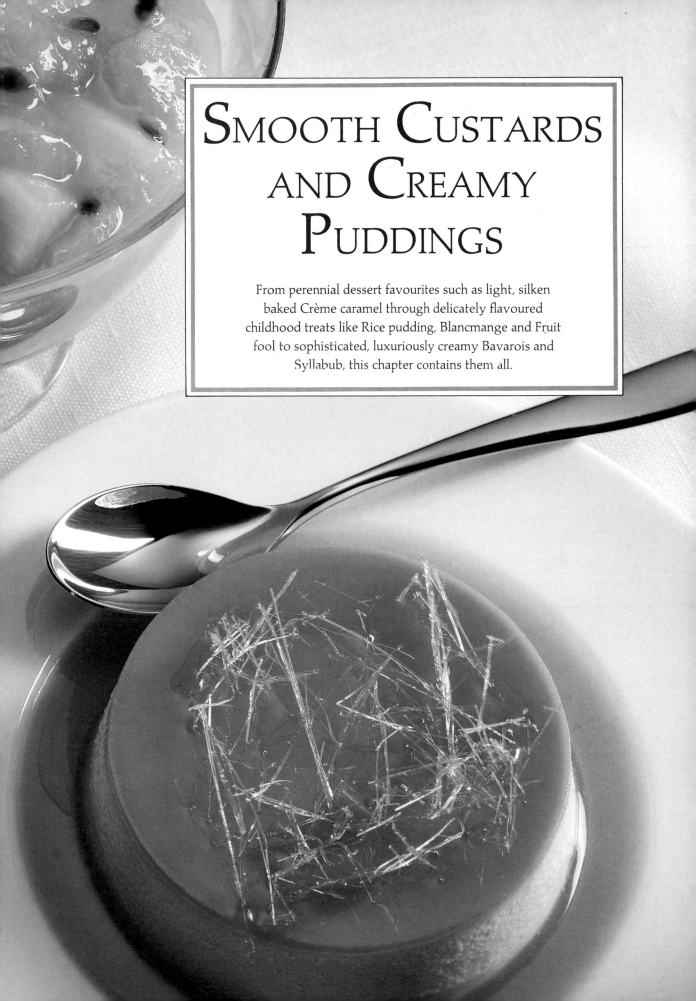

SMOOTH CUSTARDS AND CREAMY PUDDINGS

From perennial dessert favourites such as light, silken baked Crème caramel through delicately flavoured childhood treats like Rice pudding, Blancmange and Fruit fool to sophisticated, luxuriously creamy Bavarois and Syllabub, this chapter contains them all.

Egg Custard

Real egg custard forms the basis of a wide range of familiar and much loved desserts. Achieving a perfectly smooth, fine custard is not difficult, providing you take your time. Real custard cannot be hurried and will not tolerate rigorous boiling like packet custard.

Always cook custard in a heavy-based saucepan or in the top of a double boiler over a very low heat. Stir frequently to prevent it overheating and curdling. It will only thicken slightly, just enough to coat the back of the spoon lightly — don't expect it to thicken in the same way as packet custard. Watch the froth on the top of the pan — this will be absorbed into the milk as the custard thickens slightly. As soon as the sauce thickens, pour it into a cold bowl to prevent further cooking.

Egg custard can be cooked in the microwave on LOW. Use a large bowl and whisk every 30 seconds.

Baked Custard

Custards are usually baked in a bain-marie. The surrounding water prevents the delicate mixture overcooking at the sides before the middle is set. In an overcooked custard, small holes will appear in the middle of the custard first, then it will curdle and eventually separate as the whey leaks out.

Cream

Custard mixed with cream and set with gelatine (see the notes on page 188) forms the basis of bavarois. Cream whipped and flavoured makes light fools and syllabubs. Properly whipped cream is essential when a smooth, airy texture is required. Choose double or whipping cream for whipping. To achieve more volume, add 15 ml (1 tbsp) milk to each 150 ml (¼ pint) cream before starting. Chill the cream and all the utensils thoroughly beforehand. Whip quickly at first, using a balloon whisk or hand-held electric whisk, until the cream begins to look matt on the surface. Continue whipping, a little more slowly until it stands in soft peaks and does not fall off the upturned whisk. Extra care is needed if using an electric whisk. If overwhipped, the cream will look granular and the flavour will be affected. It is impossible to rescue if this happens. Overwhipped cream will not fold smoothly into mousses and bavarois.

Double and whipping cream freeze particularly well if they are first lightly whipped and then frozen in plastic containers. They will keep successfully for two months. It is best to add 15 ml (1 tbsp) milk to each 150 ml (¼ pint) cream before partially whipping. When thawed, finish whipping to the consistency required. Take care when whipping cream which has been frozen, because it is easily overwhipped. Rosettes of cream for decorating can be open frozen on non-stick baking sheets. Use while frozen to decorate cakes and trifles, then allow 45 minutes to thaw.

Serving

Smooth puddings such as fools, bavarois, syllabubs and creams are best served with crisp biscuits to give a contrast in texture, see the recipes following.

Langues de Chats

MAKES ABOUT 12

50 g (2 oz) butter or margarine
50 g (2 oz) caster sugar
1 egg
50 g (2 oz) self raising flour

1. Grease two baking sheets.
2. Cream the butter and sugar together in a bowl until pale and fluffy, then beat in the egg. Work in the flour until mixture is of a piping consistency.
3. Put the mixture into a piping bag fitted with a 1 cm (½ inch) plain piping nozzle. Pipe on to the prepared baking sheets in fingers about 6–7.5 cm (2½–3 inches) long, spaced widely apart.
4. Bake in the oven at 220°C (425°F) mark 7 for about 5 minutes until the edges of the biscuits are lightly coloured. Leave to cool on a wire rack.

To freeze: pack in a rigid container and freeze. Thaw at cool room temperature.

Florentines

MAKES 12

25 g (1 oz) hazelnuts, finely chopped
25 g (1 oz) blanched almonds, finely chopped
3 glacé cherries, chopped
30 ml (2 tbsp) sultanas, chopped
30 ml (2 tbsp) mixed peel, chopped
50 g (2 oz) butter or margarine
50 g (2 oz) caster sugar
10 ml (2 tsp) top of the milk
100 g (4 oz) plain chocolate, melted

1. Line three baking sheets with non-stick baking paper.
2. Mix together the nuts, fruit and peel.
3. Melt the butter in a saucepan, stir in the sugar and bring slowly to the boil, stirring. Remove the pan from the heat immediately, then stir in the fruit and nut mixture with the milk. Leave the mixture to cool slightly, stirring occasionally, until evenly blended and no longer oily in appearance.
4. Spoon the mixture on to the prepared baking sheets, allowing plenty of space to spread.
5. Bake in rotation in the oven at 180°C (350°F) mark 4 for about 12 minutes until golden brown.
6. Using a small oiled palette knife, immediately push in the edges to give a neat round shape. Cool for 1–2 minutes, then slide them on to a wire rack to cool.
7. Spoon a little chocolate on to the smooth side of each florentine and carefully spread to coat. Leave the chocolate until creamy but not set.
8. Draw the prongs of a fork across the chocolate in a wavy line. Wipe the non-stick paper clean and replace the florentines on to the lined baking sheet. Chill.

To freeze: see above.

BAKED CUSTARD

SERVES 4

A simply delicious family pudding. Be careful not to overcook or the custard will curdle.

568 ml (1 pint) milk
3 eggs
30 ml (2 tbsp) caster sugar
grated nutmeg

1. Grease an ovenproof dish.
2. Warm the milk in a saucepan but do not boil. Whisk the eggs and sugar lightly in a bowl, then pour on the hot milk, stirring.
3. Strain the mixture into the prepared dish. Sprinkle the nutmeg on top. Stand the dish in a roasting tin and fill with hot water to come halfway up the sides.
4. Bake in the oven at 170°C (325°F) mark 3 for about $1\frac{1}{4}$ hours or until set and firm to the touch. Serve hot or cold.

Not suitable for freezing.

Previous page: CRÈME CARAMEL (PAGE 166). Above: CRÈME BRÛLÉE.

CRÈME BRÛLÉE

SERVES 6

Delicious pots of rich baked custard, topped with a crisp caramellized sugar top. Serve with poached or fresh fruit.

600 ml (1 pint) whipping cream
4 egg yolks
100 g (4 oz) caster sugar
5 ml (1 tsp) vanilla essence

1. Put the cream in the top of a double saucepan or in a heatproof bowl over a pan of hot water. Heat gently; do not boil.
2. Meanwhile, beat the egg yolks, 50 g (2 oz) of the caster sugar and the vanilla essence together in a bowl. Add the cream and mix well together.
3. Stand six individual ramekin dishes in a roasting tin, then pour in enough hot water to come halfway up the sides of the dishes. Pour the custard mixture slowly into the ramekins, dividing it equally between them.
4. Bake in the oven at 150°C (300°F) mark 2 for about 1 hour or until set. Remove from tin and cool for 1 hour.
5. Chill for 2–3 hours, preferably overnight. Sprinkle the top of each crème brûlée with the remaining sugar and put under a hot grill for 2–3 minutes until the sugar turns to caramel. Chill again for 2–3 hours before serving.

Not suitable for freezing.

CRÈME CARAMEL

SERVES 4–6

A perennial dessert favourite, this light silken, baked custard with a rich amber, caramel sauce, can be made with most types of milk. For richer results, however, use single cream. Different flavourings such as vanilla or cardamom pods, orange rind, or even scented geranium leaves may be infused in the milk. Confident cooks may crown the custard with a froth of spun sugar. See the photograph on pages 162–163. The recipe for spun sugar is on page 56.

FOR THE CARAMEL
175 g (6 oz) granulated sugar

FOR THE CUSTARD
1 vanilla pod or a few drops of vanilla essence
568 ml (1 pint) milk
4 eggs
4 egg yolks
60 ml (4 tbsp) caster sugar or more to taste

1. To make the caramel, slightly warm six 150 ml (¼ pint) ramekin dishes. Put the granulated sugar in a heavy saucepan with enough water to just moisten. Place over a low heat and heat without boiling until the sugar is dissolved. (If boiled before dissolved, the sugar will crystallize and never form a caramel.) Prod the sugar occasionally to help it dissolve.

2. Bring to the boil and boil rapidly for a few minutes until the sugar begins to turn pale brown. DO NOT LEAVE THE SUGAR. At this stage it will turn brown very quickly and could easily catch and burn. Gently swirl the caramel to ensure even browning.

3. Once the caramel has reached the desired colour, dip the base of the pan in cool water to prevent further cooking. Pour a little caramel into each of the warm ramekins and rotate each one to coat the bottom and part way up the sides with caramel. Leave to cool.

4. To make the custard, split the vanilla pod to expose the seeds. Place in a pan with the milk and heat until almost boiling (if using vanilla essence, add after heating the milk first). Meanwhile, beat the eggs, yolks and caster sugar until well mixed. Strain on to the milk. Stir well and strain again into the ramekins.

5. Place the ramekins in a roasting tin and fill the tin with hot water to come two thirds up the sides of the dishes.

6. Bake in the oven at 170°C (325°F) mark 3 for 20–30 minutes or until just set. To test, insert the tip of a small sharp knife into the centre of a custard—if cooked it should come out clean. Also, if sufficiently set, when gently tapped the custard will wobble slightly like a jelly. Remove from the water bath. Leave to cool, then chill overnight.

7. To turn out, allow the custards to come to room temperature for 15 minutes. Free the edges by pressing with fingertips, then loosen the sides with a thin-bladed, blunt-edged knife. Place a serving dish over the top and invert. Lift off the ramekin. Serve with a fruit compote.

Not suitable for freezing.

STRAWBERRY CUSTARD FLAN

SERVES 6–8

1½ quantity Flan pastry (see page 43)

FOR THE FILLING
40 g (1½ oz) cornflour
2 eggs, separated
450 ml (¾ pint) milk
75 g (3 oz) caster sugar
few drops of vanilla essence
350 g (12 oz) strawberries, hulled

1. Roll out the pastry on a floured work surface and use to line a 23 cm (9 inch) flan dish. Chill for 30 minutes. Prick the base of the flan.

2. Bake blind in the oven at 200°C (400°F) mark 6 for 20 minutes or until pale golden and cooked through. Cool in the dish for 30–40 minutes.

3. To make the filling, mix the cornflour to a smooth paste with a little of the milk. Mix the egg yolks with the cornflour paste.

4. Put the rest of the milk in a saucepan with the sugar and vanilla essence. Bring to the boil. Remove from the heat and pour on to the cornflour mixture. Return to the pan, then bring to the boil, stirring, and boil for 2 minutes until thickened. Cover with damp greaseproof paper and leave to cool for 30 minutes.

5. Thinly slice the strawberries into the base of the pastry case, reserving a few for decoration. Whisk the egg whites until stiff, then fold into the cold custard mixture. Smooth the custard mixture evenly over the strawberries. Chill for 1 hour until set.

6. Serve the flan decorated with the reserved strawberry slices, preferably within 2 hours of completion.

Not suitable for freezing.

MINTED STRAWBERRY CUSTARDS

SERVES 6

Replace the mint with a few lemon geranium leaves, if preferred.

450 ml (¾ pint) milk
4 large sprigs mint
1 egg
2 egg yolks
45 ml (3 tbsp) caster sugar
20 ml (4 tsp) powdered gelatine
700 g (1½ lb) strawberries, hulled
15 ml (1 tbsp) icing sugar
strawberries, to decorate

1. Oil six 150 ml (¼ pint) ramekin dishes.
2. Place the milk and mint sprigs in a saucepan. Bring slowly to the boil, cover and leave to infuse for about 30 minutes.
3. Whisk the egg and yolks with the caster sugar in a bowl. Strain over the milk. Return to the pan and cook gently, stirring, until the custard just coats the back of the spoon. Do not boil. Leave to cool.
4. Sprinkle the gelatine over 45 ml (3 tbsp) water in a small bowl and leave to soak for 2–3 minutes. Place the bowl over a pan of simmering water and stir until dissolved. (Alternatively, microwave on HIGH for 30 seconds or until dissolved.) Stir the gelatine into the custard.
5. Purée and sieve the strawberries. Whisk about two thirds into the cold, but not set, custard. Pour the custard into the dishes and chill to set—about 3 hours.
6. Meanwhile, whisk the icing sugar into the remaining strawberry purée. Chill.
7. To serve, turn out the custards. Surround with strawberry sauce, then decorate with strawberries.

Not suitable for freezing.

Above: MINTED STRAWBERRY CUSTARDS.

BAKED CLEMENTINE CUSTARDS

SERVES 6

Lightly set custards flavoured with clementines and served with a clementine compote.

450 g (1 lb) clementines or satsumas
75 g (3 oz) caster sugar
568 ml (1 pint) milk
4 eggs
30 ml (2 tbsp) orange-flavoured liqueur

1. Using a potato peeler, pare the rind from one of the clementines. Place in a saucepan with 25 g (1 oz) of the caster sugar and 300 ml (½ pint) water. Bring slowly to the boil. Boil for 10 minutes. Strain, reserving the syrup.
2. Peel the remaining fruit, reserve the peel and flesh. Blend this peel, the milk, remaining sugar and eggs in a blender or food processor for 2 minutes or until the peel is very small.
3. Strain the mixture into six deep 150 ml (¼ pint) ovenproof dishes. Place in a roasting tin filled with enough hot water to come halfway up the dishes.
4. Bake in the oven at 170°C (325°F) mark 3 for about 1 hour. They should be very lightly set. Cool, then chill.
5. Meanwhile, separate the segments of fruit. Carefully remove any pith. Place the segments in a small bowl with the reserved syrup and liqueur. Cover and marinate until required.
6. To serve, decorate each custard with a few marinated segments. Serve the remainder separately.

Not suitable for freezing.

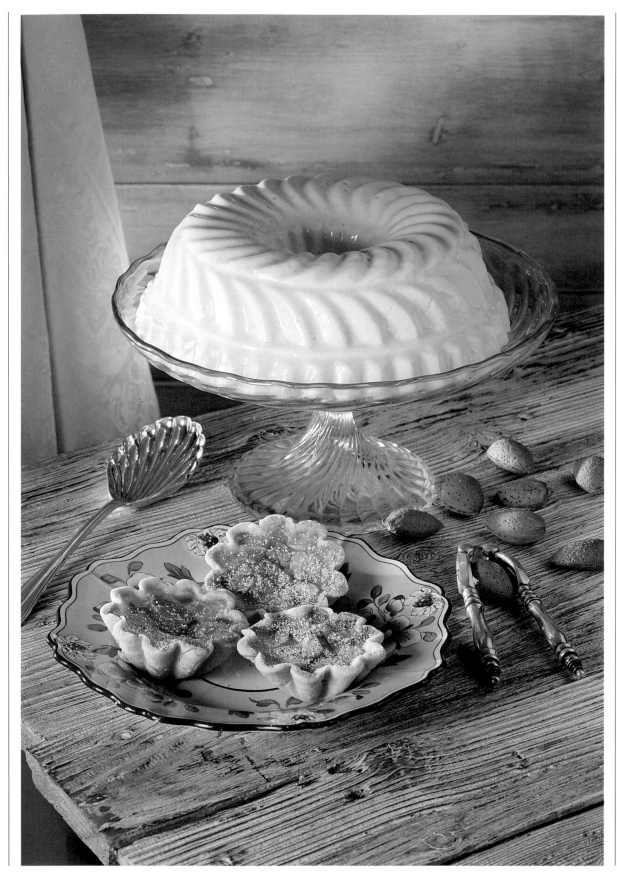

CREMA FRITTA

SERVES 4–6

Literally translated, this simple dessert means 'fried cream', which is in fact exactly what it is. In Italy, it is traditional to celebrate *Carnevale*—the day before Lent—by eating *crema fritta*. Children and young people invite friends home and everyone eats *crema fritta* in the way that people in other countries eat pancakes.

3 eggs
50 g (2 oz) caster sugar
50 g (2 oz) plain flour
225 ml (8 fl oz) milk
300 ml ($\frac{1}{2}$ pint) single cream
finely grated rind of $\frac{1}{2}$ lemon
100 g (4 oz) dry white breadcrumbs
oil, for shallow frying
caster sugar, for sprinkling

1. Grease a shallow 18 cm (7 inch) square cake tin.
2. Beat 2 of the eggs and the sugar together in a large bowl until the mixture is pale.
3. Add the flour, beating all the time. Very slowly, beat in the milk and cream. Add the lemon rind. Pour the mixture into the prepared tin.
4. Bake in the oven at 180°C (350°F) mark 4 for about 1 hour until a skewer inserted in the centre comes out clean. Leave to cool for 2–3 hours, preferably overnight.
5. When completely cold, cut into 16 cubes and remove from the cake tin.
6. Beat the remaining egg in a bowl. Dip the cubes in the egg, then in the breadcrumbs until well coated.
7. Heat the oil in a frying pan and, when hot, slide in the cubes. Fry for 2–3 minutes until golden brown and a crust is formed. Turn and fry the second side. Drain well on absorbent kitchen paper. Serve immediately, sprinkled with caster sugar.

Not suitable for freezing.

BAKED CUSTARD SPONGE

SERVES 6

You can use up slices of leftover sponge instead of trifle sponges in this family favourite.

450 ml ($\frac{3}{4}$ pint) milk
4 eggs, beaten
150 ml ($\frac{1}{4}$ pint) double cream
50 g (2 oz) caster sugar
2.5 ml ($\frac{1}{2}$ tsp) vanilla essence
100 g (4 oz) trifle sponges
50 g (2 oz) currants, sultanas or raisins
2.5 ml ($\frac{1}{2}$ tsp) grated nutmeg

1. Heat the milk in a saucepan until almost boiling. Place the eggs, cream, sugar and vanilla essence in a bowl and pour over the milk.
2. Dip the sponges into the custard and use to line the sides of a 1.1 litre (2 pint) ovenproof dish.
3. Place the dried fruit in the base of the dish and pour the rest of the custard over. Sprinkle with nutmeg.
4. Bake in the oven at 150°C (300°F) mark 2 for about 1 hour until lightly set. Serve warm with single cream.

Not suitable for freezing.

ALMOND CUSTARD TARTS

SERVES 10

Here, pastry cases made in brioche tins make good deep containers for a delicious almond custard.

1 quantity Shortcrust pastry (see page 42)
FOR THE FILLING
200 ml (7 fl oz) milk
2 eggs
50 g (2 oz) caster sugar
1.25 ml ($\frac{1}{4}$ tsp) almond flavouring
flaked almonds, toasted
icing sugar, for dusting

1. Grease ten 7.5 cm (3 inch) fluted brioche tins and place on a baking sheet.
2. Roll out the pastry thinly on a floured work surface and use to line the tins. Chill for 20 minutes.
3. Bake blind in the oven at 200°C (400°F) mark 6 for 15 minutes.
4. To make the filling, whisk the milk, eggs, caster sugar and almond flavouring together. Pour into the pastry cases. Scatter toasted almonds on top.
5. Reduce the oven temperature to 180°C (350°F) mark 4 and bake for a further 15–20 minutes until just set. Leave the tarts to cool before serving. Dust lightly with icing sugar.

Not suitable for freezing.

Above: VANILLA BAVARIAN RING (PAGE 180). Below: ALMOND CUSTARD TARTS.

CHARLOTTE RUSSE

SERVES 6

A classic French dessert, this charlotte Russe (Russian charlotte) is made with a filling of *crème bavarois*—a rich vanilla-flavoured egg custard. Sometimes the custard is flavoured with chocolate, almond-flavoured liqueur or kirsch. Fresh raspberries can also be added when they are in season.

135 g (4¾ oz) packet lemon jelly, broken into squares
45 ml (3 tbsp) lemon juice
2 glacé cherries, quartered
piece of angelica, cut into triangles
300 ml (½ pint) milk
1 vanilla pod
15 ml (3 tsp) powdered gelatine
3 egg yolks
45 ml (3 tbsp) caster sugar
about 18 sponge fingers
300 ml (½ pint) whipping cream

1. Dissolve the jelly in a measuring jug, according to the packet instructions, using the lemon juice and enough boiling water to make 600 ml (1 pint). Leave to cool for 20 minutes.
2. Spoon a thin covering of cool jelly into the base of a 1.1 litre (2 pint) charlotte tin. Chill for about 20 minutes or until set.
3. When set, arrange the cherry quarters and angelica triangles on top. Carefully spoon over cool liquid jelly to a depth of about 2.5 cm (1 inch). Chill for about 30 minutes to set, together with the remaining jelly.
4. Bring the milk slowly to the boil with the vanilla pod in a pan. Remove from the heat, cover and leave to infuse for at least 10 minutes.
5. Sprinkle the gelatine over 45 ml (3 tbsp) water in a small bowl and leave to soak for 2–3 minutes. Place the bowl over a pan of simmering water and stir until dissolved. (Alternatively, microwave on HIGH for 30 seconds or until dissolved.) Leave to cool slightly.
6. Using a wooden spoon, beat the egg yolks and sugar together until well mixed, then stir in the strained milk. Return to the pan and cook gently, stirring all the time until the custard is thick enough to just coat the back of the spoon—do not boil. Pour into a large bowl, stir in the dissolved gelatine and leave to cool for 30 minutes.
7. Trim the sponge fingers so that they just fit the tin; reserve the trimmings. Stand the fingers closely together, sugar side out, around the edge of the tin.
8. Lightly whip the cream and stir into the cool custard. Place the bowl in a roasting tin. Pour in enough iced water to come halfway up the sides. Stir occasionally for about 10 minutes until the custard is on the point of setting and has a thick pouring consistency. Pour gently into the lined mould without disturbing the sponge fingers.
9. Trim the sponge fingers level with the custard. Lay the trimmings together with the reserved trimmings on top of the custard. Cover with clingfilm and chill for at least 3 hours to set.
10. To turn out, using fingertips, ease the sponge fingers away from the tin, then tilt it slightly to allow an airlock to form between the two. Dip the base of the tin in hot water for about 5 seconds only—to loosen the jelly. Invert the pudding on to a damp plate, shake the tin gently, then ease it carefully off the finished charlotte.
11. Loosen the remaining set jelly by dipping the jug in hot water for a few seconds only. Turn out on to a board lined with damp greaseproof paper. Moisten a large knife and chop the jelly into small pieces. Spoon the jelly around the charlotte Russe.

Not suitable for freezing.

BLANCMANGE

SERVES 4

A real old-fashioned pudding. Set in one large jelly mould or in individual moulds.

60 ml (4 tbsp) cornflour
568 ml (1 pint) milk
strip of lemon rind
45 ml (3 tbsp) sugar or to taste

1. Blend the cornflour to a smooth paste with 30 ml (2 tbsp) of the milk.
2. Put the remaining milk in a saucepan with the lemon rind. Bring to the boil, then strain the milk on to the blended mixture, stirring well.
3. Return the mixture to the pan and bring to the boil, stirring all the time, until the mixture thickens. Cook for 3 minutes. Add sugar to taste.
4. Pour into a dampened 600 ml (1 pint) jelly mould or individual moulds and leave until cool. Chill for several hours until set. Turn out to serve.

VARIATIONS

Chocolate Omit the lemon rind and add 50 g (2 oz) melted chocolate to the cooked mixture.

Coffee Omit the lemon rind and add 15–30 ml (1–2 tbsp) coffee flavouring.

Orange Substitute the lemon rind with 5 ml (1 tsp) grated orange rind.

Not suitable for freezing.

MILK PUDDING

SERVES 4

There's nothing nicer than a lovingly made milk pudding—use full cream milk though, and do not omit the butter or spice. Opt for rice, tapioca, sago or semolina, whichever you have. The method is easy for them all.

50 g (2 oz) short-grain white or brown pudding rice, flaked rice or tapioca, or 40 g (1½ oz) semolina or sago
568–900 ml (1–1½ pints) milk
30 ml (2 tbsp) sugar
15 g (½ oz) butter
1.25 ml (¼ tsp) ground cinnamon, ground mixed spice or grated nutmeg

1. Grease a 1.1 litre (2 pint) ovenproof dish.
2. If using white rice, flaked rice or tapioca, place in the prepared dish and pour in 568 ml (1 pint) of the milk. If using brown rice, add an extra 300 ml (½ pint) milk. Add the sugar and butter. Sprinkle the top with the spice.
3. If using semolina or sago, heat the milk in a saucepan until lukewarm, then gradually sprinkle in the semolina or sago, stirring continuously. Add the sugar and butter and continue to cook for 10 minutes until thickened, stirring frequently. Pour into the prepared dish. Sprinkle the top with the spice.
4. Bake the rice, flaked rice or tapioca pudding in the oven at 170°C (325°F) mark 3 for 2–2½ hours (brown rice for an extra 30 minutes). Stir the pudding two or three times during the first hour, but leave for the remaining time to form a crust.
5. Bake the semolina or sago pudding in the oven at 180°C (350°F) mark 4 for 30 minutes, without stirring.
6. Serve milk puddings hot or cold, plain or topped with fresh fruit, chopped nuts or thick natural yogurt.

Not suitable for freezing.

RUM AND COFFEE JUNKET

SERVES 4

A sophisticated version of the nursery pudding. Do not use UHT, long-life or sterilized milk—it will not set.

568 ml (1 pint) plus 60 ml (4 tbsp) milk
30 ml (2 tbsp) caster sugar
10 ml (2 tsp) rennet essence
10 ml (2 tsp) rum
150 ml (¼ pint) soured cream
10 ml (2 tsp) coffee and chicory essence
plain and white chocolate, to decorate

1. Put the 568 ml (1 pint) milk in a saucepan and heat until just warm to the finger.
2. Add the sugar, rennet and rum, then stir until the sugar has dissolved.

3. Immediately, pour the mixture into four individual dishes or a 900 ml (1½ pint) shallow, edged serving dish. Put in a warm place, undisturbed, for 4 hours to set.
4. Lightly whisk the soured cream. Gradually add the 60 ml (4 tbsp) milk and the coffee essence, whisking until smooth.
5. Carefully flood the top of the junket with the coffee cream, taking care not to disturb the junket. Decorate with pared or coarsely grated chocolate. Chill for 1 hour.

Not suitable for freezing.

RISENGRØD

SERVES 4–6

This elegant Danish Christmas rice pudding contains sherry, cream and chopped almonds. A single whole almond is always put in the pudding for luck. The finder receives a present and, if single, will be the next to marry. It is traditionally served with Kirsebaersauce, a Danish hot cherry sauce.

FOR THE PUDDING
568 ml (1 pint) milk
75 g (3 oz) pudding rice
50 g (2 oz) caster sugar
4–5 drops of vanilla essence
50 g (2 oz) chopped almonds
1 glass of sherry
300 ml (½ pint) double cream
1 whole almond
FOR THE KIRSEBAERSAUCE
100 g (4 oz) granulated sugar
225 g (8 oz) cherries, stoned
15 ml (1 tbsp) arrowroot
chopped almonds, toasted, to decorate

1. To make the pudding, put the milk and rice in a saucepan and simmer for about 20 minutes until the rice is soft and most of the milk is absorbed.
2. Add the sugar, vanilla essence, almonds and sherry, then stir well. Leave to cool completely.
3. Stir in the cream. Transfer to a serving dish and push the whole almond into the pudding so that it is hidden. Cover and chill for several hours.
4. Meanwhile to make the kirsebaersauce, put the sugar in a heavy-based saucepan. Add 300 ml (½ pint) water and heat very gently until the sugar has dissolved.
5. Increase the heat and boil rapidly for 1 minute. Add the cherries and cook for 10 minutes until tender. Mix the arrowroot with 30 ml (2 tbsp) water and stir into the cherries. Simmer for 2 minutes until the sauce is clear.
6. To serve, decorate the Risengrød with almonds and accompany with the sauce.

Not suitable for freezing.

GAJAR HALVA

SERVES 4–6

This unusual Indian carrot pudding is very sweet and rich. Serve in very small portions after an Indian-style meal.

450 g (1 lb) carrots, peeled
750 ml (1¼ pints) milk
150 ml (¼ pint) single cream
75 g (3 oz) granulated sugar
15 ml (1 tbsp) treacle
45 ml (3 tbsp) ghee or melted butter
100 g (4 oz) ground almonds
seeds of 6 green cardamom pods, crushed
25 g (1 oz) sultanas
chopped pistachio nuts, to decorate

1. Roughly grate the carrots and put into a large, heavy-based saucepan. Pour in the milk and cream and bring to the boil, stirring constantly.
2. Simmer gently, stirring occasionally to prevent any sticking, for at least 2 hours until the milk has evaporated and the mixture is greatly reduced.
3. Stir in the sugar and treacle, then simmer for a further 30 minutes, stirring occasionally to prevent sticking.
4. Add the ghee, ground almonds, crushed cardamom seeds and sultanas. Cook, stirring, for another 5–10 minutes until the mixture begins to look oily on the surface.
5. Transfer to a serving dish and decorate with the pistachios. Serve hot or cold.

Not suitable for freezing.

BANANA CHARTREUSE

SERVES 4–6

The word *chartreuse* in French culinary terms can mean several different things. It is the name of a yellow or green liqueur made by the monks at the abbey of Chartreuse. *En chartreuse* is a term used to describe a game bird which is stewed with cabbage. Or, as here, it can be used to describe a dessert made with jelly.

135 g (4¾ oz) packet lemon jelly, broken into squares
3 bananas
juice of ½ lemon
about 6 shelled pistachio nuts
15 ml (1 tbsp) powdered gelatine
60 ml (4 tbsp) dark rum
150 ml (¼ pint) double cream
50 g (2 oz) icing sugar, sifted

1. Chill an 18 cm (6 inch) Charlotte mould.
2. Make up the jelly according to the packet

instructions, using only 300 ml (½ pint) boiling water. Leave to cool for 30 minutes.
3. Pour about one third of the jelly into the prepared mould. Chill for 30 minutes until set.
4. Peel 1 banana, slice thinly, then sprinkle with a little lemon juice to prevent browning.
5. Arrange the banana slices on top of the set jelly in an attractive pattern. Cut the pistachios in half lengthways and carefully place between or around the banana slices.
6. Slowly spoon over the remaining cool jelly, taking care not to dislodge the pattern of bananas and pistachios. Chill for 30 minutes until set.
7. Sprinkle the gelatine over the rum and remaining lemon juice in a small bowl. Place the bowl over a saucepan of simmering water and stir until dissolved. (Alternatively, microwave on HIGH for 30 seconds or until dissolved.) Leave to cool for 5 minutes.
8. Whip the cream with the icing sugar. Peel and mash the remaining bananas, then combine with the cream and dissolved gelatine liquid. Spoon on top of the set jelly. Chill for about 2 hours until set.
9. To serve, dip the base of the mould briefly in hot water, then invert the banana chartreuse on to a serving plate. Serve chilled.

Not suitable for freezing.

DAMASK CREAM

SERVES 4

This subtly flavoured dish, also known as Devonshire junket, is a far cry from a junket that comes from a packet. Do not serve it until you are ready to eat, as once it is cut the shape will disintegrate. Rose petals make a pretty decoration.

600 ml (1 pint) single cream
45 ml (3 tbsp) caster sugar
10 ml (2 tsp) rennet essence
large pinch of grated nutmeg
15 ml (1 tbsp) brandy
60 ml (4 tbsp) clotted or double cream
5 ml (1 tsp) rose water
rose petals, to decorate (optional)

1. Put the cream and 30 ml (2 tbsp) of the sugar in a saucepan. Heat gently until tepid, stirring until the sugar dissolves. (When the mixture is tepid it will register 36.9°C (98.4°F) on a sugar thermometer, or not feel hot or cold if you put your finger in it.)
2. Stir in the rennet, nutmeg and brandy, then pour into a serving dish. Leave for 2–3 hours until set. It is important not to disturb the junket during this time or it will not set.
3. When the junket is set, mix the remaining sugar, the cream and rose water together and spoon carefully over the top. Decorate with rose petals, if liked.

Not suitable for freezing.

TEA CREAM

SERVES 4

Earl Grey tea, a blended black tea flavoured with bergamot oil, gives this unusual tea cream a subtle, perfumed flavour. It isn't essential to use Earl Grey, however, you can use any of your favourite Ceylon or China teas, although aromatic teas are more flavoursome in cooking. Why not try jasmine tea, lapsang souchong or orange pekoe?

300 ml (½ pint) milk
15 g (½ oz) Earl Grey tea leaves
2 eggs, separated
30 ml (2 tbsp) caster sugar
15 ml (1 tbsp) powdered gelatine
150 ml (¼ pint) double cream

1. Put the milk into a saucepan, add the tea and bring to the boil. Remove from the heat and leave to infuse for 10–15 minutes or until the milk is well coloured with the tea.

2. Beat the egg yolks and sugar together, then strain on the milk and mix well. Return to the pan and cook gently for 10 minutes, stirring all the time, until the custard thickens slightly and just coats the back of the spoon.

3. Sprinkle the gelatine over 45 ml (3 tbsp) water in a small bowl and leave to soak for 2–3 minutes. Place the bowl over a pan of simmering water and stir until dissolved. (Alternatively, microwave on HIGH for 30 seconds or until dissolved.)

4. Mix the dissolved gelatine into the tea mixture. Leave for about 2 hours until beginning to set. Stir the mixture occasionally.

5. Whip the cream until thick but not stiff, then fold into the custard. Finally, whisk the egg whites until stiff, then fold into the mixture.

6. Pour the cream mixture into a dampened 600 ml (1 pint) mould. Chill for about 2–3 hours until set. Turn out on to a chilled dish and decorate with grapes and crisp biscuits, if liked.

Not suitable for freezing.

Below left: DAMASK CREAM. *Below right:* TEA CREAM.

COFFEE BAVARIAN CREAM

SERVES 6

100 g (4 oz) roasted coffee beans
900 ml (1½ pints) milk
4 egg yolks
75 g (3 oz) caster sugar
20 ml (4 tsp) powdered gelatine
300 ml (½ pint) double cream
30 ml (2 tbsp) coffee-flavoured liqueur

FOR THE DECORATION

coffee dragees
coarsely grated chocolate

1. Lightly oil a 1.4 litre (2½ pint) moule-à-manqué cake tin or soufflé dish.

2. Put the coffee beans in a saucepan and place over low heat for 2–3 minutes, shaking the pan frequently. Remove from the heat, pour all the milk into the pan, then return to the heat and bring to the boil. Remove from the heat, cover and leave to infuse for at least 30 minutes.

3. Beat the egg yolks and sugar together in a bowl until thick and light in colour. The beaters should leave a trail on the surface of the mixture when lifted.

4. Strain on the milk and stir well. Pour into the rinsed out pan and stir over low heat for 10 minutes. Do not boil. Strain into a large bowl and leave to cool for 20 minutes.

5. Sprinkle the gelatine over 60 ml (4 tbsp) water in a small bowl and leave to soak for 2–3 minutes. Place the bowl over a pan of simmering water and stir until dissolved. (Alternatively, microwave on HIGH for 30 seconds or until dissolved.)

6. Stir the dissolved gelatine into the custard. Stand this in a roasting tin of cold water and ice cubes. Stir until the mixture is cool and about to set.

7. Lightly whip 150 ml (¼ pint) of the cream to the thick pouring stage, then fold into the custard. Pour into the prepared tin. Chill for at least 3 hours or overnight until completely set.

8. With dampened fingers, gently ease the edges of the cream away from the tin. Turn the cream out on to a flat plate, shaking the tin or dish gently until the cream moves and loosens inside the tin. Carefully ease off the tin and slide the cream into the centre of the plate.

9. Whip the remaining cream until stiff, then gradually whisk in the liqueur. Spoon into a piping bag fitted with a 1 cm (½ inch) star nozzle and pipe rosettes around the top edge of the cream. Decorate with coffee dragees and grated chocolate. Serve chilled.

Not suitable for freezing.

ZABAGLIONE

SERVES 6

A classic, rich Italian dessert to serve after a light main course. It should be served as soon as it is made so that it remains light, fluffy and slightly warm. Serve with Sponge fingers, see the recipe below.

4 egg yolks
65 g (2½ oz) caster sugar
100 ml (4 fl oz) Marsala

1. Beat the egg yolks and sugar together in a large bowl. Add the Marsala and beat until mixed.

2. Place the bowl over a saucepan of simmering water and heat gently, whisking the mixture until it is very thick and creamy.

3. To serve, pour the zabaglione into six glasses and serve immediately, with sponge fingers.

Not suitable for freezing.

SPONGE FINGERS

MAKES ABOUT 32

75 g (3 oz) caster sugar
3 eggs, separated
5 ml (1 tsp) vanilla essence or almond flavouring
75 g (3 oz) plain flour
25 g (1 oz) cornflour
pinch of salt
icing sugar, for dredging

1. Grease two large baking sheets.

2. Using an electric whisk, beat half of the caster sugar and the egg yolks in a bowl until very pale and creamy.

3. Whisk the egg whites until stiff, then gradually add the remaining sugar, whisking between each addition. Fold into the egg yolk mixture, using a large metal spoon. Fold in the vanilla essence.

4. Sift the flours and salt together, then sift into the mixture. Fold in lightly, using the spoon.

5. Spoon the batter into a piping bag fitted with a 1 cm (½ inch) plain nozzle. Pipe 10 cm (4 inch) fingers on to the prepared baking sheets. Dredge the fingers with icing sugar.

6. Bake in the oven at 150°C (300°F) mark 2 for about 20 minutes or until crusty on the surface. Transfer to wire racks and cool. Store in an airtight container.

To freeze: wrap and freeze the cooled fingers. Thaw, wrapped, at room temperature.

Opposite: ZABAGLIONE SERVED WITH SPONGE FINGERS.

OLD ENGLISH SYLLABUB

SERVES 4

Bring out the full fragrance of the spices by grinding them just before use. Decorate the syllabub with fresh edible flower petals such as nasturtium, geranium and rose, or with borage flowers.

1 clove
1 allspice
2.5 cm (1 inch) cinnamon stick
little grated nutmeg
50 g (2 oz) caster sugar
finely grated rind and juice of 1 lemon
90 ml (6 tbsp) pale cream sherry
300 ml ($\frac{1}{2}$ pint) double cream
24 ratafia biscuits

1. Very finely grind the clove, allspice and cinnamon stick with a pestle and mortar, then sift through a fine sieve.
2. Put the ground spices, nutmeg, sugar, lemon rind, lemon juice and sherry into a bowl. Stir well until the sugar dissolves, then cover and leave to stand for 1 hour.
3. Strain the sherry mixture through a fine nylon sieve into a clean bowl. Pour in the cream in a continuous stream, whisking all the time. Whip the double cream until it is just thick enough to hold a trail when the whisk is lifted.
4. Place four ratafias in each of four serving glasses, then fill each glass with the spicy syllabub. Chill for about 1 hour. Decorate with the remaining ratafias and a few fresh flower petals.

Not suitable for freezing.

LIME SYLLABUB

SERVES 4–6

Serve this well flavoured syllabub with Langues de chat biscuits (see page 164). Lemon may be used instead of lime, but if so, use only one.

thinly pared rind and juice of 3 limes
150 ml ($\frac{1}{4}$ pint) white wine
30 ml (2 tbsp) brandy
75 g (3 oz) caster sugar
300 ml ($\frac{1}{2}$ pint) double cream
lime twists, to decorate

1. Put the lime rind and juice, white wine, brandy and sugar into a bowl. Stir well until the sugar has dissolved. Cover and leave to stand for about 2 hours.
2. Remove the rind from the wine mixture with a slotted spoon and discard. Pour the cream into the wine in a continuous stream, stirring with a whisk. Whip the cream until thick and it holds a trail when the whisk is lifted.
3. Pour the syllabub into serving glasses and chill. Decorate with lime twists.

Not suitable for freezing.

ALMOND BAVAROIS AND PLUM SAUCE

SERVES 6

Add almond flavouring with care, as it can be overpowering.

900 ml (1$\frac{1}{2}$ pints) milk
6 egg yolks
75 ml (5 tbsp) caster sugar
20 ml (4 tsp) powdered gelatine
150 ml ($\frac{1}{4}$ pint) double or whipping cream, lightly whipped
2.5–5 ml ($\frac{1}{2}$–1 tsp) almond flavouring
450 g (1 lb) ripe red plums
toasted flaked almonds, to decorate

1. Oil a 1.4 litre (2$\frac{1}{2}$ pint) ring mould.
2. Place the milk in a pan and bring almost to the boil. Whisk the egg yolks and half the sugar together in a bowl until blended.
3. Add the milk, then return to the pan. Cook gently, stirring all the time, until the custard thickens slightly. Do not boil or the custard will curdle. Strain into a bowl and leave until cold.
4. Sprinkle the gelatine over 60 ml (4 tbsp) water in a small bowl and leave to soak for 2–3 minutes. Place the bowl over a pan of simmering water and stir until dissolved. (Alternatively, microwave on HIGH for 30 seconds or until dissolved.)
5. Stir the dissolved gelatine into the cold custard. Light whip the cream and add to the custard with the almond flavouring. Pour into the prepared mould and chill until set.
6. Meanwhile, slice the plums, discarding the stones. Place in a medium saucepan with 150 ml ($\frac{1}{4}$ pint) water and the remaining sugar. Cover and simmer until mushy. Purée in a blender or food processor until smooth. Leave to cool and chill.
7. Turn out the bavarois, decorate with flaked almonds and serve with the plum sauce.

To freeze: pack and freeze the sauce only. Thaw overnight at cool room temperature.

Opposite: OLD ENGLISH SYLLABUB.

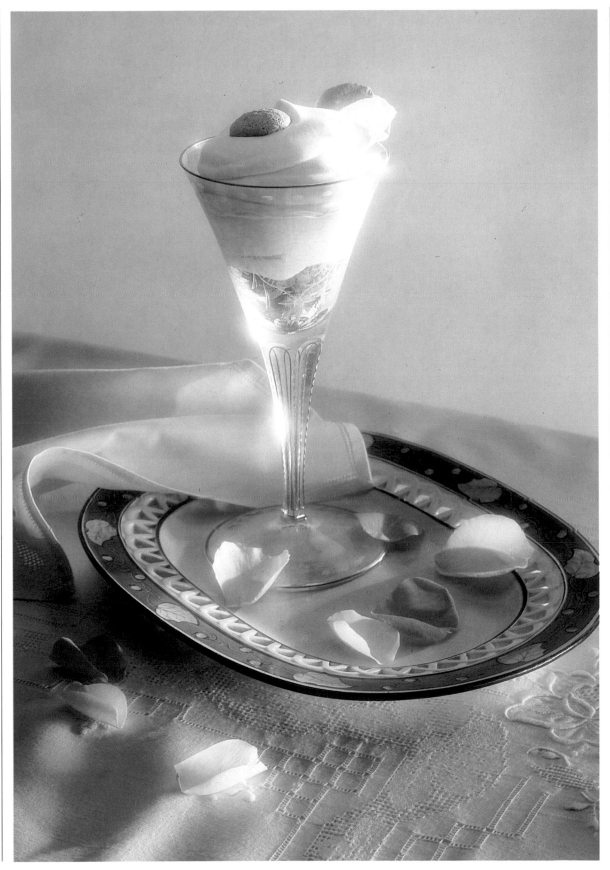

STRAWBERRY BAVAROIS

SERVES 6–8

It is essential to use really well flavoured strawberries for this bavarois—frozen strawberries may be used, but only as a last resort. This elegant dessert is perfect for summer entertaining.

350 g (12 oz) strawberries, hulled
22.5 ml (1½ tbsp) powdered gelatine
6 egg yolks
50 g (2 oz) caster sugar
300 ml (½ pint) milk
300 ml (½ pint) double cream

FOR THE STRAWBERRY SAUCE

225 g (8 oz) strawberries, hulled
50 g (2 oz) caster sugar
15 ml (1 tbsp) raspberry-flavoured liqueur (optional)

FOR THE DECORATION

150 ml (¼ pint) double cream, whipped
strawberries

1. Press the strawberries through a very fine nylon sieve to make a purée, over 300 ml (½ pint).
2. Sprinkle the gelatine over 60 ml (4 tbsp) water in a small bowl and leave to soak for 2–3 minutes. Place the bowl over a pan of simmering water and stir until dissolved. (Alternatively, microwave on HIGH for 30 seconds or until dissolved.)
3. Lightly whisk the egg yolks and sugar together in a bowl. Bring the milk almost to the boil, then whisk it into the egg yolks. Place the bowl over a pan of simmering water and cook the custard, stirring, until it thickens enough to coat the back of the spoon. (Alternatively, microwave on HIGH for 2½–3 minutes, stirring every 30 seconds with a wire whisk.)
4. Strain the custard through a nylon sieve into a clean bowl and add the dissolved gelatine, stirring. Set the custard aside until cold, but not set, stirring to prevent a skin forming.
5. Whip the cream until it just holds soft peaks. Stir the strawberry purée into the custard, then gently fold in the whipped cream. Pour the mixture into a 1.4 litre (2½ pint) mould. Chill until set.
6. Meanwhile to make the sauce, slice the strawberries and put them into a bowl. Sprinkle with the sugar and liqueur, if using. Cover and leave to stand for about 1 hour. Press through a nylon sieve to form a purée. Pour into a serving jug and chill.
7. To unmould the bavarois, quickly dip the mould, right up to the rim, into hot water. Place a serving plate on top, then invert the mould and the plate together, giving the mould a sharp shake to free the bavarois. Decorate with whipped cream and whole, halved or sliced strawberries. Serve the bavarois with the chilled strawberry sauce.

To freeze: pack and freeze the sauce only. Thaw overnight at cool room temperature.

COEURS À LA CRÈME

SERVES 4–6

Light, delicate and refreshing, this may be eaten with cream, or with soft summer fruit, ideally, tiny wild strawberries. This dessert takes its name from the small heart-shaped white porcelain colanders in which it is made.

225 g (8 oz) curd or ricotta cheese
300 ml (½ pint) crème fraîche
few drops of vanilla essence
25 g (1 oz) caster sugar
2 egg whites

1. Line four small heart-shaped moulds with muslin.
2. Press the cheese through a nylon sieve into a bowl. Lightly whip the cream, vanilla essence and sugar together. Mix into the cheese.
3. Whisk the egg whites until stiff, then fold into the cheese mixture.
4. Turn the mixture into the prepared moulds. Leave to drain overnight in the refrigerator. Turn out and serve with strawberries and single cream.

Not suitable for freezing.

CREAM CROWDIE

SERVES 4

In Scotland, crowdie can mean a cream cheese or a kind of porridge. This recipe for cream crowdie is so called because it contains oatmeal, which the Scots use for making porridge.

50 g (2 oz) medium oatmeal
300 ml (½ pint) double cream
60 ml (4 tbsp) clear honey
45 ml (3 tbsp) whisky
350 g (12 oz) raspberries, hulled

1. Place the oatmeal in a grill pan (without the rack) and toast until golden brown, stirring occasionally with a spoon. Leave for 15 minutes until cool.
2. Whip the cream until just standing in soft peaks. Stir in the honey, whisky and cooled toasted oatmeal.
3. Reserve a few raspberries for decoration, then layer up the remaining raspberries and cream mixture in four tall glasses. Cover with clingfilm and chill for at least 1 hour.
4. Allow to come to room temperature for 30 minutes before serving. Decorate each glass with the reserved raspberries.

Not suitable for freezing.

Opposite: COEURS À LA CRÈME.

VANILLA BAVARIAN RING

SERVES 6

This vanilla flavoured bavarois is set in a pretty ring mould and served undecorated. However, it can be decorated with cherries or grapes dipped in caramel; piped chocolate scrolls; fresh fruits, or edible flower petals.

15 ml (1 tbsp) powdered gelatine
6 egg yolks
50 g (2 oz) caster sugar
300 ml ($\frac{1}{2}$ pint) single cream
5 ml (1 tsp) vanilla essence
300 ml ($\frac{1}{2}$ pint) double cream

1. Sprinkle the gelatine over 45 ml (3 tbsp) water in a small bowl and leave to soak for 2–3 minutes. Place the bowl over a pan of simmering water and stir until dissolved. (Alternatively, microwave on HIGH for 30 seconds or until dissolved.)

2. Lightly whisk the egg yolks and sugar together in a bowl. Bring the single cream and the vanilla essence almost to the boil, then whisk into the egg yolks. Place the bowl over a pan of simmering water and cook the custard, stirring, until it thickens enough to coat the back of the spoon. (Alternatively, microwave on HIGH for 2–2$\frac{1}{2}$ minutes, stirring every 30 seconds with a wire whisk.)

3. Strain the custard through a nylon sieve into a clean bowl and add the dissolved gelatine, stirring. Leave the custard to cool, stirring frequently to prevent a skin forming.

4. Whip the cream until it just holds soft peaks, then fold into the custard. Pour into a 1.1 litre (2 pint) ring mould. Chill until set.

5. To unmould the bavarois, dip the mould briefly, right up to the rim, into hot water. Place a serving plate on top, then invert the mould.

Not suitable for freezing.

Illustrated on page 168

LEMON BALM SYLLABUB

SERVES 6–8

Use freshly picked lemon balm for the best flavour.

30 ml (2 tbsp) finely chopped lemon balm leaves
600 ml (1 pint) double cream
150 ml ($\frac{1}{4}$ pint) sweet white wine
grated rind and juice of 2 lemons
5 ml (1 tsp) caster sugar or to taste
sprigs of lemon balm, to decorate

1. Using an electric whisk, whisk together all the ingredients until the consistency of custard is obtained.

2. Chill for 2–3 hours. To serve, spoon the syllabub into tall glasses and decorate with sprigs of lemon balm.

Not suitable for freezing.

HOME-MADE YOGURT

Home-made yogurt makes a delicious dessert served on its own or as an accompaniment to fruit and fruit pies. It is not necessary to invest in a commercial yogurt machine; a wide-necked insulated jar and a thermometer are the only essential equipment. Use either skimmed or semi-skimmed milk, skimmed milk powder, raw, pasteurized milk, sterilized or UHT. (UHT is already sterilized so it is the most convenient to use and results in a richer texture. It does not have to be boiled; just heated to the correct temperature.) Condensed and evaporated milks do not always give such good results. You can buy special yogurt starter cultures, but it is simpler at first to use bought natural yogurt. For your next batch, keep back a little from the first yogurt you made. You can do this about three times, then buy a new starter tub of natural yogurt. To obtain a thick, creamy yogurt, add skimmed milk powder (see recipe). Flavour the finished yogurt with fruit, fruit purée or serve Greek-style with honey and a few chopped nuts.

NATURAL YOGURT

MAKES ABOUT 600 ml (1 pint)

568 ml (1 pint) milk
25 ml (1½ tbsp) natural yogurt
30 ml (2 tbsp) skimmed milk powder (optional see above)

1. Use absolutely clean, well rinsed containers and utensils. Warm an insulated jar. Pour the milk into a saucepan and bring to the boil. (If you want a thick yogurt, keep the pan on a very low heat after this for 15 minutes.) Remove from the heat and allow to cool to 45°C (113°F). If you are using UHT or sterilized milk, bring them up to 45°C (113°F).
2. Spoon the natural yogurt into a bowl and stir in a little of the cooled milk. Add the skimmed milk powder, if using, to make a smooth paste. Stir in the remaining milk.
3. Pour into the warmed insulated jar. Cover and leave for 8–9 hours, undisturbed.
4. Transfer the yogurt into small pots or cartons and place in the refrigerator immediately. It will keep for up to 10 days.

Not suitable for freezing.

LEMON CURD CREAMS

SERVES 6

It really is worth making the effort to prepare your own fresh tasting lemon curd but if time is at a premium a good quality bought variety will do!

FOR THE LEMON CURD

finely grated rind and juice of 2 lemons
2 eggs, whisked
50 g (2 oz) butter, cut into pieces
100 g (4 oz) caster sugar

FOR THE CUSTARD

3 eggs, whisked
45 ml (3 tbsp) caster sugar
300 ml (½ pint) single cream
150 ml (¼ pint) milk
150 ml (¼ pint) double cream, lightly whipped, to decorate

1. To make the lemon curd, place the lemon rind, 90 ml (6 tbsp) strained lemon juice, eggs, butter and sugar into a medium heatproof bowl. Place the bowl over a saucepan of simmering water and cook gently, whisking occasionally, until the curd thickens slightly—it should just coat the back of a spoon.

2. Strain the curd into a cold bowl, push a piece of damp greaseproof paper on to the surface of the curd and leave to cool.
3. Spoon about 30 ml (2 tbsp) lemon curd into the base of six 150 ml (¼ pint) ramekin dishes.
4. To make the custard, whisk the eggs, sugar, cream and milk together. Strain, then gently pour into the ramekins being careful not to disturb the lemon curd.
5. Stand the ramekins in a roasting tin and pour in hot water to come halfway up the sides. Cover the top of the roasting tin with foil.
6. Bake in the oven at 180°C (350°F) mark 4 for about 45 minutes or until the custards are just set. Do not overcook or the mixture will curdle and separate.
7. Take the ramekins out of the roasting tin and cool. When cold, cover and chill well before serving decorated with lightly whipped cream.

Not suitable for freezing.

BAKED SAFFRON YOGURT

SERVES 8

These individual, golden-tinted yogurts make an attractive finale to an Indian meal. They are also excellent for children at tea-time, served with fruit.

300 ml (½ pint) milk
pinch of saffron threads
6 green cardamom pods
2 eggs
2 egg yolks
383 g (13.5 oz) can condensed milk
300 ml (½ pint) natural yogurt
1 large ripe mango, to decorate

1. Bring the milk, saffron and cardamoms to the boil in a pan. Remove from the heat, cover and infuse for 10–15 minutes.
2. Beat the eggs, egg yolks, condensed milk and yogurt together in a bowl.
3. Strain in the milk, stirring gently to mix. Divide between eight ramekin dishes in a roasting tin. Add hot water to come halfway up the sides.
4. Bake in the oven at 180°C (350°F) mark 4 until firm to the touch.
5. Cool the baked yogurt desserts completely. Chill for at least 2 hours before serving.
6. To serve, run a blunt-edged knife around the edge of each yogurt, then turn out on to individual dishes.
7. Peel the skin off the mango sections. Slice thinly on either side of the central stone. Serve with the yogurts.

Not suitable for freezing.

GERANIUM CREAM WITH RED SUMMER FRUITS

SERVES 8

This rich cream, which is a mixture of double cream and full fat soft cheese, is delicately scented with geranium leaves. The red summer fruits served with it—a combination of raspberries, strawberries (wild if possible) and redcurrants—look beautiful, with their jewel-like colours surrounding the white cream.

150 ml ($\frac{1}{4}$ pint) double cream
4 sweet geranium leaves, bruised
450 g (1 lb) full fat soft cheese
75 g (3 oz) caster sugar or to taste
700 g (1$\frac{1}{2}$ lb) red summer fruits, such as raspberries, wild strawberries, small strawberries and redcurrants, chilled
caster sugar, for sprinkling
sweet geranium leaves, to decorate

1. Gently heat the cream and geranium leaves in the top of a double boiler, or in a bowl placed over a saucepan of hot water, for 10–15 minutes, until it reaches simmering point. Do not allow it to boil. Remove from the heat, cover and leave to cool.

2. Strain the cream, then gradually stir it into the cheese, stirring until smooth. Rinse the geranium leaves, dry them and stir into the cream mixture. Cover and leave in a cool place for 12 hours.

3. Remove the geranium leaves and stir in sugar to taste. Spoon the cream into a mound on a cold serving plate. Spoon the fruits around. Serve sugar for sprinkling over the fruits separately. Decorate with geranium leaves.

Not suitable for freezing.

GOOSEBERRY CHARLOTTE

SERVES 6

There are many varieties of gooseberry, round or long, hairy or smooth, cooking or dessert. Their pale green colour and unique flavour make them unbeatable for fruit charlottes and fools.

450 g (1 lb) gooseberries, topped and tailed
75 g (3 oz) caster sugar
10 ml (2 tsp) powdered gelatine
2 egg yolks
300 ml ($\frac{1}{2}$ pint) milk
300 ml ($\frac{1}{2}$ pint) double cream
angelica, to decorate
20 Langue de chat biscuits (see page 164), trimmed to size

1. Oil a 15 cm·(6 inch) soufflé non-metal straight sided dish and line the base with greaseproof paper.

2. Place the gooseberries in a small saucepan with 60 ml (4 tbsp) water. Cover and simmer for about 10 minutes until the fruit softens to a pulpy consistency. (Alternatively, microwave, covered, on HIGH for 6 minutes until soft.)

3. Purée the gooseberries in a blender or food processor, then sieve to remove the pips. Stir in 50 g (2 oz) of the sugar.

4. Sprinkle the gelatine over 30 ml (2 tbsp) water in a small bowl and leave to soak for 2–3 minutes. Place the bowl over a pan of simmering water and stir until dissolved. (Alternatively, microwave on HIGH for 30 seconds or until dissolved.)

5. Meanwhile, make the custard. Beat the egg yolks and remaining sugar together in a bowl until light in colour. In a small saucepan, warm the milk, and pour over the eggs and sugar, stirring until blended.

6. Return to the pan and cook over a low heat, stirring all the time, until the custard thickens sufficiently to lightly coat the back of the spoon—do not boil.

7. Remove from the heat and add the dissolved gelatine. Pour the custard out into a large bowl and mix in the gooseberry purée. Leave to cool for 45 minutes.

8. Lightly whip the cream. When the gooseberry mixture is cold, but not set, stir in half the cream until evenly blended. Pour the gooseberry mixture into the prepared dish. Chill for 1–2 hours to set. When firm, turn out on to a flat serving plate.

9. Spread a thin covering of the remaining cream around the edge of the charlotte.

10. Spoon the rest of the cream into a piping bag fitted with a 1 cm ($\frac{1}{2}$ inch) large star nozzle. Pipe the cream around the top edge of the charlotte. Decorate with angelica. Just before serving, arrange the biscuits carefully around the outside.

To freeze: wrap and freeze at the end of step 8. Thaw overnight in the refrigerator, then finish as above.

Above: GOOSEBERRY CHARLOTTE. Below: GERANIUM CREAM WITH RED SUMMER FRUITS.

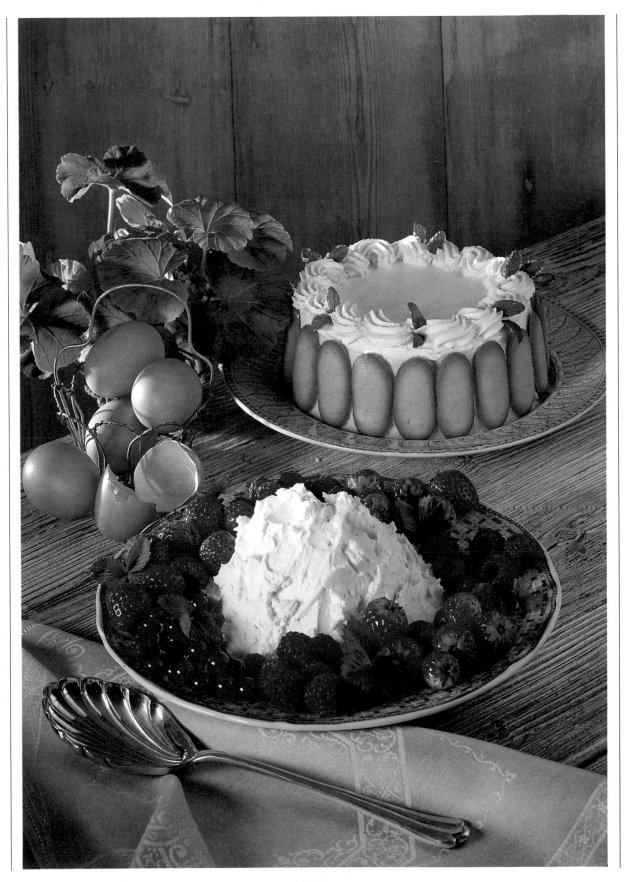

BREAD AND BUTTER PUDDING

SERVES 4

This recipe has been made for centuries and has always been popular, partly because it is such a good way to use up day-old bread. It can be made with white or brown bread.

6 thin slices bread, crusts removed
50 g (2 oz) butter or margarine
50 g (2 oz) currants or sultanas, or mixture of both
40 g (1½ oz) caster sugar
2 eggs
568 ml (1 pint) milk

1. Grease a 1.1 litre (2 pint) ovenproof dish.

2. Thickly spread the bread slices with the butter. Cut into fingers or small squares. Put half into the prepared dish. Sprinkle with all the fruit and half the sugar.

3. Top with the remaining bread, buttered side uppermost. Sprinkle with the rest of the sugar.

4. Beat the eggs and milk well together. Strain into the dish over the bread. Leave to stand for 30 minutes, so that the bread absorbs some of the liquid.

5. Bake in the oven at 170°C (325°F) mark 3 for 45 minutes—1 hour until set and the top is crisp and golden.

VARIATION

Osborne Pudding Spread the bread with orange marmalade and flavour the milk with the finely grated rind of 1 orange and 15 ml (1 tbsp) brandy or rum.

Not suitable for freezing.

Below: BREAD AND BUTTER PUDDING.

ENGLISH TRIFLE

SERVES 6–8

A perfect trifle should be a rich confection of fruit, light sponge, alcohol, real egg custard and whipped cream. The recipe has altered little over the centuries—at one time the custard was topped with syllabub, and fruit has not always been included.

4 trifle sponges
60 ml (4 tbsp) cherry jam
15 ratafia biscuits
60 ml (4 tbsp) sherry
2 bananas
grated rind and juice of ½ lemon
225 g (8 oz) cherries, stoned
450 ml (¾ pint) milk
3 eggs
50 g (2 oz) caster sugar
150 ml (¼ pint) double cream

FOR THE DECORATION

glacé cherries
25 g (1 oz) chopped nuts, toasted

1. Cut the trifle sponges in half and spread with jam, then sandwich together. Arrange in the base of a glass serving dish.

2. Cover with ratafias and sprinkle with sherry. Peel, slice and coat the bananas in lemon juice. Arrange the bananas and cherries on top of the ratafias.

3. Heat the milk in a medium saucepan until almost boiling. (Alternatively, microwave on HIGH for 5 minutes.) Whisk the eggs, lemon rind and sugar together in a bowl until pale. Pour on the hot milk, stirring continuously.

4. Return to the pan and heat gently, stirring continuously, until the custard thickens enough to coat the back of a wooden spoon—about 20 minutes. Do not allow to boil. (Alternatively, microwave the custard on MEDIUM for 7–8 minutes, whisking frequently.) Set aside to cool.

5. Pour the custard over the trifle and leave until cold.

6. Whip the cream until stiff and pipe on the top of the trifle. Decorate with glacé cherries and nuts.

Not suitable for freezing.

Above: ENGLISH TRIFLE.

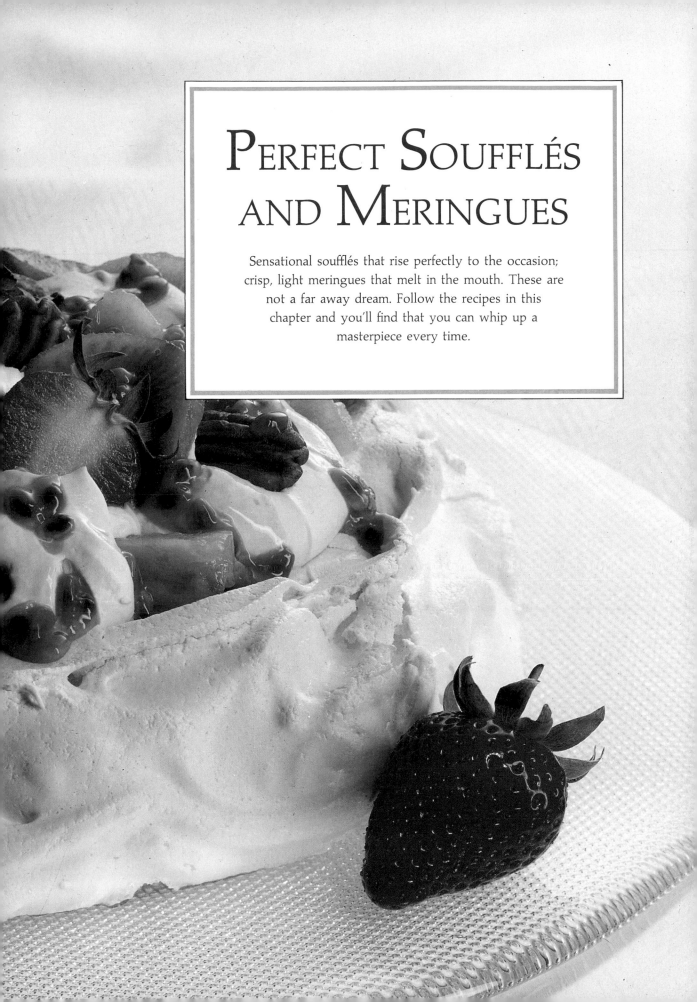

PERFECT SOUFFLÉS AND MERINGUES

Sensational soufflés that rise perfectly to the occasion;
crisp, light meringues that melt in the mouth. These are
not a far away dream. Follow the recipes in this
chapter and you'll find that you can whip up a
masterpiece every time.

Awe inspiring soufflés, crisp light meringues and marshmallow soft pavlovas are wonderful creations, guaranteed to bring sighs of delight from dinner guests.

Hot Soufflés

A hot soufflé is the true soufflé. The tiny bubbles of air, trapped within the egg whites, expand as they are heated, puffing up the base mixture, to which they were added, by as much as two thirds of its original size. When making hot soufflés, it is important to follow the recipe precisely; do not try to cut corners.

- *All the equipment must be spotlessly clean and dry. This is especially important when whisking the egg whites, as the volume will be poor if there's a trace of grease in the bowl or on the whisk.*
- *Either a hand whisk or an electric one can be used but be careful not to overbeat the whites with an electric whisk. (Egg whites whisked by hand in a copper bowl produce a greater volume, and have a much stronger make up, but as the majority of home cooks do not own a copper bowl this is not practical.)*
- *The mixture should stand in soft peaks, and the tips of the peaks should flop over gently when held upon the whisk. Overbeaten egg whites look dry and powdery and will be difficult to fold in evenly.*
- *The basic sauce mixture must still be warm when the whisked whites are folded in. If necessary, the sauce can be prepared in advance and gently reheated before adding the egg whites. Much of the volume of the whites will be lost if they are folded into a cold, stiff mixture.*
- *Quickly fold in one large spoonful of the egg whites first to loosen the basic sauce. Always add the egg whites with a large metal spoon, using a light cutting and folding action.*
- *Make sure that the dish is well greased—this helps it rise. Before baking, a hot soufflé dish should be two-thirds to three-quarters full.*
- *Make sure that the temperature in the oven remains constant and that there are no draughts while the soufflé is baking—which means no peeking! A hot soufflé is cooked when it is risen and golden, and just firm to the touch. Test it in the oven, in case it needs more time. The creamy middle should be a little gooey—if it is dry it tastes like overcooked scrambled egg.*
- *Finally, a hot soufflé should be served immediately, always keep your guests waiting for the soufflé rather than the soufflé waiting for them.*

Cold Soufflés

Cold soufflés are very light mixtures set high above a soufflé dish, as imitations of hot soufflés. They are not true soufflés but mousses set with gelatine. The preparation of the dish is all important. Do not tie the paper collar so tightly as to flute the paper and so spoil the final appearance of the soufflé. It should stand upright and be even all round. To remove the paper from the cold soufflé once the mixture has set, rinse a round bladed knife in hot water and slip it, upright between the paper and the soufflé, peeling away the paper and the knife.

The rules regarding whisking egg whites for hot soufflés apply to cold soufflés too. Similarly, cream should be whipped until it just holds its shape. If it is overbeaten it will be impossible to achieve a smooth mixture. Make sure it is well chilled.

Gelatine

Gelatine sets cold soufflés. It is not difficult to use, providing a few simple rules are followed. Before adding it to a mixture it must be softened, by soaking in cold water, this will make it swell. (Sprinkle the gelatine over the water, never the other way round or you will get lumpy gelatine.) Once soaked it can be added to a hot mixture and stirred until dissolved.

Before gelatine can be added to a cold mixture, it must be dissolved. Do this by standing the bowl over a saucepan of simmering water. Heat gently until it dissolves (just like melting chocolate). Alternatively, dissolve in a microwave. Properly dissolved gelatine will be transparent. To test this, dip a teaspoon in, turn it over and any undissolved granules will show on the back of the spoon. Never allow gelatine to boil.

Always add dissolved gelatine to a mixture which is lukewarm or at room temperature. If added to a cold mixture, it will set on contact, in fine threads. The soufflé will not set properly or will set too quickly before you have a chance to fold in the egg whites or cream.

Allow at least 4 hours for it to set, longer if it contains fruit. For a firm set, allow 12 hours.

Meringues

The light, crisp texture of meringues is the perfect foil to creamy fillings and slices of soft fruit. Meringues are made with whisked egg whites to which sugar is incorporated. They are a perfect way to use up leftover egg whites because meringues will keep in an airtight tin for as long as six weeks.

The egg whites must be whisked until they are very stiff and will hold an unwavering peak on the end of the whisk. The sugar can be added in two halves or can be whisked in a little at a time. This type of meringue is known as meringue Suisse. Meringue cuite is made by putting the unwhisked whites and sugar in a bowl, then whisking them over gently simmering water until stiff and thick. As soon as the mixture becomes thick, the bowl should be removed from the heat. This meringue has a smooth texture and wonderful gloss. It also holds its shape well. Italian meringue is made by whisking a hot sugar syrup into egg whites. It is rarely used in home cooking.

Hot Vanilla Soufflé

SERVES 4

Once used, rinse off the vanilla pod. Leave to dry on absorbent kitchen paper, then wrap and refrigerate for use once more. The flavour will not be quite as strong the second time around.

50 g (2 oz) butter or margarine, plus extra for greasing
1 vanilla pod or 5 ml (1 tsp) vanilla essence
300 ml (½ pint) milk
40 g (1½ oz) plain flour
50 g (2 oz) caster sugar
5 eggs, separated
icing sugar, for dusting

1. Tie a double strip of greaseproof paper around a 1.4 litre (2½ pint) soufflé dish to make a 7.5 cm (3 inch) collar. Brush the inside of the dish and the paper with melted butter.
2. Split the vanilla pod to reveal the seeds. Place in a saucepan with the milk and bring to the boil. Remove from the heat, cover and leave to infuse for about 20 minutes.
3. Strain the milk. Melt the butter in a large heavy-based saucepan. Add the flour and cook for 1 minute, then blend in the milk. Bring to the boil, stirring all the time, and cook for about 1 minute.
4. Cool slightly, then beat in the sugar, egg yolks and vanilla essence, if using.
5. Whisk the egg whites until stiff but not dry. Beat one spoonful into the sauce mixture to lighten it, then carefully fold in the remaining egg whites.
6. Gently pour the soufflé mixture into the prepared dish. Level the top with a palette knife and make a few cuts through the outer edges of the mixture—this helps it to rise evenly. Stand the dish on a baking sheet.
7. Bake in the oven at 190°C (375°F) mark 5 for about 35–40 minutes or until well risen, just set and well browned. (It can take as long as 50 minutes in a gas oven.) Remove the paper and dust lightly with icing sugar. Serve straight away with single cream.

Not suitable for freezing.

Orange Liqueur Soufflé

SERVES 4

This soufflé is not quite as light as the plain vanilla one as the liqueur weighs it down. However, it is still wonderful to devour!

50 g (2 oz) butter or margarine, plus extra for greasing
60 ml (4 tbsp) orange marmalade
40 g (1½ oz) plain flour
300 ml (½ pint) milk
25 g (1 oz) sugar
5 eggs, separated
75 ml (5 tbsp) orange-flavoured liqueur
icing sugar, to decorate

1. Tie a double strip of greaseproof paper around a 1.4 litre (2½ pint) soufflé dish to make a 7.5 cm (3 inch) collar. Brush the inside of the dish and the paper with melted butter.
2. Finely chop the marmalade, especially any larger pieces of peel.
3. Melt the butter in a large heavy-based saucepan. Add the flour and cook for 1 minute then blend in the milk. Bring to the boil, stirring all the time, and cook for about 1 minute.
4. Cool slightly, then beat in the marmalade, sugar and egg yolks. Carefully stir in the liqueur until evenly mixed.
5. Whisk the egg whites until stiff but not dry. Beat one spoonful into the sauce mixture to lighten it, then carefully fold in the remaining egg white.
6. Gently pour the soufflé mixture into the prepared dish. Level the top with a palette knife and make a few cuts through the outer edges of the mixture—this helps it to rise evenly. Stand the dish on a baking sheet.
7. Bake in the oven at 190°C (375°F) mark 5 for about 35–40 minutes or until well risen, just set and well browned. (It can take as long as 50 minutes in a gas oven.) Remove the paper and dust lightly with icing sugar. Serve straight away with single cream.

Not suitable for freezing.

Previous page: PAVLOVA (PAGE 202).

INDIVIDUAL CHOCOLATE MINT SOUFFLÉS

SERVES 4–6

For added luxury, pour in a little single cream to serve.

25 g (1 oz) butter or margarine, plus extra for greasing
150 ml (¼ pint) milk
12 After Eight mints
20 g (¾ oz) plain flour
25 g (1 oz) caster sugar
3 eggs, separated

1. Lightly grease six 150 ml (¼ pint) ramekin dishes.
2. Heat the milk and mints in a pan until evenly blended.
3. Melt the butter in a large heavy-based saucepan. Add the flour and cook for 1 minute, then blend in the milk. Bring to the boil, stirring all the time, and cook for 1 minute.
4. Cool slightly, then beat in the sugar and egg yolks.
5. Whisk the egg whites until stiff but not dry. Beat one spoonful into the sauce to lighten it, then carefully fold in the remaining egg white. Spoon into the prepared dishes. Stand the dishes on a baking sheet.
6. Bake in the oven at 190°C (375°F) mark 5 for 15–20 minutes or until lightly set. Serve straight away.

Not suitable for freezing.

CHOCOLATE CINNAMON SOUFFLÉ

SERVES 4

This soufflé is especially good served with a few sliced strawberries or orange segments.

50 g (2 oz) butter or margarine, plus extra for greasing
75 g (3 oz) plain chocolate
300 ml (½ pint) plus 15 ml (1 tbsp) milk
40 g (1½ oz) plain flour
2.5 ml (½ tsp) ground cinnamon
5 eggs, separated
25 g (1 oz) caster sugar
icing sugar, for dusting

1. Tie a double strip of greaseproof paper around a 1.4 litre (2½ pint) soufflé dish to make a 7.5 cm (3 inch) collar. Brush the inside of the dish and the paper with melted butter.
2. Break the chocolate into small pieces. Place in a heatproof bowl with the 15 ml (1 tbsp) milk. Stand the bowl over a pan of simmering water and heat gently until the chocolate melts. (Alternatively, microwave on LOW for 3–4 minutes until melted, stirring occasionally.) Remove from the heat.
3. Melt the butter in a large heavy-based saucepan. Add the flour and cook for 1 minute, then blend in the remaining milk and the cinnamon. Bring to the boil, stirring all the time, and cook for about 1 minute.
4. Cool slightly, then beat in the egg yolks, sugar and chocolate.
5. Whisk the egg whites until stiff but not dry. Beat one spoonful into the sauce mixture to lighten it, then carefully fold in the remaining egg whites.
6. Gently pour the soufflé mixture into the prepared dish. Level the top with a palette knife and make a few cuts through the outer edges of the mixture—this helps it to rise evenly. Stand the dish on a baking sheet.
7. Bake in the oven at 190°C (375°F) mark 5 for about 35–40 minutes or until well risen, just set and well browned. (It can take as long as 50 minutes in a gas oven.) Remove the paper and dust lightly with icing sugar. Serve straight away.

Not suitable for freezing.

MINI LEMON AND RASPBERRY SOUFFLÉS

SERVES 4–6

Small soufflés have the benefit of short cooking making their timing easier.

25 g (1 oz) butter or margarine, plus extra for greasing
225 g (8 oz) raspberries, hulled
25 g (1 oz) icing sugar
20 g (¾ oz) plain flour
150 ml (¼ pint) milk
finely grated rind and juice of 2 medium lemons
25 g (1 oz) caster sugar
3 eggs, separated

1. Grease six 150 ml (¼ pint) ramekin dishes.
2. Purée the raspberries and icing sugar in a blender or food processor. Rub through a nylon sieve. Divide between the prepared dishes.
3. Melt the butter in a medium saucepan. Add the flour and cook for 1 minute, then blend in the milk. Bring to the boil, stirring all the time, and cook for about 1 minute.
4. Cool slightly, then beat in the lemon rind, 45 ml (3 tbsp) lemon juice, the caster sugar and egg yolks.
5. Whisk the egg whites until stiff but not dry. Beat one spoonful into the sauce to lighten it, then carefully fold in the remaining egg white. Spoon into the prepared dishes. Stand the dishes on a baking sheet.
6. Bake in the oven at 190°C (375°F) mark 5 for 15–20 minutes or until lightly set. Serve straight away.

Not suitable for freezing.

Opposite: CHOCOLATE CINNAMON SOUFFLÉ.

ORANGE SEMOLINA SOUFFLÉS

SERVES 6

These individual soufflés, baked in orange shells, are good served with thinly sliced oranges sprinkled with a little orange-flavoured liqueur or orange flower water.

5 large juicy oranges
25 g (1 oz) granulated sugar
25 g (1 oz) semolina
3 eggs, separated
icing sugar, for dusting

1. Finely grate the rind and squeeze the juice from 2 of the oranges into a measuring jug. You will need 300 ml (½ pint) juice. Make up with juice from one of the remaining oranges if there is not enough.

2. Halve the remaining oranges. Scoop out any loose flesh still attached to the skins and eat separately or use in another recipe. You need six clean orange halves to serve the soufflés in. Cut a thin slice from the bottom of each so that they stand flat.

3. Place the orange juice and rind, sugar and semolina in a pan and simmer until thickened, stirring all the time. (Alternatively, microwave on HIGH for 5 minutes, stirring frequently.)

4. Cool slightly, then stir in the egg yolks. Whisk the egg whites until stiff and fold into the mixture. Spoon into the reserved orange shells and stand on a baking sheet.

5. Bake in the oven at 200°C (400°F) mark 6 for 15—20 minutes or until risen and golden brown. Dust with icing sugar and serve straight away.

Not suitable for freezing.

APRICOT AND ALMOND SOUFFLÉ

SERVES 4

The dried apricot purée gives a wonderful depth of flavour to this light soufflé. Serve with single cream flavoured with a little almond liqueur.

50 g (2 oz) butter or margarine, plus extra for greasing
175 g (6 oz) no-soak dried apricots
pared rind of 1 lemon
40 g (1½ oz) plain flour
200 ml (7 fl oz) milk
40 g (1½ oz) sugar
5 eggs, separated
flaked almonds, to decorate

1. Tie a double strip of greaseproof paper around a 1.4 litre (2½ pint) soufflé dish to make a 7.5 cm (3 inch) collar. Brush the inside of the dish and the paper with melted butter.

2. Put the apricots and lemon rind in a saucepan with enough water to cover. Cover and simmer for about 20 minutes or until really tender. Drain, reserving the liquid. Purée the apricots with 100 ml (4 fl oz) of the cooking liquor. Sieve to make a really smooth purée.

3. Melt the butter in a large heavy-based saucepan. Add the flour and cook for 1 minute, then blend in the milk. Bring to the boil, stirring all the time, and cook for about 1 minute—the sauce will be very thick.

4. Cool slightly, then beat in the apricot purée, sugar and egg yolks.

5. Whisk the egg whites until stiff but not dry. Beat one spoonful into the sauce mixture to lighten it, then carefully fold in the remaining egg whites.

6. Gently pour the soufflé mixture into the prepared dish. Level the top with a palette knife and make a few cuts through the outer edges of the mixture—this helps it to rise evenly. Sprinkle with a few flaked almonds. Stand the dish on a baking sheet.

7. Bake in the oven at 190°C (375°F) mark 5 for about 35—40 minutes or until well risen, just set and well browned. (It can take as long as 50 minutes in a gas oven.) Remove the paper and serve straight away.

Not suitable for freezing.

SALZBURGER NOCKERLN

SERVES 4

This soufflé is a speciality of the Salzkammergut region of Austria. The soufflé is baked in a shallow dish, about 2.5 cm (1 inch) deep, and is mounded in the dish to represent the mountains of the area.

3 egg yolks
finely grated rind of 2 lemons
30 ml (2 tbsp) lemon juice
25 g (1 oz) plain flour
4 egg whites
50 g (2 oz) caster sugar
icing sugar, for sifting

1. Grease a shallow 23 cm (9 inch) round or oval dish.

2. Whisk the egg yolks and lemon rind together until thick. Whisk in the lemon juice, then fold in the flour.

3. Whisk the egg whites until stiff but not dry, then gradually whisk in the caster sugar, whisking until shiny. Fold a little of the egg whites into the lemon mixture, then carefully fold in the remainder.

4. Spoon the soufflé mixture, in three mounds, in the prepared dish. Place the dish on a baking sheet.

5. Bake in the oven at 190°C (375°F) mark 5 for 12—14 minutes until lightly set. Dust with icing sugar and serve straight away.

Not suitable for freezing.

Opposite: ORANGE SEMOLINA SOUFFLÉS.

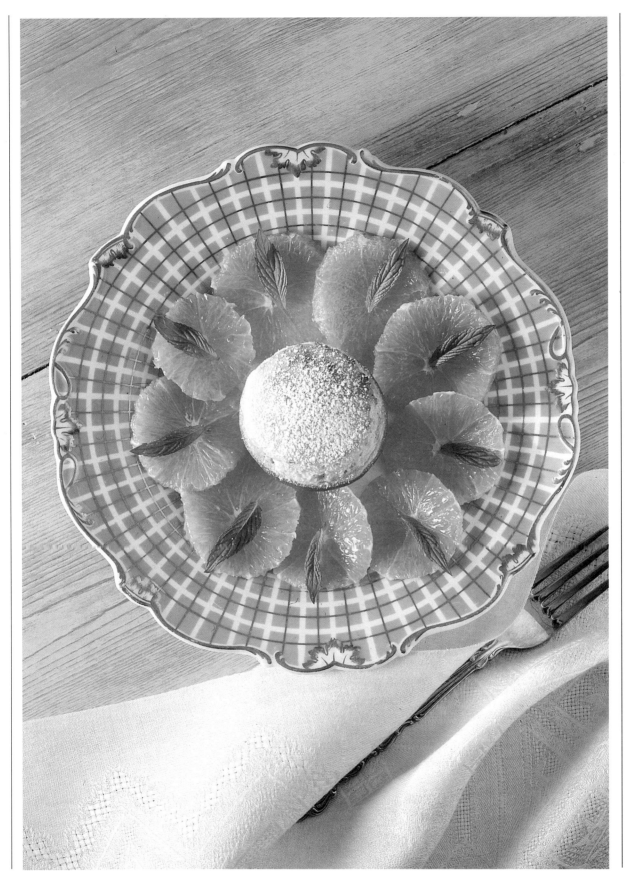

INDIVIDUAL APPLE SOUFFLÉS

SERVES 6

The apple sauce mixture can be prepared ahead, ready to add the whisked egg whites at the last minute.

icing sugar, for dusting
350 g (12 oz) cooking apples
50 g (2 oz) butter or margarine
25 g (1 oz) caster sugar
30 ml (2 tbsp) plain flour
150 ml ($\frac{1}{4}$ pint) milk
3 eggs, separated
30 ml (2 tbsp) apple brandy
apple slices, to decorate (optional)

1. Lightly grease six 150 ml ($\frac{1}{4}$ pint) ramekin dishes. Dust them out with icing sugar.

2. Peel, quarter, core and roughly chop the apples. Place in a small saucepan with 25 g (1 oz) of the butter and the sugar. Cover tightly and cook gently until the apples are very soft. Uncover and cook over a moderate heat, stirring frequently until all excess moisture evaporates. (Alternatively, cover and microwave on HIGH for 5 minutes, or until really soft, stirring.) Mash or beat until smooth; cool slightly.

3. Melt the remaining butter in a pan, add the flour and cook for 2 minutes. Remove from the heat and stir in the milk. Cook, stirring, for 2–3 minutes. (Alternatively, put everything in a bowl and microwave on HIGH for 3–4 minutes or until boiling and thickened, whisking.)

4. Remove from the heat, cool slightly, then stir in the apple purée and egg yolks. Gently mix in the apple brandy. Whisk the egg whites until stiff but not dry. Stir one large spoonful into the apple mixture, then gently fold in the remaining egg whites. Divide between the prepared ramekin dishes so that each is three-quarters full.

5. Bake in the oven at 180°C (350°F) mark 4 for about 30 minutes or until just set and golden brown. Dust quickly with icing sugar and decorate with apple slices, if using. Serve straight away with single cream.

Not suitable for freezing.

Below: INDIVIDUAL APPLE SOUFFLÉS.

CHILLED LEMON SOUFFLÉ

SERVES 6

Sharp with the tang of lemon, this delicious cold dessert has a creamy, crunchy pistachio casing, making a rich yet beautifully light soufflé.

grated rind and juice of 3 lemons
6 eggs, separated
100 g (4 oz) caster sugar
30 ml (2 tbsp) powdered gelatine
600 ml (1 pint) double cream
pinch of salt
100 g (4 oz) granulated sugar
75 g (3 oz) pistachio nuts
slices of star fruit, to decorate

1. Tie a double strip of greaseproof paper around a 900 ml (1½ pint) soufflé dish to make a 7.5 cm (3 inch) collar. Lightly brush the inside of the paper with oil. Lightly oil a baking sheet.
2. Whisk the lemon rind, egg yolks and 75 g (3 oz) of the caster sugar together in a medium bowl until pale and creamy.
3. Sprinkle the gelatine over 105 ml (7 tbsp) lemon juice and leave to soak for 2–3 minutes. Place the bowl over a pan of simmering water and stir until dissolved. (Alternatively, microwave on HIGH for 30 seconds or until dissolved.) Stir the dissolved gelatine into the egg yolk mixture.
4. Lightly whip 450 ml (¾ pint) of the cream until it just begins to hold its shape. (Do not refrigerate or it will become too cold.) Place the gelatine mixture over a bowl of iced water and stir until the mixture is on the point of setting—just beginning to thicken. Remove the bowl from the ice and fold in the cream.
5. Whisk the egg whites in a large bowl with a pinch of salt (to strengthen the whites) until stiff but not dry. Add the remaining caster sugar and whisk again until very stiff and standing in firm peaks. Stir a spoonful of egg whites into the yolk mixture to loosen it. Then, with a large metal spoon, quickly and carefully fold in the rest of the whites until evenly mixed.
6. Gently pour the mixture into the prepared dish and level the top. Chill for at least 4 hours until set.
7. Meanwhile, melt the granulated sugar very slowly in a small pan until it bubbles and turns golden brown. Stir in the pistachio nuts. Immediately pour on to the prepared baking sheet and leave to one side to cool.
8. Whip the remaining cream until it holds its shape, reserve (45 ml) 3 tbsp. Fill a piping bag fitted with a star nozzle with the remainder. Keep refrigerated until decorating the soufflé.
9. When set, carefully ease the paper collar away from the soufflé with a knife dipped in hot water.
10. Place the caramel and nut mixture in a polythene bag and lightly crush with a rolling pin or break up into a food processor and roughly chop.
11. Spread a thin layer of the reserved whipped cream around the edge of the soufflé and press the crushed nut mixture on to the sides. Pipe rosettes of cream at regular intervals around the edge of the soufflé then top each one with a slice of star fruit, sitting at an angle almost hiding the rosette. Chill until ready to serve. (No longer than 2 hours or the caramel will start to weep.)

To freeze: remove the paper collar after chilling soufflé mixture for at least 4 hours (see step 6). Open freeze the soufflé, then overwrap loosely. Thaw overnight in the refrigerator, then finish as above.

THREE FRUIT SOUFFLÉ

SERVES 6–8

grated rind and juice of 1 lemon
grated rind and juice of 1 orange
juice of 1 grapefruit
15 ml (3 tsp) powdered gelatine
4 eggs, separated
100 g (4 oz) caster sugar
300 ml (½ pint) double cream
crushed sweet biscuits and crystallized oranges and lemon slices, to decorate

1. Tie a double strip of greaseproof paper around a 18 cm (6 inch) soufflé dish to make a 7.5 cm (3 inch) collar.
2. Pour the fruit juices into a heatproof bowl and sprinkle in the gelatine. Stand the bowl over a saucepan of hot water and heat gently until dissolved. (Alternatively, microwave on HIGH for 30 seconds or until dissolved.) Cool.
3. Put the fruit rinds, egg yolks and sugar in a large heatproof bowl and stand over the pan of gently simmering water. Whisk until the mixture is thick and leaves a trail.
4. Remove the bowl from the pan and whisk in the gelatine liquid. Leave until beginning to set, whisking occasionally.
5. Whip the cream until it will stand in soft peaks. Whisk the egg whites until stiff. Fold the cream into the soufflé, then the egg whites, until evenly blended.
6. Pour into the prepared dish and level the surface. Chill until set.
7. Carefully remove the paper. Press the crushed biscuits around the exposed edge, then decorate with crystallized fruit.

To freeze: open freeze at the end of step 6, then overwrap loosely. Thaw overnight in the refrigerator, then finish as above.

CHOCOLATE ORANGE SOUFFLÉ

SERVES 6–8

Dark plain chocolate is the best kind to use for mouth-watering desserts like this one, which call for a good depth of flavour. Cold soufflés and mousses, concocted from whipped cream and egg whites, have been popular puddings since the 17th century.

450 ml (¾ pint) milk
150 g (5 oz) plain chocolate
3 eggs, separated, plus 1 egg white
75 g (3 oz) sugar
15 ml (1 tbsp) powdered gelatine
grated rind and juice of 1 orange
300 ml (½ pint) whipping cream
15 ml (1 tbsp) chocolate-flavoured liqueur
grated chocolate, to decorate

1. Tie a double strip of greaseproof paper around a 900 ml (1½ pint) soufflé dish to make a 7.5 cm (3 inches) collar. Lightly brush the inside of the paper with oil.
2. Put the milk in a saucepan and break the chocolate into it. Heat gently until the chocolate melts, then cook over a high heat until almost boiling.
3. Whisk the egg yolks and sugar together in a bowl until pale and thick. Gradually pour on the chocolate milk, stirring. Return to the pan and cook for about 20 minutes, stirring continuously, until it coats the back of a wooden spoon. Do not boil.
4. Sprinkle the gelatine over 45 ml (3 tbsp) water in a small bowl and leave to soak for 2–3 minutes. Place the bowl over a saucepan of simmering water and stir until dissolved. (Alternatively, microwave on HIGH for 30 seconds or until dissolved.) Stir the dissolved gelatine into the custard with the orange rind and juice. Leave to cool.
5. Whip the cream until it just holds its shape, then fold most of the cream into the cold mixture. Whisk the egg whites until stiff, then fold into the mixture.
6. Pour the soufflé mixture into the prepared dish and leave to set. Carefully ease away the paper collar just before serving.
7. Stir the liqueur into the remaining cream and use to decorate the soufflé. Sprinkle the top with grated chocolate.

To freeze: open freeze at the end of step 6, then overwrap loosely. Thaw overnight in the refrigerator, then finish as above.

ICED STRAWBERRY SOUFFLÉ

SERVES 8

450 g (1 lb) strawberries, hulled
60 ml (4 tbsp) almond-flavoured liqueur
30 ml (2 tbsp) lemon juice
15 ml (1 tbsp) icing sugar
50 g (2 oz) small ratafia biscuits
450 ml (¾ pint) double cream
15 ml (1 tbsp) powdered gelatine
4 eggs, separated
175 g (6 oz) caster sugar

1. Tie a double strip of greaseproof paper around a 1.1 litre (2 pint) straight sided soufflé dish to make a 7.5 cm (3 inch) collar. Lightly brush the inside of the paper with oil. Place a straight sided 450 g (1 lb) jam jar in the centre of the dish.
2. Marinate the strawberries in the liqueur, lemon juice and icing sugar for 30 minutes. Purée half the strawberries, then sieve to remove the seeds.
3. Finely crush half the ratafias. Lightly whip 300 ml (½ pint) of the cream until it just holds its shape. Whip the remaining cream.
4. Sprinkle the gelatine over 45 ml (3 tbsp) water in a small bowl and leave to soak for 2–3 minutes. Place the bowl over a saucepan of simmering water and stir until dissolved. (Alternatively, microwave on HIGH for 30 seconds or until dissolved.)
5. Meanwhile whisk the egg yolks and caster sugar together with an electric whisk until very light and creamy. Fold in the strawberry purée, whipped cream and dissolved gelatine.
6. Whisk the egg whites until stiff but not dry, then fold into the strawberry mixture.
7. Pour the mixture into the prepared dish, keeping the jam jar in the centre. Chill for 1–2 hours to set. Freeze until firm for at least 3 hours.
8. To serve, about 2 hours before eating, fill the jam jar with hot water. Gently twist and remove it from the centre of the dish. Fill the centre with the remaining strawberries. Carefully ease away the paper collar and coat the sides with crushed ratafias. Decorate with the remaining whipped cream and the whole ratafias. Refrigerate for about 2 hours before serving.

To freeze: freeze until firm in step 7, then remove the jam jar as step 8. Overwrap and freeze. Finish as above and transfer to the refrigerator for about 2 hours before serving.

Frozen Passion Fruit Soufflé

SERVES 8

A velvety smooth soufflé to make the perfect ending to a dinner party, it should be made the day before. The soufflé can be decorated with whipped cream and pistachio nuts, but as its impressive qualities are in the texture and fresh flavour, it really doesn't need to be dressed-up.

16 passion fruit
6 egg yolks
175 g (6 oz) caster sugar
600 ml (1 pint) double cream

1. Tie a double strip of greaseproof paper around a 900 ml (1½ pint) soufflé dish to make a 7.5 cm (3 inches) collar. Lightly brush the inside of the paper with oil.

2. Cut each passion fruit in half and scoop out the flesh and seeds into a nylon sieve, placed over a small bowl. Press with a spoon to extract all of the juice—about 150 ml (¼ pint).

3. Whisk the egg yolks in a large bowl with an electric mixer until very thick.

4. Put 60 ml (4 tbsp) of the passion fruit juice into a small saucepan with the caster sugar. Stir over a low heat until the sugar has dissolved. Bring to the boil and boil until the temperature reaches 110°C (230°F) on a sugar thermometer.

5. Whisk the syrup in a steady stream into the egg yolks, then continue whisking until the mixture cools and thickens. Gradually whisk in the remaining passion fruit juice, whisking until the mixture is thick and mousse-like.

6. Whip the cream until it just holds its shape. Fold the cream into the passion fruit mixture until no trace of white remains. Pour into the prepared dish, then freeze until firm. Once frozen, cover the top of the soufflé with clingfilm.

7. To serve, remove the soufflé from the freezer 20–30 minutes before serving and carefully ease away the clingfilm and paper collar. Decorate the soufflé with whipped cream, if liked.

Above: FROZEN PASSION FRUIT SOUFFLÉ.

ICED ROSE PETAL SOUFFLÉS

SERVES 8

You can either make individual soufflés or one large one. Do not make more than two or three days in advance.

50 g (2 oz) well scented rose petals, dried
100 g (4 oz) caster sugar
200 g (7 oz) fromage blanc
75 g (3 oz) crème fraîche
few drops of rose water (optional)
4 egg whites
small rose petals, to decorate

1. Tie a double strip of greaseproof paper around eight 150 ml (¼ pint) ramekin dishes to make 7.5 cm (3 inch) collars. Lightly brush the inside of the paper with oil.

2. Blend the rose petals and sugar in a blender or food processor until the petals are reduced to very small pieces.

3. Mix the fromage blanc and crème fraîche together. Taste and add a few drops of rose water to increase the flavour, if necessary.

4. Whisk the egg whites until stiff but not dry, then gently fold into the fromage blanc mixture with the sugared rose petals.

5. Divide the mixture between the prepared dishes. Freeze until firm, then cover the tops.

6. About 25 minutes before serving, carefully ease away the paper collars. Leave the soufflés in the refrigerator until required. Serve decorated with small rose petals.

APRICOT SOUFFLÉ

SERVES 6–8

This delightful chilled apricot soufflé is flavoured with a hint of almond.

225 g (8 oz) no-soak dried apricots
175 g (6 oz) caster sugar
30 ml (2 tbsp) almond-flavoured liqueur
15 ml (1 tbsp) powdered gelatine
4 eggs, separated
300 ml (½ pint) double cream
FOR THE DECORATION
ratafia biscuits
whipped cream

1. Tie a double strip of greaseproof paper around a 900 ml (1½ pint) soufflé dish to make a 7.5 cm (3 inch) collar. Lightly brush the inside of the paper with oil.
2. Put the apricots in a saucepan with 120 ml (8 tbsp) water and 50 g (2 oz) of the sugar. Heat gently until the sugar has dissolved, then cover and simmer for about 30 minutes until tender. Leave to cool slightly, then rub through a sieve or purée in a blender or food processor. Stir in the liqueur and leave to cool for about 30 minutes.
3. Sprinkle the gelatine over 60 ml (4 tbsp) water in a small bowl and leave to soak for 2–3 minutes. Place the bowl over a pan of simmering water and stir until dissolved. (Alternatively, microwave on HIGH for 30 seconds or until dissolved.) Cool slightly.
4. Put the egg yolks and remaining sugar in a large bowl and stand over the pan of gently simmering water. Whisk until the mixture is thick and holds a trail when the whisk is lifted. Remove from the heat and whisk until cold.
5. Whip the cream until it stands in soft peaks. Whisk the egg whites until stiff.
6. Stir the dissolved gelatine into the apricot purée, then fold this into the egg yolk mixture until evenly blended. Next fold in the whipped cream, then egg whites.
7. Pour the soufflé mixture into the prepared soufflé dish and level the surface. Chill for at least 4 hours until set.
8. Carefully ease away the paper collar. Crush some ratafia biscuits and use to press around the exposed edge. Decorate with whipped cream and whole ratafias.

To freeze: open freeze after removing the paper collar, then overwrap. Thaw overnight in the refrigerator. Decorate as above.

CHILLED GINGER WINE SOUFFLÉS

SERVES 6

Brandy snaps make a good accompaniment to these soufflés.

450 ml (¾ pint) milk
4 eggs, separated
50 g (2 oz) demerara sugar
2.5 ml (½ tsp) ground ginger
15 ml (1 tbsp) powdered gelatine
90 ml (6 tbsp) ginger wine
300 ml (½ pint) whipping cream
25 g (1 oz) stem ginger, roughly chopped
slices of stem ginger, to decorate

1. Tie a double strip of greaseproof paper around six 150 ml (¼ pint) ramekin dishes to make 7.5 cm (3 inch) collars.
2. Heat the milk in a pan to almost boiling. Beat the egg yolks, sugar and ground ginger together in a bowl until well mixed.
3. Pour the milk on to the egg yolk mixture. Return to the pan and cook over gentle heat, without boiling, until the mixture just coats the back of a spoon. Pour into a bowl and leave to cool.
4. Sprinkle the gelatine over 45 ml (3 tbsp) water in a small bowl and leave to soak for 2–3 minutes. Place the bowl over a saucepan of simmering water and stir until dissolved. (Alternatively, microwave on HIGH for 30 seconds or until dissolved.) Stir the dissolved gelatine into the mixture with the ginger wine. Chill until on the point of setting.
5. Divide the cream in half and lightly whip separately. Stir one portion of cream and the stem ginger into the soufflé mixture.
6. Whisk the egg whites until stiff and fold into the mixture. Spoon into the prepared dishes. Chill to set.
7. Gently ease away the paper collars and decorate the soufflés with whirls of cream and slices of stem ginger.

Not suitable for freezing.

Left: PEACH AND WALNUT MERINGUE CAKE (PAGE 208). Right: ICED ROSE PETAL SOUFFLÉS.

MERINGUE MEDLEY

MAKES 44 SMALL MERINGUES

Made with meringue cuite, these little meringues are favourites with adults and children alike.

FOR THE MERINGUE

6 egg whites
350 g (12 oz) caster sugar
15 ml (1 tbsp) finely chopped pistachio nuts

FOR THE FILLING

300 ml (½ pint) double cream
15 ml (1 tbsp) orange-flavoured liqueur
25 g (1 oz) pecans, walnuts or hazelnuts, finely chopped
15 ml (1 tbsp) raspberry purée
75 g (3 oz) plain chocolate, melted (see page 78)

1. Line several baking sheets with non-stick baking paper.
2. To make the meringue, whisk the egg whites and caster sugar, together in a large bowl standing over a large pan of simmering water until very stiff and shiny. Remove from the heat and continue whisking until the meringue will hold unwavering peaks—on no account let the meringue become too hot.
3. Fill a large piping bag fitted with a large star nozzle with meringue and pipe out as follows:
To make whirls: pipe 24 whirls of meringue on the prepared baking sheets, about 4 cm (1½ inches) in diameter.
To make oblong spirals: pipe the meringue in a spiral fashion to make 24 spirals about 7.5 cm (3 inches) long. Or, if you find it easier, pipe a joined line of shells to the same length.
To make pistachio fingers: simply pipe 20 straight lines of meringue about 7.5 cm (3 inches) long on the prepared baking sheets, then sprinkle with chopped pistachios.
4. Bake in the oven at 140°C (275°F) mark 1 for 2–2½ hours until dry. Change the sheets around in the oven during cooking to ensure that they all dry evenly. Allow the meringues to cool, then remove from the paper and complete as follows or store in an airtight tin until required.
Whirls: whisk 150 ml (¼ pint) of the double cream with the liqueur until it will hold soft peaks, then fold in the chopped nuts. Sandwich the meringues together, in pairs, with the nut cream, then place in small paper cases for serving.
Spirals: whisk the remaining cream until thick, then fold in the raspberry purée. Put the cream into a piping bag fitted with a large star nozzle. Sandwich the meringues together, in pairs, with piped cream. Put the meringues into small paper cases for serving.
Pistachio fingers: dip the base of each meringue in the melted chocolate to coat it evenly, removing excess chocolate by gently pulling the meringue across the back of a knife. Place on greaseproof paper until set.

To freeze: freeze the meringues before filling. Thaw overnight at cool room temperature, then finish as above.

CROQUEMBOUCHE OF MERINGUE

SERVES 8–10

This unorthodox Croquembouche makes a stunning centrepiece for a summer buffet party or a stunning finale to a special meal. The meringues can be made well in advance and stored in an airtight container. The cream can be mixed and flavoured, then stored in the refrigerator for several hours before serving. However, once the Croquembouche is assembled, it should be served within 1 hour.

FOR THE MERINGUES

4 egg whites
225 g (8 oz) icing sugar, sifted
15 g (½ oz) cocoa powder

FOR THE FILLING

900 g (2 lb) full fat soft cheese
finely grated rind of 2 oranges
few drops of vanilla essence
60 ml (4 tbsp) orange-flavoured liqueur
caster sugar, to taste

FOR THE DECORATION

fresh summer fruits, such as redcurrants, strawberries, blackcurrants, tayberries
fresh or crystallized flowers or petals

1. Line two large baking sheets with non-stick paper.
2. To make the meringue, place the egg whites and sugar in a large bowl standing over a pan of simmering water. Using a hand held electric whisk, whisk the meringue until thick and standing in stiff peaks. Remove from the heat and continue whisking for 2 minutes.
3. Spoon half of the meringue mixture into a large piping bag fitted with a star nozzle and pipe small star shapes, about 2.5 cm (1 inch) in diameter, on to one of the prepared baking sheets.
4. Sift the cocoa powder into the remaining meringue mixture. Fold in, using a large metal spoon. Spoon into the piping bag and pipe star shapes as above.
5. Bake all the meringues at 110°C (225°F) mark ¼ for 2½–3 hours or until dry. Leave to cool on a wire rack.
6. To make the filling, beat the soft cheese, orange rind, vanilla essence, liqueur and sugar to taste together. Pile most of the mixture in a pyramid shape on a cake stand or large serving plate.
7. Stick meringues on to the soft cheese pyramid until completely covered. Spread a little of the reserved cheese mixture on to the flat side of the remaining meringues and attach to the first meringues, forming a tall, thin pyramid about 20.5 cm (8 inches) high. Decorate with fresh fruits and flowers.

To freeze: freeze the meringues. Thaw at cool room temperature, then finish as above.

Opposite: MERINGUE MEDLEY.

MERINGUE BASKET

SERVES 6–8

The unfilled basket will keep well for several days in an airtight container.

FOR THE MERINGUE

4 egg whites
225 g (8 oz) icing sugar

FOR THE FILLING

300 ml (½ pint) whipping cream
30 ml (2 tbsp) kirsch
about 450 g (1 lb) prepared fresh fruit in season, such as strawberries, raspberries, blackberries, starfruit

1. Line three baking sheets with non-stick baking paper (turn rimmed baking sheets upside down and use the bases) and draw a 19 cm (7½ inch) circle on each. Turn the paper over so that the pencilled circle is visible but does not come into contact with the meringues.
2. To make the meringue, place 3 of the egg whites in a large bowl standing over a pan of simmering water. Sift in 175 g (6 oz) of the icing sugar. Whisk the egg whites and sugar until the mixture stands in very stiff peaks. Do not allow the bowl to get too hot or the meringue will crust around edges.
3. Spoon one third of the meringue mixture into a piping bag fitted with a large star nozzle. Secure the paper to the baking sheets with a little meringue. Pipe rings of meringue, about 1 cm (½ inch) thick, inside two of the circles on the paper. Fill the bag with the remaining meringue and, starting from the centre, pipe a continuous coil of meringue on the third sheet of paper to make the base of the basket.
4. Bake all in the oven at 100°C (200°F) mark ¼ for 2½–3 hours until dry. Swap the positions of the meringues during this time so that they cook evenly.
5. Use the remaining egg white and sugar to make meringue as before and put into the piping bag. Remove the cooked meringue rings from the paper and layer up on the base, piping a ring of fresh meringue between each. Return to the oven for a further 1½–2 hours.
6. Leave to cool, then slide on to a wire rack and peel off the base paper. Just before serving, stand the meringue shell on a flat serving plate.
7. To make the filling, lightly whip the cream and fold in the kirsch. Spoon half into the base of the meringue basket and top with fruit. Whirl the remaining cream over the top and decorate with more fruit.

To freeze: freeze the meringue basket before filling. Thaw overnight at cool room temperature, then finish as above.

VARIATION

Mini Meringue Baskets Prepare the baking sheets as above, but draw sixteen 5 cm (2 inch) circles or eight 10 cm (4 inch) circles on the paper. Make the meringue as above, using 3 egg whites and 175 g (6 oz) icing sugar. Pipe a continuous coil of meringue on each circle to make the bases, then pipe a ring on top of each circle. Bake as step 4 above for 2½ hours to dry out.

PAVLOVA

SERVES 8

This luscious meringue is generally believed to have been created in Australia in the 1930s to celebrate the visit of Anna Pavlova, the great prima ballerina.

FOR THE MERINGUE

3 egg whites
175 g (6 oz) caster sugar
5 ml (1 tsp) cornflour
5 ml (1 tsp) vinegar
2.5 ml (½ tsp) vanilla essence

FOR THE FILLING

2 passion fruit
2 kiwi fruit
225 g (8 oz) strawberries
225 g (8 oz) fresh pineapple
450 ml (¾ pint) double cream or Greek yogurt and double cream, mixed
walnuts, pecans or almonds, to decorate

1. Line a baking sheet with greased foil or non-stick baking paper.
2. To make the meringue, whisk the egg whites in a large bowl until very stiff. Add 50 g (2 oz) of the sugar and whisk until very stiff. Add another 50 g (2 oz) sugar and whisk once more until the mixture returns to its stiff texture. Spoon in the remaining sugar and whisk again until shiny and standing in stiff peaks. Do not rush this process or the meringue will become too soft.
3. Fold in the cornflour, vinegar and vanilla essence.
4. Pile or pipe the meringue in a 23 cm (9 inch) round or oval on to the prepared baking sheet, making sure there is a substantial dip or hollow in the centre to hold the filling. It should look rather like a nest.
5. Bake in the oven at 130°C (250°F) mark ½ for 1¼–1½ hours or until pale brown and dry but a little soft in the centre. Press lightly with a finger to test if the meringue is cooked. Leave to cool slightly, then peel off the foil or paper and place on a serving dish to cool completely. At this stage the meringue will probably crack and sink a little—this is to be expected with a Pavlova. (When completely cold, the meringue can be overwrapped in foil and stored for a couple of days if wished.)
6. To make the filling, halve the passion fruit and scoop out the pulp. Peel and slice the kiwi fruit. Halve the strawberries. Slice the pineapple, discard skin and core, and roughly chop the flesh. Whip the cream until it just holds its shape and, if using, mix with the yogurt.
7. Either fold the fruit into the cream and spoon into the Pavlova or fill the centre with cream—it may have to be whipped a little longer if used in this way—and arrange the fruit on top. Scatter with nuts to decorate and serve immediately, or within an hour or so.

Not suitable for freezing.

Illustrated on pages 186–187

CHOCOLATE CHIP MERINGUES

SERVES 6

Serve these chocolate speckled meringues with a bowl of strawberries or a fresh fruit salad.

4 egg whites
225 g (8 oz) caster sugar
100 g (4 oz) plain chocolate, grated
300 ml (½ pint) double or whipping cream

1. Line a baking sheet with non-stick baking paper.
2. Whisk the egg whites in a bowl until stiff but not dry. Whisk in 20 ml (4 tsp) of the caster sugar, keeping the mixture stiff. Fold in the remaining sugar with the grated chocolate.
3. Spoon out 12 meringues on to the prepared baking sheet, allowing them room to spread.
4. Bake in the oven at 130°C (250°F) mark ½ for about 1¼ hours until dry. Peel off the paper and cool on a wire rack. Store, if wished, in an airtight container.
5. To serve, whip the cream until softly stiff and use to sandwich together the meringues.

To freeze: freeze the meringues before filling. Thaw overnight at cool room temperature, then finish as above.

MERINGUE AND ICE CREAM EXTRAVAGANZA

SERVES 10–12

A more elaborate version of the meringue basket on page 202, filled with ice cream and decorated with frosted fruits, flowers and leaves.

FOR THE MERINGUE

1 meringue basket, made with 3 egg whites and 175 g (6 oz) icing sugar to the end of step 4 (see page 202)
3 egg whites
175 g (6 oz) icing sugar

FOR THE FILLING AND DECORATION

1 quantity ice cream of your choice (see pages 216–224)
Frosted fruits, flowers and leaves (see page 10)

1. Line a baking sheet with non-stick baking paper.
2. Using the egg whites and sugar, make a stiff meringue mixture as page 202.
3. To assemble the meringue basket, stand the rings of meringue on the base. Stand on the prepared baking sheet.
4. Using a palette knife, spread a little of the uncooked meringue mixture around the outside of the basket, filling in the gaps between the rings.
5. Spoon the remaining meringue into a piping bag fitted with a large star nozzle. Working from the base to the top of the basket, pipe vertical lines of meringue to cover the sides completely. Pipe scrolls or rosettes around the top to neaten the edge.
6. Bake in the oven at 100°C (200°F) mark ¼ for about 2 hours until dry. Leave the basket to cool completely.
7. To make the filling, leave the ice cream at room temperature to soften slightly. When the basket is cold, quickly fill with the ice cream. Return to the freezer for 1 hour until firm. Decorate and serve.

To freeze: pack the meringue basket in a rigid container and freeze. Thaw at cool room temperature.

CHOCOLATE MERINGUE GÂTEAU

SERVES 6–8

FOR THE MERINGUE

3 egg whites
175 g (6 oz) caster sugar

FOR THE FILLING

2 egg yolks
50 g (2 oz) caster sugar
50 g (2 oz) plain chocolate, melted (see page 78)
50 g (2 oz) unsalted butter, softened
150 ml (¼ pint) double cream
Chocolate curls (see page 78), to decorate

1. Draw two 20.5 cm (8 inch) circles on non-stick baking paper and place on separate baking sheets.
2. To make the meringue, whisk the egg whites in a large bowl until stiff. Whisk in 75 g (3 oz) of the sugar. Whisk again for 5 minutes until stiff. Carefully fold in the remaining sugar.
3. Spoon the mixture into a piping bag fitted with a large star nozzle and pipe the mixture on to the circles on the baking sheets. Or, using a palette knife, spread the mixture evenly.
4. Bake in the oven at 110°C (225°F) mark ¼ for about 1¼ hours until dry. Cool on the sheets for 30 minutes.
5. To make the filling, beat the egg yolks in a bowl. Put the sugar and 45 ml (3 tbsp) water into a small pan and heat to dissolve the sugar.
6. Bring to the boil and boil to 110°C (230°F) on a sugar thermometer, or until the mixture reaches the soft ball stage. Check by plunging a teaspoonful into a bowl of iced water. It should form a ball in your fingers.
7. Pour the syrup on to the egg yolks in a steady stream, whisking all the time. Continue to whisk until thick and mousse-like.
8. Cool the chocolate for 5 minutes. Gradually beat the butter and melted chocolate into the syrup mixture.
9. Carefully peel the paper from the meringues, then use the chocolate filling to sandwich the rounds together. Whip the cream until stiff and pipe on to the gâteau. Decorate with chocolate curls.

To freeze: freeze the meringues before filling. Thaw overnight at cool room temperature, then finish as above.

Brown Sugar and Hazelnut Meringues

MAKES ABOUT 40

Meringues made with brown sugar have a rich flavour and are a delicate pale brown in colour. Serve them sandwiched together with ice cream or cream, or as an accompaniment to fruit salads or compotes.

25 g (1 oz) hazelnuts
3 egg whites
175 g (6 oz) light brown soft sugar
FOR THE FILLING
Ice cream (see pages 216–224)

1. Line two large baking sheets with non-stick baking paper.
2. Toast the hazelnuts under the grill until golden brown. Tip on to a clean tea towel and rub off the loose skins. Chop roughly.
3. Whisk the egg whites in a bowl until stiff. Whisk in the sugar, 15 ml (1 tbsp) at a time. Spoon the meringue mixture into a piping bag fitted with a large star nozzle and pipe about 40 small swirls on to the prepared baking sheets. Sprinkle with the hazelnuts.
4. Bake in the oven at 110°C (225°F) mark $\frac{1}{4}$ for about 2–3 hours or until dry. Swap the position of the sheets halfway through the cooking time to ensure even browning. Leave to cool.
5. Sandwich the meringues together in pairs with a little ice cream. Arrange on a freezerproof plate or a baking sheet and freeze for up to 2 hours before serving. Serve with a sauce, if liked.

Queen of Puddings

SERVES 4

A delicate old English favourite.

4 eggs
568 ml (1 pint) milk
100 g (4 oz) fresh breadcrumbs
45–60 ml (3–4 tbsp) raspberry jam
75 g (3 oz) caster sugar

1. Separate 3 of the eggs and beat together the 3 egg yolks and one whole egg. Add to the milk in a bowl and mix well. Stir in the breadcrumbs.
2. Spread the jam on the base of a pie dish. Pour over the milk mixture and leave for 30 minutes.
3. Bake in the oven at 150°C (300°F) mark 2 for 1 hour until set.
4. Whisk the egg whites in a bowl until stiff. Fold in the sugar. Pile on top of the custard and return to the oven for a further 15–20 minutes until the meringue is set.

Not suitable for freezing.

Meringue and Ganache Gâteau

SERVES 14–16

This very rich gâteau makes a lovely party-time special.

FOR THE MERINGUE
4 egg whites
225 g (8 oz) caster sugar
FOR THE FILLING
350 g (12 oz) plain chocolate
475 ml (16 fl oz) double cream
30–45 ml (2–3 tbsp) orange-flavoured liqueur, brandy or rum
icing sugar, for sifting

1. Line four baking sheets with non-stick baking paper. Draw a 20.5 cm (8 inch) circle in the centre of each sheet of paper.
2. To make the meringue, whisk the egg whites in a bowl until stiff, but not dry. Gradually whisk in the sugar, a little at a time, whisking well until very stiff and shiny. Divide the meringue equally between the prepared baking sheets, then spread evenly to form neat rounds.
3. Bake in the oven at 140°C (275°F) mark 1 for 1–1$\frac{1}{4}$ hours until dry, swapping over the baking sheets during cooking to ensure that they dry out evenly. Leave to cool.
4. Meanwhile to make the filling, break the chocolate into small pieces. Put into a large saucepan with the cream. Heat gently, stirring, until the chocolate melts and blends with the cream to form a smooth rich cream. Do not allow to boil.
5. Pour the chocolate cream into a bowl and leave to cool, stirring frequently to prevent a skin forming. When cold, add the liqueur and whisk well until light and fluffy.
6. Place one of the meringue layers on a flat serving plate, then spread with a generous layer of the whipped chocolate cream. Continue until the meringue rounds are sandwiched together.
7. Spread the remaining chocolate cream all over the meringue to cover completely. Mark the cream into swirls with a palette knife. Sift the icing sugar lightly over the gâteau. Chill until slightly chilled, but do not let the chocolate cream set too hard. Serve the gâteau still slightly chilled.

To freeze: freeze the meringues before filling. Thaw overnight at cool room temperature, then finish as above.

Opposite: BROWN SUGAR AND HAZELNUT MERINGUES.

VACHERIN AU CHOCOLAT ET AUX MARRONS

SERVES 10–12

The meringues can be made in advance and stored in an airtight container. Do not sandwich them with the filling more than 2 hours before serving.

FOR THE MERINGUE
175 g (6 oz) hazelnuts
6 egg whites
350 g (12 oz) caster sugar

FOR THE FILLING AND DECORATION
225 g (8 oz) plain or bitter chocolate
60 ml (4 tbsp) dark rum
350 g (12 oz) sweetened chestnut purée
300 ml (½ pint) double or whipping cream
Chocolate caraque (see page 78) or grated chocolate, to decorate

1. Grease three 20.5 cm (8 inch) sandwich tins and line the bases with non-stick baking paper.

2. To make the meringue, first toast the hazelnuts lightly under the grill, shaking the pan frequently. Transfer the nuts to a clean tea towel and rub gently while still hot to remove the skins. Grind until very fine.

3. Put the egg whites in a large bowl and whisk until very stiff and standing in peaks. Whisk in 175 g (6 oz) of the sugar until the meringue is glossy. Fold in the remaining sugar with the hazelnuts. Spoon the meringue into the prepared sandwich tins. Level the tops.

4. Bake in the oven at 180°C (350°F) mark 4 for 35–40 minutes until crisp.

5. Invert the tins on to a wire rack and turn out the meringues. Peel off the lining papers carefully. (Don't worry if the meringues are cracked.) Leave to cool.

6. To make the filling, break the chocolate in small pieces. Place in a heatproof bowl standing over a pan of simmering water. Add the rum and heat gently until the chocolate melts. Remove from the heat and gradually blend in 225 g (8 oz) of the chestnut purée.

7. Put a meringue round, soft side uppermost, on a serving plate. Spread with half of the chocolate and chestnut mixture, then top with the second meringue round, crisp side uppermost. Spread with the remaining mixture, then top with the last round.

8. Whip the cream until it holds its shape. Reserve 30 ml (2 tbsp) of the cream and swirl the remainder all over the gâteau to cover the top and sides completely.

9. Blend the remaining chestnut purée into the reserved cream, then pipe around the edge. Decorate with chocolate caraque or grated chocolate. Chill before serving.

Not suitable for freezing.

HAZELNUT MERINGUE GÂTEAU

SERVES 6–8

This simple gâteau is perfect for the novice meringue-maker. The sharp flavour of the raspberries contrasts well with the nutty meringue.

FOR THE MERINGUE
3 egg whites
175 g (6 oz) caster sugar
50 g (2 oz) hazelnuts, skinned, toasted and finely chopped

FOR THE FILLING
300 ml (½ pint) double cream
350 g (12 oz) raspberries, hulled
icing sugar, for sifting
finely chopped pistachio nuts, to decorate

1. Line two baking sheets with non-stick baking paper, then draw a 20.5 cm (8 inch) circle on each one.

2. To make the meringue, whisk the egg whites in a bowl until very stiff, but not dry. Gradually whisk in the caster sugar, a little at a time, whisking well between each addition until stiff and very shiny. Carefully fold in the chopped hazelnuts.

3. Divide the meringue equally between the prepared baking sheets, then spread neatly into rounds. With a palette knife, mark the top of one of the rounds into swirls—this will be the top meringue.

4. Bake in the oven at 140°C (275°F) mark 1 for about 1½ hours until dry. Turn the oven off, and allow the meringues to cool in the oven.

5. To make the filling, whip the cream until it will hold soft peaks. Carefully remove the meringues from the baking paper. Place the smooth meringue round on a large flat serving plate, then spread with the cream. Arrange the raspberries on top of the cream, then place the second meringue on top. Sift icing sugar over the top of the gâteau, then sprinkle with the nuts. Serve the gâteau as soon as possible.

To freeze: freeze the meringues before filling. Thaw at cool room temperature, then finish as above.

Opposite: HAZELNUT MERINGUE GÂTEAU.

PEACH AND WALNUT MERINGUE CAKE

SERVES 8

FOR THE MERINGUE
4 egg whites
225 g (8 oz) caster sugar
15 ml (1 tbsp) ground cinnamon
225 g (8 oz) walnut pieces, finely chopped

FOR THE FILLING
30 ml (2 tbsp) granulated sugar
225 g (8 oz) ripe peaches, thinly sliced
pared rind of 1 lemon
50 g (2 oz) redcurrants
30 ml (2 tbsp) kirsch
450 ml (¾ pint) double cream
icing sugar, for dusting
Frosted redcurrants (see page 10), to decorate

1. Line three baking sheets with non-stick baking paper.
2. To make the meringue, whisk the egg whites in a bowl until stiff but not dry. Gradually whisk in 100 g (4 oz) of the caster sugar, keeping the mixture stiff. Fold in the remaining caster sugar with the cinnamon and 100 g (4 oz) of the walnuts.
3. Divide the meringue between the prepared baking sheets and, with a round-bladed knife, spread the mixture into three 18 cm (7 inch) rounds.
4. Bake in the oven at 190°C (375°F) mark 5 for 5 minutes. Reduce the oven temperature to 140°C (275°F) mark 1 and bake for a further 1–1¼ hours until dry. Cool in the oven, then carefully ease off the paper.
5. To make the filling, dissolve the granulated sugar in 75 ml (3 fl oz) water in a pan over a very gentle heat. Add the peaches, lemon rind and redcurrants. Bring to the boil, then cover and simmer for 5 minutes until the juices begin to run. Uncover and simmer for about 5 minutes.
6. Cool, then purée in a blender or food processor. Sieve the fruit into a bowl and stir in the kirsch.
7. Lightly whip the cream until it just holds its shape. Place one meringue round on a serving plate. Spread a quarter of the whipped cream over the meringue. Spread half of the peach purée over the cream. Top with another round and cover with cream and fruit purée as before. Finish with the remaining round.
8. With a round-bladed knife, cover the sides of the meringue cake with cream. Press on the remaining walnuts. Decorate with whirls of cream. Cover loosely and chill for at least 1 hour before serving, but no longer than 3–4 hours. Dust with icing sugar and decorate.

To freeze: freeze the meringues before filling. Thaw at cool room temperature, then finish as above.

Illustrated on page 198

LEMON MERINGUE PIE

SERVES 6–8

Lemon meringue pie comes in various forms. This delicious version has a lemon filling which is cool, smooth and tangy.

1 quantity Pâte sucrée (see page 43)

FOR THE FILLING
rind and juice of 4 large lemons
65 g (2½ oz) cornflour
50–75 g (2–3 oz) caster sugar
3 egg yolks

FOR THE MERINGUE
3 egg whites
175 g (6 oz) caster sugar

1. Roll out the pastry on a lightly floured work surface to a round 2.5 cm (1 inch) larger than a 23 cm (9 inch) fluted flan tin. Line the dish with the pastry, pressing it well into the flutes. Trim the edge, then prick the pastry well all over with a fork. Chill for 30 minutes.
2. Bake blind at 220°C (425°F) mark 7 for 25–30 minutes until cooked and lightly browned. Leave to cool. Leave the oven on.
3. Meanwhile to make the filling, put the lemon rind and 600 ml (1 pint) water in a saucepan. Bring to the boil, then remove from the heat, cover and leave to stand for at least 30 minutes.
4. Remove all of the lemon rind from the pan, then stir in the lemon juice. Blend the cornflour with a little of the lemon liquid to form a smooth paste, pour it into the pan and stir well. Bring the lemon mixture to the boil, stirring continuously. Reduce the heat and continue cooking until thickened. Stir in the sugar to taste, then beat in the egg yolks. Pour the lemon filling into the pastry case.
5. To make the meringue, whisk the egg whites in a bowl until stiff, but not dry. Gradually whisk in the sugar, a little at a time, whisking well between each addition, until very stiff and shiny.
6. Put the meringue into a large piping bag fitted with a large star nozzle, then pipe it attractively on top of the lemon filling. Alternatively, spoon the meringue on to the filling and shape it into swirls with a palette knife.
7. Bake in the oven for 5–10 minutes until the meringue is very lightly browned. Remove the pie from the oven and leave to cool, then refrigerate until cold.

Not suitable for freezing.

Opposite: LEMON MERINGUE PIE.

KEY LIME PIE

SERVES 8

A favourite pie from America's deep South. It is sometimes made with a biscuit crust.

1½ quantity Flan pastry (see page 43)

FOR THE FILLING
200 g (7 oz) granulated sugar
25 g (1 oz) butter
25 g (1 oz) cornflour
finely grated rind and juice of 4 limes
3 egg yolks
30 ml (2 tbsp) milk
grated lime rind, to decorate

FOR THE MERINGUE
3 egg whites
90 ml (6 tbsp) caster sugar

1. Roll out the pastry and use to line a 23 cm (9 inch) fluted flan dish. Chill for 30 minutes.
2. Bake blind in the oven at 200°C (400°F) mark 6 for 10–15 minutes. Remove the beans and bake for a further 10 minutes or until pale brown. Leave to cool.
3. To make the filling, put the sugar, butter and 300 ml (½ pint) water in a saucepan and heat gently until the sugar has dissolved, stirring all the time. Do not boil.
4. Meanwhile, blend the cornflour to a smooth paste with the lime rind and juice. Stir a little of the sugar mixture into the blended cornflour, then return to the pan. Heat gently, stirring all the time, until boiling and thickened. Cool slightly, then stir in the egg yolks, one at a time, and the milk. Leave to cool.
5. Pour the cold filling into the pastry case.
6. To make the meringue, whisk the egg whites in a bowl until stiff. Continue whisking, adding the sugar 15 ml (1 tbsp) at a time. Spoon the meringue on to the filling. Using a palette knife, spread it to the edges of the pastry case to seal in the filling. Pull the meringue into peaks with a teaspoon.
7. Bake in the oven at 200°C (400°F) mark 6 for about 15 minutes or until the meringue is lightly browned. Leave to cool, then sprinkle with the lime rind.

Not suitable for freezing.

ALMOND MERINGUE WITH NECTARINES

SERVES 6

Almonds ground at home from whole almonds have a stronger flavour than shop-bought, ready ground ones.

FOR THE MERINGUE
75 g (3 oz) whole almonds
4 egg whites
225 g (8 oz) caster sugar
pinch of cream of tartar

FOR THE FILLING
50 g (2 oz) granulated sugar
4 ripe nectarines
300 ml (½ pint) whipping cream
30–45 ml (2–3 tbsp) peach brandy
icing sugar, for dusting

1. Line two baking sheets with non-stick baking paper.
2. To make the meringue, first blanch the almonds in boiling water to remove the skins. Dry well, then finely grind in a nut mouli or food processor.
3. Whisk the egg whites in a bowl until stiff. Add 15 ml (1 tbsp) of the caster sugar and the cream of tartar and whisk again for about 1 minute. Fold in the remaining caster sugar with the ground almonds.
4. Spread the mixture evenly into two 20.5 cm (8 inch) rounds on the prepared baking sheets.
5. Bake in the oven at 140°C (275°F) mark 1 for 1–1½ hours until firm and golden. Leave to cool.
6. Meanwhile to make the filling, dissolve the granulated sugar in 150 ml (¼ pint) water in a pan. Boil for 1 minute. Halve 2 of the nectarines. Add to the syrup, cover and poach until tender. Lift out of the liquid and discard the liquid. Remove the stones and purée the nectarines in a blender or food processor until smooth. (If wished, press through a nylon sieve.) Cool.
7. Stone and slice the remaining nectarines. Carefully remove the paper from the meringue rounds. Whip the cream until stiff and fold in the fruit purée, adding peach brandy to taste. Use to fill the meringues, layering with the nectarine slices. Dust with icing sugar.

To freeze: freeze the meringue before filling. Thaw overnight at cool room temperature, then finish as above.

BAKED ALASKA

SERVES 6–8

A spectacular dessert for a special dinner party, the recipe for Baked Alaska originated in the United States, where it is also sometimes called Norwegian Omelet or *omelette norwégienne* in French. Although impressive to serve, Baked Alaska is in fact surprisingly easy to make; the essential thing is to allow yourself unhurried time in the kitchen before serving—Baked Alaska cannot be kept waiting once it is cooked!

225 g (8 oz) fresh or frozen raspberries
30 ml (2 tbsp) orange-flavoured liqueur
20.5 cm (8 inch) sponge flan case (see page 125)
483 ml (17 fl oz) block vanilla ice cream

FOR THE MERINGUE

4 egg whites
175 g (6 oz) caster sugar

1. Place the raspberries on a shallow dish and sprinkle over the liqueur. Cover and leave to macerate for 2 hours, turning occasionally.

2. Place the sponge flan on a large ovenproof serving dish and spoon the raspberries and juice into the centre.

3. To make the meringue, whisk the egg whites in a bowl until stiff, but not dry. Add 20 ml (4 tsp) of the caster sugar and whisk again, keeping the mixture stiff. Sprinkle over the remaining sugar and fold through gently.

4. Fit a piping bag with a large star nozzle and fill with the meringue mixture.

5. Place the block of ice cream on top of the raspberries, then immediately pipe the meringue on top. Start from the sponge base and pipe the meringue around and over the ice cream until it is completely covered, leaving no gaps.

6. Immediately bake in the oven at 230°C (450°F) mark 8 for 3–4 minutes. At this stage the meringue should be nicely tinged with brown. Watch the meringue carefully as it burns easily. Do not overcook or the ice cream will become too soft. Serve at once, before the ice cream begins to melt.

Not suitable for freezing.

Below: BAKED ALASKA.

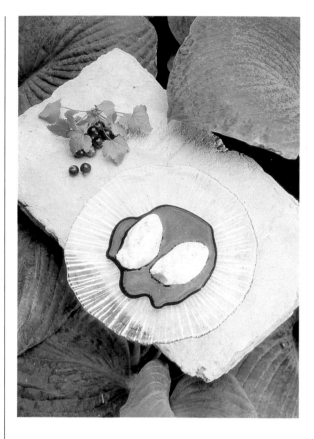

spoons as moulds. Slide about six or eight at a time into the liquid and poach gently for 2–3 minutes. The meringue will puff up then shrink back a little. When cooked, it will be firm if lightly touched. Remove with a fish slice and drain on absorbent kitchen paper. Poach the remaining mixture. Store in a cool place for not more than 2 hours.

5. To serve, spoon a little blackcurrant sauce on to individual serving dishes. Float a few 'islands' on top and sprinkle with nutmeg.

To freeze: pack and freeze the sauce at the end of step 1. Thaw overnight at cool room temperature, then chill.

MERINGUE ROULADE
MAKES 10 SLICES

FOR THE MERINGUE ROULADE
3 egg whites
175 g (6 oz) caster sugar

FOR THE FILLING
225 g (8 oz) raspberries, hulled
15 ml (1 tbsp) icing sugar
300 ml (½ pint) double cream

FOR THE DECORATION
150 ml (¼ pint) double cream
cocoa powder
few raspberries, hulled
mint, chervil or geranium leaves

1. Grease a 33 × 23 cm (13 × 9 inch) Swiss roll tin and line with greaseproof paper.

2. To make the meringue, using a hand held whisk, whisk the egg whites in a bowl until stiff. Gradually whisk in the sugar, whisking after each addition until thoroughly incorporated. The mixture should be thick and glossy. Spoon the meringue into the prepared tin and level the surface.

3. Bake in the oven at 190°C (375°F) mark 5 for 10–15 minutes or until risen and firm to the touch.

4. Turn the roulade out on to a sheet of greaseproof paper. Peel away the lining paper and leave until cold.

5. To make the filling, mix 100 g (4 oz) of the raspberries with the sugar and crush lightly with a fork. Whip the cream until stiff then fold in the crushed raspberries. Spoon the cream evenly over the cold meringue. Sprinkle with the remaining raspberries.

6. Starting at one of the narrow ends of the meringue, roll up, using the greaseproof paper to help. Transfer to a serving plate.

7. To make the decoration, whip the remaining cream until stiff and spoon into a piping bag fitted with a large star nozzle. Pipe the cream down the centre of the roulade. Sift over a little cocoa powder, then decorate with the raspberries and herb leaves.

Not suitable for freezing.

Above: FLOATING SPICE ISLANDS.

FLOATING SPICE ISLANDS
SERVES 8
Poached meringues are floated on a blackcurrant sauce.

FOR THE SAUCE
350 g (12 oz) blackcurrants, stalks removed
75 g (3 oz) granulated sugar
30 ml (2 tbsp) blackcurrant-flavoured liqueur

FOR THE MERINGUE
2 egg whites
50 g (2 oz) caster sugar
grated nutmeg
pinch of salt

1. To make the sauce, place the blackcurrants, granulated sugar and 60 ml (4 tbsp) water in a small saucepan. Cover tightly and cook gently until the fruit softens. Rub through a nylon sieve, then leave to cool. Stir in the liqueur. Cover and chill.

2. Meanwhile to make the meringue, whisk the egg whites in a bowl until stiff, but not dry. Gradually whisk in the caster sugar, keeping the mixture stiff. Fold in 1.25 ml (¼ tsp) grated nutmeg.

3. Pour 2 cm (¾ inch) water into a large frying pan and bring to a gentle simmer. Add the salt.

4. Shape the meringue into small egg shapes, using two

SWISS FLAN

SERVES 6–8

The tip of every meringue star in this dessert is dotted with a bead of redcurrant jelly to give a jewelled effect. Therefore, a little skill with a piping bag is needed as each star must have a clean point.

---

1 quantity Pâte sucrée (see page 43)

FOR THE FILLING

225 g (8 oz) granulated sugar

---

juice of 1 lemon

---

900 g (2 lb) dessert apples

FOR THE MERINGUE

3 egg whites

---

175 g (6 oz) caster sugar

---

30 ml (2 tbsp) redcurrant jelly or seedless raspberry jam

---

1. Roll out the pastry on a lightly floured work surface to a round 2.5 cm (1 inch) larger than a 23 cm (9 inch) fluted flan tin. Line the tin with the pastry, pressing it well into the flutes. Trim the edge, then prick the pastry well, all over, with a fork. Chill for 30 minutes.

2. Bake blind in the oven at 220°C (425°F) mark 7 for 20–25 minutes until cooked and lightly browned. Cool. Reduce the temperature to 140°C (275°F) mark 1.

3. To make the filling, put the sugar and lemon juice into a wide saucepan with the water. Heat gently until the sugar has dissolved, then bring to the boil and simmer gently for 5 minutes.

4. Peel, quarter, core and slice the apples about 0.5 cm ($\frac{1}{4}$ inch) thick. Add the apples slices, in batches, to the sugar syrup and poach until just tender. Lift out with a slotted spoon and drain on absorbent kitchen paper.

5. Leaving the pastry case in the flan tin, arrange the apple slices neatly inside the flan case.

6. To make the meringue, put the egg whites and sugar into a bowl standing over a pan of simmering water. Whisk until stiff. Remove from the heat and continue whisking until the meringue forms stiff peaks.

7. Put the meringue into a piping bag fitted with a large star nozzle, then pipe stars over the top of the apple-filled flan, making sure that each star is finished with a clean point. Continue to pipe the meringue, in decreasing circles, until it builds up to a point.

8. Bake in the oven for 1 hour until the meringue is set, but not browned—it must remain as white as possible.

9. Put the redcurrant jelly into a small paper piping bag and cut a small hole in the base of the bag. Pipe a small bead of jelly on the tip of every meringue star. Serve the flan warm or cold.

Not suitable for freezing.

Below: SWISS FLAN.

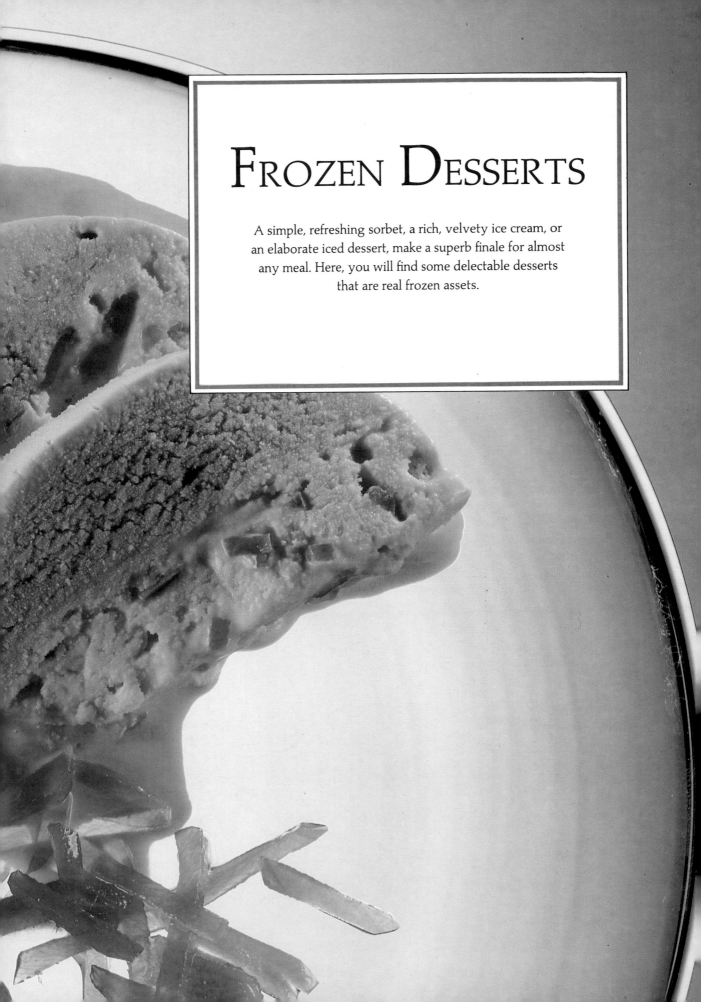

FROZEN DESSERTS

A simple, refreshing sorbet, a rich, velvety ice cream, or
an elaborate iced dessert, make a superb finale for almost
any meal. Here, you will find some delectable desserts
that are real frozen assets.

There is nothing to beat the rich flavour and creamy texture of home-made ice cream, or the mouthwatering fruitiness of home-made sorbet.

The knack of successfully making smooth frozen desserts largely involves making sure that no large ice crystals form during freezing. This means that it is necessary to periodically whisk the freezing mixture by hand, if you do not own an ice cream machine, which will do the job for you.

To Freeze Ice Cream By Hand

The following freezing times based on 900 ml (1½ pint) ice cream are given as a guide. If making a larger quantity of ice cream, the times should be increased.

1. Set the freezer to maximum or fast freeze about 1 hour before you intend to freeze the mixture.
2. Make the ice cream as directed in the recipe.
3. Pour the mixture into a shallow non-metal, freezer container. Cover and freeze for about 3 hours or until just frozen all over. It will have a mushy consistency.
4. Spoon into a bowl and mash with a fork or flat whisk to break down the ice crystals. Work quickly so that the ice cream does not melt completely.
5. Return the mixture to the shallow container and freeze again for about 2 hours or until mushy.
6. Mash again as step 4. If any other ingredients are to be added, such as, nuts, chocolate drops, then fold it in at this stage.
7. Return to the freezer and freeze for about 3 hours or until firm.
8. Remove from the freezer and leave at room temperature for 20–30 minutes to soften before serving. (Do not forget to return the freezer setting to normal.) Ice cream can be stored in the freezer for up to 3 months.

Ice Cream Machines

An ice cream machine will freeze an ice cream or sorbet mixture and churn it at the same time, thus eliminating the physical effort. The results will be smooth and even textured.

There are several types of ice cream machine available, some use a salt solution and others a disc which needs to be frozen before use. Always follow manufacturer's instructions.

Generally speaking, the cooled mixture should be poured into the machine when the paddles are moving, otherwise it tends to freeze on to the base and sides of the bowl, stopping the paddles working. When making ice cream this way, if the recipe calls for whipped cream, it should be ignored. The cream can simply be added from the carton with the custard. When making sorbet, any egg white should be lightly whisked with a fork and added at the start of the churning process. Freezing time is usually about 20–30 minutes. The ice cream or sorbet should then be transferred to the freezer and frozen for 1–2 hours to allow the flavours to develop before serving. Soften them slightly at room temperature before serving.

It is vital to clean ice cream machines thoroughly after using to prevent development of bacteria. Wash bowls, lids, paddles and spatulas in the hottest water temperature possible. Be sure to wash and dry all parts which come into contact with salt to prevent corrosion.

VANILLA ICE CREAM
SERVES 4–6

This recipe is the basis for many ice creams. If preferred, cook custard in a bain marie or a bowl standing over a pan of simmering water. To make a low calorie version, make the custard with 568 ml (1 pint) skimmed milk, flavoured with a vanilla pod or vanilla essence, 30 ml (2 tbsp) skimmed milk powder, 30 ml (2 tbsp) custard powder and 15–30 ml (1–2 tbsp) sugar. Omit the cream and freeze as below.

1 vanilla pod or vanilla essence
300 ml (½ pint) milk
3 egg yolks
50–75 g (2–3 oz) caster sugar
300 ml (½ pint) double cream

1. Split the vanilla pod to reveal the seeds. Put the milk and vanilla pod into a heavy-based saucepan and bring almost to the boil. (Alternatively, put the ingredients in a large bowl and microwave on HIGH for 3 minutes or until almost boiling.) Remove from the heat, cover and leave to infuse for about 20 minutes. (If using vanilla essence, add during step 3 below.)
2. Beat the egg yolks and sugar together in a bowl until well blended. Stir in the milk and strain back into the pan. Cook the custard over a gentle heat, stirring all the time, until it thickens very slightly. (Alternatively, microwave on LOW for 12–15 minutes or until slightly thickened, stirring frequently.) It is very important not to let the custard boil or it will curdle. Pour out into a bowl and leave to cool.
3. Whisk the cream into the cold custard mixture, with about 1.25 ml (¼ tsp) vanilla essence, if using (omit if vanilla pod already used).
4. Freeze the ice cream mixture by hand or in an ice cream machine (see opposite). Leave at cool room temperature for 20–30 minutes to soften before serving.

Previous page: BUTTERSCOTCH AND GINGER ICE CREAM (PAGE 220). *Opposite, from left to right:* STRAWBERRY AND MINT ICE CREAM, MANGO ICE CREAM (PAGE 218), BANANA AND DATE ICE CREAM, CHOCOLATE AND ORANGE LIQUEUR ICE CREAM.

VARIATIONS

Fruit Ice Cream   Add 300 ml (½ pint) fruit purée, sweetened to taste, to the cooled custard. Complete as before. Serves 4—6.

Chocolate and Orange Liqueur Ice Cream   Prepare Vanilla ice cream to the end of step 3, omitting the vanilla. Break up 100 g (4 oz) plain chocolate. Place in a bowl with 30 ml (2 tbsp) orange-flavoured liqueur and melt over a pan of simmering water. (Alternatively, microwave on LOW for 4—6 minutes, stirring occasionally.) Stir occasionally until smooth. Cool slightly. Add the chocolate to the custard mixture and complete as before. Serves 4—6.

Double Chocolate Ice Cream   Put the milk in a saucepan with 100 g (4 oz) plain chocolate and heat gently until the chocolate melts, then cook over high heat until almost boiling. Complete as for Vanilla ice cream to step 3. Freeze by hand to the end of step 5 (see page 216). Mash again, then stir in 50 g (2 oz) plain chocolate drops. Freeze until firm. Serves 4—6.

Chocolate Flake Ice Cream   Crumble 2 large chocolate flakes. Stir half into the cooled custard with the cream. Complete as before. Stir in the remaining flake just before the ice cream is completely frozen. Serves 4—6.

Cinnamon Ice Cream   Add 10 ml (2 tsp) ground cinnamon and a cinnamon stick to the milk instead of the vanilla pod. Complete as before. Serves 4—6.

Gooseberry and Orange Ice Cream   Prepare Vanilla ice cream to the end of step 3, omitting the vanilla. Stew 450 g (1 lb) gooseberries with 45 ml (3 tbsp) icing sugar, the grated rind of 1 orange and 60 ml (4 tbsp) orange juice. Purée, sieve and cool. Add gooseberry purée and complete as before. Serves 6.

Banana and Date Ice Cream   Prepare Vanilla ice cream to the end of step 3, omitting the vanilla. Peel 450 g (1 lb) bananas and purée in a blender or food processor with 45 ml (3 tbsp) lemon juice and 30 ml (2 tbsp) honey. Add the banana purée to the custard mixture. Freeze by hand to the end of step 5 (see page 216). Mash 175 g (6 oz) roughly chopped dates (either fresh or dried), add to the banana mixture and complete as before. Serves 6—8.

Coconut Ice Cream   Finely chop 175 g (6 oz) creamed coconut. Add to the milk and warm until dissolved, whisking until smooth, then add 30 ml (2 tbsp) lemon juice. Complete as for Vanilla ice cream, omitting the vanilla. Serves 4—6.

Strawberry and Mint Ice Cream   Slice 450 g (1 lb) strawberries. Sprinkle over 30 ml (2 tbsp) icing sugar with 30 ml (2 tbsp) lemon juice. Cover and macerate for about 1 hour. Purée in a blender or food processor, then press through a nylon sieve. For the custard, bring the milk to the boil with a handful of fresh mint. Cover and leave to infuse for at least 30 minutes. Strain. Complete as for Vanilla ice cream, omitting the vanilla and adding the strawberry mint purée at the end of step 3. Serves 6—8.

Mango Ice Cream Cut the flesh from 2 medium ripe mangoes, discarding the skin and stone. Purée in a blender or food processor until smooth with the juice of 1 large lime, then press through a nylon sieve. Chill. Prepare Vanilla ice cream to the end of step 3, omitting the vanilla. Add the mango purée and complete as before. Serves 8.

Avocado and Pistachio Ice Cream Prepare Vanilla ice cream to the end of step 3. Purée 1 medium ripe avocado with the finely grated rind and juice of 1 lime, 45 ml (3 tbsp) icing sugar and the cream. Stir into the cooled custard. Fold in 50 g (2 oz) chopped pistachio nuts, if freezing in an ice cream machine. If freezing by hand, freeze to the end of step 5 (see page 216), then mash and fold in the nuts. Freeze as before. Serves 6.

Peanut and Toffee Ice Cream Put the milk in a saucepan with 75 ml (3 tbsp) golden syrup and 30 ml (2 tbsp) soft dark brown sugar. Heat gently until the sugar has dissolved, stirring occasionally. Complete the custard as before, then stir in 75 ml (3 tbsp) crunchy peanut butter. Serve straight from the freezer. Serves 4–6.

Coffee Ice Cream Add 150 ml ($\frac{1}{4}$ pint) strong fresh coffee to the cooled custard or 10 ml (2 tsp) instant coffee granules to the milk instead of the vanilla pod. Complete as before. Serves 4–6.

BLACKCURRANT RIPPLE ICE CREAM

SERVES 8

Follow this basic method to make other ripple ice creams.

568 ml (1 pint) milk
1 vanilla pod
6 egg yolks
350 g (12 oz) sugar
600 ml (1 pint) whipping cream
450 g (1 lb) blackcurrants, stalks removed

1. Put the milk and vanilla pod in a heavy-based pan and bring almost to the boil. Remove from the heat, cover and leave to infuse for at least 20 minutes.

2. Beat egg yolks and 175 g (6 oz) of the sugar together in a bowl. Stir in the milk and strain back into the pan. Cook the custard over a gentle heat, stirring all the time, until thickened slightly. Do not boil. (Alternatively, microwave on LOW for 12–15 minutes, stirring occasionally. Do not boil.)

3. Pour into a chilled, shallow freezer container and leave to cool. Freeze by hand to the end of step 3 (see page 216).

4. Whip the cream until stiff. Mash the ice cream, then fold in the cream. Freeze for 2 hours until mushy.

5. Cook the blackcurrants, remaining sugar and 120 ml (8 tbsp) water in a pan until soft. Purée in blender or food processor, then sieve to remove the seeds. Leave to cool.

6. Whisk the ice cream to a spreading consistency. Spoon a layer into freezer container. Pour over some of the blackcurrant purée. Continue to layer. Freeze until firm.

7. Leave at cool room temperature for 20–30 minutes to soften before serving.

PISTACHIO AND ALMOND ICE CREAM

SERVES 6

This is a very special ice cream, traditionally served at wedding banquets in India. It is best reserved for dinner parties, but only serve it after a fairly light main course as it is very rich.

1.4 litres (2$\frac{1}{2}$ pints) milk
15 ml (1 tbsp) rice flour
175 g (6 oz) granulated sugar
25 g (1 oz) pistachio nuts
50 g (2 oz) ground almonds
few drops of rose water
150 ml ($\frac{1}{4}$ pint) double cream
shredded pistachio nuts, to decorate

1. Pour the milk into a large, heavy-based saucepan. Bring to the boil, then simmer gently for about 45 minutes or until the milk reduces by half. Cool slightly.

2. Mix the rice flour with a little of the cooled milk until smooth. Return to the pan and bring to the boil, stirring. Cook for 15 minutes, stirring frequently until the consistency of thin batter. Strain, add the sugar and stir until dissolved. Leave to cool.

3. Cover the pistachio nuts with boiling water. Leave to stand for 1–2 minutes, then drain. Ease the skins off the pistachios with the fingers. Shred the nuts finely.

4. Stir the pistachios, ground almonds and rose water into the milk mixture. Whip the cream lightly, then fold into the mixture. Pour into a shallow freezer container.

5. Freeze the ice cream mixture by hand (see page 216) or in an ice cream machine.

6. Leave at cool room temperature for 20–30 minutes to soften before serving. Serve in scoops or cut into slices, decorated with shredded pistachios.

Opposite: PISTACHIO AND ALMOND ICE CREAM.

GRAPEFRUIT AND MINT ICE CREAM

SERVES 4–6

The ice cream will be smoothest if you can freeze the mixture in an ice cream machine, because it breaks down the ice crystals as it mixes the ice cream.

25 g (1 oz) mint leaves
568 ml (1 pint) milk
25 g (1 oz) custard powder
75 g (3 oz) caster sugar
finely grated rind and juice of 2 pink grapefruit
150 ml ($\frac{1}{4}$ pint) double cream, lightly whipped

1. Reserve a few sprigs of mint for decoration and refrigerate these in a polythene bag. Roughly chop the remainder.

2. Put 450 ml ($\frac{3}{4}$ pint) of the milk and the chopped mint into a heavy-based saucepan and bring almost to the boil. Remove from the heat, cover and leave to infuse for about 10 minutes.

3. Whisk the custard powder, sugar and remaining milk together in a bowl until smooth. Strain the milk on to the mixture, then return to the pan. Bring to the boil, stirring constantly, and cook for 1–2 minutes. (Alternatively, microwave on HIGH for 4–5 minutes, stirring frequently.) Pour into a bowl and leave to cool, whisking occasionally to prevent a skin forming.

4. Stir the grapefruit rind and 300 ml ($\frac{1}{2}$ pint) juice into the cold custard with the cream.

5. Freeze by hand (see page 216) or in an ice cream machine.

6. Leave at cool room temperature for 20–30 minutes to soften before serving. Scoop into individual serving dishes and decorate with the reserved mint sprigs.

GOOSEBERRY MARSHMALLOW ICE CREAM

SERVES 6

This ice cream is easy to make as it doesn't need churning.

100 g (4 oz) white marshmallows
170 g (6 oz) can evaporated milk
450 g (1 lb) fresh or frozen gooseberries, prepared
75 g (3 oz) caster sugar
150 ml ($\frac{1}{4}$ pint) double cream, lightly whipped
50 g (2 oz) Lyle's golden syrup

1. Place the marshmallows and evaporated milk in a small heatproof bowl standing over a pan of simmering water to melt the marshmallows. (Alternatively, microwave on HIGH for 1–2 minutes, stirring occasionally.) Stir until smooth, then leave to cool.

2. Place half the gooseberries and 30 ml (2 tbsp) water in a pan. Cover and cook gently for about 5 minutes, or until the skins burst and the fruit softens. (Alternatively, microwave, covered, on HIGH for 4–5 minutes.)

3. Stir the sugar into the warm fruit, then purée in a blender or food processor until just smooth. Sieve and leave to cool. Stir into the marshmallow mixture with the cream.

4. Spoon the ice cream mixture into a deep freezer container. Cover and freeze for about 5 hours until required. Do not churn.

5. Meanwhile, prepare the sauce. Place the remaining gooseberries, golden syrup and 30 ml (2 tbsp) water in a small pan. Cover and cook gently until the gooseberries are soft. (Alternatively, microwave on HIGH, covered, for 4–5 minutes.) Sieve and return to the pan.

6. Serve the ice cream straight from the freezer with the warm sauce.

BUTTERSCOTCH AND GINGER ICE CREAM

SERVES 6–8

1 vanilla pod or vanilla essence
300 ml ($\frac{1}{2}$ pint) milk
50 g (2 oz) caster sugar
45 ml (3 tbsp) dark brown soft sugar
25 g (1 oz) butter
300 ml ($\frac{1}{2}$ pint) double cream
25 g (1 oz) stem ginger, finely chopped
25 g (1 oz) meringues, roughly crushed
15 ml (1 tbsp) brandy

FOR THE DECORATION
50 g (2 oz) ratafia biscuits
slices of stem ginger

1. Follow the basic Vanilla ice cream recipe to the end of step 2. Divide the custard in half. Leave to cool.

2. Warm the brown sugar and butter together in a small pan until both have melted, then cook for 1 minute. Mix with half of the custard and leave to cool.

3. Freeze by hand (see page 216) to step 6, keeping the mixtures separate.

4. Lightly whip the cream. Fold half into the vanilla ice cream with the ginger and meringues. Freeze for about 1 hour until firm but not solid.

5. Fold the remaining cream and the brandy into the butterscotch mixture. Spoon into a 1 litre ($1\frac{3}{4}$ pint) Balmoral or loaf tin. Freeze for about $1\frac{1}{4}$ hours until firm.

6. Spoon the vanilla ice cream mixture evenly over the butterscotch layer and freeze until firm.

7. Dip the tin in warm water and unmould on to a freezerproof serving plate, mopping up any runny ice cream. Decorate with ratafias and stem ginger. Leave in the refrigerator for 10–15 minutes to soften before serving. Serve sliced.

Illustrated on pages 214–215

BLACKBERRY ICE CREAM

SERVES 6–8

Choose a mild honey like clover rather than one of the scented varieties.

450 g (1 lb) blackberries, fresh or frozen
30 ml (2 tbsp) thick honey
410 g (14.5 g) can evaporated milk, chilled
150 ml (¼ pint) whipping cream
30 ml (2 tbsp) orange-flavoured liqueur
45 ml (3 tbsp) lemon juice

1. Pick over the fresh blackberries, wash and drain well.
2. Place the blackberries and honey in a small saucepan. Cover and cook gently until the fruit is soft and pulpy. Purée in a blender or food processor, then rub through a nylon sieve. Leave to cool.
3. Whip the evaporated milk until thickened slightly. Whip the cream to the same consistency, then fold gently together. Stir in the cold fruit purée with the liqueur and lemon juice.
4. Freeze by hand (see page 216) or in an ice cream machine.
5. Leave at cool room temperature for 20–30 minutes to soften before serving. Scoop into individual glass dishes and serve with single cream and crisp biscuits.

TUTTI FRUTTI ICE CREAM

SERVES 8–10

For a short-cut version of this ice cream, use a 425 g (15 oz) can custard instead of making the egg custard. With vanilla-flavouring added and the heady flavour of fruit macerated in rum, no-one will guess the custard came out of a can! If you are making the ice cream with children in mind, use orange juice instead of rum and add 25 g (1 oz) chocolate drops to the mixture in step 5, when adding the macerated fruit.

90 ml (6 tbsp) dark rum
50 g (2 oz) sultanas
50 g (2 oz) stoned dates
50 g (2 oz) glacé cherries
50 g (2 oz) no-soak dried apricots
568 ml (1 pint) milk
1 vanilla pod or few drops of vanilla essence
6 egg yolks
175 g (6 oz) caster sugar
600 ml (1 pint) double cream, whipped

1. Pour the rum into a screw-top jar or a bowl. Add the sultanas, then roughly snip the dates, cherries and apricots into the jar or bowl. Make sure all the fruit is coated with rum. Cover and leave to macerate for 2–3 hours, shaking or tossing occasionally until the rum is absorbed.

2. Put the milk and vanilla pod or essence into a heavy-based saucepan and bring almost to the boil. Remove from the heat, cover and leave to infuse for 15 minutes.
3. Beat the egg yolks and sugar together in a bowl until pale and thick. Stir in the milk and strain back into the pan. Cook the custard over a gentle heat, stirring all the time, until it coats the back of a wooden spoon. Do not boil. (Alternatively, microwave on LOW for 12–15 minutes, stirring occasionally. Do not boil.) Cover and leave to cool.
4. Pour into a chilled, shallow freezer container and freeze by hand to the end of step 5 (see page 216).
5. Whip the cream. Mash the ice cream, then fold in the cream and macerated fruit. Freeze until firm. (If using an ice cream machine, put the custard, cream and macerated fruit into the machine together.)
6. Leave at cool room temperature for 20–30 minutes to soften before serving.

QUICK RHUBARB ICE CREAM

SERVES 6

A pretty, pink ice cream made with storecupboard ingredients. It is easy too because it doesn't need churning.

540 g (1¼ lb) can rhubarb in syrup
30 ml (2 tbsp) redcurrant jelly
397 g (14 oz) can condensed milk
150 ml (¼ pint) Greek yogurt

1. Purée the rhubarb, syrup and redcurrant jelly in a blender or food processor until really smooth. Stir the condensed milk and yogurt into the rhubarb mixture until evenly blended.
2. Pour into a shallow freezer container, don't use a metal dish. Freeze until firm, then overwrap and return to the freezer until required.
3. Leave at cool room temperature for 20–30 minutes to soften before serving.

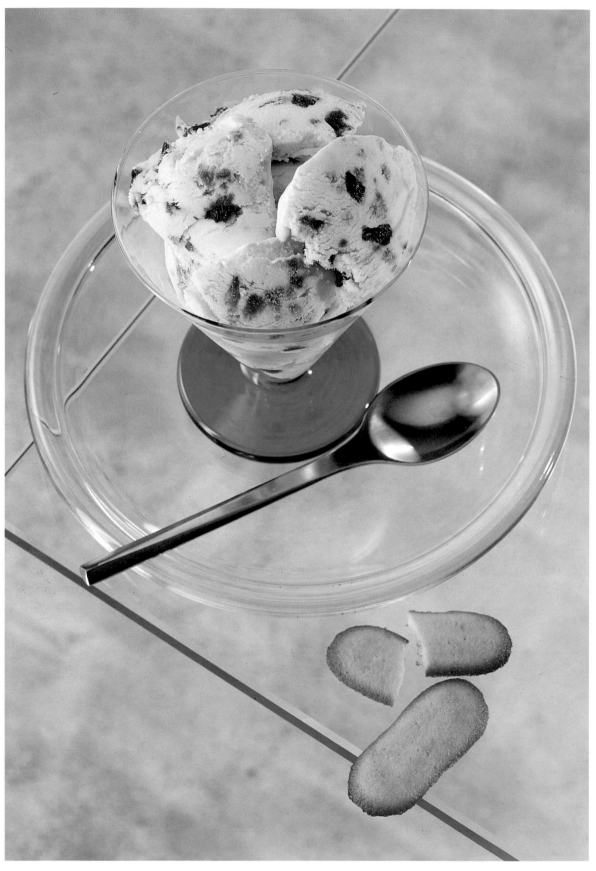

PRUNE AND BRANDY ICE CREAM

SERVES 8

Serve this sumptuous ice cream with small, crisp biscuits such as Langues de chats (see page 164).

225 g (8 oz) no-soak dried prunes
90 ml (6 tbsp) brandy
30 ml (2 tbsp) lemon juice
100 g (4 oz) caster sugar
450 ml (¾ pint) milk
1 vanilla pod
5 egg yolks
40 g (1½ oz) butter
50 g (2 oz) fresh brown breadcrumbs
30 ml (2 tbsp) demerara sugar
450 ml (¾ pint) whipping cream, whipped

1. Cut all the prune flesh off the stones, then snip into small pieces. Place in a bowl with the brandy, lemon juice and 25 g (1 oz) of the caster sugar. Stir well to mix, then cover and leave to soak.

2. Put the milk and vanilla pod into a heavy-based pan and bring almost to the boil. Remove from the heat, cover and leave to infuse for 10 minutes.

3. Beat the egg yolks and remaining caster sugar together in a bowl until pale and frothy. Stir in the milk and strain back into the pan. Cook the custard over a gentle heat, stirring all the time, until thickened slightly. Do not boil. (Alternatively, microwave on LOW for 11–13 minutes, stirring occasionally. Do not boil.) Leave to cool.

4. Melt the butter in a small frying pan, add the breadcrumbs and demerara sugar and cook over a moderate heat, stirring frequently until the crumbs turn golden brown and become crisp. Immediately, spoon the mixture out on to a plate. Leave to cool.

5. Freeze the ice cream mixture by hand to the end of step 5 (see page 216). Mash the ice cream, then fold in the whipped cream, the soaked prunes with any juices, and the crumb mixture. Freeze until firm.

6. Leave at cool room temperature for 20–30 minutes to soften before serving.

VARIATION

Fig and Port Ice Cream Use 225 g (8 oz) no-soak dried figs in place of the prunes and 90 ml (6 tbsp) port in place of the brandy.

SNOWCAP ICED PUDDING

SERVES 6–8

150 ml (¼ pint) kirsch
60 ml (4 tbsp) water
about 15 sponge fingers
¾ quantity Chocolate flake ice cream (see page 217)
225 g (8 oz) ripe cherries, stoned and roughly chopped
¾ quantity Vanilla ice cream (see page 216)
150 ml (¼ pint) double cream

1. Cut out a circle of greaseproof paper and use it to line the base of a 1.1 litre (2½ pint) pudding basin.

2. Mix the kirsch with the water and dip the sponge fingers one at a time into the mixture. Use to line the sides of the pudding basin, trimming them to fit so that there are no gaps in between. Fill the base with leftover pieces of sponge. Refrigerate for 15 minutes.

3. Stir any remaining kirsch liquid into the chocolate ice cream and mash the ice cream well with a fork to soften it slightly and make it smooth without any ice crystals.

4. Spoon the chocolate ice cream into the basin and work it up the sides of the sponge fingers to the top of the basin so that it forms an even layer. Freeze for about 2 hours until firm.

5. Mix the cherries into the vanilla ice cream and mash well with a fork as in step 3.

6. Spoon the vanilla ice cream into the centre of the basin and smooth it over the top so that it covers the chocolate ice cream and sponge fingers. Cover with foil and freeze overnight.

7. To serve, whip the cream until it will just hold its shape. Run a knife around the inside of the basin, then turn the ice cream out on to a well chilled serving plate.

8. Spoon the cream over the top and let it just start to run down the sides, then freeze immediately for about 15 minutes or until the cream has frozen solid. Serve straight from the freezer.

Opposite: PRUNE AND BRANDY ICE CREAM.

ROSE PETAL ICE CREAM

SERVES 4–6

A delicious ice cream scented with the fragrance of rose petals. To make a rose petal infusion, pick off the white bases, then clean, but do not wash, the petals from 2–4 fragrant roses. Bruise them with 50 g (2 oz) sugar, then pour on 150 ml ($\frac{1}{4}$ pint) boiling water. Leave overnight to infuse. Strain and use or freeze for use later.

350 ml (12 fl oz) whipping cream
strip of lemon rind
1 egg
3 egg yolks
50 g (2 oz) caster sugar
rose petal infusion (see recipe introduction)

1. Put the cream and strip of lemon rind in a pan and slowly bring to boiling point.
2. Beat the whole egg, egg yolks and sugar together in a bowl. Stir in the cream and strain back into the pan. Cook the custard over a gentle heat, stirring all the time, until it coats the back of a spoon. (Alternatively, microwave on LOW for 10–12 minutes, stirring occasionally.) Leave to cool.
3. Mix the ice cream mixture with the rose petal infusion. Freeze by hand or in an ice cream machine (see page 216).
4. Leave at cool room temperature for 20–30 minutes to soften before serving.

BROWN BREAD ICE CREAM

SERVES 6

The addition of lemon in this recipe for brown bread ice cream adds a pleasing tang.

30 ml (2 tbsp) custard powder
100 g (4 oz) light brown soft sugar
300 ml ($\frac{1}{2}$ pint) milk
finely grated rind and juice of 1 lemon
150 ml ($\frac{1}{4}$ pint) double cream
150 ml ($\frac{1}{4}$ pint) single cream
1 egg white
30 ml (2 tbsp) oil
25 g (1 oz) butter
100 g (4 oz) fresh brown breadcrumbs

1. Mix the custard powder and 50 g (2 oz) of the sugar to a smooth paste with a little milk. Bring the remaining milk almost to the boil in a pan. Stir into the custard powder, then return to the pan. Bring to the boil, stirring all the time, and cook for 2 minutes. (Alternatively, microwave on HIGH for 4–5 minutes, stirring frequently.) Pour out into a bowl and cool slightly.

2. Whisk in the lemon rind and 45 ml (3 tbsp) juice. Leave to cool completely.
3. Whip the creams together until they just begin to hold their shape. Whisk the custard until smooth, then gently whisk in the creams. Stiffly whisk the egg white and fold in.
4. Freeze by hand up to step 5 (see page 216).
5. Meanwhile heat the oil and butter in a frying pan, add the breadcrumbs and remaining sugar and cook over a moderate heat, stirring occasionally, until the crumbs brown well and begin to crisp. This can take as long as 15 minutes. Turn out into a bowl and leave to cool.
6. Mash the ice cream, then stir in the cold crumbs. Freeze until firm.
7. Leave at cool room temperature for 20–30 minutes to soften before serving.

DEEP FRIED ICE CREAM

SERVES 12

A fun dessert for children to enjoy. Do not attempt it with soft scoop ice cream!

1 litre (1$\frac{3}{4}$ pint) vanilla ice cream cutting block
2 eggs, beaten
275 g (10 oz) digestive biscuits, crushed
oil, for deep frying

1. Cut the ice cream into 5 cm (2 inch) squares.
2. Working quickly, coat the ice cream pieces in the beaten egg, then cover completely in biscuit crumbs.
3. Place on a baking sheet and freeze for about 2 hours or until firm. Repeat step 2. Return to the freezer and freeze for at least 5 hours or overnight until really hard.
4. Heat the oil to 190°C (375°F). Remove the ice cream from the freezer. Deep fry in batches for about 30 seconds. Serve immediately with a fruit sauce.

LEMON GERANIUM ICE CREAM

SERVES 4–6

Not only do lemon-scented geraniums provide a marvellous display of colour all through the summer, but their leaves can be used to add a deliciously aromatic flavour to this unusual ice cream.

300 ml (½ pint) milk
10–12 lemon-scented geranium leaves, crushed
3 egg yolks
100 g (4 oz) icing sugar, sifted
300 ml (½ pint) whipping cream
lemon-scented geranium leaves, to decorate

1. Put the milk and geranium leaves in a heavy-based pan and bring almost to the boil. (Alternatively, microwave on HIGH for 2–3 minutes until boiling.) Remove from the heat and leave to infuse for 30 minutes. Remove the geranium leaves.

2. Whisk the egg yolks and sugar together in a bowl until pale and frothy. Stir in the milk and strain back into the pan.

3. Cook the custard over a gentle heat, stirring all the time, until it coats the back of a wooden spoon. Do not boil. This takes about 20 minutes. (Alternatively, microwave on LOW for 10–12 minutes, stirring occasionally. Do not boil.)

4. Freeze by hand up to step 5 (see page 216).

5. Whip the cream until stiff. Mash the ice cream, then fold in the cream. Complete step 6, then freeze until firm.

6. Leave at cool room temperature for 20–30 minutes to soften before serving. Decorate with geranium leaves.

Below: LEMON GERANIUM ICE CREAM.

HERB SCENTED HONEY ICE CREAM

SERVES 4–6

This ice cream, with a luxurious velvety, smooth texture, is very rich, so serve in small portions after a light main course.

150 ml (¼ pint) herb or wild flower honey
450 ml (¾ pint) double cream
sprig of rosemary
1 bay leaf
4 egg yolks

1. Put the honey, cream, rosemary and bay leaf in a pan and heat very gently until just boiling, stirring occasionally. (Alternatively, microwave in a large bowl on HIGH for 3–4 minutes.) Leave to infuse for 15 minutes.

2. Using an electric whisk, whisk the egg yolks in a bowl until pale and frothy.

3. Quickly bring the honey and cream mixture to boiling point again in the saucepan, or on HIGH for 1½–2 minutes. Remove the herbs, then pour on to the eggs, whisking all the time. Return to the pan and heat gently until thick enough to coat the back of a spoon. (Alternatively, microwave on LOW for 12–15 minutes until thickened, stirring frequently.) Leave to cool.

4. Freeze by hand or in an ice cream machine (see page 216). Serve straight from the freezer.

ORANGES EN SURPRISE

SERVES 6

An extremely easy and quick frozen pudding.

6 large oranges
300 ml (½ pint) double cream
50 g (2 oz) icing sugar
90 ml (6 tbsp) orange-flavoured liqueur
90 ml (6 tbsp) chunky orange marmalade
fresh bay leaves or Chocolate rose leaves (see page 78), to decorate

1. Cut a slice off the top of each orange and reserve. Scoop out all the flesh, pips and juice from the oranges and discard (the juice can be used for drinking or in other recipes). Wash, then dry thoroughly. Set aside.

2. Whip the cream and icing sugar together in a bowl until standing in stiff peaks. Mix the liqueur and marmalade together, then fold into the cream until evenly distributed.

3. Spoon the cream mixture into the orange shells, mounding it up over the top. Freeze for at least 4 hours, preferably overnight (to allow the flavours to develop).

4. Serve straight from the freezer, decorated with reserved orange lids, bay leaves or chocolate rose leaves.

FROZEN YOGURT

SERVES 4–6

This ice will be more granular if made by hand rather than in an ice cream machine.

2 egg whites
25–50 g (1–2 oz) caster sugar
600 ml (1 pint) Greek yogurt or thick Home-made natural yogurt (see page 181)
30 ml (2 tbsp) milk
5 ml (1 tsp) vanilla essence

1. Whisk the egg whites and sugar together until stiff.

2. Mix the yogurt, milk and vanilla essence together in a bowl, then fold in the egg whites.

3. Freeze in an ice cream machine or by hand (page 216).

VARIATIONS

Frozen Fruit Yogurt   Add 300 ml (½ pint) fruit purée to the yogurt mixture, the complete as above.

Frozen Muesli Yogurt   Blend 100 g (4 oz) muesli, 30 ml (2 tbsp) milk and 30 ml (2 tbsp) clear honey with the yogurt, then complete as above.

MAPLE AND PECAN ICE CREAM

SERVES 6

Serve this rich ice cream in small portions.

450 ml (¾ pint) milk
150 ml (¼ pint) maple syrup
5 egg yolks
50 g (2 oz) caster sugar
75 g (3 oz) pecan nuts
300 ml (½ pint) soured cream

1. Put the milk and maple syrup in a heavy-based pan and bring almost to the boil, stirring occasionally. (Alternatively, microwave on HIGH for 3–4 minutes.)

2. Using an electric whisk, whisk the egg yolks and sugar in a bowl until very pale and fluffy. Pour on the hot milk, whisking all the time.

3. Return to the pan and cook the mixture over a gentle heat, stirring all the time, until thick enough to coat the back of a spoon. (Alternatively, return to the bowl and microwave on LOW for 12–15 minutes, until thickened, stirring frequently.) Leave to cool.

4. Meanwhile, lightly toast the pecan nuts under a hot grill. Cool, then chop finely.

5. When the custard is cold, fold in the soured cream. If using an ice cream machine, fold in the nuts and freeze. If freezing by hand, freeze up to the end of step 5 (see page 216). Mash the ice cream, then stir in the nuts. Freeze until firm. Leave at cool room temperature for 20–30 minutes to soften before serving.

QUENELLES OF PRALINE ICE CREAM WITH APRICOT COULIS

SERVES 2

If you have difficulty in shaping the ice cream into quenelles, shape into scoops instead using an ice cream scoop.

FOR THE ICE CREAM

75 g (3 oz) unblanched almonds
115 g (4½ oz) caster sugar
3 eggs, separated
300 ml (½ pint) whipping cream
2.5 ml (½ tsp) vanilla essence

FOR THE APRICOT COULIS

225 g (8 oz) fresh apricots, halved
30 ml (2 tbsp) Southern Comfort
caster sugar, to taste

1. Lightly oil a baking sheet.

2. To make the praline, put the almonds and 75 g (3 oz) of the sugar in a heavy-based saucepan. Heat gently until the sugar melts and caramelizes to a rich golden brown. Turn on to the prepared sheet and leave until cold and set. Break up with a rolling pin, then crush to a fine powder in a nut mill or food processor.

3. Put the egg yolks in a bowl over a pan of gently simmering water. Put the remaining sugar in a clean heavy-based pan. Add 120 ml (4 fl oz) cold water and heat gently until the sugar has dissolved. Increase the heat and boil for 3–5 minutes, without stirring, until a light syrup is formed. Remove from the heat and whisk into the egg yolks until thick, using an electric whisk.

4. Remove the bowl from the heat and whisk until cold. Stir in the cream, vanilla essence and praline. Stiffly whisk the egg whites, then fold into the mixture until evenly incorporated.

5. Freeze by hand or in an ice cream machine (see page 216).

6. To make the apricot coulis, put the apricots in a heavy-based pan with just enough water to cover the bottom. Cover and poach until soft. Press the flesh through a nylon sieve into a bowl. Stir in the Southern Comfort and sugar to taste. Cover and chill.

7. Leave the ice cream in the refrigerator for 30 minutes to soften. Shape into six quenelles with dessertspoons. Arrange three quenelles on each individual plate and return to the freezer. When ready to serve, remove the plates from the freezer and flood with the chilled apricot coulis.

Above: QUENELLES OF PRALINE ICE CREAM WITH APRICOT COULIS.

Meringue Surprise Cassis

SERVES 6–8

Use shop-bought meringues or make your own following the recipe on page 200, using half the ingredients.

15 ml (1 tbsp) arrowroot
6 egg yolks
50 g (2 oz) vanilla sugar
300 ml (½ pint) milk
300 ml (½ pint) double cream
2 egg whites
16 baby meringues

FOR THE SAUCE
350 g (12 oz) frozen blackcurrants
juice of 1 lemon
50 g (2 oz) icing sugar or to taste
45 ml (3 tbsp) blackcurrant-flavoured liqueur

1. Line the base of an 18 cm (6 inch) charlotte mould, soufflé dish or cake tin with non-stick baking paper.
2. Put the arrowroot in a bowl and blend to a paste with the egg yolks and vanilla sugar.
3. Put the milk in a pan and bring almost to the boil. Stir slowly into the egg yolk mixture.
4. Stand the bowl over a pan of simmering water and stir until the custard is thick enough to coat the back of a wooden spoon. Remove from the heat, cover the surface of the custard closely with clingfilm, to prevent a skin forming, and leave for 1 hour.
5. Whip the cream until it just holds its shape, then fold into the cold custard. Whisk the egg whites until stiff, then fold in until evenly incorporated.
6. Crush ten of the meringues roughly and fold into the custard mixture until evenly distributed.
7. Pour the custard mixture into the prepared mould. Cover, then freeze for at least 4 hours or overnight until solid.
8. To make the sauce, reserve a few whole frozen blackcurrants for decoration. Put the remaining frozen blackcurrants and the lemon juice in a heavy-based pan and heat gently until defrosted, shaking the pan constantly. Cook gently for 10 minutes, then tip into a sieve and press with the back of a spoon to extract as much juice as possible.
9. Sift the icing sugar into the blackcurrant juice, then stir in the liqueur. Leave until cold, taste and add more sugar if liked.
10. To serve, run a knife around the dessert in the mould, then carefully turn out on to a serving plate. Remove the paper.
11. Pour a little of the sauce over the dessert, then decorate with the reserved blackcurrants and the remaining meringues. Serve at once, with the remaining sauce handed separately.

Christmas Pudding Ice Cream

SERVES 4–6

All the nicest things that go into the Christmas pudding—dried fruit, rum, port and spices—are used in this unusual recipe.

100 g (4 oz) mixed no-soak dried fruit
60 ml (4 tbsp) light or dark rum
30 ml (2 tbsp) port
finely grated rind and juice of 1 orange
450 ml (¾ pint) single cream
3 egg yolks
100 g (4 oz) caster sugar
150 ml (¼ pint) whipping cream
5 ml (1 tsp) ground mixed spice

1. Mix the dried fruit, rum, port and orange rind and juice together in a bowl. Leave to macerate overnight.
2. Gently heat the single cream in a small saucepan to simmering point. (Alternatively, microwave on HIGH for 5 minutes.)
3. Whisk the egg yolks and sugar together in a bowl until pale and thick. Gradually pour on the hot cream, stirring continuously.
4. Strain the mixture into a medium heavy-based or double saucepan and cook for about 20 minutes over a gentle heat, stirring all the time, until it coats the back of a wooden spoon. Do not boil. (Alternatively, microwave on LOW for 12–15 minutes, stirring frequently.) Leave to cool.
5. Whip the cream until stiff, then fold into the cold custard with the dried fruit mixture and mixed spice.
6. Freeze by hand to the end of step 6 (see page 216) or in an ice cream machine.
7. Beat the ice cream again, then turn into a 1.1 litre (2 pint) bombe mould. Cover and freeze for a further 2 hours until firm.
8. Dip briefly in hot water to unmould, then turn out on to a cold serving plate. Transfer to the refrigerator to soften for 30 minutes before serving.

Opposite: Christmas Pudding Ice Cream.

RASPBERRY REDCURRANT FREEZE

SERVES 4–6

Serve this pretty ice cream with a red fruit salad and crisp biscuits.

350 g (12 oz) fresh or frozen raspberries
225 g (8 oz) jar redcurrant jelly
300 ml ($\frac{1}{2}$ pint) soured cream

1. Put the raspberries and jelly in a saucepan and heat gently, stirring frequently, until the fruit is soft. (Alternatively, microwave on HIGH for 4–5 minutes, stirring occasionally.)

2. Purée in a blender or food processor, then sieve to remove the seeds. Chill for about 1 hour until cold.

3. Whisk in the soured cream. Freeze by hand or in an ice cream machine (see page 216).

4. Leave at cool room temperature for 20–30 minutes to soften before serving.

ICED RASPBERRY MOUSSE

SERVES 6–8

225 g (8 oz) raspberries, hulled
2 egg yolks
50 g (2 oz) caster sugar
7.5 ml (1$\frac{1}{2}$ tsp) powdered gelatine
150 ml ($\frac{1}{4}$ pint) whipping cream
1 egg white
15 ml (1 tbsp) orange-flavoured liqueur

FOR THE DECORATION
mint leaves
raspberries, hulled

1. To purée the raspberries, press through a sieve.

2. Using an electric mixer, whisk the egg yolks and caster sugar together in a bowl until very thick. Slowly add the raspberry purée and continue whisking until the mixture is very thick again.

3. Sprinkle the gelatine over 30 ml (2 tbsp) water in a small bowl and leave to soak for 2–3 minutes. Place the bowl over a saucepan of simmering water and stir until dissolved. (Alternatively, microwave on HIGH for 30 seconds or until dissolved.)

4. Lightly whip the cream. Whisk the egg white. Stir the dissolved gelatine, cream, egg white and liqueur into the raspberry mixture.

5. Divide between six to eight small freezerproof serving dishes and freeze for at least 5 hours until firm.

6. Transfer to the refrigerator for 30–45 minutes to soften before serving. Decorate with mint leaves and surround with raspberries.

To freeze: pack at the end of step 5.

ICED LEMON MOUSSE

SERVES 6

5 ml (1 tsp) powdered gelatine
3 eggs, separated
100 g (4 oz) caster sugar
finely grated rind and juice of 2 lemons
150 ml ($\frac{1}{4}$ pint) natural yogurt

FOR THE DECORATION
lemon twists
chopped pistachio nuts

1. Sprinkle the gelatine over 30 ml (2 tbsp) water in a small bowl and leave to soak for 2–3 minutes. Place the bowl over a pan of simmering water and stir until dissolved. (Alternatively, microwave on HIGH for 30 seconds or until dissolved.)

2. Whisk the egg yolks, sugar and lemon rind together in a bowl until thick, using an electric whisk if possible.

3. Gradually add the lemon juice, about 90 ml (6 tbsp), to the egg yolk mixture, whisking well between each addition. Keep the mixture as thick as possible. Stir the dissolved gelatine into the lemon mixture.

4. Stand the bowl in a roasting tin of iced water and stir occasionally until the lemon mixture begins to set.

5. Whisk one egg white until stiff. Add to the lemon mixture with the yogurt.

6. Gently pour the mixture into six small ramekin dishes and freeze. When firm, overwrap and return to the freezer.

7. Ten minutes only before serving, transfer the lemon mousse to the refrigerator to soften. Decorate with lemon twists and chopped pistachio nuts.

ICED ORANGE SABAYON

SERVES 6

6 egg yolks
175 g (6 oz) demerara sugar
90 ml (6 tbsp) orange-flavoured liqueur
200 ml (7 fl oz) unsweetened orange juice
Chocolate leaves (see page 78), to decorate

1. Beat the egg yolks and sugar together in a bowl until pale and creamy. Stir in the liqueur and orange juice.

2. Transfer the mixture to a medium heavy-based saucepan and stir over low heat until the mixture thickens and just coats the back of the spoon. Do not boil. (Alternatively, microwave on LOW for 4–6 minutes or until just thickened, stirring frequently. Do not boil.)

3. Pour the mixture into six individual freezerproof soufflé dishes or ramekins and leave to cool for at least 30 minutes. Freeze for 3–4 hours until firm. Wrap in clingfilm and return to the freezer.

4. Serve straight from the freezer, decorated with chocolate leaves.

CASSATA

SERVES 8

Recipes for Cassata are confusing, because there are two different types. The recipe given here is for Cassata Gelata, which is an ice cream bombe. The other type is known as Cassata Siciliana and is a chilled dessert made from layers of ricotta cheese and sponge cake. Making Cassata is not difficult but it does take several hours. Start the recipe at least 2 days before you intend to serve it; complete up to the end of step 6 on day one, then complete the remaining steps on day two. Freeze the Cassata overnight ready for serving the next day.

300 ml (½ pint) milk
3 egg yolks
75 g (3 oz) caster sugar
50 g (2 oz) plain chocolate
225 g (8 oz) ripe strawberries, hulled
1.25 ml (¼ tsp) vanilla essence
300 ml (½ pint) double cream
red food colouring
15 g (½ oz) pistachio nuts
4 glacé cherries, cut into small pieces
30 ml (2 tbsp) chopped mixed peel
30 ml (2 tbsp) orange-flavoured liqueur

1. Set the freezer to fast freeze. Bring the milk to boiling point in a pan. Beat the egg yolks and sugar together in a bowl until thick and pale in colour.
2. Stir in the milk and strain back into the pan. Cook the custard over a gentle heat, stirring all the time, until it thickens slightly. Do not boil. Leave to cool for 30 minutes.
3. Break the chocolate into small pieces. Place in a bowl standing over a pan of simmering water and heat until the chocolate melts. (Alternatively, microwave on LOW for 2–3 minutes or until melted, stirring occasionally.) Add two thirds of the cool custard to the chocolate, stirring to blend.
4. Purée the strawberries in a blender or food processor. Sieve into the remaining custard and stir in the vanilla essence.
5. In a separate bowl, lightly whip 150 ml (¼ pint) of the cream. Stir two thirds of this through the cold chocolate mixture and the remainder into the strawberry, adding red food colouring to the latter if necessary.
6. Pour the mixtures into separate shallow freezer containers and freeze by hand to step 5 (see page 216).
7. Put a 1.1 litre (2 pint) pudding basin or bombe mould in the freezer. Leave the chocolate ice cream at cool room temperature for 20 minutes to soften slightly. Line the basin evenly with chocolate ice cream, using a round-bowled spoon. Freeze for about 1 hour until firm.
8. Take the strawberry ice cream out of the freezer and leave at cool room temperature for 20–30 minutes to soften slightly. Work the strawberry ice cream with a spoon to make it more pliable (it will be firmer than the

chocolate ice cream), then use to make a second lining of ice cream in the basin. Freeze, covered, for 1–2 hours until firm.
9. Meanwhile pour boiling water over the pistachio nuts. Leave to stand for 10 minutes, then skin and chop roughly. Place the cherries, nuts, peel and liqueur in a bowl. Cover and macerate for 2 hours.
10. In a separate bowl, whip the remaining cream until stiff, then fold in the cherry mixture. Spoon into the centre of the cassata. Cover and freeze for 4 hours or until firm.
11. Dip the pudding basin briefly in hot water to loosen the cassata. Slip a knife around the top edge to ensure it is loose and invert on to a serving platter. Leave in the refrigerator for about 40 minutes to soften before serving. Serve the cassata in wedges.

FROZEN BRANDY CREAMS

SERVES 4

This works equally well with other liqueur flavours, such as almond or coffee.

4 egg yolks
150 g (5 oz) caster sugar
90 ml (6 tbsp) brandy
150 ml (¼ pint) double cream
coffee dragées, to decorate

1. Mix the egg yolks, sugar and brandy together in a medium bowl, stirring well.
2. Place the bowl over a pan of simmering water. Stir the mixture all the time for about 15 minutes until it thickens slightly and will just coat the back of the spoon. Do not overheat or the eggs may curdle. Remove from the heat and leave to cool for 30 minutes. (Alternatively, microwave on LOW for 4–6 minutes or until thickened. Cool.)
3. Lightly whip the cream and stir half into the cold brandy mixture. Pour into four small freezerproof soufflé or ramekin dishes. Cover and freeze for at least 5 hours until firm.
4. To serve, decorate each ramekin with a whirl of the remaining whipped cream, then top with a coffee dragée. Serve immediately.

PERNOD PARFAIT

SERVES 8

Small moulds of frozen cream flavoured with aniseed and topped with a crisp, lacy biscuit.

4 egg yolks
350 ml (12 fl oz) Stock syrup (see page 237)
30 ml (2 tbsp) Pernod
450 ml (¾ pint) whipping cream
150 ml (¼ pint) whipping cream, to decorate

FOR THE BISCUITS
25 g (1 oz) butter or margarine
25 g (1 oz) caster sugar
15 ml (1 tbsp) golden syrup
25 g (1 oz) plain flour
2.5 ml (½ tsp) Pernod

1. Using an electric whisk, beat the egg yolks in a bowl until pale and fluffy. Meanwhile, bring the syrup back up to boiling point. Pour the hot syrup in a thin stream on to the egg yolks and continue beating. Beat until the mixture is cool. Beat in the Pernod.

2. Whip the cream until it just holds its shape, then fold into the egg mixture. Pour into eight freezerproof serving bowls or ramekin dishes. Cover and freeze for 5 hours or overnight until firm.

3. Meanwhile to make the biscuits, line 2 baking sheets with non-stick baking paper. Melt the butter, sugar and syrup over a low heat in a small pan. Remove from the heat and stir in the flour and Pernod.

4. Put about 16 small spoonfuls of the mixture, spread well apart on the prepared baking sheets.

5. Bake in the oven at 180°C (350°F) mark 4 for 7–10 minutes until bubbly and golden. Leave to cool slightly, then remove from the paper and pinch into petal shapes. Store in an airtight container until ready to serve.

6. To serve, whip the cream until it just holds its shape, then pipe a swirl on to each parfait. Top each with a biscuit. Serve immediately with the remaining biscuits.

INDIVIDUAL COFFEE BOMBES WITH TRUFFLE CENTRES

SERVES 6

These delicious bombes with a surprise centre will not fail to impress. Substitute the coffee ice cream with any of the others on pages 217–218, if preferred.

1½ quantity Coffee ice cream (see page 218)

FOR THE FILLING
25 g (1 oz) cake crumbs
25 g (1 oz) ground almonds
50 g (2 oz) plain chocolate
45 ml (3 tbsp) double cream
30 ml (2 tbsp) rum or brandy
Chocolate leaves or caraque, to decorate (see page 78)

1. Set the freezer to fast freeze. Put six 175 ml (6 fl oz) individual freezerproof pie or pudding moulds in the freezer to chill.

2. Leave the ice cream at room temperature for 20–30 minutes or until soft enough to spread.

3. Meanwhile, to make the truffle filling, mix the cake crumbs and almonds together in a bowl. Put the chocolate and cream in a small bowl standing over a pan of simmering water and stir until melted. (Alternatively, microwave on LOW for 3–4 minutes or until melted, stirring occasionally.) Add the chocolate mixture to the crumb and almond mixture with the rum. Mix well.

4. Spread the softened ice cream around the base and sides of the pie moulds, leaving a cavity in the centre for the truffle mixture. Freeze for 1 hour or until firm.

5. Fill the centre of each mould with the truffle mixture and level the surface. Cover and freeze for 1 hour or until firm.

6. To serve, dip the moulds briefly in hot water, then unmould on to serving plates. Return to the freezer for 10 minutes to firm up. Decorate and serve.

Above: INDIVIDUAL COFFEE BOMBE WITH TRUFFLE CENTRE.
Below: PERNOD PARFAIT.

APRICOT AND RAISIN BOMBE

SERVES 8

A delicious fruit and nut filled bombe served with an apricot sauce.

FOR THE BOMBE

50 g (2 oz) no-soak dried apricots
100 g (4 oz) raisins, roughly chopped
50 g (2 oz) whole blanched almonds, roughly chopped
60 ml (4 tbsp) medium dry sherry
450 ml (¾ pint) milk
3 eggs
75 g (3 oz) caster sugar
300 ml (½ pint) whipping cream
25 g (1 oz) meringues, lightly crushed

FOR THE SAUCE

175 g (6 oz) no-soak dried apricots
300 ml (½ pint) orange juice
1 bay leaf
5 ml (1 tsp) lemon juice

1. Line the base of a 1.6 litre (2¾ pint) pudding basin with greaseproof paper.

2. Snip the apricots into small pieces and place in a bowl. Add the raisins, almonds and sherry. Cover and leave to soak for 2–3 hours.

3. Meanwhile gently heat the milk in a pan. Lightly whisk the eggs and sugar together in a bowl. Stir in the milk and strain back into the pan. Cook the custard over a gentle heat, stirring all the time, until it thickens slightly and just coats the back of the spoon. Do not boil. Leave to cool.

4. Lightly whip the cream and fold into the cool custard. Freeze by hand up to step 5 (see page 216). Mash the ice cream, then stir in the fruit mixture and liquor and crushed meringue.

5. Spoon the mixture into the prepared basin. Return to the freezer and freeze for about 4½ hours or until firm.

6. Meanwhile to make the apricot sauce, place the apricots, orange juice and bay leaf in a small pan. Bring to the boil, cover and simmer gently for about 10 minutes. Cool slightly, remove the bay leaf, then purée in a blender or food processor until smooth. Add the lemon juice and pour into a jug to cool. Chill.

7. To serve, dip the basin briefly in hot water, then invert on to a serving plate. Serve with the chilled apricot sauce.

To freeze: pack the bombe and sauce separately. Thaw the sauce overnight at cool room temperature. Chill before use.

FROZEN CHESTNUT BOMBE

SERVES 8–10

It is important to return the unmoulded bombe to the freezer for 10 minutes (see step 5), it helps the cream to adhere to the sides of the bombe.

FOR THE BOMBE

1 quantity Vanilla ice cream (see page 216)
285 g (10 oz) can whole chestnuts, drained
30 ml (2 tbsp) icing sugar
150 ml (¼ pint) soured cream
100 g (4 oz) macaroons
45 ml (3 tbsp) rum

FOR THE DECORATION

300 ml (½ pint) whipping cream
15 ml (1 tbsp) rum
marrons glacés or dragées
herb leaves

1. To make the bombe, remove the ice cream from the freezer and leave at cool room temperature for 45 minutes to soften.

2. Purée the chestnuts, icing sugar and soured cream in a blender or food processor until smooth. Add the ice cream and purée.

3. Roughly crush the macaroons and sprinkle with the rum. Fold into the ice cream mixture.

4. Pour into a 1.1 litre (2 pint) bombe mould or pudding basin. Cover and freeze for at least 5 hours or until firm.

5. To serve, dip the mould or bowl briefly in hot water, then unmould on to a serving plate. Return to the freezer for 10 minutes.

6. To make the decoration, whip the cream and rum until stiff. Spoon into a piping bag fitted with a large star nozzle. Pipe around the base of the bombe and up and over the sides. Decorate with marrons glacés or dragées and herb leaves. Leave in the refrigerator for 1 hour to soften before serving.

Above: FROZEN CHESTNUT BOMBE. *Below:* FROZEN CHOCOLATE AND MANGO CAKE (PAGE 236).

FROZEN CHOCOLATE AND MANGO CAKE

SERVES 8–10

Use this as a basic recipe to make other ice cream cakes of your choice.

1 chocolate Swiss roll sponge, made with 2 eggs (see page 125)
½ quantity Mango ice cream (see page 218)
¼ quantity Chocolate flake ice cream (see page 217)

FOR THE DECORATION
Chocolate caraque (see page 78)
mango slices

1. Trim the Swiss roll sponge and cut into three pieces the width and length of a 1.1 litre (2 pint) loaf tin.
2. Take the ice creams out of the freezer and leave at room temperature for 30 minutes or until soft enough to spread. Spread half the mango ice cream into the loaf tin and level the surface.
3. Place one piece of sponge on top of the mango ice cream in the loaf tin. Spread with the chocolate flake ice cream. Return to the freezer for 15 minutes to firm.
4. Place a second piece of sponge on top of the chocolate flake ice cream. Spread with the remaining mango ice cream. Top with the last piece of sponge. Cover and freeze for at least 3 hours or until firm.
5. One hour before serving, dip the tin briefly in hot water then unmould on to a serving plate. Leave in the refrigerator for 1 hour before serving. Decorate with chocolate caraque and slices of mango. Serve sliced.

Illustrated on page 234

FROZEN CHOCOLATE TERRINE WITH BRANDIED PRUNES

SERVES 14

225 g (8 oz) no-soak stoned dried prunes
150 ml (¼ pint) cold tea
45 ml (3 tbsp) brandy
225 g (8 oz) plain chocolate
4 eggs, separated
75 g (3 oz) icing sugar, sifted
25 g (1 oz) cocoa powder, sifted
300 ml (½ pint) double cream

1. Place the prunes, tea and brandy in a bowl and leave to soak for 3–4 hours or overnight. Drain, reserving the liquid, then roughly chop the prunes.
2. Break the chocolate into small pieces. Place in a small bowl standing over a pan of simmering water and heat until the chocolate melts. (Alternatively, microwave on LOW for 6–8 minutes or until melted, stirring occasionally.) Leave to cool.
3. Using an electric whisk, whisk the egg whites and icing sugar together in a bowl to make a stiff meringue. Fold in the cocoa powder.
4. Whip the double cream until it just holds soft peaks. Whisk the egg yolks until pale and fluffy, then whisk in the chocolate.
5. Carefully fold the egg yolk and chocolate mixture into the meringue, followed by the cream. Fold in the soaked prunes and the reserved liquid.
6. Pour the mixture into a 1.1 litre (2 pint) terrine. Cover and freeze for at least 5 hours or until firm.
7. To serve, dip the terrine briefly in hot water, then turn out on to a serving plate. Serve cut into slices with single cream.

ICED BLACK FOREST GÂTEAU

SERVES 8

The sponge quickly softens at room temperature to give a delicious base for the gâteau.

FOR THE SPONGE
2 eggs
75 g (3 oz) caster sugar
50 g (2 oz) plain flour
25 g (1 oz) cocoa powder, sifted

FOR THE FILLING AND DECORATION
454 g (16 oz) can stoned cherries
30 ml (2 tbsp) kirsch
1 quantity Vanilla ice cream (see page 216) or 600 ml (1 pint) tub soft scoop vanilla ice cream
40 g (1½ oz) toasted flaked almonds
Chocolate curls (see page 78)

1. Grease a 20.5 cm (8 inch) round cake tin and line the base with greaseproof paper. Dust out with a little caster sugar and flour.
2. To make the sponge, using an electric whisk, beat the eggs and caster sugar in a bowl until pale and thick. Gently fold in the flour and cocoa. Spoon into the tin.
3. Bake in the oven at 180°C (350°F) mark 4 for about 30 minutes or until firm to the touch. Turn out on to a wire rack to cool.
4. To make the filling, drain the cherries, reserving the juice. Mix 90 ml (6 tbsp) juice with the kirsch. Finely chop the cherries.
5. Cut the cake into two layers and place the base on a flat plate. Spoon on half the kirsch juices and all the cherries. Top with spoonfuls of ice cream, then the second layer of cake and remaining juices. Sprinkle with flaked almonds and chocolate curls.
6. Return immediately to the freezer and freeze for at least 3 hours. Overwrap once firm. Leave at cool room temperature for about 40 minutes to soften before serving. Cut into wedges.

GRANITA ALL' ARANCIA
(ORANGE WATER ICE)
SERVES 6
This light, refreshing iced dessert makes the perfect finale to a rich entertaining menu.

175 g (6 oz) sugar
450 ml (¾ pint) water
10 large oranges
1½ lemons

1. To make the sugar syrup, place the sugar and water in a medium saucepan. Heat gently until the sugar dissolves, then boil gently for 10 minutes without stirring.

2. Meanwhile, using a potato peeler, thinly pare off the rind from four of the oranges and the lemons. Add the orange and lemon rind to the sugar syrup and leave until cold.

3. Squeeze the juice from the four oranges and the lemons. Strain into a measuring jug—there should be 450 ml (¾ pint).

4. Strain the cold syrup into a shallow freezer container and stir in the fruit juices. Mix well. Cover and freeze for about 4 hours until mushy in texture.

5. Remove from the freezer and turn the frozen mixture into a bowl. Beat well with a fork to break down the ice crystals. Return to the freezer container and freeze for at least 4 hours or until firm.

6. Meanwhile, using a serrated knife, cut away the peel and pith from the remaining oranges.

7. Slice the oranges down into thin rings, ease out and discard any pips. Place the oranges in a serving bowl, cover tightly with clingfilm and refrigerate until serving time.

8. Place the water ice in the refrigerator for 45 minutes to soften before serving. Serve with the fresh orange slices.

VARIATIONS

Granita al Limone *(Lemon Water Ice)* With 6–8 lemons as a basis, follow the recipe using the pared rind of four lemons and enough juice to give 450 ml (¾ pint).

Granita di Fragole *(Strawberry Water Ice)* With 700 g (1½ lb) strawberries, puréed and sieved, and the pared rind and juice of 1 orange as a basis, follow the recipe, using the strawberry purée and orange juice instead of the orange and lemon juices in step 3.

Granita di Caffé *(Coffee Water Ice)* Put 30 ml (2 tbsp) sugar and 50 g (2 oz) finely ground Italian coffee in a jug. Pour over 600 ml (1 pint) boiling water and leave to stand for 1 hour. Strain the coffee through a filter paper or muslin, then follow the recipe after the straining in step 4.

Granita di Pescanoce *(Nectarine Water Ice)* Poach 900 g (2 lb) halved ripe nectarines in the syrup. Remove stones, then purée until smooth. Press through a sieve. Freeze as step 4 above, then add 30 ml (2 tbsp) peach brandy. Finish as above.

SORBETS

Stock Syrup Put 100 g (4 oz) granulated sugar in a heavy-based saucepan. Add 300 ml (½ pint) water and heat gently until the sugar dissolves. Do not stir the ingredients but occasionally loosen the sugar from the base of the pan to help it dissolve. Bring to the boil and boil for 2 minutes. Cool and use as required in the following recipes. *Makes about 350 ml (12 fl oz).*

LEMON SORBET
SERVES 3–4

350 ml (12 fl oz) Stock syrup (see above)
pared rind and juice of 3 lemons
1 egg white

1. Prepare the stock syrup as far as dissolving the sugar. Add the lemon rinds and simmer gently for about 10 minutes. Leave to cool completely.

2. Stir in the lemon juice and strain into a shallow freezer container. Cover and freeze for about 3 hours until mushy.

3. Whisk the egg white until stiff. Turn the sorbet into a bowl and beat gently to break down the ice crystals. Fold in the egg white.

4. Return to the freezer container, cover and freeze for 4 hours or until firm.

5. Leave in the refrigerator for about 40 minutes to soften slightly before serving.

To freeze in an ice cream machine, see page 216.

VARIATION

Orange or Lime Sorbet Make as above, using the pared rind and juice of 2 oranges or 5 limes instead of the lemons.

PEAR SORBET
SERVES 6
A little kirsch spooned over this sorbet at serving time enhances the subtle flavour of the pears.

700 g (1½ lb) ripe pears, peeled and cored
350 ml (12 fl oz) Stock syrup (see above)
300 ml (½ pint) soured cream

1. Poach the pears in the stock syrup in a pan for 15–20 minutes or until tender. Leave to cool. Purée in a blender or food processor.

2. Freeze as for Lemon sorbet, adding the soured cream when you would add the egg whites. Serve straight from the freezer.

VARIATION

Apple Sorbet Make as above using 700 g (1½ lb) eating apples.

MIXED BERRY SORBET

SERVES 6

Frozen redcurrants can be used instead of fresh and they do not need defrosting beforehand.

---

225 g (8 oz) redcurrants, stalks removed

225 g (8 oz) strawberries, hulled

150 ml (¼ pint) Stock syrup (see page 237)

150 ml (¼ pint) sparkling white wine

2 egg whites

---

1. Place the redcurrants, strawberries and 30 ml (2 tbsp) water in a pan. Cover and cook for about 10 minutes until soft. Press the blackcurrants and strawberries through a sieve to form a purée.
2. Stir the stock syrup and wine into the fruit purée. Freeze as Lemon sorbet, adding the egg whites as directed.

PLUM SORBET

SERVES 6

Any variety of dessert plum can be used.

---

550 g (1¼ lb) Victoria plums, halved and stoned

350 ml (12 fl oz) Stock syrup (see page 237)

15 ml (1 tbsp) lemon juice

1 egg white

---

1. Add the plums to the stock syrup in a pan. Cover and simmer for about 20 minutes or until very soft. Cool, then purée in a blender or a food processor. Press through a nylon sieve to remove the skins.
2. Stir in the lemon juice. Freeze as for Lemon sorbet, adding the egg white as directed.

PASSION FRUIT SORBET

SERVES ABOUT 6

This sorbet has a very exotic taste.

---

10 medium passion fruit

60 ml (4 tbsp) orange juice

350 ml (12 fl oz) Stock syrup (see page 237)

2 egg whites

---

1. Halve the passion fruit and scoop out the flesh and seeds. Purée briefly in a blender or food processor with the orange juice. Press through a nylon sieve—there should be about 200 ml (7 fl oz) juice.
2. Add to the stock syrup. Freeze as for Lemon sorbet, adding the egg whites as directed.
3. After 1 hour, check and refold in the egg whites, if necessary, as the mixture tends to separate.

PINEAPPLE SORBET

SERVES 4

Stock syrup made with 100 g (4 oz)
sugar and 150 ml (¼ pint) water (see page 237)

450 ml (¾ pint) pineapple juice

juice of 1 orange

1 egg white

---

1. Mix the stock syrup, pineapple juice and orange juice together.
2. Freeze as for Lemon sorbet, adding the egg white as directed.

POMEGRANATE SORBET

SERVES 4

A marvellously fragrant sorbet.

4–5 pomegranates

350 ml (12 fl oz) Stock syrup (see page 237)

1 egg white

---

1. Squeeze the juice from the pomegranates. You need at least 300 ml (½ pint).
2. Mix with the stock syrup. Freeze as for Lemon sorbet, adding the egg white as directed.

MANGO SORBET

SERVES 8

---

2 large ripe mangoes

350 ml (12 fl oz) Stock syrup (see page 237)

juice of 1 large lime

1 egg white

---

1. Peel the mangoes and remove the flesh from the stone. Purée the flesh in a blender or food processor. Press through a sieve. Mix with the stock syrup and lime juice.
2. Freeze as for Lemon sorbet, adding the egg white as directed. Serve straight from the freezer.

Above: RASPBERRY SORBET (PAGE 241). Centre: MANGO SORBET. Below: PINEAPPLE SORBET.

ROSE GERANIUM SORBET

SERVES 4

You will only need a small handful of rose geranium leaves. Do not use too many—they have a strong flavour.

small handful rose geranium leaves
350 ml (12 fl oz) Stock syrup (see page 237)
juice of 1–2 small lemons
1 egg white

1. Add the rose geranium leaves to the stock syrup in a pan. Bring quickly to the boil, then leave to infuse.
2. When the syrup is cold, remove the leaves and add lemon juice to taste. Freeze as for Lemon sorbet, adding the egg white as directed.

GUAVA SORBET

SERVES 4–6

The pink fleshed variety of guava has the best flavour and colour for sorbets.

about 700 g (1½ lb) ripe guavas
350 ml (12 fl oz) Stock syrup (see page 237)
juice of 1 lime
1 egg white

1. Peel the guavas and roughly chop the flesh. Purée the flesh in a blender or food processor. Press through a nylon sieve to remove the seeds.
2. Mix with the stock syrup and lime juice. Freeze as for Lemon sorbet, adding the egg white as directed. Serve straight from the freezer.

MINT SORBET

SERVES 4–6

Serve this as a cool, refreshing dessert or as a palate cleanser between courses.

4 sprigs of mint
350 ml (12 fl oz) Stock syrup (see page 237)
juice of 2 lemons
15 ml (1 tbsp) finely chopped fresh mint
1 egg white

1. Add the mint sprigs to the stock syrup in a pan. Bring to the boil, then leave to infuse.
2. When the syrup is cold, strain it then add the lemon juice and chopped mint. Freeze as for Lemon sorbet, adding the egg white as directed.

BLACKCURRANT SORBET

SERVES 8

One of the strongest flavoured sorbets, this is ideal after spicy curries.

450 g (1 lb) blackcurrants, stalks removed
30 ml (2 tbsp) blackcurrant-flavoured liqueur
30 ml (2 tbsp) lemon juice
350 ml (12 fl oz) Stock syrup (see page 237)
2 egg whites

1. Blend the blackcurrants, liqueur, lemon juice and half the stock syrup together in a blender or food processor. Press through a nylon sieve.
2. Add the remaining stock syrup. Freeze as for Lemon sorbet, adding the egg whites as directed.

KIWI FRUIT SORBET

SERVES 6

Serve this sorbet decorated with slices of kiwi fruit.

6 kiwi fruit, peeled
150 ml (¼ pint) Stock syrup (see page 237)
2 egg whites

1. Purée the kiwi fruit and syrup in a blender or food processor. Press through a sieve to remove the pips.
2. Freeze as for Lemon sorbet, adding the egg whites as directed.

APRICOT AND MINNEOLA SORBET

SERVES 8

Minneolas are one of the new varieties of 'easy peelers'. You can also use satsumas or tangerines.

two 420 g (15 oz) cans apricot halves in syrup
pared rind and juice of 1 minneola
2 egg whites

1. Drain the apricots, reserving the syrup. Simmer the minneola rind in the apricot syrup for 2–3 minutes. Leave to cool, then strain.
2. Purée the apricots with 60 ml (4 tbsp) minneola juice in a blender or food processor. Press through a nylon sieve. Add the apricot syrup.
3. Freeze as for Lemon sorbet, adding the egg whites as directed.

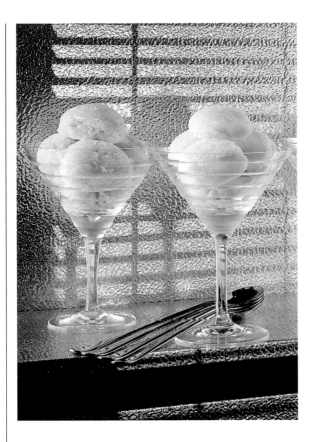

Left: APRICOT AND MINNEOLA SORBET. *Right:* MELON AND GINGER SORBET.

COLA SORBET

SERVES 4–6

350 ml (12 fl oz) Stock syrup (see page 237)
300 ml (½ pint) cola
1 egg white

1. Mix the stock syrup with the cola.
2. Freeze as for Lemon sorbet, adding the egg white as directed.

CHAMPAGNE SORBET

SERVES 4–6
A refreshing way to end a special occasion meal.

350 ml (12 fl oz) Stock syrup (see page 237)
juice of 1 lemon
350 ml (12 fl oz) champagne
1 egg white

1. Mix the stock syrup, lemon juice and champagne together.
2. Freeze as for Lemon sorbet, adding the egg white as directed.

MELON AND GINGER SORBET

SERVES 6
Ginger lovers thought this sorbet was delicious; others weren't so keen! The type of melon used determines the colour of the sorbet.

1 medium green or orange-fleshed melon, such as Ogen, Galia or Canteloupe
50 g (2 oz) stem ginger
30 ml (2 tbsp) lemon juice
350 ml (12 fl oz) Stock syrup (see page 237)
2 egg whites

1. Purée the melon flesh, ginger and lemon juice in a blender or food processor. Press through a nylon sieve.
2. Add the stock syrup. Freeze as for Lemon sorbet, adding the egg whites as directed.

RASPBERRY SORBET

SERVES ABOUT 6
This full flavoured sorbet is a favourite with both adults and children alike. It works equally well with loganberries or strawberries. The hint of kirsch adds a touch of luxury to this dessert.

450 g (1 lb) raspberries
30 ml (2 tbsp) lemon juice
30 ml (2 tbsp) kirsch
350 ml (12 fl oz) Stock syrup (see page 237)
2 egg whites

1. Purée the raspberries with the lemon juice and kirsch in a blender or food processor. Press through a nylon sieve.
2. Add to the stock syrup. Freeze as for Lemon sorbet, adding the egg whites as directed.

LYCHEE SORBET

SERVES 6
This sorbet has a wonderful fragrant taste, even though the lychees used are canned ones.

567 g (1 lb 4 oz) can lychees in syrup
30 ml (2 tbsp) lemon juice
1 egg white

1. Purée the lychees, their syrup and the lemon juice in a blender or food processor. Press through a nylon sieve.
2. Freeze as for Lemon sorbet, adding the egg white as directed.

SAUCES AND CREAMS

Enliven the plainest pancake or enhance a simple ice cream with our tempting selection of hot and cold sauces and creams. Ignore the fear and mystique surrounding sauce making, with our easy-to-follow recipes you will never fail to create a luscious, glistening topping for all your desserts.

SWEET WHITE SAUCE

MAKES 300 ml (½ pint)

25 ml (1½ tbsp) cornflour
300 ml (½ pint) milk
25 ml (1½ tbsp) sugar or to taste

1. Blend the cornflour with 15–30 ml (1–2 tbsp) of the milk to a smooth paste.
2. Heat the remaining milk until almost boiling in a saucepan. (Alternatively, microwave on HIGH for 1½ minutes.) Add to the cornflour mixture, stirring.
3. Return to the pan and bring to the boil, stirring. Cook for 1–2 minutes after the mixture has thickened to a glossy sauce. (Alternatively, microwave on HIGH for 3–4 minutes, stirring every minute.) Add sugar to taste.

VARIATIONS

When adding extra liquid to the sauce, make a thicker sauce by increasing the cornflour to 30 ml (2 tbsp).

Flavour with any of the following when sauce has thickened:
5 ml (1 tsp) ground mixed spice
30 ml (2 tbsp) jam
grated rind of ½ orange or lemon
30 ml (2 tbsp) single cream
15–30 ml (1–2 tbsp) rum.
Chocolate Sauce Blend 15 ml (1 tbsp) cocoa powder with the cornflour.

To freeze: pack in a rigid container. Thaw at cool room temperature overnight. Reheat gently in a saucepan or microwave on HIGH for 2–3 minutes.

FRUIT PURÉE SAUCE

MAKES ABOUT 450 ml (¾ pint), DEPENDING ON FRUIT

Serve poured over sorbets or mousses or flood a flat plate with the sauce and lay slices of ice cream or gâteau on top.

450 g (1 lb) ripe fruit, prepared, such as raspberries, blackcurrants, redcurrants, strawberries, mango, pawpaw, apricots, kiwi, passion fruit pulp
Stock syrup (see page 237), to taste
lime or lemon juice, to taste
fruit liqueur or brandy (optional)

1. Purée the fruit in a blender or food processor. Add enough sugar syrup and lime or lemon juice until the sauce has the desired consistency and flavour.
2. Press through a fine sieve to remove seeds, then stir in liqueur to taste, if using.

To freeze: pack in a rigid container. Thaw overnight in the refrigerator.

ORANGE SABAYON SAUCE

SERVES 4

This deliciously light and fluffy sauce may be served hot or cold. If serving cold, serve within 1 hour of making or it will separate.

5 egg yolks
75 g (3 oz) caster sugar
75 ml (3 fl oz) orange-flavoured liqueur

1. Put all the ingredients in a bowl placed over a saucepan of simmering water and whisk constantly until the sauce is thick and creamy.
2. Remove from the heat, place the bowl in a bowl of cold water and whisk constantly until the sauce cools to lukewarm.
3. Serve warm, or cool completely, whisking occasionally and serve cold.

Not suitable for freezing.

CHOCOLATE FUDGE SAUCE

MAKES ABOUT 450 ml (¾ pint)

Serve this rich, sticky sauce with profiteroles, ice cream and bananas.

75 ml (5 tbsp) single cream
25 g (1 oz) cocoa powder
100 g (4 oz) caster sugar
175 g (6 oz) Lyle's golden syrup
25 g (1 oz) butter or margarine
pinch of salt
2.5 ml (½ tsp) vanilla essence

1. Combine all the ingredients, except the vanilla essence, in a saucepan over low heat and mix well. Slowly bring to the boil, stirring occasionally. Boil for 5 minutes, then add the vanilla essence.
2. Cool the sauce slightly before serving.

To freeze: pack in a rigid container. Thaw at cool room temperature. Reheat gently, stirring all the time. Alternatively, reheat from frozen, in a heavy-based saucepan, stirring all the time.

Previous page: FRUIT PURÉE SAUCE USING RASPBERRIES.

EGG CUSTARD SAUCE

MAKES 300 ml (½ pint)

The classic accompaniment to hot and cold puddings.
The sauce can be flavoured with vanilla or lemon.

2 eggs
15 ml (1 tbsp) caster sugar
300 ml (½ pint) milk
1 vanilla pod, split, or 5 ml (1 tsp) vanilla essence or few strips of thinly pared lemon rind

1. Beat the eggs, sugar and 45 ml (3 tbsp) of the milk together in a bowl.
2. Heat the rest of the milk with the vanilla pod or lemon rind, if using, in a pan until lukewarm. (Alternatively, microwave on HIGH for 2 minutes or until hot.) Beat into the eggs.
3. Pour the mixture into a double saucepan or bowl standing over a pan of simmering water. Cook, stirring continuously, until the custard thickens enough to thinly coat the back of a spoon. Do not boil. (Alternatively, microwave on HIGH for 1 minute, then on LOW for 4½ minutes, whisking frequently.) Remove the vanilla pod or lemon rind, if using.
4. Pour into a cold jug and stir in the vanilla essence, if using. Serve hot or cold. The sauce thickens slightly on cooling.

To freeze: pack in a rigid container. Thaw in the refrigerator overnight. Serve cold. Do not reheat.

BUTTERSCOTCH NUT SAUCE

MAKES ABOUT 150 ml (¼ pint)

Serve with steamed or baked puddings and ice cream.

10 ml (2 tsp) custard powder
15 ml (1 tbsp) Lyle's golden syrup
15 ml (1 tbsp) soft dark brown sugar
15 g (½ oz) butter or margarine
few drops of lemon juice
30 ml (2 tbsp) chopped nuts

1. Blend the custard powder with 150 ml (¼ pint) water in a bowl.
2. Put the syrup, sugar and butter in a saucepan and heat gently until melted. Remove from the heat and mix in the custard powder mixture. Bring to the boil, stirring, and add a little lemon juice and the nuts.
3. Serve the sauce hot or cold.

To freeze: pack in a rigid container. Thaw at cool room temperature. Reheat gently, stirring all the time. Alternatively, reheat from frozen in a heavy-based saucepan, stirring all the time.

LEMON SAUCE

MAKES ABOUT 350 ml (12 fl oz)

juice and grated of 1 large lemon
15 ml (1 tbsp) cornflour
30 ml (2 tbsp) sugar
knob of butter
1 egg yolk

1. Make up the lemon juice to 300 ml (½ pint) with water. Add the lemon rind.
2. Blend a little of the liquid with the cornflour and sugar until smooth.
3. Bring the remaining liquid to the boil and stir into the cornflour mixture. Return all the liquid to the pan and bring to the boil, stirring until the sauce thickens and clears. Add the butter.
4. Cool, then beat in the egg yolk. Reheat without boiling, stirring all the time.

Not suitable for freezing.

COFFEE CREAM SAUCE

MAKES ABOUT 200 ml (7 fl oz)

10 ml (2 tsp) instant coffee powder
150 ml (¼ pint) double cream
15 ml (1 tbsp) milk
30 ml (2 tbsp) caster sugar
few drops of vanilla essence

1. Dissolve the coffee powder in 10 ml (2 tsp) hot water in a bowl. Leave to cool slightly.
2. Stir in the cream, milk, sugar and vanilla essence. Whisk until the cream begins to hold its shape.

Not suitable for freezing.

APRICOT SAUCE

MAKES 200 ml (7 fl oz)

Serve this speedy sauce with poached fruit or ice cream.

425 g (15 oz) can apricots in natural juice
10 ml (2 tsp) brandy

1. Drain the apricots, reserving the juice. Purée the apricots with 60 ml (4 tbsp) of the juice in a blender or food processor until smooth.
2. Pour the purée into a saucepan and add the brandy. Heat gently for 2–3 minutes. (Alternatively, microwave on HIGH for 1–2 minutes.)

To freeze: pack in a rigid container. Thaw at cool room temperature. Serve cold.

MELBA SAUCE

MAKES 450 ml ($\frac{3}{4}$ pint)

Serve hot or cold with ice cream and fresh fruit.

450 g (1 lb) raspberries, hulled
60 ml (4 tbsp) redcurrant jelly
15 ml (1 tbsp) icing sugar
30 ml (2 tbsp) arrowroot

1. Rub the raspberries through a sieve into a saucepan. Add the jelly and icing sugar and bring to the boil.
2. Blend the arrowroot with 15 ml (1 tbsp) cold water to a smooth cream. Stir in a little of the raspberry mixture. Return the mixture to the pan and bring to the boil, stirring with a wooden spoon, until it thickens and clears.

To freeze: pack in a rigid container. Thaw at cool room temperature.

WALNUT RUM SAUCE

MAKES ABOUT 450 ml ($\frac{3}{4}$ pint)

This sauce is equally good hot or cold. Serve with vanilla, coffee or chocolate ice cream.

175 g (6 oz) dark brown soft sugar
10 ml (2 tsp) instant coffee powder
90 ml (6 tbsp) single cream or evaporated milk
25 g (1 oz) butter or margarine
15 ml (1 tbsp) Lyle's golden syrup
15 ml (1 tbsp) rum
50 g (2 oz) walnuts, roughly chopped

1. Combine the sugar, coffee, cream, butter and golden syrup together in a saucepan. Cook over a low heat to dissolve the sugar.
2. Bring to the boil and simmer, stirring, for 2–3 minutes or until thickened. Stir in the rum and walnuts.

To freeze: pack in a rigid container. Thaw at cool room temperature. Serve cold.

MOUSSELINE SAUCE

MAKES ABOUT 150 ml ($\frac{1}{4}$ pint)

Serve with fruit desserts, chocolate gâteau or light steamed puddings.

1 egg
1 egg yolk
45 ml (3 tbsp) sugar
15 ml (1 tbsp) sherry
60 ml (4 tbsp) single cream

1. Place all the ingredients in a bowl over a pan of boiling water and whisk until pale, frothy and a creamy thick consistency. Serve at once.

Not suitable for freezing.

CARAMEL SAUCE

MAKES ABOUT 300 ml ($\frac{1}{2}$ pint)

Serve with poached apples or pears.

100 g (4 oz) light brown soft sugar
150 ml ($\frac{1}{4}$ pint) single cream
25 g (1 oz) stem ginger, cut into thin strips

1. Melt the light soft brown sugar in a small, heavy-based saucepan over a gentle heat.
2. Take the pan off the heat, cover your hand with a cloth and carefully stir in 120 ml (4 fl oz) water. Cook gently for another minute, stirring continually to make a smooth sauce.
4. Cool slightly, stir in the cream and ginger and serve immediately.

Not suitable for freezing.

Opposite: MELBA SAUCE..

CRÈME PÂTISSIÈRE

MAKES ABOUT 600 ml (1 pint)

A rich, thick, custard used as a filling for cakes. small pastries and flans. Its light, smooth, cool texture contrasts and complements both sponge cakes and pastries alike. The basic mixture is flavoured with vanilla, but it can also be flavoured with liqueurs, chocolate, coffee, orange or lemon rind. Add liqueurs, such as kirsch or brandy, to the cold custard, but do not add too much or the custard will become thin. Chocolate, coffee, orange or lemon rind should be heated with the milk. It is always best to make the custard the day before required, to ensure that it is thoroughly chilled.

300 ml (½ pint) milk
5 ml (1 tsp) vanilla essence
3 egg yolks
50 g (2 oz) caster sugar
35 g (1¼ oz) plain flour
1 egg white
150 ml (¼ pint) double cream

1. Put the milk and vanilla essence into a saucepan and bring almost to the boil.
2. Whisk the egg yolks and 15 g (½ oz) of the sugar together in a bowl until pale and thick. Fold in the flour. Gently whisk in the milk and strain back into the pan.
3. Cook the custard over a gentle heat, stirring all the time, until thickened. Pour the hot custard into a clean bowl, then cover the surface closely with clingfilm to prevent a skin forming. Allow the custard to cool completely, but not to set too firmly.
4. Whisk the egg white until stiff, then gradually whisk in the remaining caster sugar. Whip the cream until thick.
5. Whisk the cooled custard until smooth, gradually fold in the egg white mixture, then the cream. Cover the crème pâtissière with clingfilm and thoroughly chill before using.

Not suitable for freezing.

QUICK CRÈME PÂTISSIÈRE

MAKES 300 ml (½ pint)

2 eggs
50 g (2 oz) caster sugar
30 ml (2 tbsp) plain flour
30 ml (2 tbsp) cornflour
300 ml (½ pint) milk
few drops of vanilla essence

1. Whisk the eggs and sugar together in a large bowl, using an electric whisk, until pale and creamy and the mixture leaves a trail when the whisk is lifted. Sift the flour and cornflour into the bowl and beat in with a little of the milk until smooth.
2. Heat the rest of the milk in a pan until almost boiling. (Alternatively, microwave on HIGH for 2–2½ minutes until almost boiling.) Pour on to the egg mixture, stirring all the time.
3. Return the custard to the pan and stir over a low heat until the mixture boils. Add vanilla essence to taste and cook for a further 2–3 minutes until thickened. (Alternatively, microwave on HIGH for 1½–2 minutes until very thick, stirring frequently.) Cover and leave to cool before using.

Not suitable for freezing.

CRÈME CHANTILLY

MAKES 300 ml (½ pint)

The addition of sugar and vanilla essence before whipping, turns double cream into crème Chantilly, making the cream smoother and more flavourful. It is used extensively for filling and decorating cakes, large and small pastries, and desserts, or as an accompaniment to fruit salads or poached fruit.

300 ml (½ pint) double cream, well chilled
15 ml (1 tbsp) icing sugar, sifted
2.5–5 ml (½–1 tsp) vanilla essence

1. Put the cream, sugar and vanilla essence to taste into a well chilled bowl.
2. Whip until the cream forms soft peaks, or a little thicker if required for piping. Take care not to overwhip the cream or it will turn buttery and be unusable.

Not suitable for freezing.

Opposite: ORANGE SABAYON SAUCE.

TOFFEE SAUCE

MAKES ABOUT 300 ml (½ pint)
Serve with bananas and ice cream.

50 g (2 oz) caster sugar
100 g (4 oz) butter or margarine
150 ml (¼ pint) double cream
50 g (2 oz) Lyle's golden syrup
vanilla essence

1. Put the sugar, butter or margarine, cream and golden syrup in a bowl, and add vanilla essence to taste.
2. Stand over a saucepan of water and heat gently. Stir until the butter and sugar have melted and the ingredients are well mixed. (Alternatively, microwave on HIGH for 3–5 minutes, or until melted, stirring frequently.) Serve hot.

Not suitable for freezing.

SYRUP SAUCE

MAKES ABOUT 150 ml (¼ pint)
Serve with steamed and baked puddings.

60–75 ml (4–5 tbsp) Lyle's golden syrup
juice of ½ lemon

1. Put the syrup and 45 ml (3 tbsp) water in a saucepan. Stir over gentle heat until blended.
2. Simmer for 3–4 minutes. (Alternatively, microwave on HIGH for 2–3 minutes, stirring occasionally.) Add the lemon juice. Serve hot.

To freeze: pack in a rigid container. Thaw at cool room temperature. Reheat gently, stirring all the time. Alternatively, reheat from frozen in a heavy-based saucepan, stirring all the time.

CRÈME AU BEURRE

MAKES ABOUT 275 g (10 oz)
Use this rich butter cream to fill gâteaux, pastries and choux buns.

75 g (3 oz) caster sugar
2 egg yolks, beaten
175 g (6 oz) butter

1. Place the sugar and 60 ml (4 tbsp) water in a heavy-based saucepan. Heat very gently to dissolve the sugar, without boiling. When completely dissolved, bring to boiling point and boil steadily for 2–3 minutes, to reach a temperature of 107°C (225°F).
2. Put the egg yolks in a bowl. Pour the syrup in a thin stream on to the egg yolks, whisking all the time. Continue to whisk until the mixture is thick and cold.
3. In another bowl, cream the butter until very soft and gradually beat in the egg yolk mixture.

VARIATIONS

Chocolate   Melt 50 g (2 oz) plain chocolate with 15 ml (1 tbsp) water. Cool slightly and beat in.

Coffee   Beat in 15–30 ml (1–2 tbsp) coffee flavouring.

Fruit   Crush 225 g (8 oz) fresh strawberries, raspberries etc, or thaw, drain and crush frozen fruit. Beat into the basic mixture.

Orange or Lemon   Add grated rind and juice to taste.

To freeze: pack in a rigid container. Thaw in the refrigerator. Beat thoroughly before using.

Opposite: SYRUP SAUCE.

BRANDY OR RUM BUTTER

SERVES 8

Serve sweet butters with Christmas pudding or
fruit pies.

75 g (3 oz) light brown soft sugar
75 g (3 oz) icing sugar
175 g (6 oz) softened butter
about 30 ml (2 tbsp) brandy or rum

1. Gradually beat the sugars into the butter in a bowl
until evenly blended.
2. Add the brandy or rum, about 5 ml (1 tsp) at a time,
beating well between each addition. Spoon into a
serving bowl, cover tightly and chill.
3. Take the brandy butter out of the refrigerator 30
minutes before serving.

VARIATIONS

Lemon Butter Omit the brandy or rum. Use caster
sugar in place of brown sugar. Add the finely grated
rind and juice of 1 lemon.

Orange Butter Make as above using the grated rind
and juice of 1 orange.

Lime Butter Make as above using the grated rind
and juice of 1–2 limes.

*To freeze: pack and freeze. Thaw overnight at cool room
temperature. Chill again before serving.*

ALMOND BUTTER

SERVES 4

This works equally well with toasted and finely ground
hazelnuts. Serve with warm apple or pear pies or hot
waffles and pancakes.

100 g (4 oz) butter, softened
100 g (4 oz) caster sugar
25 g (1 oz) ground almonds, lightly toasted
15 ml (1 tbsp) almond-flavoured liqueur

1. Cream the butter and sugar together in a bowl until
light and fluffy.
2. Stir in the almonds and liqueur.
3. Pile into a small dish and chill well before serving.

*To freeze: pack and freeze. Thaw overnight at cool room
temperature. Chill again before serving.*

CHOCOLATE NUT BUTTER

SERVES 4

Serve with hot pancakes and waffles.

100 g (4 oz) butter
10 ml (2 tsp) caster sugar
15 ml (1 tbsp) grated chocolate
30 ml (2 tbsp) chopped walnuts, hazelnuts or pecan nuts

1. Beat the butter until very light and fluffy, then beat
in the remaining ingredients.

*To freeze: pack and freeze. Thaw overnight at cool room
temperature. Chill again before serving.*

*Opposite: BAKED CHOCOLATE MARBLE SPONGE (PAGE 102)
WITH CHOCOLATE FUDGE SAUCE.*

INDEX